To The Setting Of The Sun: The Story Of York

Best Regards —
George R. Sheets
Feb. 27, 1982

The 19th-century watercolors of William Wagner provide modern York residents with a sharp view of the city's past. This panoramic view of York by Wagner was used on the face of the York Bank's $10 bill. Courtesy, The Historical Society of York County.

To The Setting Of The Sun: The Story Of York

By Georg R. Sheets

©1981 by Windsor Publications.
All rights reserved.
Published 1981
Printed in the United States of America

First Edition

Library of Congress Cataloging in Publication Data

Sheets, Georg R., 1947-
   To the setting of the sun.

   Bibliography: p. 232
   Includes index.
   1. York (Pa.) — History. 2. York (Pa.) —
Description. I. Title.
F159.Y93S53   973.8'41   81-52021
ISBN 0-89781-013-6   AACR2

This detail of a Wagner engraving depicts the old building of the York Bank. The engraving, used on the bank's $5 bill, dates from the 1850s. Courtesy, The Historical Society of York County.

CONTENTS

Foreword, by Governor Dick Thornburgh — 6
I Out of the Wilderness — 9
II The Founding of York Town — 21
III Capital of Revolutionary America — 35
IV Center of Trade and Commerce — 55
V Railroads Above and Below the Ground — 75
VI Post-Civil War Prosperity — 95
VII World War I and the
"Roaring Twenties" — 117
VIII The Depression Years — 135
IX The Rise of the Greater York Area — 145
Color Plates — 161
Partners in Progress, by Jerry Sweitzer — 177
Acknowledgments — 230
Bibliography — 231
Index — 232

FOREWORD

Pennsylvania prides itself on the beauty of its natural environment, the wealth of its historical attractions and, most of all, the friendliness and productivity of its people.

This year, as the Keystone State celebrates its 300th birthday, it is particularly fitting that we pay tribute to close-knit communities such as

York, whose residents have made vast contributions to the social, educational, cultural, and economic progress of our great state.

We must study the past if we are to understand the future. By learning about the history of York, all of us can gain a keener understanding of the people of this Commonwealth and of their traditions.

— Dick Thornburgh, Governor

In the early 1800s the new County Hospital and Poor House were built, the latter "for the employment and support of the poor in York County." This 1830 view of the structures is by William Wagner. Courtesy, The Historical Society of York County.

One of the first white men to meet the Susquehannock Indians was Captain John Smith. He wrote of the natives, "Such great and well proportioned men are seldome seene...." Courtesy, The Historical Society of York County.

CHAPTER I
OUT OF THE WILDERNESS

The history of York is a richly colored mosaic stretching over three centuries. It takes its tone and rhythm from great and quiet moments, and its texture and breadth from inhabitants and visitors as varied as human nature itself. Once an Indian hunting ground, then a frontier village, the town of York was destined to serve for nine months as the capital of the New Republic and would further distinguish itself throughout its development from a planned pioneer settlement of thrifty, energetic, and religious individuals to a highly diversified community of more than 300,000 people. York's heritage and modern-day story are both marked by bountiful contributions to the American spirit.

The story of York weaves together the tales of powerful Indians, passionate soldiers, anxious Congressmen, skilled craftsmen, artists, inventors, industrialists, Confederate generals, bold schoolgirls, peaceful churchgoers, self-proclaimed witches, eccentric businessmen, and thousands of other men, women, and children.

Located in southcentral Pennsylvania, York is 50 miles north of Baltimore, 200 miles southwest of New York City, 90 miles west of Philadelphia, and about 10 miles west of the Susquehanna River. The Maryland border, surveyed by Mason and Dixon, lies south of York about 18 miles from center city.

The Susquehanna—450 miles long—flows from New York State's Otsego Lake southeast through Pennsylvania, then empties into the Chesapeake Bay at Havre de Grace, Maryland. The river was the region's single most important factor in attracting people—first Indians, then the early explorers and settlers.

The Indians' story begins millenia before York's three centuries of recorded history, when nomadic hunters migrated across the land bridge of the Bering Sea (through what is now Alaska) and followed Ice Age animals over North America.

During the 15th century, tribes classified by archaeologists as Late Woodland arrived in New York State. This group of Indians spoke the Iroquois language. Intertribal conflicts apparently caused a splinter group to move away from the main body and migrate southward into southern New York and northern Pennsylvania. This group began to increase in size but further conflicts with the main group forced its members to move southward again.

About the year 1575, Indians reached the area of the Susquehanna and built a stockaded town on the east side of the river in Washington Borough. The Susquehannocks, as they were called, built "long houses" made of two parallel rows of posts 20 feet apart. Each post was tied to the one facing it in the opposite row. The pole frame, 60 to 80 feet long, was then covered with slabs of bark. Beds were built inside along the walls, and storage pits were dug beneath them. Like the Iroquois from whom their culture derived, the Susquehannocks were a matriarchal society and female members of the same family shared the long house. The only other clues to the nature of their life in the Susquehanna Valley are the broken shards of pottery, arrowheads, and other artifacts buried by the centuries.

Captain John Smith was one of the first Europeans to describe these people. Smith, who had had considerable experience with other Indians, was impressed by their size, their cleanliness, and their independence. The English explorer, in 1608, wrote: "Sixty of those Sasquehanocks came to us with Skins, Bowes, Arrows, Targets, Beads, Swords and Tobacco pipes for presents. Such great and well proportioned men are seldome seene, for they seemed like Giants to the English yea and to the neighbours, yet seemed of an honest and simple disposition with much adoes restrained from adoring us as Gods. These ar the strangest people of all those Countries, both in language and attire; for their language it may well beseeme their proportions, sounding from them as a voyce in a vault." He wrote that the Indians' proportions made them seem to the English "the godliest men we ever beheld."

The Indians used the river as a trade route, as a battleground, and as a source of food and transportation. A few of them made settlements along its banks and used the interior land for another source of food—game and plants—both of which were abundant in the forests and fields. They roamed the land freely, and sometimes a small group or a family would break away from the main tribe and settle in distant places, so it is not unlikely that a few of them lived on the banks of the Codorus in what is now York.

About 1665 the Susquehannocks, still engaged in wars with their northern neighbors, erected one town and perhaps two in York County directly across the river from their Washington Borough site. The Indians along the river developed extensive trade with the Europeans, who brought guns, powder, kettles, iron knives, axes, glass beads, and liquor. Furs were the Indians' chief trading commodity and these animal pelts became much in demand at European and Indian markets.

Soon the Indians stopped producing their own pottery and tools, relying on European substitutes that proved to be more durable. The Susquehannock culture, also weakened by increasing alcoholism, deteriorated.

The Indians' lands near the Susquehanna River had an enormous variety of flora and fauna. According to Bruce B. Smith, a biology professor known for his work along the Susquehanna and the Codorus Creek, the plant and wildlife has remained largely unchanged through the years. There were, and still are, rhododendrons, azaleas, violets, honeysuckles, bulrushes, skunk cabbage, rushes, onion, jonquils, pussy willows, buckwheat, star grass, amaryllis, blueberries, and cranberries. Remnants remain of the huge forests of poplar, cottonwood, walnut, oak, beech, elm, silver maple, sugar maple, red maple, and dogwood—where the Indians hunted deer, bear, rabbits, and squirrels. The plants and animals were similar along Codorus Creek, the Susquehanna's tributary that cuts right through present-day York, passing at one point within a block of City Hall before leaving town and stopping in the Maryland community of Havre de Grace.

But in 1608, when John Smith had encountered the Indians, the Susquehanna River Valley was Indian country, a kind of buffer area between southern and northern Indian groups. A steady influx of explorers and settlers would soon change that.

In 1609 the British explorer Henry Hudson sailed into Delaware Bay, searching for a trade route to the Far East. He left the region, which lay less than 100 miles from the future York townsite, but the reports he sent back to Europe encouraged the Dutch sea captain, Cornelius Hendrickson, to sail up the Delaware River in 1615 to what is now Philadelphia. His travels would later have far-reaching implications to the history of the York area, but it was another explorer, Etienne Brule (then working as an interpreter for

Although no records exist, this artist's rendition of a Susquehannock Indian shows the large physical stature that was often described by early explorers in Pennsylvania. Courtesy, Sunday News.

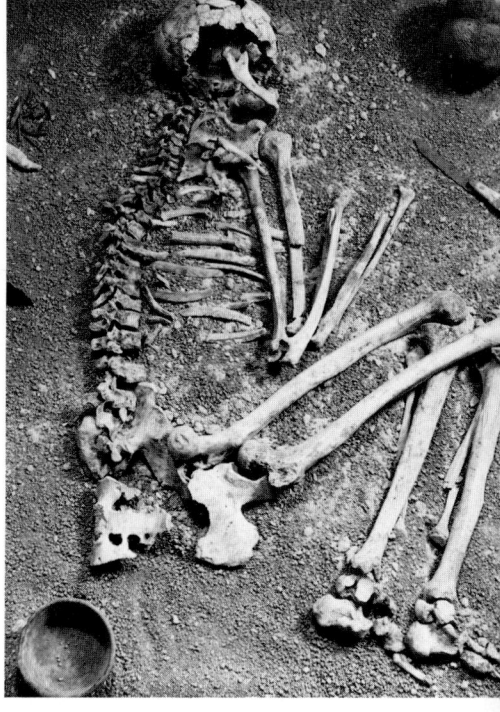

Samuel de Champlain), who became the first white man actually to set foot in the future Commonwealth of Pennsylvania.

Brule had been sent to the tribes of the Susquehanna in 1616 to ask for reinforcements in a proposed attack against Onondaga Fort, one of the strongholds of the Five Nations of the Iroquois Indians in what is now New York State. While waiting for the Indians to prepare themselves, he "busied himself in exploring the country." He followed the Susquehanna "to the sea," which probably meant "to the Chesapeake Bay," a journey that must have included areas of what is now York County.

At the same time Swedish settlers were following Captain Hendrickson's route up the Delaware and in 1643 became Pennsylvania's (although not York's) first permanent settlers. The lands passed from Swedish hands to Dutch in 1655, and to the English in 1664.

The Swedes, English, and Dutch put down settlements among the area's "aboriginal" natives. The Susquehannocks were still using lands along the river and they were continually occupied by disputes with their neighbors to the north, the Five Nations. Even though Brule reported meeting, in 1618, "a large number of [Susquehannock] people who are of good natural disposition," their friendliness was not extended toward the Five Nations (consisting of the Senecas, Cayugas, Onondagas, Oneidas, and Mohawks).

A priest working in the Susquehannock territory told of how 60 Susquehannock boys, about 15 to 16 years old, surprised and killed two northern warriors, and "following up their advantage pursued the rest of the war party in canoes and killed fourteen more and wounded many others."

The Five Nations treated the Susquehannocks with equal cruelty. John de Lamberville, a missionary, wrote this account of how Susquehannocks were tortured: "The hot irons were applied [to their bodies]. One of whom having been burnt during the night from his feet to his knees in a cabin, still prayed to God with me the next day, being fastened to a stake in the square of the town. . . . It is impossible to behold without horror their flesh roasting and men who make a vile meal of them like hungry dogs." Even though some accounts of early Indian activities are known to be exaggerated, archaeologists have found evidence that cannibalism among the early Indian inhabitants and hunters of the Susquehanna Valley was not unknown. (The word "Mohawk," for instance, came from the Algonquin term meaning "man-eaters.")

Above
This reconstruction of a Susquehannock grave, from about 1650-1657, is similar to those found at Long Level, York County. The clay pot and the brass kettle represent grave offerings, while the beads, brass objects, iron, and knife are personal or ornamental objects that evidence interaction with the early European visitors in the county. (HSYC)

Above left
These clay pots were unearthed at the archaeological dig at Long Level. (HSYC)

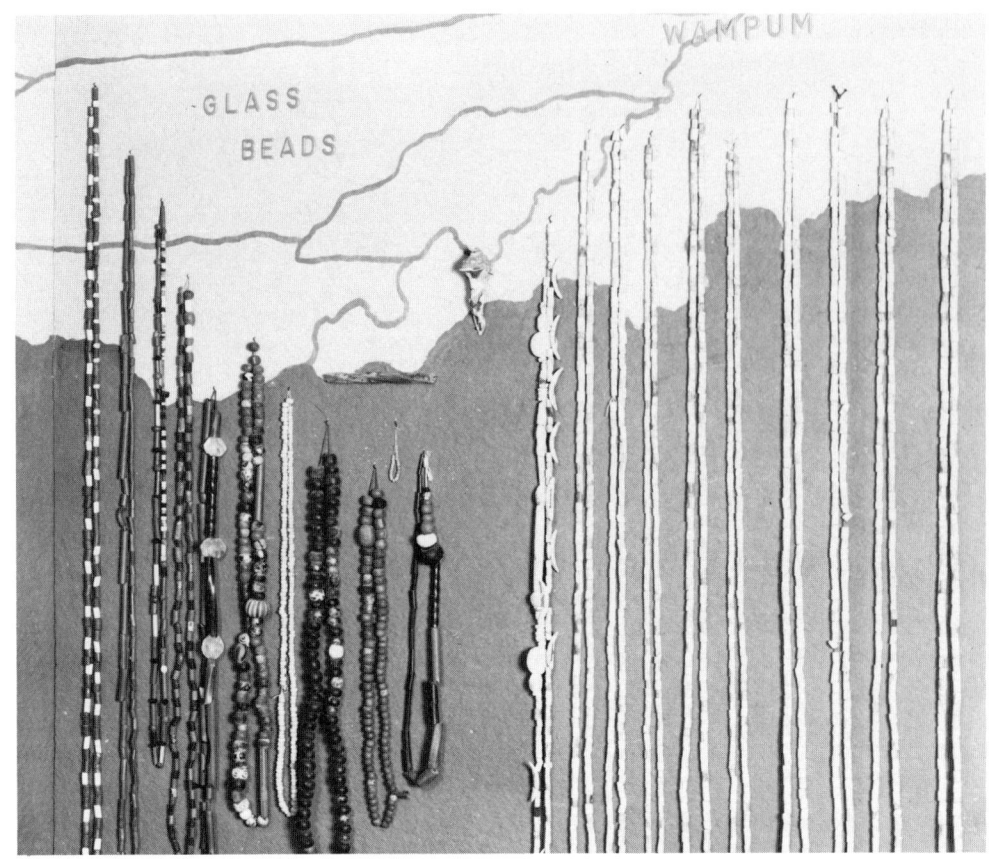

Right
Susquehannock Indian artifacts found at the Long Level site included glass beads and wampum. (HSYC)

Below
William Penn, called "the peaceful founder of Pennsylvania," is seen in a portrait by Henry Inman. King Charles II warned Penn of the so-called "savage" Indians, but Penn's nonviolent Quaker faith gave him the confidence that he could live in peace with the Indians. The date of the portrait is unknown, but it was painted after Penn's death, since his religious beliefs would allow no graven images to be created. From Richman, *Penn Pictures.*

Despite the tactics used against them, the Susquehannocks managed to beat the Five Nations back, reaching the height of their own power between 1660 and 1667. A publication of the Pennsylvania Historical Commission asserts: "Had they taken full advantage of their strength they might have changed our history considerably. As a result of their rise the warlike activities of the Five Nations were curtailed."

Meanwhile the English were still arriving in Pennsylvania. English mercenaries had captured the land around the Susquehanna in 1664 and given it to the Duke of York, but King Charles II transferred the land to William Penn, in 1681, to pay a debt that he owed to Penn's father. William Penn was a devout Quaker with a firm belief in religious freedom, for which he had been thrown out of school and sent to prison at least three times— once in the Tower of London. Penn was anxious to reach his newly acquired lands, which promised not only religious freedom but also personal rights, property privileges, and self-government. He had decided to call the lands "Sylvania," but King Charles II added the name "Penn" to honor William's father. William Penn set sail for "Pencilvania" (as it was spelled on early documents), arriving there in 1682.

But Penn "the Proprietor" immediately encountered problems. In 1632 King Charles I had granted lands south of Pennsylvania, now called Maryland, to Cecilius Calvert, Lord Baltimore. Boundary disputes resulting from the adjacency of the grants were to trouble Penn and Baltimore for many years, and they would have special impact on the greater York area, since it lay only about 18 miles from the Maryland boundary. When Penn died in 1718, he was still not assured of the safety of his province.

Boundary disputes with Maryland squatters were not the only property problems in store for Penn or for York. One of Penn's first desires in the New

World was to purchase the Susquehanna River and all the lands lying on both sides of it from the Indians. The lands did not, at that time, belong to the Indians living on them, because they had been lost in a brutal war with members of the Five Nations. Penn engaged Colonel Thomas Dongan, once governor of what is now New York State, to travel north to enter into negotiations with the Indians there.

Dongan, "in consideration of one hundred pounds sterling," conveyed the lands to Penn in 1696. Dongan's agreement with the Five Nations included "all that tract of land lying on both sides of the river Susquehanna . . . adjacent, in or near the Province of Pennsylvania . . . beginning at the mountains or head of said river, and running as far as and into the bay of Chesapeak."

Widagh and Addagyjunkquagh, kings (or "sachems") of the Susquehannocks, confirmed Dongan's deed in 1700, but the neighboring Conestogoe Indians —another Iroquois splinter group— were displeased with the transaction, asserting that the Five Nations had no right to make such a sale. They also disputed the portion of the deed which read, "for all the [river] Susquehanna and all the islands therein, and all the lands lying on both sides of the said river, *and next adjoining to same,* to the utmost confines of the lands which are, or formerly were, the right of the people or nation called the *Susquehanna* Indians."

The words "next adjoining to same" left open the question of who owned the lands west of the river, including what would become York. The Five Nations insisted, regardless of the agreement of 1700, on treating the lands and the river as their own territory.

The fact that more than 30 years would pass before the issue of land ownership was settled also did not stop the English from treating the area as their own. In 1722 the heirs of William Penn approved a plan to survey an area west of the Susquehanna River. The area was to be set aside as a "manor" for use by the Penns since they had been authorized to reserve "10,000 acres from every 100,000" over which they would have direct control. The 64,000 acres surveyed extended from the river into what is now York. The land was named Springettsbury Manor for Penn's grandson, who was also his heir. The establishment of its borders formally opened the West to white settlers, who, until the land's purchase from the Indians, had no legal right to settle west of the river. (The word "manor" was then commonly used in England to describe any unit of land for which the owner could expect rents, levy fines, and exact privileges. The Penns, for example, had the privilege of collecting "quitrents"—rents that the settlers paid instead of performing various feudal services—until 1775 on most Pennsylvania lands. They retained their ownership privileges on the manors, however, long after 1775 and last collected quitrents from those areas in 1793.)

Among the first settlers to cross the Susquehanna to take up lands in the newly opened frontier were John and James Hendricks, English by birth. Although no one knows precisely when they made their settlement, it could have been as early as 1728. Even though the lands west of the Susquehanna were not yet fully purchased from the Indians, agents for the Penns had granted certain individuals authority to settle there with the understanding that title to the lands would come later.

The laying out of Springettsbury Manor not only clarified settlement rights in the western lands, it also established boundaries (albeit loosely defined ones) whereby officials could deal with the bothersome "Maryland intruders." Lord Baltimore's followers had, for many years, presented themselves farther and farther north, and their audacity often involved them in "bloody fracases" in the region that Penn's agents strongly claimed as "Penn's

A meeting between William Penn and the Indians, symbolizing "mutual trust," is depicted in this segment of a mural painted by Paul Domville. The mural is now in the collection of the William Penn Museum in Harrisburg. Courtesy, Pennsylvania Historical and Museum Commission.

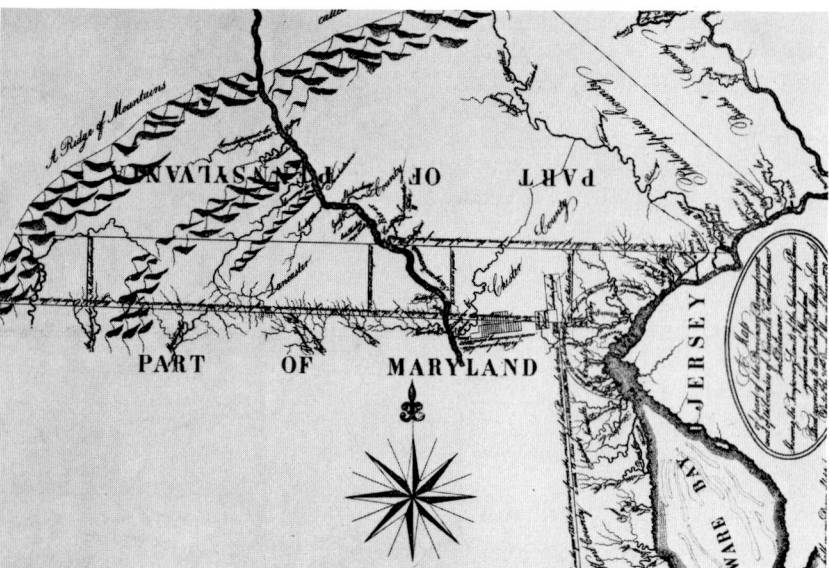

Above
The motto "mercy and justice" appeared on the Penn family coat of arms. The Penns were from the west of England. From *Pennsylvania; Colonial and Federal*, Vol I, 1903.

Above right
The temporary line between Pennsylvania and Maryland is shown on this early map. The provinces were "fixed according to an Order of His Majesty in Council, dated the 25th day of May in the Year 1738, surveyed in the year 1739." (HSYC)

woods." Thomas Cresap, one of the more adventurous Marylanders, seized Pennsylvania lands unabashedly, causing murderous battles, until he himself was seized in 1736 and locked up by the sheriff of Lancaster County.

Although the first settlers west of the Susquehanna were English (and Marylandish), they were soon followed by large numbers of Germans who settled near the site taken up by the Hendrickses on what is now Kreutz Creek. The area originally was called Grist Creek after one of its earliest settlers, John Grist. The Kreutz Creek settlement extended from the Susquehanna southwest to the seven-mile-long area now known as Stony Brook. The Canadochly settlement, probably as old as the Kreutz Creek settlement, encompassed the present-day areas of Yorkana, East Prospect, and Delroy. It had been called the Conojehela Valley by the Indians, who had an established village on the opposite shore in Washington Borough. Corruption of the Indian name, Conojehela, led to different versions of the name, such as "Canajockley," "Jockley," and, finally, "Canadochly."

The English settlers took up land just west of the area now called Spring Grove. The area was surveyed by Penn's surveyor, Joseph Pidgeon, and took the name Pigeon Hills, a name that is still used today.

Most of the settlers moving into these new lands had strong motivation for making a new life. Many had been subject to religious persecution in their native lands, and had watched family members die in the political turmoil of the times. For those Germans who had come from the Palatinate region of Germany, Penn's plan for a free land seemed all the more attractive because of experiences in their homeland that were still fresh in their minds.

The Electoral Palatinate was a beautiful and fertile area of what is now West Germany, often referred to as the Middle Rhineland. During the 17th and early 18th centuries, this rich agricultural region, famed now for its wines, was subject to military invasions and the ravaging of its countryside by periodic religious wars and battles for political control. After the Palatinate became involved in the War of the Grand Alliance in 1685, King Louis XIV of France (which bordered the Lower Rhineland in the south) ordered a full-scale invasion and the devastation of the Rhenish Palatinate.

In 1688 Louis XIV sent 50,000 men into the province with orders to level the lush countryside, with its clean, prosperous towns and villages, until the area was, in his words, "a desert." The invasion, which took place in the winter, forced thousands of townsmen and farmers to flee to the fields,

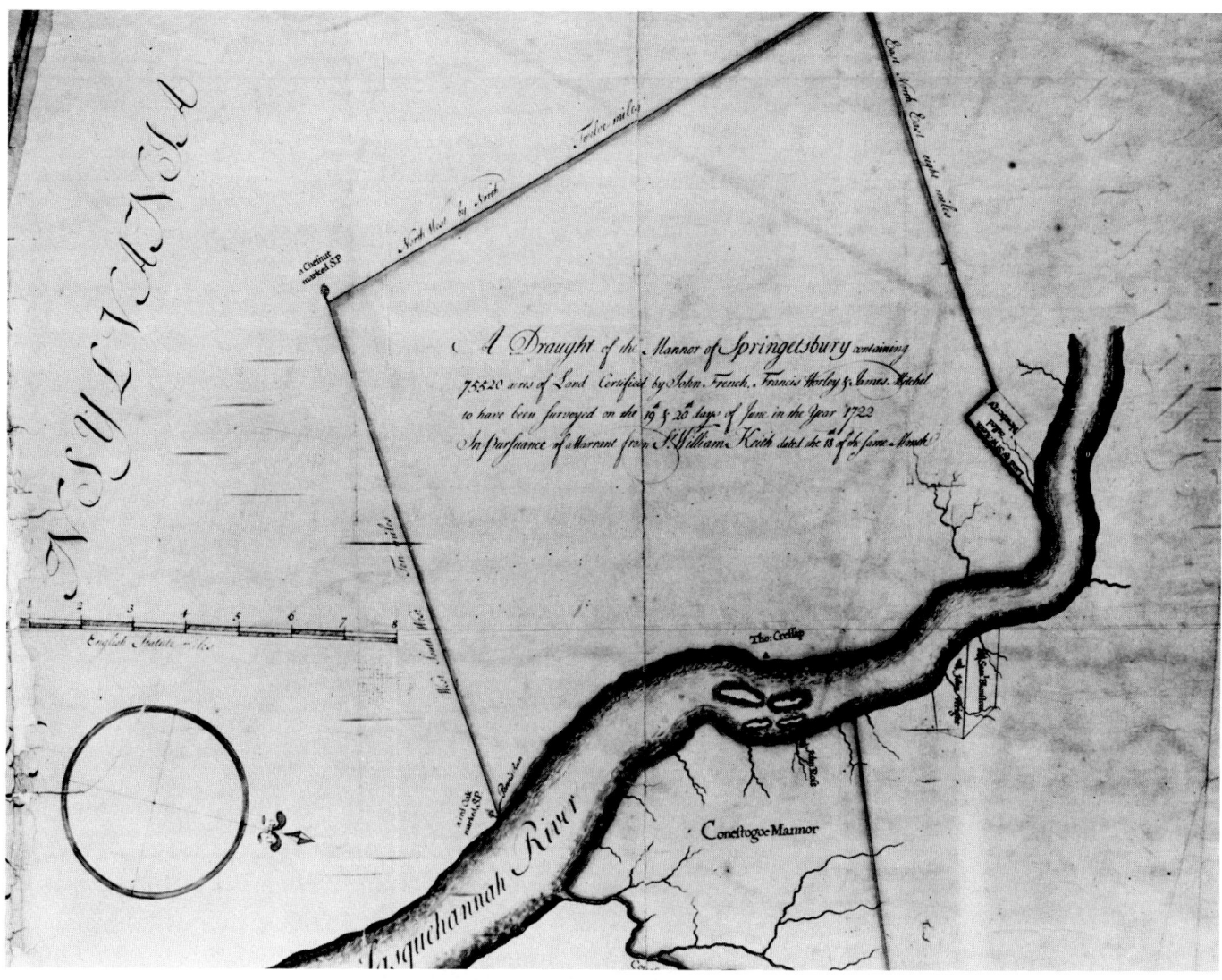

A Draught of the Manor of Springettsbury, includes 75,520 acres of land surveyed on June 19 and 20, 1722. (HSYC)

where many perished from hunger or exposure. The following spring, as the invasion continued, the remaining peasants were forced to plow under their crops.

Other invasions, and religious persecution, ensued in the coming years, so that a steady stream of immigrants found their way to the New World, often by way of sympathetic England. William Penn himself went on recruiting missions to the Palatinate and, as early as 1683, Pennsylvania had its first settlement of Palatine immigrants at Germantown, north of Philadelphia. When Governor Keith informed later arrivals of the already established settlement, many started their journey for that region, coming within 30 miles of the future York settlement. The stream of migration from Germany continued until 1775, and included not only members of the Lutheran and Reformed churches of the Palatinate, but also Mennonites from Germany and Switzerland, and the German Baptists from the Upper Rhine. Even though they could not secure rights to the land until 1733—when Samuel Blunston, the Penns' agent, began issuing licenses for settlements west of the Susquehanna— several hundred Palatines had already settled in York County.

Between 1700 and 1775 approximately 200,000 Scotch-Irish, most of them "rigid" Presbyterians, arrived in America. Comprising the second-largest immigrant group (after the English), many went to Pennsylvania for its available farmland. A large number of them made their home in what they called the York Barrens, a nearly diamond-shaped area whose points are the towns of Craley, Peach Bottom, Delta, and New Freedom. The word "barrens" has been variously defined as "vacant," "not yet bought," "infertile," or "burnt." The last definition referred to the Indians' standard practice of burning vast acreages of forest to force game into a smaller area of woodlands for easier hunting.

Whether the York Barrens was physically "bare" or not, its topography held a fascination for the Scotch-Irish and also the Welsh, who used skills acquired in their homelands to establish slate mines and quarries for the extraction of limestone. They set up family dwellings and later, after the 1736 treaty, settlers moving west from Chester County (the county bordering Lancaster County on the east, as York County later bordered it on the west) moved into the greater York area's Newberry Township. Many were Quakers who founded communities that are now called Newberrytown, Lewisberry, Goldsboro, Etters, Yocumtown, and York Haven. These early settlers called the region "the Red Land" because the soil and rocks were reddish brown. They built crude cabins among the wigwams of their Indian neighbors, who taught them how to raise corn and to use the lush woodland to full advantage.

Among those first settlers were Thomas Hall, John McFeeson, John Rankin, Ellis Lewis, and Joseph Bennett. A descendant of Lewis later laid out the town of Lewisberry and Bennett's name was given to a small stream. History takes particular note of the arrival of Rankin, Bennett, and Lewis. Their story, which has been questioned by modern historians, recounts how they arrived on the east bank of the Susquehanna, concerned that the river would not allow them to cross on horseback. The terrible threat of having to leave their horses behind hung over them. After an intense discussion, they solved the problem by fastening together two canoes. The horses then crossed the Susquehanna with their front feet in the first canoe and their hind feet in the second.

Just southwest of the Pigeon Hills settlement, during the same period, a group of Marylanders, many of whom were Catholics, were settling on land known as Digges Choice. John Digges, an Irish nobleman who lived in Prince Georges County, Maryland, obtained from the fourth Lord Baltimore, Charles Calvert, a grant of 10,000 acres which was later to encompass the Borough of Hanover. With the assistance of a respected Indian chief named Tom, Digges carved out a 6,822-acre area encompassing lands that were eventually included in York and Adams counties. Lord Baltimore's grant had authorized him to approve settlements in parts of western Maryland before the Penns obtained title to the lands west of the Susquehanna. The questionable nature of the Penn and Baltimore borders, ironically, allowed organized settlements on what was to become Pennsylvania lands by Marylanders.

An initial preoccupation for the settlers throughout the newly opened lands was the building of shelters. Two of the earliest remaining houses in York County were built of stone, although log cabins and "half-timber" houses would dominate the county's architectural scene in a few years. In the town of Hallam (from "Hellam" for the township in which Hallam was located), about six miles east of York's city limits, stands the Martin Shultz House, a Germanic stone cabin that is probably one of the earliest houses in the Kreutz Creek Valley. At about the same time, Johann and Christina Shultz built a two-story stone house south of Stony Brook, and began a new life in lands set aside for a new province.

Life in early York County was hardly easy. The early inhabitants had bitter winters and brutally hot summers to contend with, besides the threat of Indian and Maryland invaders. The streams often flooded and dry periods sometimes

The Johann Shultz house, built by the brother of Martin Shultz in 1734 and located south of Stoney Brook, as it looks after restoration. The house had a Germanic central-chimney system. (HSYC)

ruined an entire summer's work in the newly cleared fields. Still the lands in the Kreutz Creek area were fertile, so farmers, including women and children, worked the land and sent up prayers for favorable conditions.

Two of the county's best-known early historians, W.C. Carter and A.J. Glossbrenner, tell us, in their *History of York County, From Its Erection to the Present Time: (1729–1834)*, that the county's early inhabitants lived primitively, even to their clothing. "Their dress was simple," the historians relate, "consisting of a shirt, trousers and a frock," all of tow. In summer they wore only the shirt and trousers; as the weather got colder, they added frocks, "which were bound closely about their loins, usually with a string of the same material as the garments."

"There was neither a shoemaker nor a tanner in any part of what is now York County," according to Carter and Glossbrenner:

> *A supply of shoes for family use was annually obtained from Philadelphia; itinerant cobblers, travelling from one farm house to another, earned a livelihood by mending shoes. . . . The first settled and established shoemaker in the county was Samuel Landys, who had his shop somewhere on the Kreutz creek. The first, and for a long time the only tailor was Valentine Heyer. . . . The first blacksmith was Peter Gardner. The first schoolmaster was known by no other name than that of "Der Dicke Schulmeister."*

The homes of these early settlers were primitive, too. Typical Germanic architecture used a central chimney system; the fireplace cooking area, which also provided light, was often extended through the wall to the adjoining room for heating purposes. Iron-plate stoves were later introduced to house the heating fire opposite the cooking area. Candles and "betty lamps," which burned animal fat, enhanced the light that was given off by the fireplace.

Many of the settlers had brought with them iron-bound chests containing basic cooking implements and other items, such as cloth, small farming tools, candlemaking tools, the family Bible, and sometimes seed with which to start farming in the New World. Furniture was simple, but often incorporated traditional design elements, such as heart shapes and distelfink birds, both of which were thought to bring good luck to the homes of settlers who had also brought, besides basic tools, ideas and customs from their native lands.

People like these farmers and craftsmen were coming to the York area in

Early York County settlers made their simple clothes from flax and wool, using homemade instruments like the ones shown in this display at The Historical Society of York County. (HSYC)

increasing numbers largely because of promotional material, ranging from pamphlets to playing cards, which described Pennsylvania to the inhabitants of Europe. The promise of religious freedom, a better way of life, and "Goodly land, fertile and well-watered" (as the promotional pieces said) drew the Germans from the Palatinate and Scotch-Irish, but also French Huguenots and English (particularly Quakers) to Pennsylvania.

One of York's esteemed modern historians, Joe E. Kindig III, writes that by the time York was laid out in 1741, "it was predominantly a German community.... [The settlers] were of the peasant class and numbered among their group farmers, millers, tanners, and tradesmen who had accepted William Penn's promise of new land and religious freedom. They brought with them ... not the Baroque culture of the wealthy city merchants, but the peasant culture of medievalism." This culture was transplanted intact. As Kindig points out: "Since few of them [the Germans] did more than pass immediately through Philadelphia, on finding the English language not to their liking, they arrived in York County uninfluenced by English culture and customs."

Ferryboat operators worked at several points up and down the Susquehanna, and the newcomers, usually on horseback and sometimes carrying small children, reached the west side of the river much fatigued but jubilant with the thought of putting down stakes on land they could call home. Some settlers bargained with fellow-countrymen, who had already settled in Chester County, to use their covered wagons in transporting families and their belongings west of the river.

Many Germans, and some Englishmen, followed Indian trails to find homes. Some came to the area where the Monocacy crossed the Codorus and discovered that—with its fertile fields, majestic hills, good supply of fish from the Codorus, and woodlands filled with game and plant life—it would make a fine place to settle.

The early record books of the Christ Lutheran Church list the names of "24 heads of family," most of whom had emigrated from Wuerttemberg, Germany. They established a congregation and worshiped together as early as 1733. Among those first congregation members were Christian Groll, Philip Ziegler, Georg Schwaab (later Swope), John Adam Diehl, Jacob Scherer, Georg and Mathias Schmeiser (later Smyser), Martin Bauer, Georg Adam Zimmerman, Georg Ziegler, Christoph Kraut, Joseph Beyer, Jacob Ziegler, and Valentine and Heinrich Schultz.

In spite of the enthusiastic activity involving the establishment of settlements and the founding of congregations, the question of whether these settlements were legal was still in discussion. The ownership of the land had been in dispute since the treaty between Penns' agent, Dongan, and the Five Nations in 1700. Action was finally taken in 1736, when a great council was called to put an end to the quarrels of official ownership between the Penns and the Indians. Gathering in Philadelphia, the sachems and representatives of all the Five Nations renewed old treaties, and, on October 11, wrote a new deed in the name of William Penn's successors: his son Thomas and his two grandsons, John and Richard. In return for the land, the Indians were given:

>500 lbs powder, 600 lbs lead, 45 guns, 60 strouds water match coats, 100 blankets, 100 duffle match coats, 200 yds. of half thick, 100 shirts, 40 hats, 40 prs. of shoes and buckles, 40 pairs of stockings, 100 hatchets, 500 knives, 100 houghs [hoes], 60 kettles, 100 tobacco tougs, 100 scissors, 500 awe blades, 120 combs, 2,000 needles, 1,000 flints, 24 looking glasses, 2 lbs. of vermillion, 100 tin pots, 200 lbs of tobacco, 25 gals. rum, 1,000 pipes, 24 dozen of gartering.

The new deed made it clear for the first time that the Susquehanna Valley region of Pennsylvania belonged exclusively to the Penns. It was signed by 23 chiefs of the nations of Seneca, Oneida, Onondaga, and Tuscurora. It granted to the Penns all the land north of the Susquehanna "to the hills or mountains called, in the language of the Five Nations, Taymentesachta [the eastern slopes of the Allegheny Mountains] . . . and "all the river Susquehanna, and all the lands lying on the west side of the said river to the setting of the sun. . . ."

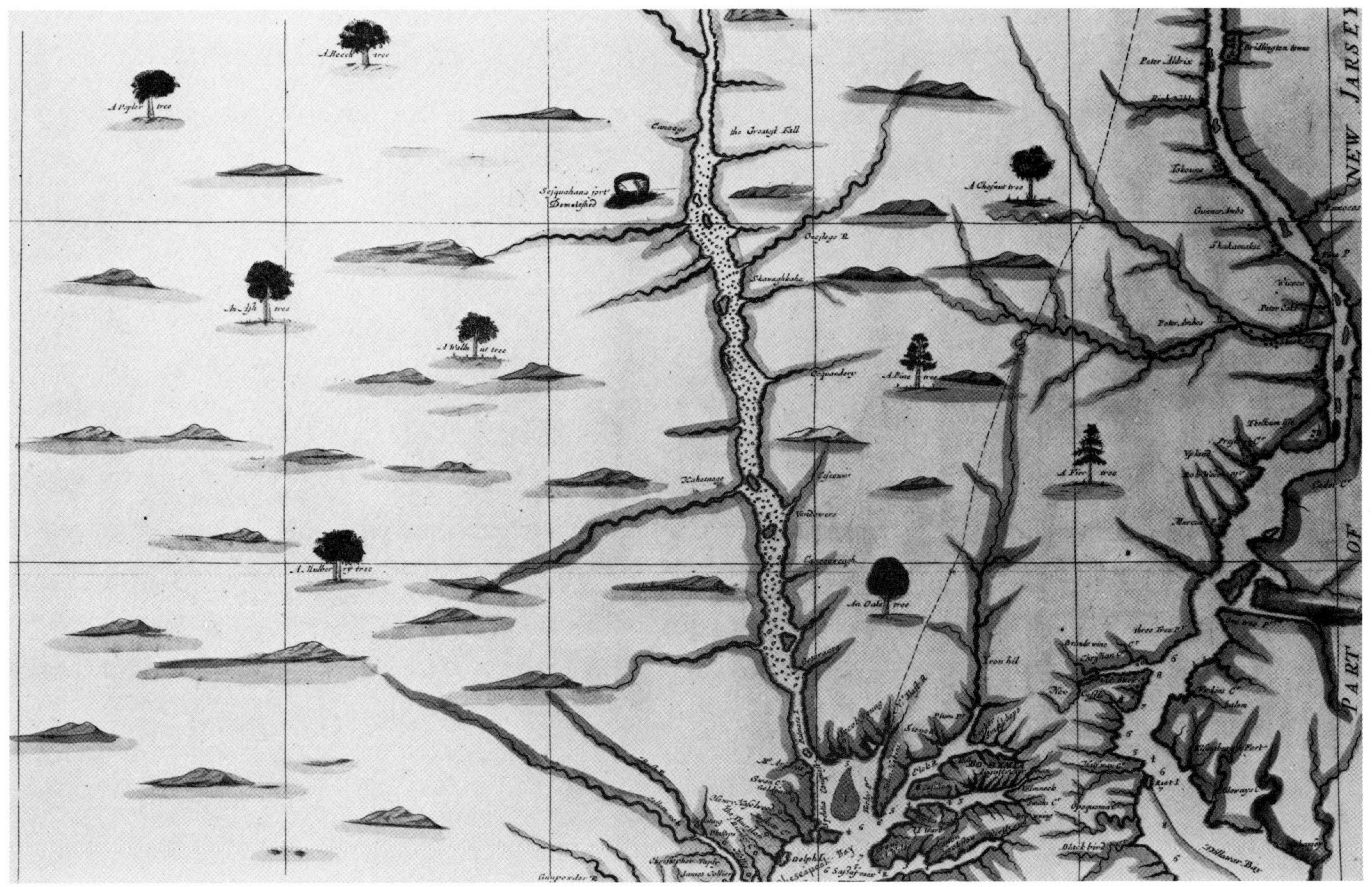

This map of some of the south and east boundaries of early Pennsylvania, date unknown, was intended "to give an account of some of the Province in America, so far as the Relations received from Persons that have been upon the place, could give any light towards it." (HSYC)

John Fisher was a carpenter and one of York's earliest clockmakers and artists. His superb craftsmanship can be seen in this tall case clock, made in 1790. (HSYC)

CHAPTER II
THE FOUNDING OF YORK TOWN

Once the settlements west of the Susquehanna officially belonged to the Penns, the Pennsylvania proprietaries and governors were more open to requests from the area's pioneer residents that an organized town be laid out. In 1739 a petition for the erection of the county of York was presented to the proprietaries. This petition was brought by Ulrich Whisler and Baltzar Spangler, two German immigrants who had built log houses near the Plank Road southeast of what is now downtown York, and was granted in 1741. The Penns then authorized Thomas Cookson, the deputy surveyor for Lancaster County (which York was a part of until 1749), to lay out a town in the "checkerboard" pattern that had been used for Philadelphia a half-century earlier.

With the assistance of Whisler and Spangler, who acted as chainbearers, Cookson laid out the town according to the prescribed plan: lots were to be 230 feet long by 65 feet wide; alleys were to be 20 feet wide; and two streets, which crossed each other to form the central intersection, were to be 80 feet wide. At the corners of the cross streets, 65 square feet were to be cut off to make a "Square," "for any public building or market."

Cookson was from Yorkshire, England, and it was probably his suggestion that led to the name of the proposed town. "York town," as it was then called and written on public documents, also manifested Cookson's English background in the names of its streets. Thus there were streets called King, Queen, Prince (now Princess), and Duke, and, of course, George Street, which had been referred to as Prison Street, or Union Street, before being renamed in honor of King George II.

In addition to being a town, York was considered a "manor," and administered by the Penns in much the same way as Springettsbury and other manors were. Applicants to the town lots had to agree to pay a rental fee of seven shillings a year and to construct "a substantial dwelling of 16 feet square at least, built with lime and sand, within the space of one year." The proprietaries could also collect other quitrents, which in the case of York were often only token in nature, consisting of a peppercorn or barleycorn "paid" each year. York was the second of seven towns established by the proprietaries during their period of governance. The first had been Philadelphia, founded in 1682. After York, in 1741, came Reading in 1749, Carlisle in 1751, Easton in 1752, Bedford in 1766, and Sunbury in 1772.

In payment for their assistance in laying out the town, Spangler and Whisler were granted the lots of their choice, thereby establishing them as the first official residents of the first town west of the Susquehanna. Baltzar Spangler chose a site on the northwest corner of what is now York's Continental Square, where he built a residence and operated the community's first inn and tavern, the Black Horse. The Black Horse was also used, while still in an unfinished state, as the first polling place in York in 1750. Ulrich Whisler, a miller by trade, waited several years before taking up his lot near the Codorus at the intersection of Main Street (now Market Street) and Water Street (now

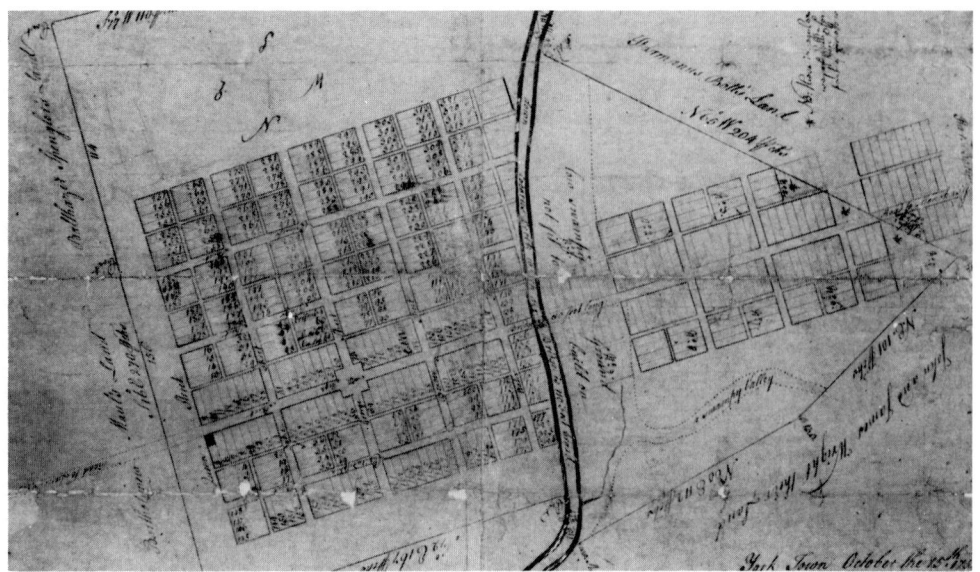

This early composite map depicts York town as surveyed by Thomas Cookson in 1741. The map shows lots for landowners, the road to Monocacy, and the land outside the town that belonged to Hermanus Bott, Baltzar Spangler, and John and James Wright. (HSYC)

Pershing Avenue). The reconstructed Colonial Court House is now located on property that includes Whisler's original lot.

Others "taking up" lots with Spangler in 1741 were: John Bishop, Jacob Welsch, Michael Schwaab (later Swope), Matthias Onvesant, Andrew Coaler (originally Kohler or Koller), Henry Hendricks, Joseph Hinsman, Christopher Croll, Michael Laub, Zachariah Shugart, Nicholas Stuke, Arnold Stuke, Samuel Hoake (later Hoke), George Swope (who took four lots when no one else took more than two lots and most applied for just one), Jacob Crebill (later Graybill), Michael Eichelberger, and Hermanus Bott. Michael Eichelberger later sold his lot to his brother, Martin, who operated another of York's early public inns and taverns. Now known as the Golden Plough, the tavern was authentically restored in the years 1963–1965. Hermanus Bott obtained a patent for 297 acres of land west of the Codorus and laid out his own town of about 50 lots in subsequent years. Bottstown, with its population of 300, was annexed to the borough of York in 1884.

Shortly after York was laid out, its residents began holding market in Centre Square (now Continental Square) at the intersection of Market and George streets. Although the exact date of authorization is not known, the Penns granted approval to the market through their lieutenant governor, Robert Hunter Morris.

York's first farmers had been Indian squaws, who scratched the land with sticks so that they could plant seed. The Indians passed on their knowledge of the land to some of the earliest immigrants, many of whom knew little about the art of growing things and were forced into farming in order to feed themselves and their families. But Yorkers' farming skills were rudimentary, to say the least, until the arrival of the first waves of German immigrants, who brought with them more advanced agricultural techniques that they had learned in Europe. The German farmers worked exceptionally hard, as did their wives, and many contemporaries remarked that the Germans were the most efficient and industrious farmers to come to the New World.

When the Germans applied their farming skills to Pennsylvania's rich lands, the results were rapid and extraordinary, so much so that Pennsylvania soon became an exporter of food to other colonies. In York their success brought a request for the Penns to allow them to make the farmers' market a twice-weekly event. The Penns granted the request, but designated Wednesday and Saturday as the only market days, thus pleasing both the predominantly German farmers and the citizens from other countries who objected to their

Above
The Golden Plough Tavern, left, built circa 1741, and the General Gates House, built circa 1751, are two surviving reminders of York's Colonial past. The Golden Plough Tavern is the only remaining example of half-timber architecture in York County. (HSYC)

Above right
The kitchen of the Golden Plough Tavern was the center of activity because of the heat and light generated from its central fireplace. Martin Eichelberger ran the tavern for travelers passing through the county. (HSYC)

practice of trading on the sabbath. The farmers' market tradition has survived to this day, making it (along with religious observance and government activity) one of the oldest public institutions in York.

The first markets were held in the open air; as a result, when it rained or snowed, the mud in Centre Square, churned by hundreds of humans and animals, grew ankle deep. Farmers from the outlying areas, who came into York town on market days, peddled their wares from the backs of wagons and from makeshift "stands" on the curbs. During dry spells in the summer, dust flew everywhere, covering the vendors' produce and meat. The building of the market shed, authorized in 1754, alleviated the problems caused by dust and mud, but extremes of heat and cold still made the market activities grueling during several months of the year. The business of market was carried on in prices that often included fractions. Since money was not plentiful, due to the relative isolation of the community and the economic level of most of its residents, bartering was often undertaken in lively sessions.

The market was not the only area of York life that was growing, however. Yorkers were a churchgoing people, and new congregations were springing up throughout the greater York area. Before church buildings and meeting houses were built, worshipers assembled in private homes or, occasionally, in taverns or barns. The churches became important social as well as religious outlets, often serving as focal points in the development of community.

In 1743 Christ Lutheran Church, founded 10 years earlier, built a log structure that also housed one of York's first schools. In 1743, too, a group of Germans built "Die Evangelische Luthensche Kanawagische Germeinde" (The German Evangelical Lutheran Church on the Conewago). This church was located in Hanover Borough (now called St. Matthew's) and its first pastor, the Reverend David Chandler, lived in the middle of a vast Lutheran parish extending from the Susquehanna River on the north to the Potomac River on the south, and including congregations in the greater York area as well as places such as Frederick, Maryland. Among the church's first "subscribers," or financial supporters, were Frederick Gelwicks, Michael Carl, Philip Morgernstern, Christoffel Schlegel (later Christopher Slagle), and Nicholaus Beidinger (later Bittinger), some of whose names are still associated with the congregation.

A short time later, perhaps as early as 1744, a Moravian missionary named Jacob Lischy was ministering to the families of the Kreutz Creek Settlement,

Above
Organized in 1733, the congregation of Christ Lutheran Church built a log structure a decade later that doubled as one of the first schools in York. In 1763 a stone church building replaced the earlier one. (HSYC)

Above right
St. Matthew's Lutheran Church, originally the German Evangelical Lutheran Church on the Conewago, was built in Hanover Borough. It was part of a large Lutheran parish that extended from the Susquehanna River on the north to the Potomac River on the south. (HSYC)

including the members of York's German Reformed Congregation, who did not yet have a church building. No one knows exactly when the Congregation was formed, but Lischy writes in his journal of 1744 that "this congregation has been for several years without a pastor." In 1745 church trustees Jacob and Samuel Welsch "took up a lot in the town of York for a meeting house." The lot fronted on High Street, located just west of the current church, now known as Trinity Reformed or "Old Trinity."

After churchmen and businessmen bought up the first 23 lots in 1741, no additional lots were spoken for until the spring of 1746, when 44 were taken up. Between 1748 and 1750, many more applications were made and York town began to take on the appearance of a prosperous community.

In the vicinity of Centre Square were the shops of shoemakers, carpenters, gunsmiths, blacksmiths, clockmakers, harnessmakers, toolmakers, distillers, and weavers. Tanners chose the area along the Codorus, two blocks west of the Square, to establish their shops. The soaking and boiling of hides required a large supply of water, which the Codorus provided, and wood, which was available from the heavily forested nearby land. To expedite travel and development in the area of the Codorus, a bridge was built in 1743. This first bridge was little more than a wooden span crossing the Codorus at High (now Market) Street.

The work of the artisans and shopkeepers who thrived along the Codorus and the Monocacy Road soon earned for York the reputation as a community of fine craftsmen. John Fisher, for example, was a carpenter and also one of York's earliest clockmakers and artists. His shop stood on North George Street about half a block north of the Square and just south of what is now the Ramona Restaurant. In Fisher's shop, the clockmaker-artist-carpenter built a particularly splendid clock embodying astronomical devices. The Fisher work now stands in an outstanding collection of clocks owned by Yale University. Besides Fisher, York had at least a dozen other fine clockmakers, including Rudolph Spangler (son of Kaspar Spangler, and nephew of Baltzar Spangler), Godfrey Lenhart, Elisha Kirk, and Jonathan Jessop. Clocks bearing the signatures of these men are highly sought after in York County today.

While small craftsmen lived and worked in York's increasingly crowded center, early manufacturers needed more space to work, so they developed their products outside of town. Gristmills and sawmills sprang up all over the area, beginning in the 1730s. Many farmers also grew flax to help supply the inhabitants' need for clothing, rope, and sacks. The fibers of the flax plant were used to make linen or were combined with wool to make "linsey-woolsey," a more elegant fabric much coveted by the women of York.

Alongside the flax fields were wide expanses of rye and Indian corn, which gave rise to York's early spirits industry. Records reveal that there were 16 distillers in Dover Township and 18 in Manchester Township by

1770. John George Charles Barnitz, married to Anna Barbara Spangler, started a brewery and left it to his two sons, Charles and John, when he died in 1796. The elder son, Charles, renounced his share of the business in favor of his brother. John married Catherine Hay, daughter of Colonel John and Julia Maul Hay, during the Revolution.

The Barnitz family, headed by David Grier Barnitz, purchased the manor of Springettsbury in 1841 from William Penn's descendant Granville Penn, who was until then the "lord" of the manor. David Grier Barnitz was obliged to pay two beaver skins per year to Granville Penn "if demanded."

All the businesses being established in the manor had one problem in common: York was still part of Lancaster County, and people had to travel 25 miles to Lancaster, the county seat, crossing the Susquehanna, to do legal business or resolve problems. Complaints from citizens eventually led to the "erection" of York County in 1749 with the county seat located at York town. With the establishment of the county, the citizens also were provided with funds to raise a courthouse and a jail.

While the Court House was being built, sessions of the court were held in the homes of York County's justices. Those first justices included John Day, Thomas Cox, John Wright, Jr., (who had settled at Wrightsville), Matthew Dill (who later founded Dillsburg [1800]), Patrick Watson, George Stevenson (who would later serve as York town's first prothonotary, clerk of the courts, register of wills, and "recorder of deeds"), Georg Swope (one of the fathers of York's first church in 1733), and Hance Hamilton (a Scotch-Irish immigrant who had settled near Wrightsville and who was appointed York's first sheriff). Hamilton was to serve as sheriff until an election for the office was held in 1750.

John Gibson's 1886 history of York County tells of that October 1750 election, the first of any kind in York. Richard McAllister ran against Hamilton, who wanted to remain sheriff after the term of his appointment expired. Hamilton, Gibson says, "was urgently supported by the Scotch-Irish," while McAllister, "although a Scotch-Irishman himself, was the candidate of the Germans. . . . The voting place on this occasion was the unfinished public inn of Baltzar Spangler." Why York's German population supported a Scotch-Irishman in these times when nationality was often foremost in people's minds is not known. The candidate favored by the Germans, as it turned out, had little chance of winning the election, regardless of his national ties.

"By the noon hour," Gibson continues, "hundreds of gallant frontiersmen . . . with great determination and impetuosity began to clamor for their

Below
This carved wooden head of Captain John Carlton, attributed to John Fisher, has human hair, silver, and brass, circa 1786. (HSYC)

Below right
The York County Court House, erected in 1754, was located in York town's Centre Square. The Continental Congress met at the site from September 30, 1777 to June 27, 1778. This authentic reproduction of the Court House stands today at the corner of Pershing Avenue and Market Street. Photo by G.H. Laird. (HSYC)

Below, far right
York artisan John Fisher's painting of the Pennsylvania Coat of Arms is now in the collection of York College of Pennsylvania. It is believed to be the oldest, painted Pennsylvania coat of arms in existence. Courtesy, York College of Pennsylvania.

favorite candidates, and crowded around the voting place." Sheriff Hamilton tried to control the situation by stopping the election, which only made things worse:

> *A general commotion and confusion ensued. A lusty German, insisting on his right to vote, tripped up the heels of one of the Scotch-Irish guards. An affray began. . . . Saplings cut along the Codorus were used as offensive and defensive weapons. Hamilton and his party fled west of the Codorus. During the remainder of the day the Scotch-Irish were not seen east of the creek. There were a few limbs broken and considerable blood was shed, but no lives were lost.*

Gibson ends by noting, "The Quakers, of whom there were a great many present from the northern part of the county . . . took no part in the affray." He explains that because Hamilton could not turn in an election report to the provincial government in Philadelphia, the governor commissioned him sheriff. He served in that post until 1753, when he was succeeded by John Adlum, but Hamilton was reelected in 1755.

York no doubt needed a sheriff during those early years, since land disputes and other legal problems were alarmingly common. Recorder of deeds George Stevenson reported, in April of 1751, that only 50 lots had been used in compliance with the original agreements. Three of those lots were occupied by churches—two by the German Lutheran and one by the German Reformed. Many individuals had taken up lots, but not built on them, as the Penns' dictates required. Some of the lot holders probably did not have the money to fulfill their building obligation; others procrastinated until after the one-year time limit had expired. Houses were sometimes constructed on lots to which the builders had no title. Some Yorkers with ready capital watched carefully until they saw a lot or building that did not meet specifications, then tried to acquire the property through a legal procedure called "forfeiture of rights."

Considering the rising number of legal wrangles that the York community found itself embroiled in, the completion of the new Court House in 1754 was timely. The Court House had been built in Centre Square. William Willis, a Quaker who was one of the first English Friends to settle near York, had been contracted for the brickmaking and bricklaying. Another Quaker, Henry Clark, provided wood "scantlings" for the building. John Meem and Jacob Klein, both Germans, were employed as carpenters; and Robert Jones, a Quaker, had been hired to haul 7,000 shingles from Philadelphia to complete the Court House roof.

To detain those awaiting legal proceedings and punish those convicted of offenses, the new jail was completed two years later. The jail, intended only as a temporary structure, had high stone walls and a wooden roof. It was located at the corner of George and King streets, the present-day site of Sunny's Surplus Store. In 1768 a three-story jail of blue limestone replaced the temporary structure.

But more public and humiliating punishments than imprisonment often awaited York's criminals. In front of the Court House were the pillory, a wooden frame with holes for the head and wrists, and the stocks, which confined the person's ankles. Residents accused of breaking the law were sometimes confined to the pillory and stocks, where they were subject to the scorn of hundreds of people passing through Centre Square. ("Scorn," in those times, often meant dirt picked up from the horse-trod streets.) Offenders were sometimes also lashed, physically mutilated, or hanged.

Records tell of the 15 lashings given to a York woman, Margaret Wilmouth, for stealing a silk handkerchief. Another woman, Elisabeth Irwin, was accused of murder, imprisoned for 20 weeks, then hanged. A crime that was considered nearly as serious as murder was counterfeiting the king's money. James Pitt was convicted of altering a two-shilling bill of credit to a ten-shilling note. For his eight-shilling crime, Pitt had both his ears cut off and nailed to the pillory, where he had to stand for one hour before receiving 39 lashes. He was also fined £100, which he could not pay, so he was sold into servitude for a period of four years.

In York, at this time, individuals were commonly sold to pay for court costs, or as payment to creditors. Imprisoned persons also had the right to sell themselves or their children to obtain their release.

Bondservants, who had sold themselves to pay for transportation to the New World or to satisfy debts, were punished especially hard when accused of trying to escape from their masters. In one case of bondservant punishment, Robert Gamel Hath was sentenced to two additional years of servitude to Baltzar Spangler, Jr., when Hath was apprehended after running away from town. Another servant, Thomas Haughy, was accused of absenting his duties for two months and 11 days, and had to serve an extra seven years.

Despite the quarrelsome and sometimes illegal ways of the York area's early residents, they remained an essentially religious people. The early 1750s saw a new flurry of religious activity and church building that helped give rise to the modern York axiom, "There's a church on every corner."

In 1752 the First Moravian Church was formally organized. The congregation met in a tavern until 1755, when it built a church on Prince and Water streets (now Princess Street and Pershing Avenue). At that location it also operated a school. The church established a burial place in back of the church, which it called "God's Acre." The Moravian dead were buried in seven sections: a section for married men and widowers, one for single men, one for male children, one for married women and widows, one for single women, one for female children, and one for "strangers." The cemetery divisions were made to remind living Moravians that there is no marrying in heaven and that all "the saints" will eventually enjoy a single reunion.

A Presbyterian congregation was formed in late 1753, or early 1754, known as Guinston, 12 miles from York. An Episcopal congregation was established in York, probably in 1755, by a missionary of the Church of England, the Reverend Thomas Barton; three prominent Yorkers—Samuel Johnston, Thomas Minshall, and Joseph Adlum—were appointed trustees.

St. John's Episcopal Church was established in York by the Reverend Thomas Barton, an English missionary, circa 1755. Samuel Johnston, Thomas Minshall, and Joseph Adlum, all prominent Yorkers, were appointed trustees. (HSYC)

Still standing today, the Warrington Friends Meeting House is a York County landmark. (HSYC)

Early Catholic records indicate that more than 100 German Catholics and about 70 Irish Catholics lived in York County in the 1750s and probably celebrated mass in private homes. The Amish, the Mennonites, the Dunkards, and Brethren also formed churches throughout York County.

This burst of religious activity faded out when the effects of the French and Indian War (1754-1763) began to reach the York area. Living peacefully with the Indians had not been a major problem for the area's whites. But when the French, aided by Indian allies near Canada, crossed Lake Erie and began to move southeast toward York County, the citizens of the York area were naturally alarmed.

Britain's king, informed of the French and Indian troubles by the Pennsylvania Assembly, sent General Edward Braddock to help the Colonists. Assemblyman Benjamin Franklin, who had urged the furnishing of money to carry on the war, assured Braddock that the Assembly had appropriated £5,000 to support Braddock's army. Unfortunately, as Franklin related in a proclamation to the people of York, Lancaster, and Cumberland counties, "money had not been provided nor any steps taken for that purpose" by either the Assembly or the governor. The Assembly, mostly made up of peace-loving Quakers, was not enthusiastic about supplying war materiel. On learning that Braddock had only 25 wagons in which to transport equipment and supplies over the Alleghenies, Franklin took it upon himself to recruit wagons and pack horses. He came to York and Lancaster, and sent his son William to Carlisle in Cumberland County, with the aforementioned proclamation, which read, in part:

> Friends and Countrymen:
>
> Having been at the camp at Frederick a few days since, I found the General and officers of the army extremely exasperated on account of their not being supplied with horses and wagons. . . .
> It was proposed to send an armed force immediately into these counties, to seize as many of the best wagons and horses as should be wanted, and compel as many persons into the service as should be necessary to drive and take care of them.

I apprehended that the progress of a body of soldiers through these counties on such an occasion, their resentment against us, would be attended with many and great inconveniences to the inhabitants; and therefore more willingly undertook the trouble of trying first what might be done by fair and equitable means.

The people of these back counties have lately been complaining that a sufficient currency was wanting; you have now an opportunity of receiving and dividing among you a very considerable sum; for if the service of this expedition should continue (as it's more than probable it will) for 120 days, the hire of these wagons and horses will amount to upwards of thirty thousand pounds. . . .

If this method of obtaining the wagons and horses is not likely to succeed, I am obliged to send word to the General in fourteen days, and I suppose Sir John St. Clair, the Hussar, with a body of soldiers, will probably enter the province, of which I shall be sorry to hear, because

I am very sincerely and truly
Your friend and well-wisher,

B. FRANKLIN

Within two weeks, 150 wagons and teams and 259 pack horses were on their way to Braddock. They carried 1,200 barrels of flour from Cumberland and York County gristmills.

The war raged on, and in 1756 York area citizens organized a number of military companies to aid the cause. George R. Prowell, perhaps York County's best-known historian, records three companies of 60 men each, three of 100 each, one of 50, and one of 106. In addition to the enlisted men, each company had its own captain, lieutenant, and ensign. Hance Hamilton formed his own company after resigning as sheriff in 1755; in 1756 he marched to Pennsylvania's western frontier to join the fighting. Companies were also formed by the Reverend Thomas Barton of the newly established York, Carlisle and York Springs Episcopal Church; by the Reverend Andrew Bay of the Presbyterian Church at Marsh Creek; by Dr. David Jameson, York's pioneer physician; and by Thomas Armor, a court justice.

As the war edged closer to the York area, some settlers fled eastward across the Susquehanna, while others assembled inside York town itself. The town had been fortified against attack. But the fighting, reaching its peak and then fading out between 1758 and 1760, never did touch York. The Treaty of Paris in 1763 ended French control of America's western frontier, which at that time was York County's western half, and peace returned to Pennsylvania.

Life as usual also returned to York. New businesses were established, new church buildings were erected, and new squabbles over land and lots were heard in the streets and in the courts. Dick's Bloomery, established in 1756, was one of the first iron furnaces in the York area and may have been built to feed the war-born demand for rifle balls, cannonballs, and other metal items.

After the war, the demand for metal goods stayed high. James Smith, York's famed lawyer and signer of the Declaration of Independence, owned the Codorus Furnace, built in 1765 and known then as Bennett's Furnace. In the 19th century it took the name Hallam Furnace and Forge. The expanding availability and use of metals combined with York County's rich cereal crops caused many farmers to erect copper stills. Area farmers became expert in blending various ingredients, and they were soon hauling their whiskey to Baltimore and other communities outside of York. The establishment of iron furnaces made other "exports" possible, such as tools, pots, kettles, spoons,

Benjamin Franklin distributed an impassioned proclamation during the French and Indian War "To the inhabitants of the Counties of Lancaster, York, and Cumberland," calling for wagons, teams, and other supplies for the English forces. Within two weeks, 150 wagons and 259 packhorses were on their way from the area to support the efforts of "His Majesty." (HSYC)

skillets, hoes, and knives, all of which were sold in great numbers. This new idea of exporting products made in York was to have a dramatic impact on the community's economy in coming years.

The iron industry spurred another successful venture in York, the making of fine guns. Early "Pennsylvania rifles" were made in York by Joseph Welshantz, Conrad Welshantz, Ignatius Leightner, Frederick Zorger, and George Eyster. No two Pennsylvania rifles were alike and the work of the early York gunsmiths helped to strengthen York's status as a community of fine craftsmen. After the Revolution, the Pennsylvania rifle was called the Kentucky Rifle, and credit for its origin became clouded.

The York area's iron furnaces also supported another important local industry, wagonmaking. There were at least half a dozen makers of Conestoga wagons working in the county by the time of the American Revolution. The Pennsylvania Germans adopted the wagon as a freight carrier, and it helped many settlers reach the Western lands with the items necessary for beginning a new life. The wagon's partner in transporting newcomers to the greater York area was usually, of course, the horse, but one could also arrive by "shank's mare," a mode of transportation named after a portion of the underside of the human foot.

The Conestoga, a much more comfortable way to travel over long distances, had a curved, boatlike body painted red. The wagons, with their white canvas tops, were often seen in long caravans, carrying loads of grain, fruit, tobacco, cider, whiskey, oil, poultry, glass, iron wares, and flour. Frederick Lawmaster, John Lever, and Daniel Weaver were among the first Conestoga wagonmakers in York, opening the community's long and rich association with the transportation business.

With the rise of the York area's iron industry, and the expansion of manufacturing that it triggered, Yorkers began talking about holding a special

Below left
Erected in 1765, Bennett's or Codorus Furnace was owned and operated by James Smith, who signed the Declaration of Independence. (HSYC)

Below
Conestoga wagons, such as the one pictured here, were made in York and helped to open Western frontiers to settlement. (HSYC)

Bottom
The rear of the York Friends Meeting House is seen in an 1893 photograph by Gilbert Cope of West Chester, Pennsylvania. The eastern portion of the Meeting House was built in 1766 and the western portion added in 1783. It is the oldest house of worship still used in York and York County. The meeting has been in continuous existence since 1764 and many notable Quakers lie buried in the churchyard. (HSYC)

exposition in which they could show off their products. In 1765 Thomas Penn, then lieutenant governor of Pennsylvania, granted the citizens of York the privilege of holding two fairs a year, in June and November, "for the purpose of buying and selling goods, wares, merchandise and cattle." The community was diversifying and the idea of selling York-made products to the people of other towns was becoming more widespread.

As commerce grew, so did the population and the need for more churches. The first formal Presbyterian services in York probably were held in 1762, when the Presbytery began sending theological students to conduct services and to minister to the needs of the small congregation there. Seventeen sixty-three saw the erection of two new stone churches for congregations that had had only wooden structures before: the German Reformed Congregation and the Christ Lutheran Church, the latter of which built its new church building on the site it still occupies today. In 1766 the York Quakers built a brick structure at what is now 135 West Philadelphia Street, the oldest building in York County still used as a house of worship. In 1783 an addition to the western side of the Meeting House greatly expanded the facility.

Devout though the people may have been, they still fought almost rapaciously over lands. A letter from recorder of deeds George Stevenson—dated June 8, 1764, and addressed to William Peters, secretary to the land office—states:

> *Yesterday at 6 P.M. Mr. Homel and myself met the two Doudels [Yorkers Michael and Jacob Doudel] together, with sundry other inhabitants of the place, to try to settle the difference between them about the lots lately granted to Michael. . . . After many things said on both sides, Michael agreed to bind himself by any reasonable instrument of writing, not to build a tan yard on the said lots. . . . But nothing would satisfy Jacob but the lots; and he offered to give Michael the two opposite lots on the other side of High Street, and to plough them and fence them. . . . This offer gave great offence to all the company, What, said they, is no body to have a lot but the two Doudels?*

All of this lot-buying, fencing, and building brought with it a greater threat of fire. S.H. Spangler, a 19th-century fireman, compiled a detailed history of York's first firefighting activities. In it Spangler notes that "in 1769 and 70 quite a number of buildings being erected, mostly of logs, which were liable to take fire, the villagers becoming aware of the necessity of making some provision to protect their property, held a meeting at the house of Baltzar Spangler, their 'Bauer Meister,' and discussed the propriety of organizing a fire company, this as in December, 1770."

Spangler tells of another meeting held in January 1771, during which a motion was made to organize a fire brigade and Spangler notes that 24 men "enrolled themselves as members," among them Baltzar Spangler, Jacob Doudel, the Reverend David Chandler, the gunsmith Ignatius Leightner, and the clockmaker Rudolph Spangler. Joseph Updegraff served as clerk at the meeting and Henry Miller was the chairman. (Chairman Miller, born in Lancaster County, had come to York in 1769 to read law with Samuel Johnston. He later participated in 47 battles and skirmishes with the British during the American Revolution, and was captain of the York Riflemen under General Washington. Captain Miller and the Riflemen were, in fact, with Washington during the arduous winter of 1777–1778 at Valley Forge. Among Miller's other positions of note were elected sheriff of York County and the supervisor of revenue for the state of Pennsylvania, appointed by then-President Washington.)

The company was named "The Sun Fire Brigade of York town," and its members agreed to meet every Saturday afternoon to participate in a drill. Those who were absent from a drill paid a two-shilling fine. Members also voted to provide each member with a bucket, basket, and staff, which they kept in the halls or entranceways of their homes. The bucket would be used for carrying water to a fire scene, and the basket (or bag) for carrying valuables out of a burning house. The staff could be used in many firefighting functions.

The company purchased its first fire wagon in 1772 and built its first engine house in 1773. The site chosen for the engine house was a lot on the Square. The red fire engine was decorated on both sides with the picture of a rising sun enclosed in a laurel wreath. The brigade's motto was "*Spectamur Agendo*," or "Let us be judged by our actions."

The creation of a fire brigade, the fights over lots, the building of churches, the growth of trade —these were all primarily local matters. There were two other events of the time that, while not strictly local in scope, did nonetheless affect York. The first was the disappearance of the Susquehannocks. Though the reason for their population decline is still a mystery, the indications are that disease brought by the white man was a major factor. Droughts came, decimating food supplies and destroying hunting land. Intertribal warfare and decreasing numbers to guard their diminishing frontiers also contributed to their fall, and the strong Susquehannocks slipped out of the annals of history.

Moving stories are told of the last groups of Susquehannocks known to exist. One tale finds a band of Susquehannocks tricked into an army encampment in Maryland where they were blamed for atrocities apparently committed by tribes from the north who had swept through that state. A 19th-century historian, S.F. Streeter, writes: "Here the Susquehannocks, to the number of nearly one hundred, with their old men, women and children, established themselves, and here they were determined to remain."

Six leaders were chosen from among the 100 Susquehannocks and they presented the white leaders with "a paper and a silver medal, with a black and yellow ribbon attached, which they said had been given to them by former governors of Maryland as a pledge of protection and friendship, as long as the sun and moon should endure." Five of the six Susquehannock leaders were killed the next day.

Another story concerning the Susquehannocks' disappearance dates from 1763. Streeter writes that the number of Susquehannocks involved amounted to "only twenty souls." "At that time," he continues, "rioters inflamed by accounts of the Indian war raging along the Pennsylvania frontier, massacred this small band where they had taken shelter in the jail yard in the city of Lancaster."

Hal Conrad, a present-day student of Pennsylvania Indians and a county editor of the *York Dispatch*, notes another story of the final days of the river Indians. "The river . . . was used by many tribes in migration to the north or south," he writes, "and provided sites for intertribal battles, which were the rule rather than the exception. The last Indians living along the Susquehanna were Shawnees, a branch of the Susquehannock tribe, and they resided at Indian Steps where they had hatcheries. Finally, when only 18 remained, they departed westward in 1765. The last glimpse of them was when the chief and his daughter climbed into a canoe and paddled away down the river."

Indian Steps Museum, an institution dedicated to the study of the Susquehannocks and other Indians, today stands in York County's Lower Chancerford Township, about 15 miles from York and along the river where the Indians carved "steps" in the bank to use as footholds while shad fishing. John Edward Vandersloot, owner and builder of Indian Steps "Cabin"

This map of Pennsylvania, including York County, "Laid down from Actual Surveys and chiefly from the map of W. Scull," was published in 1770 and "humbly inscribed to the honourable Thomas Penn and Richard Penn, Esquires." (HSYC)

in 1912, had the following words inscribed over the Museum's main door, facing the Susquehanna: "I entreat all those who pass this way to safely guard and preserve these former possessions of and monuments to an ancient Indian people." Another sharp image which Vandersloot left to York citizens was a photograph of himself, showing a powerful-looking man posed in full Indian chief regalia and standing on the rock steps that reach out into the Susquehanna.

With the disappearance of the Indians another crucial event of the time took the regional focus—the official solution of the old Pennsylvania-Maryland border conflict. In 1760 commissioners representing Lord Baltimore and the Penns agreed to authorize a survey to mark the colonies' mutual border once and for all.

Commissioners from both colonies employed Charles Mason and Jeremiah Dixon to make the survey and the two worked between 1763 and 1767 to establish the now-famous line that bears their names. Mason and Dixon established not only the southern boundary of Pennsylvania but also that of York County. This new line was marked with milestones cut in England and engraved with an "M" on one side for Maryland and a "P" on the opposite side for Pennsylvania. Five special stones were engraved with the coats of arms of Lord Baltimore and of the Penns, and these stones were placed at five-mile intervals. The Mason-Dixon line was resurveyed in 1849 and 1900, but the later surveys found no major error in the boundaries established by Mason and Dixon at the parallel of 39 degrees, 43 minutes, and 26.3 seconds.

Working with the two famous surveyors on the original job was a York County man named Archibald McLean. McLean, a surveyor by profession, served as a chief associator for Mason and Dixon, and later became chairman of the Committee of Observation and Safety for York County. A native of Antrim, Ireland, he also served as prothonotary, register of wills, and recorder of deeds for the county after George Stevenson (1749–1764) and Samuel Johnston (1764–1777).

In the Civil War the line that McLean had helped to survey—dubbed "the Mason-Dixon"—separated the free states from the slave states and took on even greater importance as Americans fought against each other. (Important as this line was, however, it did not give "Dixie" its name, as is commonly believed; the term derives from New Orleans bank notes with the English "Ten" printed on one side and the French "Dix" on the other.)

But in the meantime, Yorkers were planning to fight a different enemy: the British. The American Revolution was coming to York.

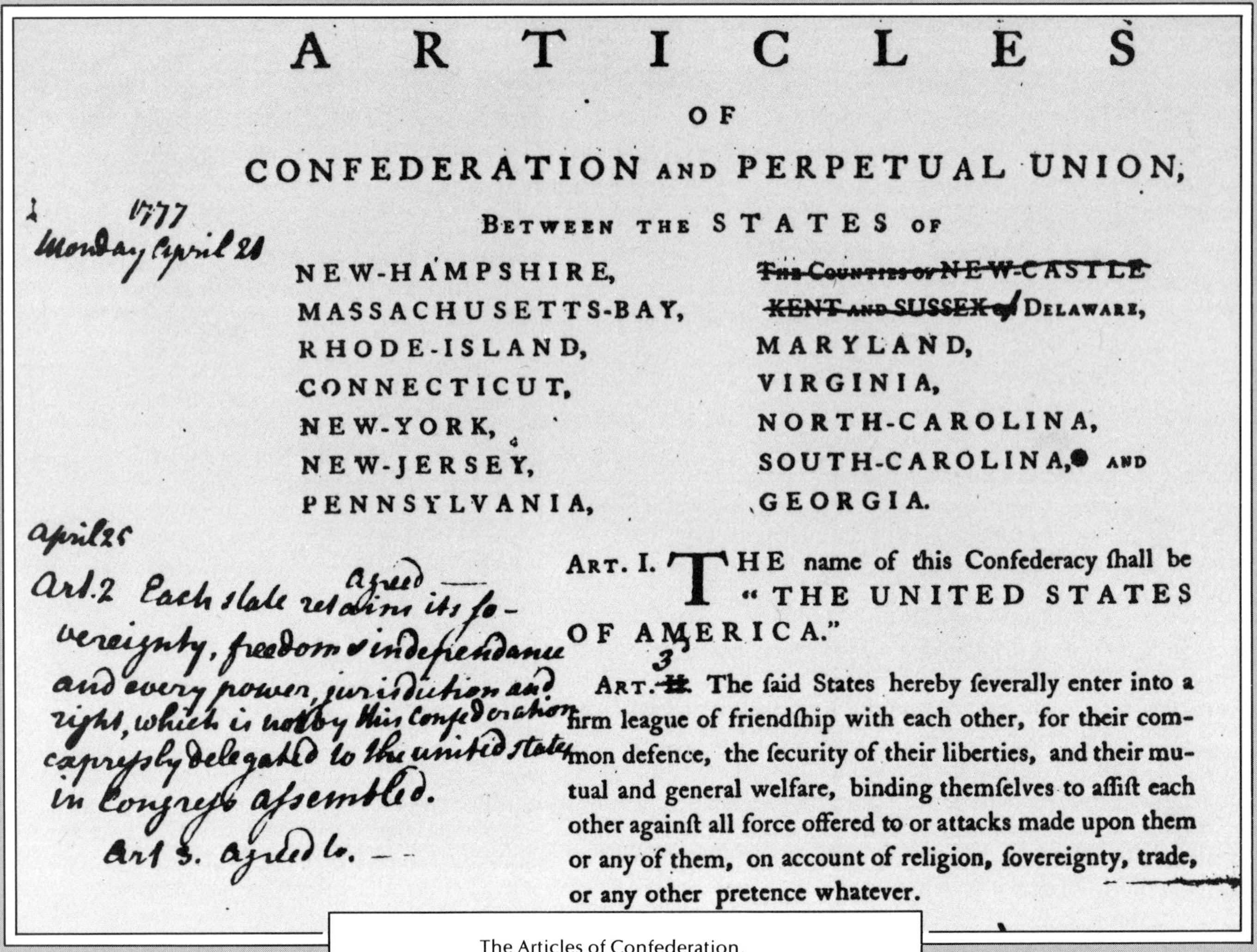

ARTICLES

OF

CONFEDERATION AND PERPETUAL UNION,

BETWEEN THE STATES OF

NEW-HAMPSHIRE,
MASSACHUSETTS-BAY,
RHODE-ISLAND,
CONNECTICUT,
NEW-YORK,
NEW-JERSEY,
PENNSYLVANIA,
~~The Counties of NEW-CASTLE KENT and SUSSEX on~~ DELAWARE,
MARYLAND,
VIRGINIA,
NORTH-CAROLINA,
SOUTH-CAROLINA, AND
GEORGIA.

[Handwritten annotations in margin:]
1777 Monday April 21

April 25
Art. 2 Each state retains its sovereignty, freedom & independance and every power, jurisdiction and right, which is not by this confederation expressly delegated to the united states in Congress assembled. Agreed—
Art 3. Agreed to.—

ART. I. THE name of this Confederacy shall be "THE UNITED STATES OF AMERICA."

ART. 3 [II]. The said States hereby severally enter into a firm league of friendship with each other, for their common defence, the security of their liberties, and their mutual and general welfare, binding themselves to assist each other against all force offered to or attacks made upon them or any of them, on account of religion, sovereignty, trade, or any other pretence whatever.

The Articles of Confederation, adopted by the Continental Congress during its stay in York, used the name "United States of America" for the first time. (HSYC)

CHAPTER III
CAPITAL OF REVOLUTIONARY AMERICA

A new spirit was alive in America. It was the spirit of revolutionary patriotism, which struck a responsive chord in York, where the citizens were highly sensitive to the invasion of their lands by outsiders. For many York citizens, horror-filled memories of King Louis XIV's armies destroying their native countryside had already merged with images of Marylanders intruding into York County and the earlier attacks of the French and the Indians. The York patriots, skilled in the use of rifles and Indian methods of warfare, were now ready to use those skills to prevent the incursion of the British "outsiders."

In 1774, after King George III failed to resolve differences between the Colonies and the British monarchy, the first Continental Congress had met in Philadelphia, where its members drew up a declaration of rights to send to the king. The declaration went unanswered and, soon afterward, Massachusetts called a Provincial Congress, which authorized the formation of troops and the collection of supplies with which the tyranny of England could be forcibly resisted.

General Thomas Gage, who had fought under Braddock in the French and Indian War, was the commander of the British regulars at Boston. On April 18, 1775, he sent 800 troops to Concord, a few miles west of Boston, to capture the supply stores there. The next day at dawn, he was met on the Lexington Common by a group of armed patriots, seven of whom died when the group refused orders to disperse and were fired upon by British troops.

When the British arrived in Concord, they were met by an even larger band of armed patriots. A tense battle ensued, the British were turned back, and, on their return to Boston, they were shot at by hundreds of Boston farmers along the way. Three hundred British soldiers died in the skirmishes, and the remaining troops barely escaped capture.

Thus began the Revolutionary War, which would occupy Yorkers, in body and mind, for nearly a decade. When the news of Lexington and Concord reached York, the populace, nearly bursting with enthusiasm for the American cause, readied themselves for action. The second Continental Congress, which had assembled in Philadelphia on May 10, now supported measures for war against Britain. On June 14 the Continental Congress adopted a resolution that eight companies of trained riflemen from Pennsylvania be raised as quickly as possible. They called for two companies each from Maryland and Virginia as well. When organized, the troops were to march to Cambridge and join the army under General George Washington.

There were already three organized military companies in York—some of the members of which were veterans of the French and Indian War—which comprised the York County militia. The required number of officers and the 68 riflemen were selected from the county's militia to head up York's first company.

Recruitment of the other soldiers for the first company took place at sites throughout the region, including the Marsh Creek area (around Gettysburg), the Monoghan settlement (now known as Dillsburg), and in the southern part of the county. In less than a week these "sturdy pioneers" were organized under Michael Doudel as captain, Henry Miller as first lieutenant, John Dill as second lieutenant, and Walter Cruise as corporal. Yorkers such as Thomas Hartley (who would become a colonel under Washington and later York's first Congressman), James Smith, John Kean, Joseph Donaldson, and Michael Hahn led the efforts to prepare the company for action.

Doudel and Miller, who were in charge of recruitment, picked only those men who could hit a small chalk mark with a flintlock from a distance of 150 yards, and it seemed that every man under 50 years of age came to prove himself. Historian George R. Prowell observes that "so many men wanted to enlist that there were more than the soldiers were authorized to accept." Luckily for Doudel and Miller, Horatio Gates—who had recently been appointed adjutant general—happened to be passing through York and he decided that it would be unwise to refuse the enlistment of "such courageous men." He looked them over and declared, "They will make soldiers!"

York's Committee of Correspondence, part of a network of such informal committees that regularly exchanged information on the current state of the fight for independence, wrote to Congress: "The men seemed actuated with the greatest zeal and thought themselves honored in having their names enrolled among the sons of liberty who are to fight for their country and in defense of their dearest rights and privileges. The only uneasiness they feel is that they are not at this moment at the scene of action."

A modern historian, Philip J. Schlegel, has compiled a complete muster roll for the York company. In the publication, "Recruits to Continentals: A History of the York County Rifle Company, June 1775 to January 1777," Schlegel lists more than 100 men as members, including Doudel, Miller, Dill, Cruise, court justice Thomas Armor, Christian Bittinger (son of one of Hanover's founders, Nicholas Bittinger), and tavernkeeper Martin Eichelberger, Jr. Schlegel points out that one of the enlistees, Peter Hammer, was under age, so his mother hired a substitute, a practice occasionally employed by Colonial families. Youths in their early teens were used by the army as drummers and flagbearers, and parents of young teenagers often saw sons just out of puberty march off to join the war.

On July 1, 1775, the men were ready to join Washington. The Reverend John Roth, pastor of the Moravian church at York, recorded in his diary that the men attended a farewell religious service at Zion Reformed Church under the Reverend Daniel Wagner. At one o'clock, after Wagner preached to the men in German and, according to Roth, entreated them to "keep God before your eyes continually and you will be assured of his guidance," the York County Rifle Company started down East Market Street on its long march.

The York company crossed the Susquehanna at Wright's Ferry and arrived at Cambridge on July 25, thereby distinguishing itself as the first military ard McAllister, the unsuccessful candidate in York's first mayoral election and the founder, in 1763, of Hanover. He had served as a member of the Committee of Observation and Safety for York County. He was married to Mary Dill, the daughter of Colonel Matthew Dill who had commanded a regiment in the French and Indian War. Richard and Mary McAllister had 11 children. Two of their sons commanded companies in the Revolution.

The nine Pennsylvania companies, including the York riflemen and a company from Franklin County commanded by two captains, James Ross and Matthew Smith, were formed into what General Washington was to call "Colonel Thompson's Battalion of Riflemen from Pennsylvania."

Born in Ireland, Colonel William Thompson had settled in Carlisle, working as a surveyor there until called to serve in the Revolution. Captain James Ross, co-commander of the Franklin County company, had been born in York County in Peach Bottom Township. He later earned a reputation as a noted orator and statesman, serving for nine years as a United States Senator. He was also a trusted confidante of and counselor to General Washington.

As in most wars, companies of men in the Revolution were massed into

James Smith, the signer of the Declaration of Independence from York, was also an organizer of "sturdy pioneers" recruited from York to fight against England in the Revolutionary War. Smith is buried today in the First Presbyterian churchyard. (HSYC)

larger bodies, then often pulled out and placed in another group for a different campaign. Such was the case with the York soldiers. After the siege of Boston in the summer of 1775, the original company of York troops, under Doudel and Miller, remained with Thompson's Battalion in Boston. Captain Doudel resigned his command and Miller was promoted to succeed him. After further reorganization and command shifts, the York company was soon engaged in a skirmish. Colonel Edward Hand recorded the incident. He writes: "Our battalion formed the picket guard of the two thousand provincial troops who on the evening of the 26th of August took possession of Ploughed Hill . . . and met with its first loss, Private Simpson. . . ."

The young private, who was from the York company captained by Ross and Smith, did not die from his wounds immediately. While near death in a battlefield tent, according to the diary of James Wilkinson: "The young man was visited by General Washington in person and by most of the officers of rank. . . ." Captain Wilkinson, who had joined Thompson's Battalion as a Boston volunteer and who would later become commander-in-chief of the post-Revolutionary army, further relates that Simpson's death "became a common sorrow in an army of twelve or fourteen thousand men." The personal visit to a dying soldier was typical of Washington's concern for his troops, especially in the early days of the Revolution.

Although the war was exacting a high price from Yorkers, including additional lives, the town's citizenry remained united in the cause of liberty. When a copy of the Declaration of Independence was brought to York soon after July 4, 1776, it was read to a cheering crowd at the Centre Square Court House and a bell atop the building rang out the news. The bell, which had been authorized for the Court House by the county commissioners in

1767, was joined by a chorus of church bells throughout the community.

Within days, however, there were few York County people left to celebrate the Declaration. The Reverend John Roth records on July 17 that "York town seems quite deserted on account of the departure for the army of all men under fifty years of age.... All business is prostrated, all shops are closed. How many prayers and tears will now be brought before the Lord, by parents for their children, by children for their parents, by wives for their husbands."

One of the war's oddities was that once local soldiers exited the town, others promptly entered it. During August, Roth writes, "Numerous bands of soldiers from Maryland, Virginia, etc., passed through the town." John Durang, a Yorker who went on to become an actor and America's first native-born professional dancer, was eight years old in 1776. In a later account of his life, *The Memoir of John Durang: American Actor 1785–1816*, he remembers the period:

> My father was encamped [with Captain George Eichelberger's company] at Lancaster, and a regiment from Virginia was in York.... The men [of this regiment were] in poor condition to meet an enemy ... some without shoes or stockings, some no coats, some with old muskets and some with fowling pieces. However, when they went on their journey, they were supplied by citizens, who could spare them clothes and provisions.

Young Durang, without permission, accompanied the Virginia soldiers to Lancaster. Arriving there in a new hunting shirt and trousers ("green with yellow fringe"), the boy was swiftly sent back to York by his father, Jacob Durang. A surgeon, storekeeper, and farmer, Jacob Durang was a typical "country gentleman" of the day.

Captain George Eichelberger, mentioned in Durang's account, was commander of the Fourth company of York County, and had served as a delegate to the provincial convention held in January of 1775. That conference was a forerunner of the one that resulted in the Declaration of Independence. Eichelberger, who kept a tavern in York, was a member of the county's Committee of Safety, a group formed to protect the families and property of those citizens who were away with the army or who were too young or infirm to protect themselves. The committee's duties also included keeping law and order in the town and collecting funds and materiel for the army. Eichelberger was married to Lydia Worley and they had seven children, including Martin, who also became a tavernkeeper. The elder Eichelberger and his brother, Jacob, had established themselves as pro-liberty activists even before Congress called troops in 1775.

Americans were not the only military men in York during 1776. The taking of prisoners of war was a reality with which the locals had to contend, since a number of prisoners were held on York County soil. Hessian soldiers were confined at Camp Security, a stockaded enclosure about four miles east of York. Just as York's earliest residents had done, prisoners there built crude huts for themselves and their wives and children, many of whom had accompanied them to America. Some of the prisoners had liberal leave policies and, after the war, a few decided to settle in York because of its already large German-speaking population and its similarities to their native land.

Other prisoners were held at the York County Jail at George and King streets, and Durang, in his memoirs, writes that "several of the officers [Hessians] boarded at my father's house." The Durangs lived on East Market Street on the site where the Hamilton Bank now stands, and young Durang says that the Hessians there "had an excellent band of music and occasionally played to my great delight and serenaded the citizens."

The York area, of course, had sources of entertainment other than the

Facing page
Top
During the Revolutionary War the British employed Hessian mercenaries, such as this grenadier, against the Americans. Many of these men brought their wives and children from Germany with them. When the soldiers were confined as prisoners at Camp Security, a few miles east of York, their families lived with them. From the Department of Prints and Drawings, British Museum.

Bottom left
Fairs, or semiannual "frolics," provided early Yorkers with entertainment. Often the fairs suffered from a bad reputation, and in 1816 they were prohibited from being held within the York Borough. This drawing by beloved York folk artist Lewis Miller depicts the "yearly market, or publick fare, held in the Borough of York, June 9th, 1801." Note the Court House and market shed in the background. (HSYC)

Bottom right
John Durang, America's first native-born professional dancer, wrote about his childhood in York, his efforts to join a Virginia regiment, and harvest fairs in the town. Durang would later become known for his various theatrical roles, including his dance to the music of the "Hornpipe," shown here in a picture from his memoirs. (HSYC)

enemy's band. Reflecting on calmer days, when the marching of soldiers and the quartering of prisoners were not necessary, Durang describes the semi-annual fairs, or frolics, where Yorkers' many diversions were often brought together in a single celebration:

> The country people flock in from all quarters, old and young, of both sexes. . . . The market place is furnished with every description of fineries, with some useful as well as ornamental goods by little merchants from Philadelphia and Baltimore, all kinds of diversions going on during the whole day, the taverns crowded, in every room a fiddle and dancing. Showfolks with their signs out, band and trumpet to invite the people to see the puppet shows, wire dancing, sleight of hand. . . . A great many marriages take place by the young country men and girls at the time of the harvest frolic.

Durang also gives the modern Yorker a peek at one of the area's early vices: "The greatest evil in this town is the collection of gamblers, who infest the country towns at the time of fairs, harvest frolics and the [horse] races. . . . They would draw the unsuspecting into their snare and yet those very same gamesters make the appearance of good moral citizens, when they walk the street."

York town's various entertainments, even in the face of war, drew the community's diverse ethnic strains and religious groups together into a shared cultural appreciation of music, parades, fairs, traveling circuses and performers, and other amusements. In fact, so strong was the community's fervor for music, especially, that if hard work, commerce, and the level-headed observance of religious strictures ruled its body, music could be said to rule its soul.

The Palatines who settled York County had brought with them a long musical heritage, as had the Moravians. Pipe organs were installed in the Lutheran and Reformed churches. Church choirs regularly gave concerts before the Revolutionary War, which brought military bands that added marches to the traditional hymns. Less religious elements were the traveling circuses, which passed through the area in wagon caravans, and York's first "dramatic" offerings, including a performance of the tragedy, *Cato,* as well as a bill offering "Mr. McGrath's Company of Comedians from Virginia and Maryland."

Local taverns also helped York earn a reputation as a town that entertained itself well. One such tavern was the Golden Lamb, located on the south side of East Market Street, which was often the scene of festive entertainments. After the Revolution, the Golden Lamb presented Frederick Durang (John's brother) performing with what was probably America's first touring company of actors.

Although Yorkers before, during, and after the Revolutionary War period gladly took time out for such diversions, they were primarily occupied with their two principal interests—farming and business. York County farmers continued to make advances in agricultural techniques and equipment. They began harvesting their crops with the German scythe, which was manufactured locally by sharpening hot iron on the edge of an anvil. The scythe proved effective on the local crops of spelt, rye, and wheat, but it was eventually replaced by another tool, the grain cradle.

The innovativeness and industry that characterized farmers in York County, and throughout Pennsylvania, had accorded them a high, even slightly romanticized, status by the 1770s. John Durang writes that "The Pennsylvania farmer stands predominant. He enjoys the sweets of his industry in the bosom of his family, his artless simplicity cements their harmony and their barn is the best house." Successful farmers were thought, in the class system of the day, to be the equal of firemen and shopkeepers, but probably a step below county and town officials, ministers, and members of the bar. Adding to their importance in the community was the fact that their barns were often used as religious meeting places for various congregations.

Barn raising, from York's beginnings, had been a cooperative effort. Indians helped some of the first white settlers construct their rather crude log barns, but as the population grew, barn raisings became something of a social event, with family, friends, and neighbors joining in the work. By the 1770s the York landscape was dotted with log barns and "Sweitzer" (Swiss) barns, which were built against a bank with the ground floor opening to one side and the top floor opening to the other. The later "bank barns" were adaptations of the Sweitzer barns built by early Yorkers, whose native lands were only miles from the Swiss barns' country of origin.

Churches, too, continued to be built. In 1776 the local Catholics purchased a property, the present-day site of Saint Patrick's Church, for use as a Mass House.

Seventeen seventy-four also was the year of the formation of another important York religious group. The River Brethren, or Brethren in Christ, originated in Lancaster County with services conducted in the home of Jacob Engel, a Mennonite, who later became the church's first bishop. After much discussion, the "brethren" meeting decided that triune-immersion (baptism by immersion three times) was the only practice acceptable to Scripture. They went to a minister of the German Baptist (Dunkard) faith and asked him to baptize the members of their group. Because the group members would not agree to join the Dunkard's church, he refused their request. The group then cast lots on the banks of the Susquehanna. The one who selected the proper ticket baptized the others and finally one of the newly baptized performed the service for him. One hundred Brethren in Christ settled in York and Lancaster counties during the period around the Revolution and the tradition of requiring women to wear small, net prayer bonnets, because of the Biblical injunction that women should keep their heads covered, is practiced today.

York County, in 1776, already had three German Baptist congregations—one on the little Conewago Creek near Hanover, one at Bermudian in Washington Township, and one in Codorus Township. The first elder of the

From the earliest days of York County history, its churches have contributed immeasurably to the welfare and strength of the community. Many early York County congregations worshipped in homes of members or in crude log meeting houses. This informal sketch depicts the Church of the Brethren, Little Conewago Congregation. (HSYC)

last-named church was Jacob Tanner, a poet, who had once mesmerized a debater with an argument set down in perfect German meter. The German Baptists —or Dunkards, from the German word *tunken*, meaning to baptize or dip —began as a group called the Pietists in North Prussia. They believed in baptism by immersion. The Dunkards, like the Brethren in Christ, the Mennonites, and the Friends, were pacifists upon arriving in York County. Some of them decided to fight during the Revolution but the majority of the members in all these groups stood by their nonviolent principles.

When York men were called away to battle, the activities of the community took on a dramatically different complexion. The women were left behind to tend market stands, farms, shops, taverns, fires, and other matters. They also had to deal with the usual chores involved in taking care of their families—spinning, sewing, weaving, cooking, making candles, and cleaning away the dust and dirt of the street. In fact, cleanliness among early York settlers *was* godliness, and German housewives in front of their homes literally sweeping the street became a common sight. The custom is still practiced by some residents today.

The war often kept the men away for long periods. Some, of course, never returned. On November 16, 1776, during the Battle of Fort Washington on Manhattan Island, nearly 400 York-area soldiers under the command of Henry Miller and Michael Swope were taken prisoner. Some of them were held for three years, suffering from hunger, cold, disease, and other afflictions. Some died and others were wounded, but since records were not always kept during those days, no accurate accounting of casualties is possible.

After the defeat at Fort Washington, commander-in-chief George Washington was forced to order his troops, which included a good many Yorkers, to retreat southward across New Jersey. On December 26 he led his men to victory in the Battle of Trenton, aided by the companies of York captains Henry Miller and Philip Albright.

Captain Albright, who had received his education at the German Lutheran School, owned a flour mill on the Codorus. He married Anna Maria Ursula Duenckle, daughter of a German aristocrat. One of the couple's daughters, Anna Maria Ursula, married George Small, who had a lumber yard. Small's lumber yard was a predecessor of the P.A. and S. Small Company.

Yorkers also distinguished themselves at the bloody Battle of Brandywine on September 11, 1777. Pennsylvania troops there were under the overall command of General Anthony Wayne. Colonel Thomas Hartley of York commanded the First Brigade of this division. Also participating in the Battle of Brandywine were Yorkers Colonel Henry Miller, Colonel David Grier, Major John Clark, Benjamin Stoddard, Evan Edwards, George Ross, Archibald McAllister (son of Richard McAllister, candidate in York's first election), Robert Hoopes, James Kenny, James Dill, Andrew Walker, and Martin Eichelberger. One thousand Americans were killed, wounded, or captured at Brandywine and an equal number killed, wounded, or captured on the British side. One of the York Countians injured was Ensign William Russel, who lost a leg by a cannonball. Colonel Miller and Major Clark requested that the state award Russel a certificate of meritorious service and a pension to help compensate him for his loss.

Colonel Thomas Hartley, born in Colebrookdale, Pennsylvania, received his early education at a classical school in Reading. When he was 18 he came to York, where he read law with Samuel Johnston, a relative of his mother. He was admitted to the York bar in 1769 and was one of York's earliest patriots. In the fall of 1775, at age 27, he was a member of the expedition to Canada, during which campaign he was promoted to lieutenant colonel under Colonel William Irvine of Carlisle. When Colonel Irvine was captured in Canada, Hartley was put in command. He returned to Carlisle with his men in March 1777.

In the fall of 1777, York County troops went on to the Battle of Paoli, about 60 miles east of York. During the engagement, 300 American soldiers were killed or wounded. General Wayne, who commanded the forces at what was called "the Massacre at Paoli," later wrote to General Washington of the Yorkers' valor, commenting that he "derived every assistance possible from those gentlemen of this occasion."

Shortly after Brandywine, the British general Howe had begun to move eastward into nearby Philadelphia, a move that would have historic consequences for York. Philadelphia, the home of the Congress, could almost hear the Redcoats approaching and delegates adjourned there on September 23, 1777, to meet in Lancaster on September 27. Congress arrived in Lancaster only to find that the Pennsylvania state government, which had also fled from Philadelphia, had already taken over Lancaster's public building. Since the Court House in York was about the same size as the one in Lancaster— 45 feet by 45 feet—and since having the Susquehanna River between themselves and the enemy seemed like a good idea, the delegates voted to adjourn at Lancaster and reconvene in York on September 30. They arrived in a town of about 1,800 people, with some 300 homes, most of them made of logs, and about a dozen "publick houses," as taverns were then called. These taverns, which also served as inns, soon grew busy and crowded, as members, aides, and guards of Congress, the Treasury, and the Board of War all tried to find lodgings and offices as close to the Court House as possible.

John Hancock, president of the Congress, stayed just across Centre Square

Below left
Colonel Thomas Hartley, commander of the troops in York during the stay of Congress, was also the first Pennsylvania lawyer to be admitted to the Supreme Court of the United States. Hartley was one of the first Yorkers to organize York Countians to fight in the Revolutionary War. (HSYC)

Below
Catherine Hartley, the wife of Thomas Hartley, was a prominent woman in Colonial York. (HSYC)

John Hancock was the president of Continental Congress when it assembled in York on September 30, 1777. Hancock, one of the most ardent supporters of the Revolutionary War, stayed at the home of Mrs. Eva Swope a few blocks west of Centre Square. (HSYC)

from the Court House at the home of Mrs. Eva Swope, the second wife of Michael Swope who had commanded the York troops at Fort Washington and was, at the time, being held as a prisoner of war. A house that later belonged to Archibald McLean at the northeast corner of the Square was chosen to house the Treasury, and James Smith volunteered his law office on South George Street as headquarters for the Board of War and the Committee on Foreign Affairs. (The site of the building used as the Treasury is now the site of Commonwealth National Bank and the James Smith property is the site of the Drovers and Mechanics Bank.) At Elizabeth Moore's Inn on the southeast quadrant of the Square, now the site of a Hamilton Bank annex and restored in 1981, Georgia delegate Edward Langworthy took lodgings and became enamored of one of the Moore daughters. He and young Mary Moore were married the next year.

The chaplains of Congress, William White and George Duffield, took advantage of the hospitality of York's ministers. The Reverend White stayed at the Christ Lutheran Church parsonage on North George Street with the Reverend John Kurtz, and the Reverend Duffield stayed on East King Street with the Reverend Daniel Wagner of Zion Reformed Church.

Increased crowding caused discontent among York's visitors. Elias Boudinot, from New Jersey, complained that the town was "full as a tick." Henry Laurens, who would succeed Hancock as the president of Congress, commented that his total accommodations in York were smaller than the hall of his home in South Carolina and that he was forced to dine on nothing but "bread and cheese and a bit of grog." James Lovell, a Massachusetts delegate, wrote that the local "lime water" had done damage to many of his countrymen's bowels and "had forced some delegates home to their native springs." Lovell's complaint stemmed from York's generous geological gift, limestone, which imparted to some early York wells a white, cloudy color and a particulate consistency. Samuel Adams (who tended to villify even America's greatest towns), complained in a letter to his wife:

> *The house where I am is so thronged that I cannot enjoy accommodations as I wish. I cannot have a room . . . The people of this country are chiefly Germans who have schools in their own language, as well as prayers, psalms and sermons, so that multitudes are born, grow up and die here without ever learning English. In politics they are a breed of mongrels or neutrals benumbed with a general torpor.*

Not every visitor shared Adams's low opinion of York and Yorkers. A letter from Board of War member Timothy Pickering to his wife, dated February 14, 1778, gives a particularly favorable picture of the household of a "widow Mihms" (probably the widow of John Meem, who had helped build the Court House). Pickering writes:

> *She is a very neat, clever, obliging old woman, and has agreed to wash and mend my linen and stockings which is a very great thing here. . . . I have not felt so much at home since I left Salem. She lived all alone and now sets from morning till night at her spinning wheel, which, by the way, is a very modest one. And when I am home writing or reading it gives me no more disturbance than the purring of a cat.*
>
> *There is a warm chamber where I lodge. In one corner [his servant] Millet has fixed me a little cabin in which he has put a straw bed. . . . In this manner I have lain every night warm and comfortable. . . .*
>
> *Millet has bought a tolerable veal at a shilling a pound, butter at two thirds of a dollar, eggs at one third of a dollar a dozen, and potatoes at a dollar a bushel. But above all he gets a quart of good milk every night and every morning which with good bread at a third of a dollar a loaf of about six pounds weight makes our breakfast and supper. . . . Thus my diet is perfectly agreeable.*

Samuel Adams, a representative to Continental Congress, had few good things to say about Yorkers and their political views. (HSYC)

As delegates and other newcomers to York settled in their lodging places, citizens readied the Court House for the Congressional sessions. The jury benches had to be pushed against the wall to make room for the delegates, and Yorkers brought in their own tables and chairs to accommodate the delegates. A table for each delegate was covered with a long cloth, which in the winter made an effective leg warmer that was augmented by a hot-coal footwarmer. A tall, cased clock—made by York's Godfrey Lenhart—timed the sessions from a corner of the room.

Historian Prowell capsulizes the Congressional sessions with these observations: "There were never more than forty members of Congress present at one time. In all there were sixty-four delegates from the thirteen original states who occupied seats in Congress from the time it came to York until it returned to Philadelphia." At the time of the first Congressional sessions in York, Prowell continues, circumstances were grim: "There was little hope that the army under Washington would eventually defeat the British forces. . . . The patriots who came here, however, continued to legislate for the army and the establishment of the freedom of the United States."

The delegates themselves were under no illusions as to the vast scope of the task ahead of them in York. A few days after they arrived, Samuel Adams wrote: "Our affairs are said to be desperate. . . . The eyes of the people of this country are upon us here." Congress had to unify and strengthen the states, which it did by organizing the country's first government and ratifying its first constitution, the Articles of Confederation. The Articles, the forerunner to the Constitution and often called the first constitutional government of the

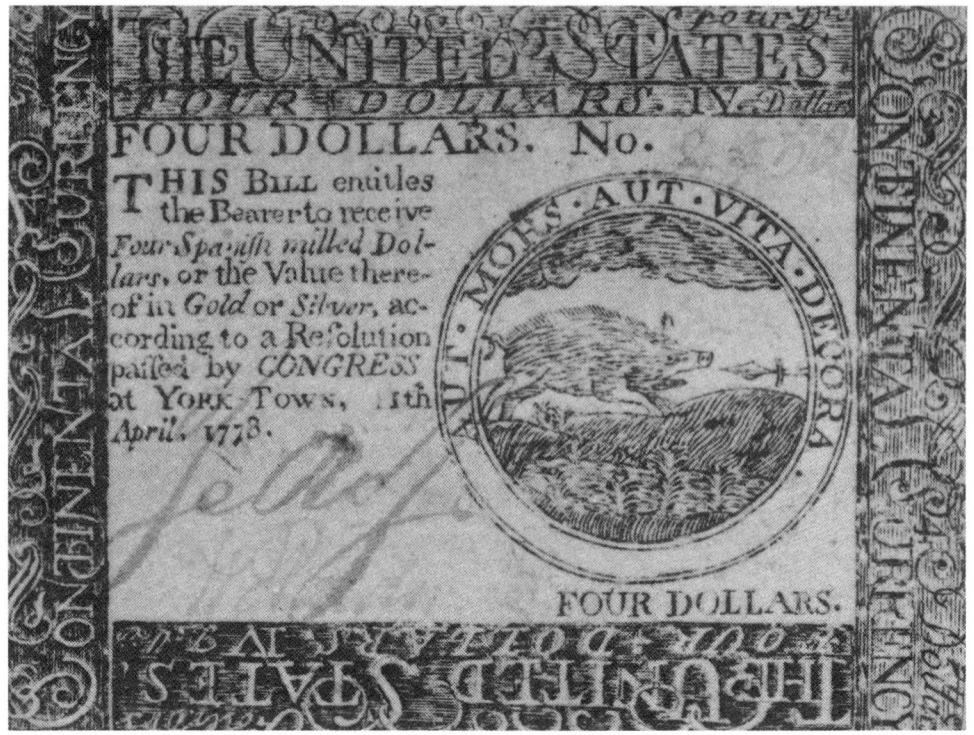

Continental currency, printed on the Hall and Sellers press in a building on the southwest corner of High and Beaver streets (now the Bon Ton Corporate Offices), used the name "United States." Before this date, currency bore the name "United Colonies." (HSYC)

New World, had been drafted and presented to Congress on July 12, 1776. In York, on October 2, 1777, the delegates agreed "that the Articles of Confederation be taken into consideration tomorrow morning at 11 o'clock."

Congressional records from October 2 through November 15 contain accounts of extensive and spirited debates, on those and other issues, as the document was hammered into a form acceptable to the Congress as a whole. Little states argued against big states; Southern states argued against Northern states; and some delegates from the same state argued against each other. The frustration and complexity of those sessions are shown in the correspondence and diaries of the times.

Henry Laurens wrote to his son: "The present question is a mode of taxation. Two days have been amused with conning it: some sensible things have been said, and as much nonsense as ever I heard in so short a space."

Richard Henry Lee reminded his colleagues of the vulnerable nature of the new confederation, saying: "I must note that in this great business of forming our first common charter, we must yield a little to each other, and not rigidly insist on having everything correspond to our own partial views. On such basis we would never be able to confederate."

In constructing the Articles, Congress had to empower the government to unify military resources, outline rules for treaties and alliances, build confidence in the government, stabilize currency in a wildly inflationary financial climate, create procedures for taxation and voting, determine the power to fix Western boundaries, and decide the issue of slavery. The delegates debated these issues and revised the Articles for more than six weeks. Then, on November 15, they adopted the Articles officially. Article I of the document read: "The Stile of this confederacy shall be 'United States of America,'" which marked the first time that term was used in an official capacity to signify the Thirteen Colonies as a single force. The Court House on York town's Centre Square had seen within its doors the adoption of America's first constitutional government. Yorkers feel justified in claiming their city as the "First Capital of the U.S.A."

While Congress was taking responsibility for America, York was taking responsibility for Congress. The Sun Fire Brigade had the honor of protecting the Congressmen during their nine months in York. Congress, probably recognizing the added burden that its presence was placing on the brigade, resolved that "an appropriation of $50.00, Continental currency, be granted to the fire company of York town which has a laurel-wreath design painted on its fire wagon." This prompted the fire company to change its name to the Laurel Company, the name under which the organization still exists today.

Congress's printing of resolutions and constitutions soon created the need for a printing facility in York. On October 17, 1777, Congress authorized its Committee of Intelligence to take "the most speedy and effectual measures for getting a printing press erected in this town—York town—for the purpose of conveying to the public the intelligence that Congress may from time to time receive."

Ten days later the Hall and Sellers press from Philadelphia, which had originally belonged to Benjamin Franklin, was brought to York. The press was set up in a building on the southwest corner of High and Beaver streets on the site, familiar to modern Yorkers, of the old Bon Ton department store. Government documents and $5 million of the inflated Continental currency were printed while Congress worked in York. The *Pennsylvania Gazette*, the official organ of Congress at that time, was also printed there.

On October 29, a couple of days after the printing press arrived, John Hancock resigned as president of Congress because of ill health. Henry Laurens of South Carolina was elected to replace Hancock in the president's chair, which was the one closest to the Court House's heating stove. Upon taking the job, Laurens joked that he "might as well be president as anyone else, since a good seat near a warm fire is some compensation for extra

Below
General Horatio Gates, head of the Board of War in 1777, plotted with other critics of General George Washington to have Washington fired from his job and replaced by Gates. The scheme, which included a plan to sway Washington's strongest supporter, the Marquis de Lafayette, is remembered in history as the "Conway Cabal." (HSYC)

Below right
Henry Laurens of South Carolina succeeded John Hancock as president of the Continental Congress and served for eight months while the Congress stayed in York. (HSYC)

CAPITAL OF REVOLUTIONARY AMERICA • 49

labor."

Laurens had been president only two days on October 31, 1777, when Congress received news from the battlefield of an important victory. Major General Horatio Gates, who had passed through York and praised its new recruits in June 1775, had soundly defeated the British under General John Burgoyne at Saratoga, New York, several days earlier.

The members of Congress were elated over the victory, although they chastised James Wilkinson, the young man who had delivered the dispatch from General Gates, for taking two weeks to arrive with the news. Wilkinson, only 20 years old at the time, had been delayed at a raucous party on his way to York. "Perhaps we should strike a medal in his honor," a member of Congress joked.

Wilkinson's drunken reveling nearly had more serious consequences than delays and the barbs of Congressmen, however. At the party he had attended, Wilkinson had been indiscreet about General Gates's efforts to undermine Washington, efforts that would be revealed as the winter of 1777 drew to a close. But, for now, Congress was jubilant about the Saratoga triumph, which later historians would call "the most decisive battle ever fought on American soil." Laurens appointed a "thanksgiving proclamation," and Congress "set apart Thursday, the 18th day of December next, for solemn thanksgiving and praise." Copies of the National Thanksgiving Proclamation were sent to all 13 states. Thus it was in York that the first national thanksgiving was decreed.

A few days later General Washington sent Colonel Thomas Hartley's regiment, composed mostly of Yorkers, to act as special guard for Congress. The delegates directed that "barracks, or sheds be erected with all possible dispatch" to house Hartley's men in York. The regiment earned the title of "Congress's Own" as a result of its service.

As popular as this move no doubt made Washington among native Yorkers, there were many individuals in town actively working to unseat him. Washington's enemies in the military and the government, foremost among whom was Gates himself, Major General Thomas Conway, and General Thomas Mifflin, were even then plotting to have Washington removed and replaced by Gates. Gates's victory at Saratoga fueled the sentiment against Washington, which had been building since the commander-in-chief's disastrous loss at Brandywine. Although the cunning Gates took credit for Saratoga, modern historians point out that he had never even been under fire, and that officers Arnold and Morgan, under Washington's direction, had actually engineered the battle.

But Congressional president Laurens wrote to Gates in October of 1777: "Your name, sir, will be written in the breasts of grateful Americans of the present age and sent down to posterity." The public concurred, and urged Congress to name Gates the head of the Board of War, a position equivalent to the present-day Secretary of Defense. Gates was thereby authorized to dictate military policy for the entire American forces. The letters, conversations, and insinuations that had passed between Gates, Conway, and the other conspirators became known as the "Conway Cabal," and it was the details of this plot that young James Wilkinson had leaked on his way to York.

When this information was passed on to Washington, by Patrick Henry and others, the commander-in-chief had written to Gates telling him that, through Wilkinson's indiscretions, he had learned of the attempts to damage him. Gates raged with anger and shot off several abusive letters to Wilkinson. Wilkinson had become an intimate friend and aide to General Gates at a very young age, and his youth was demonstrated both in his earlier loose talk and in his dramatic response to Gates's last letter, which contained particularly offensive language. In his memoirs, Wilkinson recalls the incident:

> *Immediately after receiving this letter, I repaired to York, arriving in that town by twilight on the evening of February 23, 1778, to avoid observation. During the night I met my early companion and friend, Captain Stoddert. I recounted my wrongs to him and requested him to bear a message from me to General Gates. He remonstrated against my intention to challenge to fight a duel, and warned me that I was going headlong to destruction. For the first time we parted in displeasure. Soon afterward I met with Lieutenant-Colonel Ball, of the Virginia Line, whose spirit was as independent as his fortune. He delivered Gates the following note: 'Sir—I have discharged my duty to you and my conscience. Meet me tomorrow morning behind the Episcopal Church and I will then stipulate the satisfaction which you have promised to grant. I am your humble servant, JAMES WILKINSON.'*

Lieutenant Colonel Ball was met in the doorway of the Gates home by the general. He was surprised at the message from his former aide and friend, but this was the age of dueling. Integrity and honor had to be restored, at least in Wilkinson's mind, so Gates agreed to the terms: "All right, sir," the general said to Colonel Ball, "we will meet tomorrow morning at 8 o'clock."

The next morning at the appointed time, Wilkinson walked down North Beaver Street with Ball, his "second." They saw General Gates and Captain Stoddert standing in the street in front of St. John's Episcopal Church. Gates was not armed. During the night he had decided to attempt a rapprochement with his young friend.

When Wilkinson saw them, he stopped. Captain Stoddert approached and yelled into the crisp air, "General Gates wishes to speak to you."

"I will meet him on the dueling ground in answer to the challenge which he accepted," Wilkinson yelled back.

Stoddert then came closer and pleaded with Wilkinson to walk down to the church and greet his former chief. "General Gates does not wish to fight a duel with a person for whom he entertains the highest regard and affection," Captain Stoddert said. After a tense moment, Gates and Wilkinson ran to each other and clasped hands in a triumphant renewal of their friendship.

"Come, my dear boy," General Gates said, as emotion welled up in his throat, "we must be friends again. There is no cause for ill will between us. Conway has acknowledged that he wrote a letter criticizing Washington and has since made harsher statements." The two men talked over their differences, and it was decided that Wilkinson would assume the duties of secretary to the Board of War the very next day.

When Gates had to come to York to head up the Board of War in November of 1777, three months prior to the aborted duel, he had rented a stone house next to a tavern at the northeast corner of High and Water streets. (Both house and tavern were authentically restored during the years 1961 through 1964.) Gates's wife, reputedly the richest woman in America at the time, comfortably provided for his needs at their new home near the Codorus. Records from Congress indicate that Gates was not shy about presenting extravagant expense vouchers, some of which resulted from lavish entertainments that Gates and his wife held during their stay there. Oftentimes those entertainments were designed, as in the case of a famous banquet in honor of the Marquis de Lafayette, to forward the fortunes of Gates and the Conway Cabal.

Shortly after Gates's arrival in York, to gain Lafayette's favor, the plotters had recommended to Congress that Lafayette lead an expedition to Canada, with Conway as his second-in-command. Congress approved the plan and directed Lafayette, then 22 years old, to come to York to receive his commission. He arrived in February of 1778 and, after stopping at the Court House, found conspirators John Trumbull, Richard Peters, Gates, Mifflin, General Pickering, and probably some sympathetic Congressmen, such as Benjamin Rush and James Lovell, at dinner. Tradition has it that this banquet was held on the second floor of General Gates's lodgings, where a special partition could be lifted and hooked against the ceiling to make a large banquet room.

When Lafayette entered, the diners greeted him with loud, drunken acclamations. They toasted each other and "the men of the day," conspicuously omitting Washington's name. They were ready to adjourn when Lafayette, angry at what he considered treason against Washington, arose and proclaimed, "I propose a toast to our commander-in-chief, George Washington." The conspirators shuffled their feet in awkward silence. Some pretended to drink and some refused to raise their glasses. Lafayette, having turned the tide against the Conway Cabal by effectively opposing it, bowed politely and excused himself.

These events marked the beginning of Washington's rise to a position of greater esteem and popularity than he had ever before enjoyed in America. Lafayette's visit to York and his role in support of General Washington also won him esteem and popularity—particularly in the minds of Yorkers, who adopted Lafayette as a local hero.

About the time of the cabals, York was to host three important visitors, the first of which was Thomas Paine. Paine, whose impassioned writings and tireless propaganda provided the spiritual fire of the American Revolution, is believed to have lived in York from January through May of 1778 while serving Congress as Secretary of the Committee on Foreign Affairs.

Local tradition claims that Paine lived in the "Cookes House," a stone structure built in 1761 by Johannes Guckes (Cookes) and located about a mile southwest of Centre Square. Although no one can tell how he felt about life in the House — or can even prove that he lived there at all—Paine himself documented the historic way that he spent his spare time. A letter addressed to Benjamin Franklin, dated May 16, 1778, reads in part: "After October 23, I returned to Col. Kirkbridge's [Lancaster] where I stayed a fortnight until the latter end of January, 1778. After that I went to York and published [posted] Crisis No. 5 to General Howe. I have begun No. 6 which I intend to address to [British prime minister] North."

While Paine was writing, York was receiving its second important visitor. On February 5, Baron von Steuben, a member of King Frederick the Great of Prussia's military staff, came to town. Congress, after receiving the baron with great praise, gave him the commission of lieutenant general of the American forces. He was sent to Valley Forge, where Washington graciously welcomed him and put him in charge of shaping up the "ragged and motley" American army.

In March the third famous visitor arrived: the Polish count Casimir Pulaski. While in York he worked out of headquarters near the Square at the west side of North George Street. On March 28 Congress made Pulaski a brigadier general and gave him authority to "raise and have the command of an independent corps to consist of sixty-eight horse, and two hundred foot."

Charles Fisher, son of early York clockmaker John Fisher and a friend of Pulaski, made a weathervane in the count's honor, using the silhouette of a Polish dragoon, which has become a familiar symbol to York citizens. The weathervane was installed on the cupola of the Court House and stood watch there until the Court House was torn down in 1841. It was then rescued from the building's rubble by members of the Laurel (*nee* Sun) Fire Company.

Additional help came from Europe on May 2, when Simeon Deane,

One of York's most beloved visitors, the Marquis de Lafayette, quelled General Gates's plan against General Washington by praising Washington: "Gentlemen, here is to one you have forgotten. I propose a toast to our commander in chief, General Washington." (HSYC)

Above
A weather vane depicting Count Casimir Pulaski, made by John Fisher's son Charles, was installed on the cupola of the York County Court House. (HSYC)

Above right
Oral tradition in York claims that Thomas Paine, famous pamphleteer of the Revolution, lived in York from January to May 1778 and published his famous document, *Crisis No. 5*, during his stay. (HSYC)

Above, far right
Philip Livingston, a delegate from New York State, died in York and was buried in the graveyard of the German Reformed Church. His body was later moved to the Prospect Hill Cemetery. Livingston was a signer of the Declaration of Independence. (HSYC)

brother of Silas Deane, one of three commissioners to Versailles, arrived in York from France with a letter for Congress. The letter, written by Benjamin Franklin, also a commissioner, came with copies of the Treaty of Amity and Commerce and the Treaty of Alliance. In those treaties the King of France promised to send an army, a fleet of vessels, and supplies to aid the Americans in the fight for liberty. These documents marked the first time the struggling new government was recognized abroad.

As if in contrast to these encouraging commitments of aid, sad news struck the York community. Philip Livingston, a wealthy landowner and delegate from New York, died after a burdensome illness on June 12, 1778. He was buried that evening in the graveyard of the German Reformed Church. The delegate's body later was removed to Prospect Hill Cemetery, where his burial site was marked with a monument placed there by a Livingston descendant.

After the somber occasion of Livingston's funeral, Congress's attention was drawn again to conditions on the battle front. France was pouring troops and other support into America as it had promised in the letter that Deane had delivered, and its support dealt a crucial blow to English interests.

On June 20 Congress received the news that the British had left Philadelphia. The delegates decided to return to that city, assured of the safety in reconvening the American government there. On June 27, in the little brick Court House in Centre Square, Congress adopted its last resolution in York town: "That Congress adjourn until Tuesday next to meet at the statehouse in Philadelphia."

In the following days Congressmen, government aides, servants, and other visitors left the town of York. The first village west of the Susquehanna had carved a lasting place for itself in the history of a determined new country.

John Elgar's iron steamboat, the *Codorus,* was the first metal-hull vessel built in the United States. This is an artist's rendition of the launch, on November 14, 1825, in the Susquehanna River. (HSYC)

CHAPTER IV
CENTER OF TRADE AND COMMERCE

After Congress had left York and returned to Philadelphia, life in the town resumed an even, progressive pace. Yorkers had enjoyed having important men and women living among them, but they were quite content with the greater privacy and calm occasioned by their isolation from a central role in national controversies. It was certainly not, however, a time marked by stagnation or little excitement. York built its first incorporated school, expanded community services, and offered its men several more times to the cause of liberty.

Assisting in that cause was a noted foreign dignitary who had been commissioned into the U.S. Army. Count Casimir Pulaski had been empowered by Congress to raise an independent regiment, later called Pulaski's Legion, and he came to York to recruit troops. The Polish count had a recruiting station on the west side of North George Street from February to May in 1779. He left York and marched with his troops to the South, where he was mortally wounded when the British attacked Savannah, Georgia.

York did not spend all its time engaged in national and international matters, of course. Except for the occasional foray into the war, it entered a period where it concentrated on making improvements at home.

The first order of business was a school. Reading, writing, and arithmetic were taught to York's children at the Moravian Church and at Christ Lutheran Church's German School, but many Yorkers saw the need for a more advanced program stressing the classics. The Reverend John Andrews, an English missionary, opened a classical school in the 1770s in association with Saint John's Episcopal Church. As rector, Andrews originated studies in the classics to supplement his own income. He left York in 1772, and the school he founded is considered a predecessor of the York County Academy, incorporated in 1787.

The Reverend Andrews continued to distinguish himself in academics throughout his long career. He was made vice-provost of the University of Pennsylvania in 1789 and provost in 1810. He wrote a highly praised textbook and became a close friend of Joseph Priestley, the English-born scientist and theologian who moved to America in 1794. In the 1970s York College of Pennsylvania recognized Andrews's work in York and erected a statue in his likeness on the college campus.

In 1774 the pulpit of the classical school's sponsor, the Episcopal Church, was filled by the appointment of the Reverend Daniel Batwell. The Reverend Batwell, another English missionary, openly espoused the rule of King George III and wrote that he was once ducked three times in the Codorus Creek by local people who thought little of his politics. The Reverend Batwell went back to England, where he was rewarded for his loyalty to the crown. The pulpit of St. John's was left without a minister until 1784 and, during the Revolution, the church was used as a storage place for weapons

Above
The Reverend John Andrews, an Episcopal minister, opened a classical school in the 1770s with St. John's Church. In 1787 a successor school was incorporated as the York County Academy which eventually led to the present-day institution known as York College of Pennsylvania. This portrait of the Reverend Andrews was painted by famous 18th-century artist Thomas Sully. Courtesy, University of Pennsylvania.

Above right
In Side of the Old Lutheran Church in 1800, York, Pennsylvania, a famous drawing by Lewis Miller, shows "the singing choir," the sexton, the pastor, and the firemaker among the congregation. (HSYC)

Above, far right
"The York Hotels, Kept in 1800, No better And good cooks can be found no where to prepare victuals for the table," Miller wrote. "Mrs. Lottman frying sweet potatoes and give to Lewis Miller. Some of them the first I ever tasted the where good Eating. It was in her tavern, South George Street, 1799." (HSYC)

and other military equipment.

Perhaps Yorkers took so long to establish a secondary school—after all, more than 30 years had passed since the town's founding—because life had remained simple in York town. Among the many Pennsylvania Dutch residents, there was no great call for an English school. Besides, most York towners were involved with aspects of life more immediately pressing, such as basic sustenance and shelter, than learning or culture. Some in the farming community had not yet built permanent barns or homes and others were still experimenting with the land, which, they soon learned, was not as similar to their homeland as it had at first appeared. The land in Pennsylvania would not grow the grapes the farmers were accustomed to in the mother country—a big disappointment to the settlers—but the farmers eventually found some consolation in the fact that the land could produce bountiful crops of wheat suitable for making fine flour and even finer beer.

While farmers toiled over the land in the countryside, residents of the town tended their own small gardens and the animals that lived behind their homes. The population of the town was slowly growing, though, and since wood houses with "wood and dauble" chimneys were becoming more common, the threat of fire became more worrisome.

By 1781 the number of fire companies in York town had jumped from one to three. Most prominent and long-lived of the three companies was the Sun Fire Brigade, which had renamed itself the Laurel and served York, as it does today, from the northeast corner of King and Duke streets. There were also the Federal company and the Union brigade, (later known as the Vigilant).

Little information remains about the Federal company, although a 1976 history of the York Fire Department states that "the Federal and Union . . . were dissolved" in 1780 or 1781. The Vigilant, which apparently grew out of what was left of the Union, was formed "some time between the years of 1778 and 1781." The founding dates are unclear because the flood of 1817 destroyed the brigades' early records, which were stored in the home of the Quaker clockmaker Jonathan Jessop, a member of the company and later its president.

Carter and Glossbrenner, in their history of York County, give a clear picture of the people and structures that the firemen protected in 1780. York had about 290 houses within its borders at that time and some 1,900 inhabitants, including 335 members of 32 different professions and 43 slaves (who would soon be freed by Pennsylvania's emancipation act that very year). Population of the county, which still included what is now known as Adams County, was about 27,000.

The jobs listed by Carter and Glossbrenner reveal much about the Yorkers of 1780. They must have suffered very little from theft or violent crime, since the town had only four locksmiths and the same number of gunsmiths. Although well-educated—17 teachers, not counting those in classical and theological institutions, served the community—Yorkers were probably not well-read, as they supported only three booksellers, one bookbinder, and no magazine or newspaper publishers. They were, however, well-dressed, having 16 tailors, 13 hatters, eight tanners, four dyers, five weavers, and 40 cordwainers (or leatherworkers), which constituted the town's largest single profession. In a town that had 25 tavernkeepers, 20 butchers, and hundreds of people who prepared their own meals, there was only one cutler, who made, sold, and repaired knives. Homes and farms in those days had their own knife- and ax-sharpening tools, and Pennsylvania Dutch cuisine did not require sophisticated kitchen implements because so many of the dishes were simple.

Most Yorkers were hospitable people, and sharing a meal with a visitor or putting him up for the night was a common occurrence in those days. Although treasuring their privacy, they went out of their way to make visitors feel important and welcome. One of York's distinguished visitors during the early days was the famous General Anthony Wayne. Wayne spent three months in 1781 in York recruiting troops. George Irwin lent Wayne space in his store and residence at the northwest corner of Market and Beaver streets, where the noted soldier worked until time to march off to Yorktown, Virginia. At Yorktown General Wayne participated in the defeat of Lord Cornwallis and the British army.

The following year brought another famous soldier to York with a "legion" of 200 soldiers. France's Marquis de la Rouerie had joined the Revolution under the name Charles Armand. Congress commissioned him a colonel and authorized him to raise a corps of soldiers. Half of Armand's Legion was French and the corps arrived in York after serving with Lafayette in New Jersey and later at Yorktown. Armand had been with Washington's army before his arrival in York and part of his Legion had served with York's Colonel Thomas Hartley in the expedition against the Indians in northern Pennsylvania and southern New York. Some Yorkers, in fact, had served in Armand's Legion, including surgeon John Gottleib Morris. (Morris's son, Charles, was a druggist in York for more than 50 years.) Armand and his command resided in two rows of log houses that met at the northwest corner of Philadelphia and Duke streets. The men were encamped there 11 months before they disbanded and Armand returned to France.

Besides the soldiers' quarters, various taverns, shops, civic buildings, and old churches, Carter and Glossbrenner note, York had by the 1780s added another major religious denomination. The Methodist Episcopal Church had its start as early as 1780 and a few years later Yorker Jacob Sitler erected a building for the congregation. The church soon began to hold meetings "at early candlelight"—the first evening church sessions in York. The evening sessions were controversial enough, at first, to provoke John Joseph Henry, then president of the York County courts, to declare, "there is sufficient time during the day to hold religious services." But the practice soon spread to other York churches. A few years after the congregation moved into its

building in 1807, Francis Asbury, the first bishop of the Methodist Church in America, preached in York to large and appreciative audiences. (Today one of York's most distinguished downtown churches is named in his honor.) The Methodist Episcopal Church was erected on the northwest corner of Philadelphia and Newberry streets, quite a distance in those days from Centre Square.

The principal part of the town in these days of Revolution still lay roughly in a five-block area east of the Codorus between Queen Street and the Codorus Creek. The Codorus—a source of food, recreation, and washing—was a peaceful stream, but had the potential, as Yorkers learned in 1784, to "make an awful display of its terrible destructive power." In March of that year the creek, which was still filled with huge chunks of ice from the winter freeze, rose and spilled over its banks, causing great damage to properties along its bank. After the flood Yorkers rebuilt their ruined buildings. Since public money for flood control was not even thought of in those days, the residents accepted the rampages of the Codorus as another act of God or nature, not unlike death and drought.

In 1784 two wardens of Saint John's Episcopal Church, William Bailey and William Johnston, worked to acquire a minister and, as a result, the Reverend John Campbell came to York. Campbell soon "set about repairing the church, improving the grounds, and raising to build an Academy." He purchased three lots on North Beaver Street, comprising the entire block across from the church, and ordered brick and stone for the construction of the new school. In the *Pennsylvania Gazette* of September 28, 1785, Campbell states his purpose in founding the school: "These counties are inhabited by a great number of Germans, who are daily more anxious for the education of their children in the English language, the knowledge of which may now be obtained at an easy rate; and by this means the roots of those national distinctions and prejudices, which have unhappily too long sustained, will be cut up and destroyed."

Construction soon started in a grove of locust trees. William Bailey lent the church £75 for 6,000 bricks and another sum, four pounds and 10 shillings, to pay for 2,000 shingles. Additional money for the school was raised through a lottery, despite the immoral connotation that many Yorkers connected to any form of chance. Episcopalian clockmaker Godfrey Lenhart was named treasurer of the lottery and eventually Bailey was reimbursed for the money he lent for the school.

Another Christian building, the town's very first Presbyterian church, was also constructed in 1785. Presbyterians applied to John Penn and John

Facing page
Among York's early churches were these, shown clockwise from left: Episcopal Church, Presbyterian Church, Second English Lutheran Church, German Lutheran Church, and First English Lutheran Church. (HSYC)

Penn, Jr., for a grant of land. For a transfer fee of five shillings, the Penns conveyed "the piece of ground situated on the corner of High [now Market] and Queen Streets . . . as a site for a house of religious worship and burial ground." The site is probably one of two in the town conveyed directly by the Penns and not through their attorneys. (The other lot was the one on which the Penns' agent, Thomas Cookson, built a house about 1749.)

York, during this period of growth and building, projected the image of a peaceful, productive, almost pious town, but there were occasional controversies. In 1786 an incident which historians now call "The Cow Insurrection" occurred. Jacob Bixler, a resident of nearby Manchester Township, refused to pay a tax that had been levied on farm animals. The tax collector distrained Bixler's cow and drove it to York, where he planned to sell it and take the proceeds in lieu of the tax money.

On the day of the sale, about 100 men from Bixler's neighborhood—armed with clubs, pistols, and rifles—marched into York. At the intersection of Main and Beaver streets, where the taxman was selling the cow, they were met by a large assemblage of Yorkers, also armed. A court justice, "half deprived of his senses," ran out to the crowd, shouting, "I command thee in my name to keep peace," but no one listened to him.

Frederick Hooke, one of the Bixler followers, cut a rope from around the cow's neck. A York official responded by aiming a sword thrust at Hooke, who escaped the blow. A riot ensued and, after it was over, several participants were fined. Moreover, Carter and Glossbrenner say, "Manchester and York were brought together into a fond and loving union."

Whether this "union" was a significant one or not, the complexion of York was changing from a sometimes disorderly frontier town to a well-organized center of local government, culture, and literacy. In 1787 Matthias Bartgis and T. Roberts established a printing office in York for the first time since the Hall and Sellers press had left town, and began publishing York's first newspaper, the *Pennsylvania Chronicle and York Weekly Advertiser.* Bartgis and Roberts moved their office to Harrisburg, however, when James Edie, John Edie, and Henry Wilcocks started a competing newspaper, the *Pennsylvania Herald and York General Advertiser,* two years later.

In 1787, too, the school that succeeded the Reverend Andrews's program of classical studies was formally institutionalized as the York County Academy. Education in the new country was a privilege. Every pair of hands was needed at home. By the age of 12 or 13, most young men were already employed as farmers, or as apprentices to a barber, carpenter, clockmaker, butcher, cordwainer, blacksmith, brewer, or other tradesman. Scholarships were generally only available to the children of teachers, ministers, and widows, or by the recommendation of a member of the faculty.

Headmasters, salaried on the basis of how many students they could recruit, ran the school's day-to-day business. But 21 of York's leading citizens were in charge of overseeing the school's general management, direction, and governance. The 21 included Reformed Church pastor Daniel Wagner, Presbyterian pastor Robert Cathcart, Saint John's Episcopal pastor John Campbell, Colonel Thomas Hartley, Major John Clark, and Colonel James Smith. Of the 21 men, 11 were Revolutionary War heroes.

The Academy, one of the first classical schools established west of the Susquehanna, also served the community as a center for the arts. Theatrical performances and concerts took place periodically throughout the following decades and various societies formed there provided valuable new direction in intellectual development. But the Academy's main function was education and, especially in later years as a college-preparatory school, it would train thousands of young men "who became leaders in city, state and national affairs; in professions of law, medicine, education and the ministry;

An early woodcut shows the York County Academy, which originally served as an educational institution and a center for the arts. Courtesy, York College of Pennsylvania.

and in finance and business."

A 20th-century Academy history points out that, among those who attended the Academy, were at least four judges of the York County courts, 20 others who became members of the bar, 25 who became prominent members of the medical profession, and eight who became educators. Others went on to serve as editors, authors, ministers, high-ranking military officers, and federal or state legislators. The Academy history also records that during the first 140 years of the Academy's existence, no student was graduated. Students, during their regimen of strict discipline and moral instruction, were drilled with the concept that learning never stops.

As the Academy's history suggests, alumni had far-reaching influence after their tenure at the York school. Samuel Klinefelter, for instance, studied at the Academy; at the peak of a full and varied career, he became president of Western Christian University (now Butler University). He also served as Indiana State superintendent of public instruction after pioneering schools in that state. Another alumnus, Levi Clarence Hunt, became the president of Albright College, and still another, Waldo Emerson Gentzler, became assistant provost of Columbia University in his distinguished career as an educator.

Millard E. Glatfelter, an Academy student for two years, began his career as a teacher in York County rural school but left to direct Temple University's High School. He later became the university's registrar, then its vice-president, and finally its provost. John Allen Smith proceeded to Gettysburg College after studying at the Academy and earned his medical degree from the University of Pennsylvania. He accepted a teaching position at the University of Texas, where he became "professor of all subjects taught with the microscope. . . ." Those subjects at that time included histology, embryology, bacteriology, parasitology, and clinical pathology. His work there resulted in the expansion of equipment and curriculum, and his research later with the hookworm led to mass efforts to exterminate the parasite in America's Southern states and in subtropical areas of other countries.

Edgar Fahs Smith, older brother of John Allen Smith, is probably the Academy's most distinguished alumnus. The son of a miller, he was born on the banks of the Codorus and attended the Academy, where he mastered Greek, Latin, and other subjects. During a career marked by substantial contributions to education, Smith held governmental, state, and corporate offices; wrote 13 chemistry textbooks translated into French, German, Italian, Russian and Chinese; and became provost of the University of Pennsylvania. While at the university, he completely revised the courses of study and made its school of science one of the best in the country. He also raised millions of dollars for the university and was inundated with honorary degrees, medals, decorations, and memberships in prestigious intellectual societies. Smith's image was commemorated on the University of Pennsylvania campus by the erection of a bronze statue and, in York, a high school overlooking the city was named in his honor.

The success of the Academy's students was probably linked to the seriousness with which classes were approached and to the intellectual stimulation provided by the Academy's superb faculty. A standard of excellence was set at the Academy by such instructors as Thaddeus Stevens, Samuel Bacon, Samuel S. Schmucker, and Daniel Kirkwood.

Samuel Bacon, a native of Sturbridge, Massachusetts, organized a company of Junior Volunteers at the Academy during the period of the War of 1812. The corps included young men such as David Cassatt, son of the president of York's first bank; Samuel Small, who would later establish the firm of P.A. and S. Small with his brother, Philip Albright Small, and who would also erect another important York school, the York Collegiate Institute; and other sons of York pioneers, John Armstrong, Jr., George S. Morris, Henry Miller, Jr., George P. Kurtz, and Baltzar Spangler, Jr. Professor Bacon later studied law, became deputy attorney general, and was ordained an Episcopal priest. In 1817 Bacon started York's first Sunday school, which, within a year, had 300 students. Bacon has also been credited with proposing the first professional magazine for teachers.

Samuel S. Schmucker, after his tenure at the Academy, moved to Gettysburg and founded a classical school that became Gettysburg College. He was the college's first president and also founded the Lutheran Theological Seminary in Gettysburg. Daniel Kirkwood, a Scotch-Irishman born in Harford County, Maryland, taught for three years at the Academy, instructing courses in algebra, geometry, and science. Kirkwood became a leading American pioneer in astronomy, calculating the earth's exact distance in miles from the sun, and became a highly respected authority on comets and meteors. He taught at the University of Indiana, where an observatory, a lecture hall, and a university town street were given his name.

Other faculty members made similar contributions to the worlds of medicine, science, law, and theology, as well as impressing on their students at York the fundamental joy of a keen mind put to challenging work.

The year 1787, which had seen the establishment of the York Academy as well as the town's first newpaper, also marked the date of its incorporation. On September 24, 1787, 46 years of informal organization of the government and town services ended when York was "erected" a borough. Under Pennsylvania law a community of roughly more than 2,000 citizens could incorporate itself as a borough and elect officers to manage its affairs. Upon the borough's erection, Henry Miller was elected chief burgess, David Cantler was chosen burgess, and the assistant burgesses were Baltzar Spangler, Michael Doudel, Christian Lauman, Peter Mundorf, David Grier, and James Smith. The first town clerk was George Lewis Loeffler, and Christian Stoer was the first high constable.

Under the requirements of Pennsylvania law, only the most populous area of the community was included in the boundaries of the borough, and York has been restricted in size by the original incorporation boundaries until modern times. Only through complicated annexations, which have been attempted rarely, has York been able to increase its size. In all other respects besides size, however, the borough would undergo extraordinary changes over the next several decades. Fortunately for historians, the way the borough of York looked shortly after its incorporation, and some of the ways its residents spent their time, have been preserved in the observations of a French traveler. Thomas Cazenove, who visited York in 1788, writes:

> *The town is in York valley, on Codorus Creek, a little river always rich in water, permitting several mills of all kinds in the neighborhood; the Common . . . is unusually spacious. The Court-house, placed in the middle of the square, ridiculously shuts off the view of the whole of the 2 main streets.*
>
> *As in every inland town of Pennsylvania, there is a quantity of taverns and inns, where the people come to talk and drink, morning and evening, as in the cafes of European cities. Also many stores where . . . [y]ou find everything necessary in utensils, clothing, furniture, for the lower class, but nothing dainty of choice.*

Cazenove also observed that, "James Smith, Esq. and the families of Mr. Hartley, a lawyer and congressman . . . and General Miller have been most obliging, and are the best society here. Two-thirds of the inhabitants are Germans and mechanics."

These largely uneducated "mechanics"—carpenters, wagonmakers, brick burners, and others—were often victimized by shrewd manipulators who visited York in those days. There was, for example, one Dr. Dady, a German who came to America with the Hessians during the Revolution. His eloquence in both English and German allowed him to move freely between the Englishmen and Germans in York, and his "artful ways" enabled him to dupe the more naive Yorkers. Dady, at various times, passed himself off as a minister, a conjurer of fake ghosts, and a physician who sold a "mineral dulcimer elixir."

In 1788, the year Cazenove made his observations, the capital of the nation was nearly relocated on the banks of the Susquehanna. In fact, York Borough was in consideration for the capital site. Congressman Thomas Hartley made eloquent speeches before Congress supporting the already-proposed site of Wright's Ferry (later Wrightsville), on the York County side of the river. The borough of York and York County's Peach Bottom Township had also been discussed as possible sites for the national headquarters.

William Maclay, a prominent leader in the Revolution and a member of the Supreme Executive Council of the Pennsylvania Assembly, was enthusiastic in his support of York as the national capital. He sent a letter to James Smith at York asking him to prepare a paper in support of the proposal. Smith gathered a group of community leaders, who issued a report revealing that the borough of York now had 12 public buildings (including churches), 412 private homes, 2,884 inhabitants, 46 tradesmen, 23 stores, 18 taverns, and 15 boarding houses.

In lengthy discussions the attention of Congress was again turned to Wright's Ferry. Congressman Hartley told his colleagues that Wright's Ferry, indeed, was the best site available and asserted in his analysis that the

Facing page
These early York structures are from an 1852 lithograph entitled *View of York Pa. from the Harrisburg Road* (counterclockwise): German Reformed Church, Court House, Methodist Church, Railroad Station House, and Catholic Church. (HSYC)

fertility of the soil in York County was "inferior to none in the world." Furthermore Hartley told his fellow Congressmen that, if they enjoyed a sumptuous dish of fish, he could assure them that the Susquehanna held a bountiful supply that would please the most sophisticated palate. The House of Representatives voted 28 to 21 in 1789 to locate the capital "on the banks of the Susquehanna," but complicated arguments ensued and finally the banks of the Potomac were afforded the honor.

Although York was passed over as the site of the new nation's capital, it was not forgotten by its first President. President George Washington paid York a visit in 1791. Few records of his visit exist, but modern scholars do know that Washington came to town to see his friend Thomas Hartley, who had served under the then General Washington during the Revolutionary War.

Historians have also ascertained that Washington attended services with Hartley at the German Reformed Church on West Market Street near the Square on the morning of July 3, 1791. (Washington, an Episcopalian, would have attended the Episcopal church, but its minister was out of town.) The President later wrote in his diary that he was in no danger of being converted during the service since he did not understand a word of German, the language in which the service was conducted. The windows of the Court House were illuminated by candlelight during Washington's visit.

From the time of his nomination to the Presidency, Washington found strong political support from the York community. Many of the newly erected borough's leaders had served under Washington in the Revolutionary War, and had earned deep respect for his courage in the thick of battle. His personal friendships with such Yorkers as Thomas Hartley and John Clark further strengthened the bond of allegiance to the man who would become the nation's first President. Washington, for his part, knew York well from Congress's nine-month stay there. The quashing of the Conway Cabal in York also engendered pleasant associations in Washington. Yorkers' love for Washington was richly displayed in 1799, when the country received news of the former President's death. In his memory a procession walked down the borough's streets, led by Henry Miller, the Reverend Daniel Wagner, the Reverend Robert Cathcart, and the Reverend John Campbell.

As the century drew to an end, York and Yorkers had found themselves more prominent throughout Pennsylvania. In 1796 John Fisher, York's clockmaker-artist, painted Pennsylvania's Coat of Arms for the Court House. A copy of the Fisher painting hangs in Philadelphia's Independence Hall. The original, the oldest painting of the Coat of Arms in existence, is owned today by York College of Pennsylvania.

CENTER OF TRADE AND COMMERCE • 63

John Adams, second President of the United States, served in York as a representative to Congress from Massachusetts. Adams would later visit the York County Court House as President, and congratulate Yorkers on their thrift, industry, progress, and patriotism. (HSYC)

Yorker Solomon Meyer achieved prominence with *Die York Gazette*, the county's first German newspaper and one of the first in all of southeastern Pennsylvania, which began in 1785. A number of other newspapers followed, springing up throughout the region.

As the new century appeared, it brought with it two reminders of York's past. The 1800 census revealed that the town now had 2,503 people, an increase of more than 20 percent over the 1790 census. Population in the county, which had previously been increasing at a significant rate, received a setback. Through an act of the legislature, Adams County had been carved out of York County's western side, diminishing the area of York County from 1,469 to 921 square miles. The population of the smaller county continued to grow, however, and in 1800 it stood at 25,643. In 1790, when the United States had made its first census count, there had been 37,147 people living in the county including the area that became Adams. Many of the outlying townships, in those days, had supported larger populations than the borough of York because of greater area, shifting boundaries, and further emigration, but York Borough had continued to be the center of all county activities.

In May of 1800 John Adams returned to the Court House where he had served as a Congressional delegate in 1777, but this time he came as President of the United States. Adams congratulated Yorkers on their thrift, industry, progress, and patriotism, then rode off to the newly constructed White House. As Adams left for the banks of the Potomac, a number of Yorkers no doubt had lumps of envy in their throats. A different decision 12 years earlier might have placed the White House on the banks of the Susquehanna near York, or even in York itself.

Although voting statistics for York were not kept until 1812, York had no doubt supported the Federalist Party under Adams in the 1796 election, as it had under Washington for two terms. But with the emergence of the two-party system in 1800, a trend for York County was set that would last more than 100 years. From 1800 to 1916, with few exceptions, Yorkers would cast ballots for Democratic candidates in the Presidential races, as well as electing Democrats to the U.S. Congress, the State Assembly, and the State Senate. This trend was signaled most clearly in 1800 with the election of the first "Jeffersonian Democrat" to a seat left vacant by the death of Thomas Hartley, the last Federalist to be sent to Congress from York.

The shift to the Democratic side was probably precipitated by the Federalist Party's policies that were designed to increase the power of the centralized government. Disaffection with this Federalist tendency had been engendered as early as 1791, with the hated Whiskey excise tax, which directly affected York distillers, but Washington's personal popularity had overridden the suspicion that the new federal government was becoming more like the British crown in assessing unfair taxes. Now that Yorkers had an alternative party, however, they gave it their enthusiastic support.

Besides marking a shift in political loyalties, the turn-of-the-century period also saw the culmination or initiation of a number of transportation developments that were greatly increasing York's importance as a center of trade and commerce. York was fortunate in its location, as it was an important crossroads in the middle of a commercial route going south to Baltimore, north to Harrisburg, east to Philadelphia, and west to the Fort Duquesne [Pittsburgh] area.

In 1792 the state of Pennsylvania had approved a new road linking Philadelphia to Lancaster. The 62-mile road, which was to be paid for by tolls, took two years to build and cost $465,000. The first turnpike within York County's borders was chartered in 1804 by the state legislature and was to link Wrightsville to York. The road was not completed until 1818. The York and Conewago Turnpike was built from York to York Haven in 1818, and extended along the Susquehanna River to Harrisburg in 1835. During the same era, the first bridge was built across the Susquehanna. The wooden structure with its 23 piers was completed in 1814 and greatly facilitated travel between York and Lancaster.

As commerce began to stream through York in unprecedented amounts, a series of strange local incidents brought a sense of uneasiness to the prospering community.

A series of fires threatened York in February and March of 1803. The most shocking fire struck the Academy building. No one knew, at first, how the fires had started, but Yorkers suspected arson.

It was later revealed that the fires had, indeed, been set. A black woman, Margaret Bradley, had been convicted, in February of 1803, of attempting to poison two York sisters, Matilda and Sophia Bentz. She was sentenced to four years' imprisonment, which infuriated some of York's black residents, who were convinced of her innocence. For about three weeks afterward, fires were set in buildings in town every day.

The origin of the fires remained mysterious until one black girl was instructed to set a barn on fire "at 12 o'clock." At high noon, instead of midnight as the instructions implied, she carried a pan of coals into the barn of a certain Mr. Zinn and scattered them on the hay. She was discovered, taken under arrest, and confessed to the crimes with others in her group. The conspirators were soon caught, tried, and punished.

York did not escape the slavery issue. Advertisements in the York papers prior to Pennsylvania's emancipation act of 1780 had publicized an occasional slave for sale, and other advertisements, placed in York papers by Southern plantation owners, offered rewards for escaped slaves who were believed to be passing through the York County area. York, in fact, later became a secret center for the hiding of slaves on their way to freedom. Some black people from the South were brought to York's Public Common, where they lived. The York County census (which included Adams County until 1800) had counted 471 ex-slaves in 1783 and 499 in 1790. In 1810 there were 22 and in 1820 only six were counted. York County's last black citizen who had been a slave died in Hanover in 1841.

The year after the rash of fires in York, 1804, held a sound infinitely more enjoyable to York citizens than the clangor of fire bells. The great organmaker David Tannenberg, a native of Saxony, arrived in town that year to construct a new organ for Christ Lutheran Church. Tannenberg, an accomplished violinist and fine tenor vocalist, had already built organs in Salem, North Carolina; Albany, New York; Baltimore, Reading, Philadelphia, New Holland, and Lancaster. Tragically, though, as Tannenberg was making the last adjustments on the new instrument in York, he was stricken with apoplexy, fell off his bench, and suffered head injuries that would take his life on May 19, 1804. His newly completed organ was played at his funeral service in York and the children of the Lutheran and Moravian congregations sang at his grave. Eventually Tannenberg's last organ became the property of the Historical Society of York County, which still uses it today for special events.

The people of York, during this period, were also becoming social-minded, founding the county's first and only Poor House (or Almshouse) in 1805. The state legislature had authorized the county commissioners to levy a special tax to pay for the building and operation of a house "for the employment and support of the poor in York County." A year later Yorkers Martin Gardner, Samuel Collins, Abraham Grafius, Christian Hetrich, Peter Small,

Peter Stoer, John Henneisen, Henry Grieger, and Daniel Spangler were appointed its organizers. The site that they chose for the home was "a certain plantation, and tract of land, of and from Andrew Robinson, Esq., called Elm-spring farm within one mile of the borough of York." The Almshouse buildings were constructed soon thereafter and "the poor were removed thither from all parts of the county, in April, 1806."

Financing such projects as the Almshouse and encouraging York's surge of rising commerce led in 1810 to the establishment of York's first bank. The York Bank was organized in that year, after Pennsylvania was divided into eight districts and each one was authorized to establish a bank. The York bank's 15 directors, who served until 1824, included members of the venerable Cassatt, Spangler, Hay, Eichelberger, Lenhart, Jessop, King, and Barnitz families. David Cassatt was elected the first president and was followed in that office by Jacob Hay, Charles A. Barnitz, James Lewis, Michael Doudel, Henry Welsh, G. Edward Hersh, and Grier Hersh. Early cashiers were Thomas Woodyear, John Schmidt, Samuel Wagner, George H. Sprigg, and W.H. Griffith. John C. Schmidt, a great-great-grandson of cashier Schmidt, is an officer of the bank today.

With social institutions, new churches, a new school, and a new bank, York was taking on urban characteristics. It was changing from a center of informal trade to a center of high finance, and from a center of craftsmanship to a center of fine arts. The famed engraver William Wagner, whose

Services in York's German Reformed Church were depicted by William Wagner in 1830. (HSYC)

Top
Possibly the first "Christmas Tree" pictured in the New World is included in this Lewis Miller drawing of family life. (HSYC)

Above
Lewis Miller drew and captioned the following: "Colonel George Spangler making Cherry Bounce in 1806. To a Barrel of Juice put into it Six pound of Sugar and two gallon of whiskey and let the Juice and Sugar boil in a large kettle a half an hour and Skim it." Oral tradition claims that an understood part of the recipe was the ending, "... and bounce!"

Above right
This is a self-portrait of Lewis Miller, the artist who chronicled an era with his gossipy and detailed drawings of life in York in the 1800s. (HSYC)

watercolors and engravings of York streets give modern Yorkers a sharp and penetrating view of York's past, had been born in 1800 and was learning his trade in the first decades of the 19th century. York's best-known and best-loved artist, Lewis Miller, was also at work at this time. Art critics today, who classify Miller as one of America's most treasured folk or primitive artists, tend to lose sight of the fact that he was a carpenter by trade and made his watercolors for his own enjoyment and for the pleasure of his neighbors.

Born in 1796, "Louie" Miller (as he was called) spent 80 years of his life drawing his *Chronicles*. These sketches depicted, in minute detail, the common, the grotesque, the scandalous, and the eccentric aspects of York life between 1790 and 1870. He was a prolific artist and Yorkers of the 18th and 19th centuries grew accustomed to the sight of Miller drawing in his sketchbook, while attending public events or at other times "just leaning against a lamppost." Miller himself attested to the authenticity of his works with a preface to his *Chronicles*, which reads in part: "I myself being There upon the places and Spot and put down what happened. And was Close by of the Greatest number, Saw the whole Scene enacted before my eyes."

The six volumes of Miller sketches owned by The Historical Society of York County include drawings of elephants bathing in the Codorus, a cow killing a pigeon, a farmer burning his supposedly bewitched hogs, "old Mrs. Schreck laying in the oats," a doctor extracting the skeleton from a corpse for study purposes, a York housewife's attempt to paint a chicken, York's funeral procession for President Washington in 1799, and the surrender of York to the Confederates in 1863. Miller annotated these and many other scenes in both German and English, making his works doubly valuable. In addition to the thousands of sketches, the Historical Society owns a 46-by-64-inch pediment that Miller sculpted in an eerily primitive fashion for hanging over the door of his birthplace home on the east side of South Duke

Above
A William Wagner watercolor shows the Market Shed in 1830, just west of the York County Court House. On the right is the sign of the Globe Inn. (HSYC)

Top
Lewis Miller recorded this exhibition in York, "Little Tom Thumb in the New Court House," May 28, 1849. (HSYC)

Above left
In the Pennsylvania German tradition, Lewis Miller decorated birth and marriage certificates for Yorkers. This example celebrates the birth of George Billmyer on the 4th day of June in the year 1849. (HSYC)

Street.

Miller's 80 years of work give Yorkers an unparalleled view of life in early America, and the Historical Society's collection is the envy of such museums as the Abby Aldrich Rockefeller Folk Art Center, the New York Historical Society, the Henry Ford Museum, and the Whitney Museum of American Art, all of which own less substantial collections of Miller's work. Donald A. Shelley, executive director of the Ford Museum, writes that York's Lewis Miller "suggests comparison with St. Memin and his profiles of notable Americans, with Audubon and his 'Birds of America' or with George Catlin and his on-the-spot sketches of American Indians."

Miller was 16 years old and already launched on his career in May of 1812, when the call came from President James Madison for 14,000 Pennsylvania men. Pennsylvania Governor Simon Snyder, who had spent his early manhood in York, issued the call and soon had three times more men than he needed. William Reed, a York County native, was Snyder's adjutant general, and his experience as brigade inspector of militia for York County led Snyder to choose him to organize the state militia.

The war, which was for the most part being fought hundreds of miles north of York, came frighteningly close on the night of August 24, 1814. During that evening Yorkers observed a light in the southern sky. The British were burning Washington.

The British troops were coming close—Washington was only 90 miles away—and they were planning to stay. The British sailed to North Point, 14 miles southeast of Baltimore and 60 miles southeast of York. Governor Snyder ordered the Pennsylvania militia to rendezvous at two spots—Marcus Hook on Delaware Bay and York—so that they could prepare to meet the enemy. Six thousand men, including 400 Revolutionary War veterans, gathered on York's Common and were mustered into service for six months

Above
Simon Snyder was the governor of Pennsylvania when the War of 1812 broke out. From Jenkins, *Pennsylvania: Colonial and Federal*, Vol. 3, 1903.

Above, top right
A carved pediment by Lewis Miller graced the entrance to his residence on South Duke Street. (HSYC)

Above right
St. Patrick's Church on South Beaver Street is shown in a William Wagner watercolor. The building pictured here was erected in 1810. (HSYC)

"unless sooner discharged." Among the Yorkers watching them on the Common was Lewis Miller, who stood nearby, executing a watercolor sketch of the men. That drawing has become one of Miller's most famous works. The York Volunteers, under the command of Captain Michael Spangler, marched to Baltimore and offered to help defend the city. They ended up fighting in the Battle of North Point.

On September 13, 1814, the British attacked Fort McHenry, located near Baltimore. It was during this attack that a Washington lawyer named Francis Scott Key, on his way to Baltimore to rescue a friend from imprisonment, wrote the lyrics to "The Star-Spangled Banner." The music, however, was supplied by a Yorker.

When Key arrived in Baltimore, he gave the lyrics to his brother-in-law, Captain Benjamin Eades, who took them to an old tavern that adjoined Baltimore's Holliday Street Theatre. An 18-year-old actor named Ferdinand Durang—second son of the York diarist and dancer-actor, John Durang—was at the tavern, drinking with friends who were fellow players at the theater next door. According to Chief Justice Tawney, Eades was discussing the new set of words when an idea seized Ferdinand Durang. Hunting up a volume of old flute music, he jumped up on a chair and impatiently played bits of tunes as they caught his eye. "One called 'Anacreon in Heaven,'" writes Tawney, "struck his fancy and riveted his attention. Note after note fell from his puckered lips until with a leap and a shout, he exclaimed, 'Boys, I've hit it!'" The chief justice later observes: "There rang out for the first time the song of the Star-Spangled Banner."

After the war ended in the fall of 1814, men returned home and the community resumed the business of tending fields and shops. Late in the year, 60 acres of land were added to York town when the heirs of John Hay (a president of York's first bank and the community's market master) laid out lots "after the manner of the rest of the town, extending the streets and alleys north." The lots were sold to the highest bidder and the area became known as "Hay's Addition" or "Haytown."

This welcome acquisition coincided with bad news for most of the community's citizens. Carter and Glossbrenner note that, in January of 1816, the state legislature prohibited the holding of fairs within York, declaring them "common nuisances," after a York citizen was killed in the autumn fair of 1815. Three persons were convicted of manslaughter for the death of the citizen, Robert Dunn.

Also in 1816, the York Water Company was formed, and the York bank's first president, David Cassatt, served as the Water Company's first president. (Cassatt, interestingly, was a cousin of the American painter Mary Cassatt.) The company laid out wooden pipes—logs with holes drilled through their long measure—and brought water from springs.

In addition to an annexation and a water company, the York community got its first church solely for black people during this era. As early as 1800 York had become a crossroads for escaping or manumitted slaves, and, while most of them passed through the town and proceeded to Wrightsville where they crossed the Susquehanna, some settled in York. (Others settled in communities across the river at Columbia and Marietta.) The new York residents met in each other's homes for worship services in the beginning, but by 1819 they were ready for their own house of worship. With the encouragement of other churches in town and some community leaders, they erected a church on North Duke Street. The building also was used as a school for black youths for a period of 60 years. The church's first trustees were John Joice, Richard Butler, John Lindenberger, Edward Young, and Israel Williams.

York's classical school, the York County Academy, also was expanding at this time and Thaddeus Stevens, who would later become one of America's most prominent statesmen, arrived in York to study law in Cassatt's legal offices.

While in town Stevens no doubt lived through the terrible flood of 1817. As an eyewitness reports, "the water rose five feet higher than ever known

Thaddeus Stevens, later noted as a great American statesman and debater, practiced law in York and was a teacher at the York County Academy. (HSYC)

Above
The seal of the Codorus Navigation Company chartered in 1825, is shown here. Until the railroads took over, the company shipped lumber, grain, and coal. (HSYC)

Above right
General Lafayette's arrival in York in an "open Barouch" is depicted in this 1825 drawing by Lewis Miller. (HSYC)

before in this town—where two breweries and five tanneries are swept away, and nothing left but a bleak shore—where instead of the hum of industry nothing is now to be heard but the howling of winds and the rustling of water.... Our town wears the appearance of having been the scene of military operations.... Some are engaged in burying the dead, some in hunting their valuable effects among the ruins while others are dispatched as guards to protect the property floating down the stream."

The flood was only the first in a string of problems that beset York during this period. In 1819 the economic panic that was crippling the nation also came to York, but businesses and banks withstood the disaster. In 1822 the county suffered from a prolonged drought that ended with such heavy rains that they produced another flood. Despite these disasters, the town continued to grow: the 1820 census revealed that York had 3,545 people, more than a 40 percent increase over the 1800 count. The county's population had jumped to 38,759.

A great many members of York's population were on hand a few years later to see the return of an old friend, the Marquis de Lafayette. Accompanied by his son, George Washington Lafayette, the Marquis was touring America. Lafayette arrived in York on January 29, 1825, and was met by Dr. Adam King, Colonel M.H. Spangler, and Jacob Spangler, who took him to Harrisburg. The group returned to York on February 2, and when its members arrived at the turnpike gate, they were met by six military companies and a "vast multitude of people from the town and country." Four gray horses drew a large carriage bearing the general up Market Street, where the ringing of church bells, and Yorkers eager to catch a look at the handsome war hero, greeted him. "Welcome! Thrice welcome, Lafayette," they yelled. After the procession, the Lafayette party was received at the Globe Inn, located on the southwest corner of Centre Square. A reception in the Frenchman's honor was given and a number of Yorkers who had fought under him during the Revolution made speeches praising him.

About 9 p.m., with the town brilliantly lit, Lafayette was feted at a banquet attended by "one hundred gentlemen, citizens of York and invited guests." Flags and evergreens decorated the inn's banquet rooms, and elegant chairs were placed at the tables. Lafayette talked at length to those who attended the banquet, even though he spoke English with great difficulty. Banker John Schmidt assisted the general as interpreter for the occasion.

The mood of the evening was joyous. As a writer for the *York Gazette* of February 8 put it: "The people of York County poured forth overflowing hearts of gratitude and welcome." Yorkers showered their hero with praise: "We love [Lafayette] as a man," they said, "hail him as a deliverer, revere him as a champion of freedom and welcome him as a guest." Lafayette answered: "The town of York, the seat of our American Union in our most gloomy time. May her citizens enjoy a proportionate share of American prosperity."

Although Lafayette could not have known it, his wish was already coming true. Yorkers would soon take care of a special problem: how to get trade goods in and out of the area more quickly and economically.

In 1793 public attention had been called to the importance "of removing obstructions and improving the navigation of the Susquehanna" for, among other reasons, the purpose of facilitating trade into and out of York. State and private money was appropriated for the cause but that solution was not good enough. The opening of a navigable area around the Conewago Falls, on the west bank of the Susquehanna at what is now York Haven, was, in George R. Prowell's words: "the initiatory step which inaugurated a great system of artificial navigation and internal improvement." Exhilarated with the progress already being made, a group of Baltimore businessmen formed a company to test the feasibility of running steamboats on the Susquehanna. Some York merchants joined the new company and their plans came to the attention of a master mechanic in York.

The mechanic, a Quaker named John Elgar, had begun working on the development of a steam-powered engine soon after he had joined York's Davis, Gardner and Webb foundry-machine shop. When the Baltimore-York merchant company advertised a need for steamboats, Elgar constructed a sheet-iron vessel in his shop and was ready to launch it on November 8, 1825. Elgar named his five-ton boat *The Codorus*. He loaded it on an eight-wheeled wagon and, on November 14, pulled it from the foundry as a multitude of Yorkers gathered to watch the welcoming parade. The boat was lowered into the Susquehanna and sailed upstream to Harrisburg.

Thousands gathered on the river banks to watch the vessel with its party of 100 Yorkers depart. When the boat reached Harrisburg, the party, headed by "Captain Elgar," was royally welcomed, then escorted to Buehler's Hotel for a hearty banquet. The Baltimore Company's York-born steamship had proven the Susquehanna navigable from York to the rest of the state. Yorkers, seeing the success of the growing waterways, realized that they could use their own Codorus Creek with similar success. In late 1825 a charter was granted for the construction of a slack-water navigation system from York along the creek to the Susquehanna. Incorporators included Jacob Spangler, George Small, George Loucks, Jacob Eichelberger, Michael Doudel, and Jonathan Jessop. For many years the Codorus Navigation Company oversaw the transportation of large shipments of lumber, coal, grain, and other products, before bowing later to the coming of the railroad.

While most of the Navigation Company's founders were preoccupied with the development of other businesses, Jonathan Jessop was experimenting with a new apple. Jessop had a number of fruit trees in his nursery just south of York. A friend, John Kline, told Jessop about a tree on his farm near Hallam that produced apples that had been covered with snow all winter but remained firm and tasty. Jessop grafted stems from Kline's tree onto seedlings at his farm, producing an apple that became known as the York Imperial. Jessop sold his new strain of apple trees in York, Baltimore, and Virginia, mostly to fellow Quakers. Eventually more than 60 percent of Virginia's rich apple country was growing the York Imperial.

Other agricultural advancements, including the use of burnt limestone as a fertilizer, coincided with Jessop's development of the York Imperial. The county's farmlands, thus, were keeping up with the "hum of industry" and transportation developments that were transforming the York Borough. By 1825 the York Borough had been formally incorporated; its new municipal services were firmly in place; its churches and industries had long since settled in; it had survived natural and manmade disasters and bred artistic triumphs; and it had clear connections to the outside world. York was ready for the future, a future that would turn out to be far stranger than any Yorker of the day could have imagined.

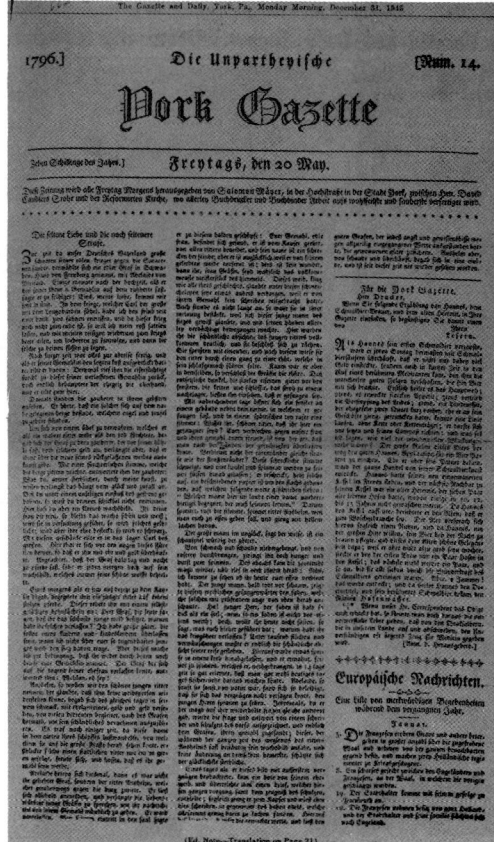

Below
This German version of *The Nonpartisan York Gazette* is dated May 20, 1796, but local historians assume the first issue was printed in late 1795. Solomon Meyer, an educated, German-born printer, saw the need for his German friends and neighbors to have a native-language newspaper and printed a four-page weekly, *Die York Gazette*. The newspaper today is recognized as the 13th oldest in the nation and is now called the *York Daily Record*. (HSYC)

Phineas Davis invented and developed the first American anthracite-burning locomotive engine and called it the "York." Davis was awarded first prize for his invention in a competition sponsored by the Baltimore & Ohio Steam Railway Company. (HSYC)

CHAPTER V
RAILROADS ABOVE AND BELOW THE GROUND

From the 1830s to the beginning of the Civil War, York experienced a period of almost unparalleled prosperity and growth. The antebellum era saw the completion or expansion of many of the transportation developments initiated at the turn of the century, the establishment of a public school system, increasing sophistication in city services and utilities, and an industrial and agricultural boom that proved resistant to financial panics and natural disasters. York was beginning to "Anglicize" and "Americanize"—though it would never completely outgrow its German village roots.

The 1830 census revealed the previous decade's expansion. While York Borough itself showed only a 10 percent increase over 1820 to 4,216 residents, the county was still expanding at a remarkable rate. Its population in 1830 stood at 42,859, up from the 1820 figure of 38,759. The fertile agricultural communities of the Susquehanna Valley, and the growing number of businesses and industries, were attracting still larger numbers of people to the area. Some of the new Yorkers came from Eastern regions of the United States, while others arrived in the continuing waves of immigration from Europe.

The era of transportation advances began, ironically, with a minor setback. An ice flood in 1832 swept away the wooden bridge spanning the Susquehanna, reminding Yorkers for the two years it took to build a replacement bridge just south of the original structure, what York had been like before easy transportation across the river was available.

The loss of the wooden bridge in 1832 was offset somewhat by the completion of the slack-water navigation system, which was first used when Gottlieb Ziegle, James Schall, and Daniel Ford launched the *Pioneer*, a 40-foot boat. Also in 1832 James Chalfont sent a 70-foot boat that could carry 150 passengers sailing down the Susquehanna toward York. On November 18 Chalfont's large, flat-bottomed riverboat, the first "ark," arrived in York carrying 40,000 feet of lumber. It was greeted by about 100 people, who celebrated its arrival with wild cheers and singing.

Canal and river traffic was a much cheaper method of transporting freight than the slow wagon trains from places like Philadelphia to the Western territories, but it was doomed to be short-lived. Canal building had been initiated in 1816, when New York announced plans to build the Erie Canal. That canal, completed in 1825, had secured for New York its preeminence as a river capital. State and local concerns began their own canal projects, however. Locally, the Susquehanna and TideWater Canal was chartered in 1835, with 24 men from Philadelphia, Baltimore, Harrisburg, and other areas serving as commissioners. Yorker Charles A. Barnitz was among the chartering group of businessmen.

A large crowd celebrated the opening of the Susquehanna and TideWater Canal. Nicholas Biddle, the noted Philadelphia financier, made a dramatic speech on the internal improvements that were leading the country toward greater wealth. The canals of Pennsylvania were coming into their own and the next 30 years showed a continual increase in traffic. The capacity of the boats increased, too, so that they were soon descending the canal with cargoes of up to 150 tons instead of the 60 tons they originally carried.

The railroad system would eventually replace the canals in their premiere position of moving freight across the land, however. The doom of the canals had been foretold as early as 1826, the year after the Erie Canal was opened, when the first U.S. railway was constructed outside Quincy, Massachusetts. The little horse-drawn railway was soon itself to be outstripped by the chartering of the Baltimore & Ohio Steam Railway Company. The Baltimore & Ohio Company would establish an intimate connection with York, and the future of American rail transport was promoted in the process. That connection was to be established by young Phineas Davis, who had come to York from New Hampshire.

Davis was an orphan boy, "in search of a situation," when he wandered into the shop of York clockmaker Jonathan Jessop. Jessop employed the young man immediately and he soon showed his inventive genius by designing a gold watch that became the talk of clockmakers in York and other towns.

During his leisure hours while working at Jessop's shop, Davis studied natural philosophy and became fascinated with an idea that he had recently heard discussed: "steam as a motor." He tinkered with many of Jessop's tools and learned from the Quaker shopkeeper's friends all he could about the production of steam energy. He soon joined York's Gardner foundry and machine shop and, while making tools and implements there, he found that many of the clockmaker's tools were just miniatures of the ones he was now operating. After experimenting for some time, his attention was turned to creating a steam-powered locomotive engine. The only locomotives being produced at that time had English-made, wood-burning engines that needed many improvements for easy use in America.

On January 4, 1831, Davis heard of an offer by the Baltimore & Ohio Steam Railway Company. The company promised a $3,500 prize to whomever would invent and manufacture a new American locomotive engine. The competition's rules stated that the engine must burn coke or coal and "consume its own smoke." Davis, now half-owner of the shop on the Codorus (the same one in which John Elgar had built York's first steamship six years earlier), set to work. On June 1, 1832, the day of the competition, he delivered his steam engine, named "the York," to Baltimore.

The *Baltimore Gazette* of July 31 describes the locomotive's trial run: "It started from the Pratt Street depot . . . with a train of fourteen loaded cars, carrying together with the engineer, a gross weight of fifty tons. The whole went off in fine style and was out of sight of the depot in six minutes. The rapid gliding of the immense train was one of the most imposing and beautiful spectacles we have ever seen."

Five other inventors entered locomotives in the competition, but on August 4, 1832, "the York," sporting steel springs invented by Davis, was awarded first prize. Davis and Gardner later built several other locomotives for the B & O. Along with Ross Winans and John Elgar, who invented not only the steamboat but also railroad-drill bearings, switch turnstiles, and plate wheels, Davis solved many of the problems connected with railroad travel and inland transportation.

Since York now had its own railroad manufacturer, the coming of the railroad line to York seemed only natural. Selling trains to the Baltimore & Ohio could prove profitable for a few York merchants and manufacturers, but the benefits of a local train line that many Yorkers could use became a priority. The desire for such a line was enhanced further on April 16, 1834, when several York shopkeepers and merchants went to Columbia, a town on the shore of the Susquehanna opposite Wrightsville, to join Governor Wolf on the first train over the just-completed Columbia, Lancaster & Philadelphia Railroad. The pleasure of train travel and the possibility of moving vast amounts of freight quickly intrigued Yorkers and they joined their neighbors in Maryland to petition the Maryland legislature to build a track to the Pennsylvania state line at York County's southern border. The track could go no further than the state line without a charter from the Pennsylvania legislature, so York County citizens began petitioning that body. Four years later Governor Wolf recommended extending the railroad into Pennsylvania and the legislature passed a bill to that effect on March 14, 1838. When the news reached York, people fired cannons, rang bells, danced in the street, formed a parade, and celebrated into the night.

Building the railroad that would prove immensely profitable for York businesses was a backbreaking task. Workers had to drill a 217-foot tunnel through solid rock and build 82 bridges over the rugged, stream-cut terrain between Baltimore and York. Further delays were caused by a strike in which workers demanded more money for their arduous and dangerous work as well as a supply of whiskey. Eventually, though, the workers finished laying the track and on August 23, 1838, the first train from Baltimore arrived in York.

That trip, and the thousands that would follow it, took only four hours. The train's daily arrival in towns soon became a public event, as passengers going to Columbia, Harrisburg, and Pittsburgh disembarked in York and continued their journey by stagecoach. York was already established as a commercial crossroads for wagon trains.

The railroad would revolutionize York in other ways, including an immediate boom in population. And, as the capacity to accommodate trade through York increased, so did the capital accrued from it. Many local businesses and industries flourished during this period, changing the look of the town as a result. One of the first indications of the new-found affluence was the appearance of more modern and expensive clothes. Carter and Glossbrenner describe York women "in silks and crepes, and jewels and gold, in lieu of [the old] tow frocks and linsey woolsey finery." York's residential neighborhoods, too, underwent a metamorphosis, as greater prosperity allowed York's leading merchants and manufacturers to build elegant homes in the town and the surrounding countryside. One such home was a beautiful Georgian-style townhouse on the corner of Duke and Market streets, a block from Centre Square.

Living in the Georgian townhouse were Philip Albright Small and his wife, the former Sarah Latimer. Sarah's father was Philadelphian Hugh Latimer, a descendant of Bishop Latimer of Worcester, England. George Small, Philip's father, had run a wholesale and retail business in York. George Small was also president of the York Water Company for two terms, during the time when it began an extensive improvement program. The 16,000 feet of bored logs that served the town as water pipes were connected to iron and lead pipes installed in York's new public buildings.

George Small owned a home on North George Street, where Philip and his younger brother Samuel had been born. Philip had attended the York County Academy and was apprenticed as a teenager to a prominent Baltimore merchant, Penrose Robinson. When he returned to York, at the age of 22, Philip was taken into his father's retail and wholesale business, which was renamed George Small and Son. In 1833, after a well-planned expansion, Samuel joined the firm, Philip was named president, and it became the P.A. and S. Small Company. Its diverse interests included purchasing grain, manufacturing flour, retailing groceries and hardware goods, and eventually iron. The firm served dozens of counties in Pennsylvania and Maryland, all without the assistance of salesmen, and at one point, P.A. and S. Small business represented one-sixth of all the freight moved over the Northern Central Railroad between York and Baltimore.

The firm's flour mills were remarkable in their own right. The Smalls built a mill on the Codorus northeast of York, another mill farther downstream north of York, and a larger concern at Goldsboro. The Smalls also operated the old Loucks mill for awhile. The P.A. and S. Small Company mills purchased, for many years, one-third of the grain grown in York County. They developed customers as far away as London and, at the peak of the flour-mill operation, shipped some 90,000 barrels of flour a year to Brazil. The Smalls went on to become partners in various Maryland iron companies, and their philanthropy would be felt throughout the York community.

A second company, established in the 1830s, proved important to York's industrial expansion. Frederick Baugher and E.I. Wolf owned a tannery on the north side of West Market Street that later became known as Eyster, Weiser and Company. The firm employed 100 men initially in tanning activities, and later expanded into foundry and machine-shop work. Dozens of other shops and industrial plants sprang up throughout York County during this period.

This depiction of the beautiful Codorus Creek was done by William Wagner in 1830, when a covered bridge crossed the Creek at Main Street (now Market Street). (HSYC)

The rest of the country, however, was suffering the widespread inflation and failure of financial institutions that would culminate in the Panic of 1837–1839. Many state financial institutions, including the Bank of the United States, went under, but York's one bank fared well during the crisis. The diversification of York businesses and the ability of many in the York community to handle finances in an efficient, conservative, and profitable manner helped York to weather hard times, as they would in the future.

The 1830s saw, as nearly every decade before it had, the visits of national leaders. For the last time, however, they would arrive by the older forms of transportation rather than the newly constructed railroad or later transportation innovations. General William Henry Harrison arrived in York in a "handsome barouche" on October 8, 1836, while campaigning for President. But as the Whig Party candidate, Harrison had little chance of winning over the strongly Democratic Yorkers. Yorkers voted against Harrison in 1836, and again in 1840 when Harrison won, only to die from pneumonia a month after his inaugural. Harrison's predecessor, Martin Van Buren, had arrived in York by horse and carriage on June 21, 1839. President Van Buren's popularity was at a low ebb during his visit to York, probably because of the unresolved difficulties of the recent financial panics. His visit coincided with the announcement of the York Bank that it had suspended specie payment. The President stayed in his hotel room at the White Hall on the corner of Market and Beaver streets, and the next morning took the York Haven turnpike on his way to New York.

More impressive to the York community, probably, than the decade's visits of national leaders was a visitation from the heavens in 1833. A spectacular meteor shower in that year is described by modern historian George Prowell as "the most remarkable known to the whole history of astronomy and the display was more brilliant in central and southern Pennsylvania than in any other part of America or Europe." Yorkers saw luminous meteors shooting from what seemed to be one point directly overhead. Within an hour's time, the entire sky was filled with shooting lights. Some Yorkers thought the world was coming to an end, but hours later, after the sky had cleared leaving no visible damage to the community, the event became only an entertaining topic of conversation.

An increasingly high percentage of that conversation, in the era's most significant social change, was in English. The English-German debate had been with York from its very beginnings. While the vast majority of York's citizens were of Germanic origin, the new province where they immigrated was originally owned and operated by British subjects. As the Pennsylvania government began to form, many Germans were dismayed because the legal language of the day was English. For 25 years, too, after the formation of York County in 1749, the presiding officers of the court had been English-speaking. Martin Eichelberger and Michael Swope were the first Germans who earned prominence in the York County courts and few German names were found among county offices for years afterward.

But in the churches, in homes and businesses, German was widely spoken until the 1830s, when the English language was used more often in church services. The Reverend Lewis Mayer had introduced English into his services in 1821 and the church's next four ministers gave sermons in both languages. The Presbyterian Church was growing, increasing the English-speaking population through larger families and new residents.

Two German newspapers, *Der Republicanische Herald* and *Die Evangelical Zeitung*, had faded from the York picture by the opening of the decade, a further sign that the English language was gaining power over the traditional German. The *People's Advocate* was one of several English newspapers

printed in York during the 1830s.

The public schools were also instrumental in the spread of English usage. An optional public school system had been established in Pennsylvania in 1834. Governor Wolf, Thomas H. Burroughs, a prominent state educator, and Thaddeus Stevens, a leading state legislator formerly from York, joined forces to win approval for the tax-supported educational system. The adoption of public schools had to be approved on the township and borough levels, and much controversy arose out of the voting process used locally. The county commissioners—Jacob Dietz, Samuel Harnish, John Schultz, Christian Inners, and Joseph Small—met with delegates from each township and borough at three separate conventions. Heated discussions, often centering around the public schools' English requirements, greeted the issue whenever it was discussed. Only Joseph Small voted for passage of the act at all three conventions.

But, after the third convention, York and Hanover boroughs, and the townships of Fairview, Chanceford, Lower Chanceford, and Peach Bottom accepted the plan. Newberry and Fawn townships voted in favor the next year, and the year after that Warrington, Hallam, Shrewsbury, Monaghan, Hopewell, Carroll, and Springfield townships accepted. West Manheim, 44 years later, was the last township to approve public schools.

The public school act established the office of county superintendent of public schools, but when the salary was set at $500, three of the four leading candidates for the job dropped out. The job went to the remaining nominee, Jacob Kirk, a Quaker from Fairview Township. By 1854 there were 247 schools in the York County system. The average salary for the 233 male teachers was $19 a month; the 33 female teachers were paid less, averaging only $13 a month. Kirk left his position after a year and was succeeded by Christopher Stair, later editor of the *People's Advocate*.

The already-established schools, especially the York Academy, also became strong influences in the community. The Academy's trustees had added a Young Ladies' Department in 1829, which taught Latin, Greek, English, and "moral, mathematical, and physical science." Besides the classroom work, the Academy's students of both sexes could participate in literary societies, perform in plays, and enter spelling bees. Spelling bees enjoyed enormous popularity and the winners of these elaborately produced events went on to state contests that afforded them a kind of celebrity status in York.

But life at the Academy was not all moral instruction and spelling bees. There are records that tell of students putting rubber in the Academy's potbellied stove and of stealing the master's coal to pack into snowballs. Sleighing parties and coasting sessions made central Pennsylvania's winters seem like fun to the Academy students and, on fairer days, they could attend outdoor circuses that often played on a lot nearby. Sometimes they attended such functions on school time. But one of the students' favorite pastimes were the periodic balloon ascensions.

Balloon ascensions appealed to the general public as well. One historian writes that the first balloon ascension in York occurred in 1798. By the 1830s the "sport" was well-established and York's inhabitants turned out by the thousands to see the big, colorful balloons lift off the Public Common or the Square. In 1842 York had two ascensions and the August *Gazette* of that year reports that 6,000 to 10,000 people witnessed the event, which took place despite the blustery weather. The dangerous but thrilling climb was made by John Wise, described at that time as "the celebrated American aeronaut." The second ascension took place in weather that was questionable, too, but the *Gazette* (the forerunner of the *York Daily Record* published

Facing page
Construction on this York County Court House began in 1839. The building was torn down in August and September, 1898, but its columns were later used on the new Court House. (HSYC)

Below
Daniel Kirkwood, the first astronomer to demonstrate the relationship between comets and meteors, was one of several of the country's foremost educators to teach at the York County Academy. (HSYC)

today) reports that Wise was so afraid of disappointing the crowd and "being mobbed" that he made the ascension anyway.

Another balloonist who entertained York was the community's own James A. Dale. Dale owned a drugstore near the Square and his hobby was "the exploration of the atmosphere." Dale made numerous ascensions from the York Square, and one of them is described in another *Gazette* article: "We never saw a more gratified multitude than were assembled on this occasion. All seemed delighted, and to be at a loss for words to express their admiration of the sight presented by the daring aeronaut. . . ." The *Gazette* describes the parting gesture of the York pharmacist as "a graceful wave of his hat to the cheers that continued to greet him as long as his features could be distinguished."

And thus balloon ascensions were added to the list of entertainments—with parades, music, and drama—that most appealed to Yorkers in this period. The last two of these entertainments were presented at the Academy by the same students who spent their spare pennies for sugar-plums, mint sticks, horehound, licorice, and rose almonds. But making music and drama were not the only means of entertainment there. Professor Daniel Kirkwood, the noted astronomer, wrote of school outings that included a stop in a hotel in Columbia for dinner, and he told of Academy students going to corn-huskings and "quiltings."

But many York Countians, especially in the rural Pennsylvania Dutch country, were little impressed by balloon ascensions and not overly worried about the spread of English. These things only affected them during occasional forays into town. The Pennsylvania Germans (also called the Pennsylvania Dutch) had developed a dialect that was a lively mixture of English and German long before the rest of York "went English." (This dialect has been preserved to the present day in communities throughout Pennsylvania, and many of its words and inflections have been incorporated in Yorker speech. In fact, many York County residents have been influenced by Pennsylvania Dutch speech, resulting in the distinctive pronunciations and singsong quality that are the bane of some young Yorkers when they go away to college. Often they first learn in universities that such common local phrases as "outen the lights" [turn off the lights] and "the milk's all" [all the milk has been used] are not considered standard English. Yorkers, even today, "spritz" [water] their lawns, "rutsch" [squirm] in their chairs, and carry "toots" [paper bags] home from the market.)

The Pennsylvania Dutch, during the antebellum period, still represented the majority of the population, and they had developed a distinctive and colorful way of life. Their culture contained within it considerable diversity, but was based on three dominant religious groups of the day: the Moravians, the "plain people," and the "church people."

The "plain people" included several Quaker-related religious denominations: the Amish, the Mennonites, the Brethren (or Dunkards), and the River Brethren.

The "church people" dominated the York population during its first 100 years. Denominations counting themselves among this group included the United Brethren, and the Lutheran, Reformed, and Evangelical faiths. The "church people," though led in all phases of their lives by their religious views, enjoyed celebrations and colorful homes. They developed an artistic approach to everyday concerns and painted chairs, cake molds, chests, stoves, clocks, Kentucky rifles, and other household items with bright designs of red, yellow, and blue. Much of the confusion surrounding the Pennsylvania Dutch to this very day stems from the identification of the "quaint" dress and customs of the "plain people" with all denominations. But for

The Willis house and barn in North York was a York County stop on the Underground Railroad. Hundreds of slaves passed through York County on their way to freedom in the North. (HSYC)

most Pennsylvania Dutch, life was far from "plain."

Many of the denominations present in York at this time soon became embroiled in the antebellum period's most controversial political issue: slavery. The oppression experienced by the forefathers of the Pennsylvania Dutch had made them keenly sympathetic to any kind of human or spiritual bondage. H.G. Wells points out, in *The Outline of History*, that "almost the first outspoken utterances against Negro slavery came from German settlers in Pennsylvania."

But opinions in the community varied, as they did everywhere in the country, and many Yorkers felt that the slavery issue was splitting the nation. They were afraid that further exacerbation would damage their good trade relations with the South. On the whole, though, Yorkers were a law-abiding people and they worked toward compromise solutions. The York County Colonization Society worked for many years on a program established by then-President James Monroe to set up in Africa a "colony for any free person of color who may choose to go there." The republic was called Liberia and its capital named Monrovia in honor of the President. Led by such York figures as Jacob and George Barnitz, Jacob Eichelberger, Charles A. Morris, John Gardner, and John Schmidt, the local group was organized a full eight years before the Pennsylvania Colonization Society.

With their sympathetic but no-nonsense views, Yorkers greeted "outside" abolitionist leaders with suspicion and sometimes scorn. When famous antislavery speakers such as Lucretia Mott came to York, they were likely to be greeted with jeers—and an occasional tomato.

But many York-area residents were so moved by the plight of the slaves that they became active in speeding "freight" along the underground railroad. Many believe, in fact, that the term "underground railroad" first came into use in the York area. Slave owners who followed their fleeing "property" northward were perplexed to find that slaves would often seem to disappear, as if the ground had swallowed them up. They are said to have exclaimed, "There must be an underground railroad somewhere!" The expression soon became a part of the American language.

Various people and places in York figured prominently in the underground railroad's operation. William Willis's house, built in 1767 southwest of Prospect Hill Cemetery (and restored in the early 1980s), became an underground-railroad "station," as did the home of Ezekiel Baptiste in the "Bald

Hills" of Newberry Township. Amos Griest and his wife Margaret Garrettson were also among the railroad's operators. Edward J. Chalfont, whose maternal grandfather was Jonathan Jessop, helped the abolitionist cause in York by distributing antislavery literature. Among the other workers on the railroad was York Academy's Thaddeus Stevens, who may have found in York the antislavery sentiments that he would carry with him into his political career.

One of the most important persons to figure in York's underground railroad was also one of the most remarkable people in York's entire history: William C. Goodridge. Goodridge lived two blocks from the Court House, at 123 East Philadelphia Street, and slaves knew him as a man with whom they could hide, which was hardly surprising since he, too, was an ex-slave. Goodridge had been born in 1805 to a slave who belonged to a Baltimore doctor. His grandmother had belonged to Charles Carroll, of Carrollton, Maryland, the namesake for Maryland's Carroll County. In 1811, when William was just six, the doctor sent him to apprentice with the Reverend William Dunn in his York tanning yard. Goodridge was to be apprenticed until the age of 21, at which time he was to receive "an extra suit and a Bible" and go off to seek his fortune.

But Goodridge was ready to leave at 16 and, with the Reverend Dunn's permission, he traveled to an Eastern town and learned the trade of barbering. He later returned to York and developed many lines of business, such as newspaper distribution (he is believed to have introduced the sale of daily papers in York) and the ordinary "above-ground" railroad. At one time he had 13 railroad cars making regular trips to Philadelphia; they also carried many escaped slaves out of York. Goodridge also erected the tallest building of the day in York, a four-story structure devoted to his various lines of business. Goodridge's success inspired considerable envy among York's other businessmen, and one merchant began construction on a larger building that he hoped would literally "overshadow" Goodridge's business complex.

It was Goodridge's courageous efforts on behalf of the "underground railroad" that would eventually spell his downfall in York, however. He frequently spirited slaves to freedom in Northern states and Canada, through his own railroad cars and by other means. Among those he helped to freedom were three fugitives who had participated in the Christiana Riots of 1857, and Osborn Perry Anderson, who had fought alongside John Brown at Harpers Ferry. While in York, Anderson hid out in Goodridge's "skyscraper" on the southeast corner of Centre Square. According to Stuart D. Gross in *Saginaw: A History of the Land and the City*, Goodridge "was so well known for his activities against slavery that a price was put on his head by irate Southern slave owners. When the army of Virginia approached York in 1863, the family fled. Some went with the father to Minnesota, but the three brothers came to Saginaw. Southern agents made several attempts to kidnap the senior Goodridge, but were not successful. He died in Minnesota in 1873."

Two of Goodridge's sons, William and Wallace, went on to make major contributions to Saginaw, Michigan, establishing a brisk trade for their photographic studio and involving themselves in a variety of community activities. The third brother, Glenalvin, soon joined his father in Minnesota, but the photographs of the "Goodridge Brothers" provided an invaluable record of Michigan frontier life.

The history of York is filled with other dramatic tales of Yorkers who worked on the underground railroad. William Wright, descendant of Wrightsville namesake John Wright, was credited with helping more than 1,000 slaves to freedom. One of those he helped was James W.C. Pennington.

When Pennington fled his master on his twenty-first birthday, he made his

This photo of the southeast corner of Centre Square shows the six-story building erected by John Hartmann in 1846, and the spire of Christ Lutheran Church. (HSYC)

way north to the home of Wright, whose name was well known among slaves in the South. The young man was apprehended near Reistertown, about 35 miles from Wright's home, and put under the care of a woman tavern owner. He negotiated with the woman for a moment of fresh air outside, gaining her confidence by taking off his hat, coat, and shoes before leaving the barroom. A boy sent to watch Pennington found him doubled over in apparent pain, crying out for water. When the boy ran to fetch the water, Pennington took off running through the cornfields. He arrived at the Wrights' home after a harrowing journey, but Wright and his wife, Phebe, immediately made Pennington feel at home. He stayed with them for several months, helping them with household chores while Wright taught him to read, write, and do arithmetic.

When Pennington left, he went to New Haven, Connecticut, where he acquired a position as janitor at Yale College. The brilliant young ex-slave also completed studies in the college curriculum, eventually moving to Germany, where a doctor of divinity degree was conferred on him. Friends of the Wrights later told them of a curious painting they had seen at an antislavery fair in London. Among the pictures for sale there was one called, "William and Phebe Wright Receiving James W.C. Pennington."

During the 1840s, while the underground railroad was striking blows for freedom, workers were laying down the lines above ground of the new York-Wrightsville Railroad. The railroad company was headed by Thaddeus Stevens, former York Academy professor. The company combined its operations with those of the Wrightsville & Gettysburg Railroad Company, so that the tracks could be extended westward from York through Abbottstown and New Oxford to Gettysburg. A state grant of $200,000 was applied to the $800,000 cost of the project.

York's growing railroad system would, at last, be used by a distinguished visitor arriving in York. The 1842 visit of the famous English writer, Charles Dickens, would be remembered by Yorkers for years to come. Dickens was only 30 years old when he arrived in York, but had achieved widespread fame and extraordinary popularity in England and its former colony. On a tour of America that he would preserve in his book, *American Notes*, Dickens

Above
English novelist Charles Dickens visited York in the spring of 1842. Local legend claims that Dickens was served "the best beefsteak he ever ate" in York. (HSYC)

Above left
Peter Wiest, after opening a "foreign and domestic dry goods store" in the York County community of Dover, set up a retail business on West Market Street. Wiest's Department Store would become a popular shopping spot in downtown York for over a hundred years. (HSYC)

stopped in York to dine at the White Hall Hotel. He later wrote that he had entered the area "by railroad; and got to a place called York, [at] about twelve. There we dined, and took a stage-coach for Harrisburgh [sic]."

Dickens liked York's stagecoaches, which he described as "like nothing so much as the body of one of the swings you see at a fair set upon four wheels and roofed and covered at the sides with painted canvas." But he seems not to have liked Yorkers; he was disappointed, generally, in the Americans he encountered. Local tradition, however, states that Dickens considered the beefsteak that he ate at the White Hall the best that he had ever eaten in America, and historian Prowell, who has retold the story, agrees. Unfortunately modern historians have been unable to find any such statement in Dickens works and the story has become another legend handed down unverified from generation to generation.

When Dickens traveled through York he undoubtedly noticed a tremendous amount of building and expansion of the area's shops and homes. Because of improved agricultural methods, a large population, and especially the better transportation provided by the railroads, the community was growing rapidly.

The year 1840 had seen the establishment of the Small and Smyser iron works, which had small shops along North Beaver Street adjoining the railroad. The company eventually became the Variety Iron Works, manufacturers of wrought-iron ornamentation. The company sent tons of wrought-iron decorations to New Orleans, where its architectural uses can still be seen in parts of the French Quarter.

At the corner of Market Street and Pershing Avenue, Jacob Hantz, once sheriff of York County, opened a hardware store which supplied tools for the town's new construction. This store later became the York Paint and Hardware Company and developed a large interstate wholesale division. Supplying lumber for the new construction going on in York County was the firm of A. and E. Wolf in New Holland (now Saginaw), about six miles north of York. The Wolfs packed lumber onto rafts traveling upstream to a landing on the west bank of the Susquehanna and thereupon unloaded the wagons and transported the wood to York. That firm eventually became the Wolf Supply Company—another business still in operation today.

Through the stories of other businesses, we discover bits of how Yorkers lived and what products they used. In the town of Dover, six miles northeast of York, Peter Wiest opened a "foreign and domestic dry goods store." Soon after, he moved to York, which had more people and thus more potential customers. He set up business at 218 West Market Street and sold "everything from buttons to butter, from rakes to cinnamon, from calico to herring." Many of Wiest's farmer customers traded him nails, which they made in their blacksmith shops, for goods in his store. Because molasses and mush was a popular dish of the day, Wiest also did a lot of his trading in molasses. He sold eggs for 10 cents a dozen, 14 pounds of flour for about 37 cents, and a customer could walk away, if he wanted to, with "five cents of whiskey." (After numerous expansions Wiest's firm became the Wiest's Department Store—a flagship store in the still booming downtown area of later years.)

Nathan Lehmayer, who became one of York's most prominent haberdashers, opened his first store in York in 1847, selling beaver hats, tailcoats, checked pantaloons, and other clothes for men and boys. (Almost a century later, in 1945, Lehmayer's, as the business was called, would move to a site next door to the Strand Theatre.)

The storekeepers, in this period, often used an informal system of bartering to provide consumers with needed supplies and food. This awkward system may have created a demand for a more organized and workable form of capital exchange, since in 1845 York saw the opening of its second bank, the York County Bank, which had 153 subscribers dividing the bank's 5,000 shares. At a meeting on May 29, the shareholders elected 13 directors, including Michael Doudel, the nephew and namesake of the Revolutionary War hero, and other community leaders such as Daniel Hartman, Christian Lanius, Charles Weiser, and Adam Smyser. They opened the bank on the north side of East Market Street nearly opposite the Court House and "four doors" from Centre Square. In five months the bank had total resources of $71,000.

Commerce was not the only area of city life undergoing expansion in the 1840s. This period saw innovations and growth in almost every aspect of Yorkers' experience. The town's first telegraph line was completed in the year 1845. Yorkers now had an alternative in long-distance communication to the use of horse and rider. A few years later when President Zachary Taylor came to town, either the York City Band or the Spring Garden Silver Coronet Band (soon to change its name to the Spring Garden Band) could have greeted him with a fanfare, for both bands were born in that year. While in town in 1849, he may have been warmed not only by York hospitality but also by the York County Gas Company, which got its start that same year.

The gas company also was incorporated in 1849 when 14 York men (including two of those who had been involved in establishment of the York County National Bank a few years before, Daniel Hartman and Charles Weiser) established the company. Dr. Alexander Small was elected the firm's first president. Gas at that time was manufactured from rosin and the incorporators sold shares of stock to partially cover the $35,000 cost of building the gas works. The era of flickering lights in homes and schools had come to York.

The next year would be just as busy. A railroad was built to haul freight from York to nearby York Haven and Harrisburg. The census revealed that York now housed about 7,000 people, a rise of nearly 70 percent over the

A "wholesale retail dry good store" stood on the southwest corner of Centre Square in 1852. (HSYC)

Above
The Odd Fellows Hall, located on the southwest corner of King and George streets, was built in the Classical Revival style in 1849. A theater occupied the second floor of the meeting hall. (HSYC)

Above right
A.B. Farquhar Company, Limited, of York produced a variety of engine-driven machines. (HSYC)

last census for the borough. The county population had climbed to 57,450. Such growth was partly attributable to the railroads, which made it easier for large numbers of people to get in and out of York. Another new development was the building of the Odd Fellows Hall on the southwest corner of King and George streets, and the Washington Hall on its second floor soon became home to many popular dramatic events. These included an appearance of Joseph Jefferson, noted actor of the day, who played Rip Van Winkle, and, later, Tom Thumb and the original Siamese Twins. (The building today houses the Hub Store.)

The 1850s saw a continuation of York's commercial advancement. While the California Gold Rush was drawing a few of York's younger sons (those who did not have inheritances of farms or shops to look forward to), a group of prominent citizens met in the Court House and organized the York County Agricultural Society to convince the state legislature to permit fairs again in York.

The first fair under the auspices of the Agricultural Society was held on the Public Common (now Penn Common) on October 5–7, 1853. The Society in 1856 held the annual fair on a new site on the south side of East King Street just east of Queen Street. That plot, later expanded by seven acres, was used for 31 years, after which the Agricultural Society—formed to operate such an exhibition of York County's agricultural products—moved to a 73-acre farm owned by Samuel Smyser in West Manchester Township. With additional purchases of land, the 120-acre property became known as the York Interstate Fair Ground. The fair was originated to display and encourage the county's agricultural production, and fair days became official festivals with county schools giving students a holiday to attend the educational exhibitions.

Today the York Inter-State Fair, still held under the auspices of the Agricultural Society but also offering "wide variety of commercial attractions," is recognized as the oldest continually operating fair in America. "School Day" at the Fair was ended in the 1960s as educators argued that the annual fete had become too commercial.

In the 1850s, too, a young man named A.B. Farquhar, a Quaker from Sandy Springs, Maryland, was starting to build an empire. His autobiography, published in 1922, tells that he came to York on April 4, 1856, and acquired an apprenticeship in the shop of W.W. Dingee and Company, which manufactured farm equipment and heavy machinery.

Farquhar's grandmother was the sister of the inventor John Elgar, who met the young Farquhar when he arrived in town. Elgar arranged to have Farquhar put up at the home of Edward Jessop, son of Jonathan Jessop and a friend of Farquhar's father. At the Jessop house on his first night in York, Farquhar met his future wife, Elizabeth, daughter of Edward Jessop, whom he would marry in 1860.

In 1860, when Farquhar was just beginning to amass his millions, the number of people in York Borough had reached about 8,600. The county population had risen to 68,200. These people were, by and large, conservative politically and regularly voted Democratic, including in the 1860 election, when they favored Stephen Douglas over Abraham Lincoln in the Presidential race. Although many Yorkers appreciated Lincoln's stand against slavery, even more felt that his policies were widening the split between North and South, thus endangering York's strong trade relationship with the South. York was well-established as a central trade route between the North and South, but its particularly close ties with neighboring Maryland (especially to the city of Baltimore) and its lucrative trade with other Southern states probably led to the development of the quasi-Southern climate in York County that some observers believe still exists.

Even though Yorkers had voted against Lincoln (and would do so again in 1864), they were still firm believers in the maintenance of the Union. It is not surprising then that when the Battle of Fort Sumter began the Civil War and forced them to choose sides, they favored the North. After Sumter, on April 12, 1861, the newly elected President Lincoln called for 75,000 volunteers to fight in the Civil War. Yorkers quickly gathered and, as in 1775 and 1812, exceeded enlistment quotas. By the close of the war, 3,780 men from the greater York area had served, including all members but one of the Spring Garden Band. The band, with its president William Frey (a descendant of Tobias Frey, founder of Freystown, now a part of York), became the 87th Regimental Band of the Pennsylvania Volunteers.

Meanwhile the Worth Infantry under the command of Captain Thomas A. Ziegle and the York Rifles under Captain George Hay were sent immediately to Maryland, where they were to guard railroad bridges. Eventually York County soldiers would participate in important engagements, such as the battles of Mechanicsville, Antietam, Frederick, Charleston, Petersburg, Richmond, Monocacy River, and Gettysburg. Some Yorkers rode with General Philip Henry Sheridan and others with Ulysses S. Grant.

As the days and battles passed, the war's focus shifted from town to town,

Below left
"The York Depot, September 28, 1861, and the Departure of Passenger Trains to Baltimore and one Regiment" at North Duke Street was done by Lewis Miller. (HSYC)

Below
A Civil War proclamation issued in York on September 8, 1862, required citizens "to assemble at suitable places within their limits, and organize military companies under the Act of 1858, to aid each other in repelling invasion of the county." (HSYC)

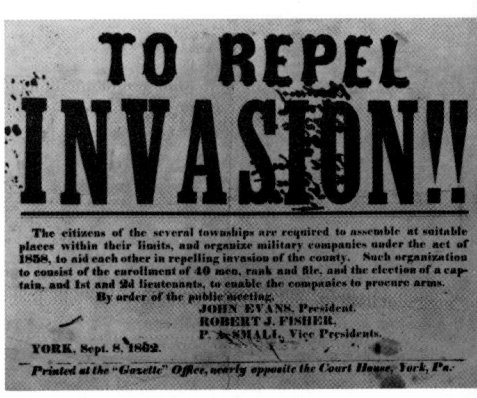

and from conflict to conflict, but in June of 1863, the war was brought frighteningly close to home.

The Confederates' main army began an invasion of Pennsylvania, planning to take Harrisburg and Philadelphia and thereby break the stronghold of Union power. General Robert E. Lee had advanced his troops over the Mason-Dixon line by June 15 and arrived in Chambersburg, about 57 miles west of York, on June 26. He ordered General R.S. Ewell to take Harrisburg and General Jubal Early to take York and move across the Susquehanna toward Philadelphia.

The next several days would be dramatic and terrifying ones for York. Streams of merchants and farmers with wagonloads of goods crowded the Gettysburg Pike (today's U.S. Route 30). They passed through the borough, crossed the river, and entered Lancaster and Chester counties. Some families buried valuables, such as silver, or hid them in wells. Some residents sent goods and valuables to Philadelphia for reclaiming later on. This escape route was soon to be cut off, however, as Confederate troops entered Wrightsville Borough to burn the bridge across the Susquehanna.

Earlier, while the Confederates were only a day from York, Farquhar relates, "the leading citizens went into session in the counting room of P.A. and S. Small's hardware store. The Smalls . . . were the big men of town and David Small, one of the proprietors of the *York Gazette*, was Chief Burgess. Among others in the meeting were W. Latimer Small, General George Hay, Samuel and Philip Small, Thomas E. Cochran [an attorney], Thomas White, and other leading citizens who had formed a Committee of Safety."

The meeting of that group of community officials and captains of local industry embodied a long-practiced custom to meet community needs, whether urgent or less demanding.

Farquhar entered the meeting and suggested that "it would be well to meet the Confederates before they entered the town—that we could make a good deal better bargain with them then than we could after they saw how little of our property we had been able to remove." Although the committeemen did not give his plan serious consideration, Farquhar told them that he would try to dicker with the Confederates anyway. He hitched up his buggy and started off.

Just beyond Abbottstown, which lay on the Pike about 14 miles southwest of York, Farquhar struck the Confederate line and by coincidence met an old classmate, Lieutenant Redik from Georgia. Farquhar asked him who was in charge and Redik informed him that the troops were under the command of General John B. Gordon. They thereupon went to see the general.

The York man later wrote that "the General was exceedingly courteous. . . . Having stated exactly the object of my mission, I said: 'General Gordon, unless you have entirely changed from the character you used to have, you are neither a horse thief nor a bank robber, and fighting is more your line than sacking a city.' " Gordon agreed, and the two made an agreement that would save York from destruction. The Civil War, after all, was a war between gentlemen, and leaders on both sides made agreements such as the one made between Farquhar and the Southern general.

When Farquhar returned to the Small's store, the Committee of Safety was still in session. He told the members of his accomplishment, but attorney Cochran argued that since Farquhar "was not authorized by the Committee to make the agreement, the Confederates would not feel bound to carry out their promises. . . . The Smalls joined me in insisting that a committee be appointed with full authority to arrange the terms, and that evening, David Small, General George Hay, Latimer Small, Thomas White, and myself, as this committee, went out to the Gettysburg Pike bearing a flag of truce."

The burning of the Wrightsville-Columbia Bridge on June 28, 1863, was depicted by artist A. Berghous. This view is from the Columbia side looking across the Susquehanna River toward Wrightsville. (HSYC)

The Confederates entered the town the next day, June 28. Cassandra Morris Small, a York girl and daughter of W. Latimer Small, described the invasion in a letter to her friend and cousin, Lissie Latimer. "Sunday morning," she writes, "Mother, Mary and I dressed for church; all the rest expected to stay home. Just as the church bells rang, the cry was heard, 'They are coming!' Oh, Lissie, what did we feel like? Humiliated! Disgraced! Men who don't often weep, wept then. They [the Confederates] came with loud music, flags flying. First we saw a picket in front of our door. Where he came from or how he got there, no one knew, he came so suddenly and quietly. [Other pickets were all along the street.] When we spoke to him, he said they were only to keep the [York] men in line."

These first soldiers carried shovels, spades, and pickaxes. The troops who arrived later had guns, but all of the soldiers, no matter where they came from, were ragged, dirty, and unshaven. Among this disheveled band some York girls recognized boyfriends from Baltimore. Thirty thousand troops in all entered the town.

General Gordon later writes of this scene in his book, *Reminiscences of the Civil War,* that " . . . the grotesque aspect of my troops was accentuated here and there, too, by barefooted men mounted double upon huge horses with shaggy manes and long fetlocks. Confederate pride, to say nothing of Southern gallantry, was subjected to the sorest trial by the consternation produced among the ladies of York. In my eagerness to relieve the citizens from all apprehension, I lost sight of the fact that this turnpike powder was no respecter of persons, but that it enveloped all alike—officers as well as privates."

Cassandra Small relates to her cousin that General Gordon's division came after the first group of men: "They halted in the Square and took down our flag. Mr. Farquhar [A.B. Farquhar] persuaded them to make our hospital buildings a camping place [they were so near residences they couldn't be burnt]." The Confederates took Farquhar's advice but nevertheless many houses were ransacked throughout the county and the Confederates appropriated horses, mules, cattle, and other items. "Our beautiful hospital!" the Small girl writes, "I would be ashamed to tell you all they did there, and to think Lissie, there are some who call themselves ladies, who went there to see them and entertained them."

These "ladies" were not the only Yorkers to welcome the Confederates. Because of York's proximity to the Mason-Dixon line, some townspeople were openly sympathetic to the Southerners and even waved red streamers as Gordon rode through the streets. Even Small, describing Gordon during his ride through town, paints a picture not of a rapacious monster but of a more

Below, far left
A.B. Farquhar, shown here in 1921, was one of York's leading industrialists. He traveled around the world, promoting both his own business and the city of York. (HSYC)

Below left
Lieutenant General John B. Gordon led his Confederate troops into York on June 28, 1863, after his advance had been stopped by the burning of the bridge at Wrightsville. By five o'clock the next morning the last of the Confederates were out of York and on their way to join General Robert E. Lee at Gettysburg. (HSYC)

Below
"The surrender of York, Pennsylvania to the Confederates" on June 28, 1863, was depicted by Lewis Miller. (HSYC)

or less humane soldier: " 'I want to say to you,' " she recalls him announcing, " 'We have not come among you to pursue the same warfare your men did in our country. You need not have any fear of us. You are just as safe as though we were a thousand miles away. That is all I have to say.' He bowed and, turning his horse, rode away."

In General Gordon's book, another remarkable event during the Confederates' invasion is recounted. Upon entering the Square, a girl not more than 12 years old walked toward Gordon's horse with a bouquet of roses. The general accepted the gift, but before riding off noticed a note inside the flowers. The note told of a secret gorge at the entry to Wrightsville that would take the general's forces unseen to a spot where they could force the Union soldiers stationed there to retreat or to surrender.

General Gordon reached Wrightsville the same evening and found that the information he had received in the bouquet of roses was indeed correct. The 1,200 Union troops immediately retreated across the bridge and burned the span behind them. Gordon noted that, as the bridge burned, no fire buckets could be found, but when the town later caught fire the buckets seemed to appear from everywhere.

Meanwhile, at about two o'clock on the first day of the Confederate invasion, General Early and his staff set up a meeting in the Court House. He demanded from York "165 barrels of flour or 28,000 pounds of baked bread, 3,500 pounds of sugar, 1,650 pounds of coffee, 300 gallons of molasses, 1,200 pounds of salt, 32,000 pounds of fresh beef or 21,000 pounds of bacon or pork . . . to be delivered at the market place on Main [now Market] Street." The general also demanded "2,000 pairs of shoes or boots, 1,000 pairs of socks, 1,000 felt hats, and $100,000 in United States money."

About $28,610 and its equivalent in merchandise were collected and given to the general, along with a "due bill" for the balance. The general appeared satisfied, although the take never reached the proportions that he had demanded and the Committee of Safety gave receipts for the contributions to the contributors. (Later the Borough reimbursed them through a special tax.)

The soldiers, who had camped not only in the hospital but also on Penn Common, the Fair Grounds, and around Louck's mill, butchered cattle and roasted them over huge fires. They set up a bakery near the United States Hospital on the Common and took flour from the mill to make bread. They also tore down wooden fences to fuel their outdoor fires. General Early asked the Committee of Safety for access to the county's deeds and records so that he could burn them. He was persuaded not to burn the records but then threatened to burn the railroad shops north of the Square.

A United States Army Hospital for the wounded was located on Penn Common at York during the Civil War. The soldiers' chapel is shown here, circa 1863. (HSYC)

This Lewis Miller drawing depicts "Camp Scott, York, Pennsylvania, May 11, 1861." (HSYC)

At about that time a foaming horse galloped into York carrying a soldier from General Lee's camp. The soldier had a dispatch from Lee that ordered Early to proceed with his men to Gettysburg. While collecting horses along the route, he marched off to Gettysburg and the decisive battle that took the town's name.

Before the Confederates vanished into the distance, they left York one more thing by which to remember them. Small relates, "as they were leaving the town on Tuesday morning, going through the main street, they tore [the Union flag they had taken down during the invasion] into strips, then others took the strips and tore them into little pieces, all singing, 'We'll Plant Our Colors on a Northern Hill.'"

Farquhar says in his autobiography that he followed the Confederates to Gettysburg as a member of the Hospital Service, and when he returned he was shocked to find Yorkers pointing and jeering at him. They accused him of being a Rebel, deciding that, as Farquhar put it, "I, as the man who had opened the negotiations, was something near to being a traitor."

Farquhar, a proud and pious man, was so hurt by this accusation that he went to Washington to seek President Lincoln's view of the situation. There he met John Hay, the President's secretary, whom he knew. Hay, who would later become Secretary of State under Presidents William McKinley and Theodore Roosevelt, tried to convince Farquhar that Lincoln was very busy and that Farquhar did not really need his help since he had acted honorably. But the York man insisted on waiting.

When President Lincoln came out of his office to go to a meeting at the War Department building, Farquhar waylaid him. He blurted out his story to the President, adding, "I am going with you; I want your advice, and to know what you think of our action." Lincoln acquiesced, and as they walked together, the President asked the 25-year-old Farquhar about his life: "'Was I married?' Lincoln asked. 'Did I have any children? Had I a business in York? What kind was it? Was it prosperous?'"

They arrived at the War Department building and entered a room where Secretary of War Edwin M. Stanton and a number of distinguished-looking generals were gathered. The President, leading Farquhar to the front of the room and giving his hand a squeeze, took him before the Secretary of War and addressed him with these good-humored words: "Stanton, I have captured that young chap who sold York, Pennsylvania, to the rebels. What are we going to do with him?"

Afterwards Farquhar returned to York and resumed his manufacturing duties, somewhat relieved by the President's blessing on his controversial action. He suffered occasional jeers from townspeople for years after the Civil War, but he was confident that he had done right.

As Farquhar's business grew, sending materials around the globe, so did many other York firms. The community already had achieved great prosperity, but it was slight compared to that which the postwar era would bring.

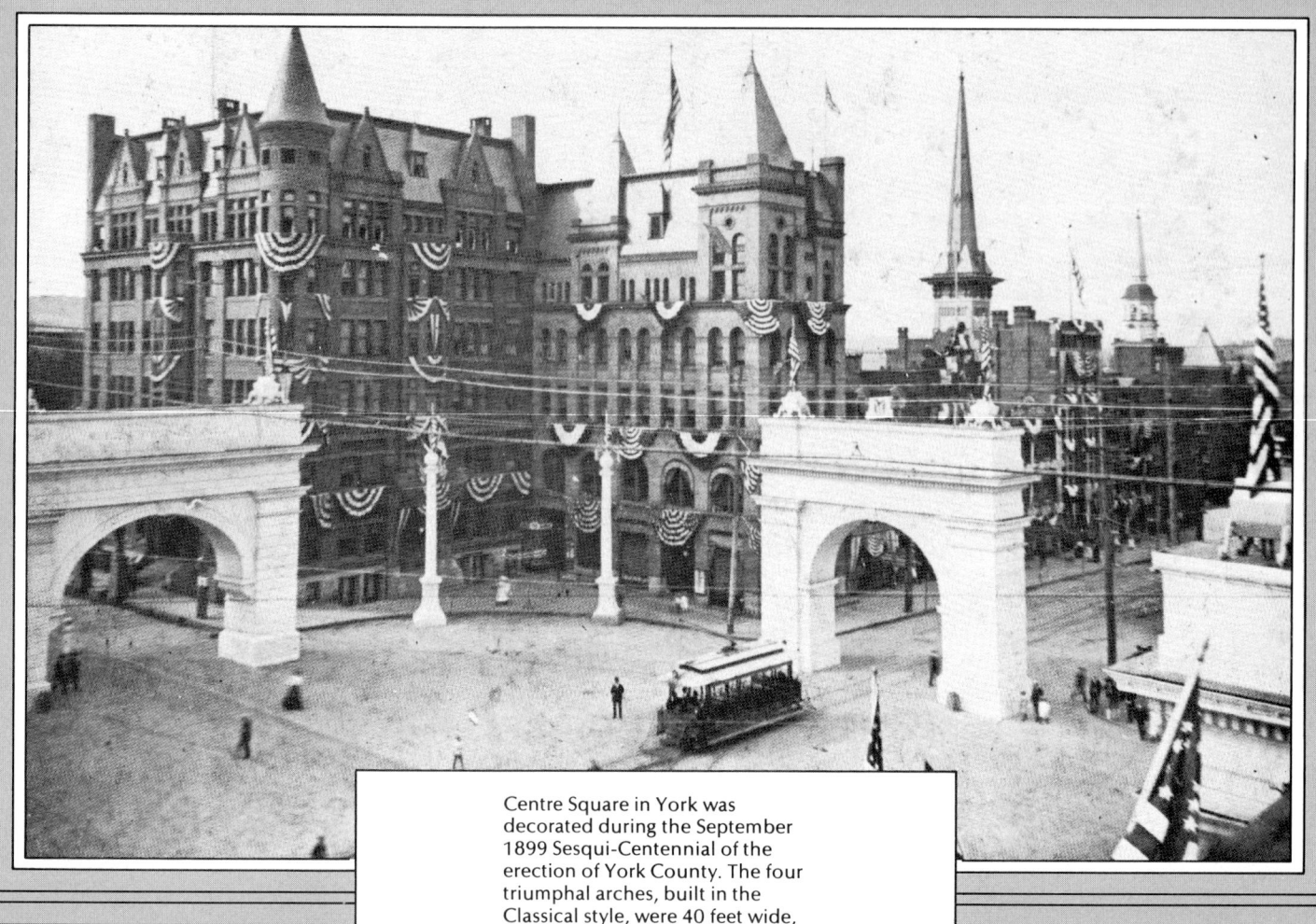

Centre Square in York was decorated during the September 1899 Sesqui-Centennial of the erection of York County. The four triumphal arches, built in the Classical style, were 40 feet wide, 30 feet high, and 12 feet deep. Flags and bunting adorned the Colonial Hotel and other buildings in the city. (HSYC)

CHAPTER VI
POST-CIVIL WAR PROSPERITY

When the Civil War ended, Yorkers put aside national politics and military matters. Instead they concentrated on developments at home and ushered in an era of tremendous growth and industrial expansion. The town's small shops, mills, foundries, and other businesses adapted to changing times and many new businesses began, further stimulating the building of the city. Construction continued to improve with larger factories and grander homes, such as those established in the 700 block of South George Street.

The designer of most of those homes, as well as many of the other buildings that would rise in York's cityscape over the next five decades, was J.A. Dempwolf. Born in Brunswick, Germany, Dempwolf came to York in 1867 at the age of 19 to work for the P.A. and S. Small Company. Seeing construction all around him, Dempwolf became interested in the building trade. He was apprenticed in 1869 to Jacob Gotwalt, a York carpenter, then went to work for Nathanial Weigel, a York building contractor. While with Weigel, Dempwolf made full-size architectural details for St. Paul's Lutheran Church then under construction at King and Beaver streets. The church building's design, by the noted Philadelphia architect Stephen D. Button, intrigued Dempwolf.

Realizing that he needed professional training, Dempwolf went to New York, where he studied architectural drawing and design in night courses at the Cooper Union Institute. He worked full time during the day. Upon graduation, Dempwolf went to Boston, where he supervised the construction of Holy Cross Cathedral. He returned to York to design St. John's German Lutheran Church on West King Street.

After completion of the church, Dempwolf went to Philadelphia to assist Stephen Button in designing some of the buildings for the Centennial Exposition to be held there the next year. In 1876 Dempwolf returned to York and, with the help of Samuel Small and other friends, opened an office in the Cassatt Building for the practice of architecture. From his office on Continental Square, Dempwolf completed designs for the York Trust Company, the York National Bank, the City Market, the Fluhrer Building, and many other landmark structures. Dempwolf, his brother Reinhart, and J.A.'s son Frederick (who also became architects), are credited with creating many of the stately and beautiful buildings that still dominate the York scene. The elder Dempwolf was active with the American Institute of Architects. He was appointed to the Pennsylvania State Arts Council, and elected that body's chairman in 1926.

Factories providing jobs for hundreds of employees sprang up in the 1860s and the community continued spreading in all directions. As the borough's population grew, so did the populations of the townships and boroughs surrounding it. One of the developments reinforcing this growth was the increasing specialization of businesses.

Richard Watt, a Scotsman, came to York in 1865 after serving as an apprentice in the painting and decorating trade. After working in one of York's first photography shops with Fitz James Evans, Watt opened his own

Above
The J.A. Singer house on East Market Street was a fine example of the Queen Anne style of architecture popular in the last quarter of the 19th century. (HSYC)

Left
Mrs. Mowbray's store at 200 West Market Street, shown here circa 1885, was called the Philadelphia Millinery. The shop, like others in the city, donned the name of a more urban area to attract customers looking for the latest in styles. (HSYC)

Far left
The David Small house at 153 East Market Street was typical of the fashionable homes of the era following the United States centennial. This photograph, taken in September 1881, shows the house draped in mourning of the death of President Garfield. (HSYC)

painting shop. In 1866 his brother Andrew joined him and they moved to 108 East Market Street to specialize in sign painting. When Richard died, their shop was continued by Andrew under the name Watt and Brother. Andrew Watt acted as president and James Webster as secretary and general manager.

Upon Andrew Watt's death, Webster became president and his son Richard Watt Webster became secretary. Realizing the need for skilled craftsmen in the trade, the two Websters opened a school for apprentices. This school's first two students, Frank P. Connolly and Ray Reisinger, both won top prizes at the Pennsylvania Master Painters' and Decorators' Association convention, held in York. Richard W. Webster opened a branch of the business in Harrisburg, and churches as far away as Brooklyn soon were employing the master craftsmen to do work for them. Watt Brothers also provided the street decoration for the town's 150th birthday celebration in 1899. Connolly later became president of his own shop.

Specialization also brought success to Christian Charles Kottcamp, a tinsmith who opened a small shop on the 100 block of North George Street, where he made cooking utensils, spouting, and roofing. Many years later, in 1895, Kottcamp realized that plumbing and heating services were coming into demand, and he sent his son Harry to pursue a course at the New York School of Plumbing and Sanitation. When Harry returned to York in 1901, he joined his father's business and, with his newly acquired knowledge in plumbing, helped expand it.

The Kottcamps moved into the plumbing and heating fields at the right time. York's new buildings were becoming more modern, and now that York's water and gas companies were well established, the community needed the

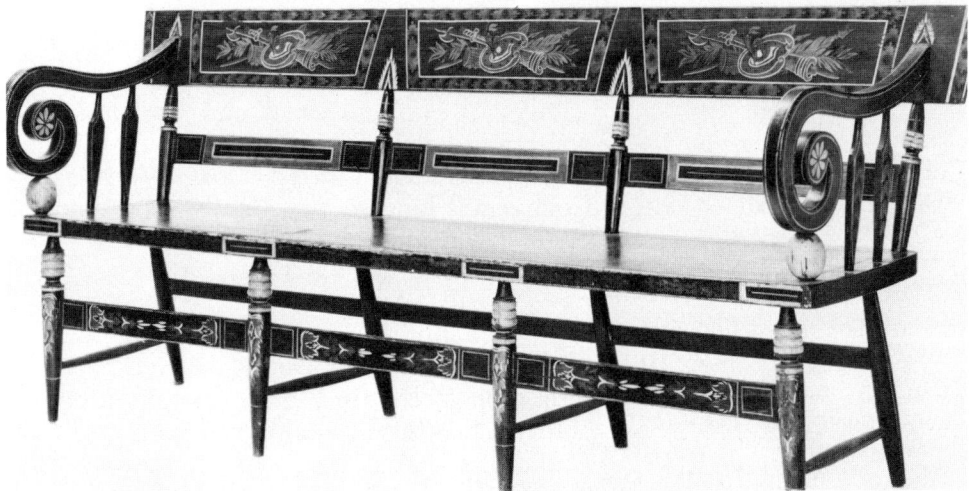

This stenciled and turned settee exemplifies the craftsmanship of York County artisans during the 19th century. (HSYC)

specialized service. Outdoor toilet facilities would linger in York's backyard environment, though, for many more years. At the time of the establishment of York's first plumbing service, the small structures behind York homes were as common a sight as the family cow or chickens.

Local farmers, after the Civil War, were enjoying their own prosperity. They were doing so well, in fact, that the Farmer's Market, which still operates on its original site at Market and Penn streets, was built in 1866 to serve the population growing in the open lands west of the Codorus. The market, incorporated by John H. Baer, Jacob Baer, John Winter, C.F. Winter, and Israel Laucks, was an instant success and was enlarged twice.

The Farmer's Market stands offered sumptuous displays of fat chickens, polished apples, fresh eggs, tender asparagus, home-cured meats, home-baked breads, pastries, and such Pennsylvania Dutch items as egg noodles, scrapple, snitz und knepp, soft pretzels, chowchow, red beet eggs, pot pie, and hog maws. Visitors found a cascade of fresh-cut flowers and just-picked produce, as well as stands showing off home-made bonnets, aprons, and household decorations. Yorkers began to consider the visit to market as important a social occasion as going to church on Sunday morning. After all, one met the same friends and neighbors there as at church, and strong and healthy bodies were needed to carry on God's work here on earth. Some families in York markets have passed their market stands down through five generations. Market in York was—and still is—a festival to be enjoyed several times a week.

Yorkers were increasingly concerned about the welfare of their children and young adults, and the late 1860s and early 1870s witnessed an unprecedented boom in institutions for community youths. Yorkers built a new Children's Home in 1865, formed the town's YMCA in 1869, opened on Duke Street the town's first public high school the next year, and in 1872 opened a second one.

Despite Yorkers' initial reluctance to welcome the public school system to the county, the inhabitants soon learned the value of mass education for its citizens. Several new public schools were opened and the parochial schools continued their work. The York County Academy still offered concentrated courses of study for the community's "gifted" students and educated generations of community leaders. York's first high school was established on South Duke Street in 1862, and in 1868 another building was erected on its back lot. Both buildings are still standing today.

With York's continuing growth a bigger high school was needed by 1872

Below
Samuel Small and his wife, Isabel Cassatt Small, founded the York Collegiate Institute in 1873. Courtesy, York College of Pennsylvania.

Bottom left
The York Manufacturing Company was formed in 1874 and eventually became the world's largest producer of refrigerators, ice-makers, and air conditioners. The company eventually became a division of Borg-Warner Corporation. (HSYC)

Bottom right
S. Morgan Smith's plant, started in the last quarter of the 19th century, became the largest in the world devoted exclusively to hydraulic turbines and allied equipment. (HSYC)

and York taxpayers contributed $35,500 for a building on Philadelphia Street opposite the Friends Meeting House. Among the school's four faculty members was historian George R. Prowell.

In 1873 Samuel Small and his wife, Isabel Cassatt Small, envisioning another privately run institution of liberal education, built still another school on the northeast corner of Duke Street and College Avenue, known as York Collegiate Institute. The Smalls appointed their own board of directors and opened with five faculty members and 50 students.

As York entered the 1870s, it housed 11,003 people, almost 30 percent more than 10 years before. The county population had zoomed to 76,134. The population rise created a demand for products that only new businesses could supply. These businesses gave York even more diversity and led to the formation of new institutions to serve them.

In 1870 Addison Shaffer started a chain shop on South Pershing Avenue. About nine years later, John C. Schmidt established a new chain company on East Walnut Street and hired Shaffer as foreman. Later Schmidt built a larger factory on State Street and used electric welders and mechanical formers that greatly improved his manufacturing process. The chain manufacturer then acquired plants in other Pennsylvania cities, as well as in Ohio, and formed the Standard Chain Company. That company eventually was sold to the American Chain Company, which used York as its headquarters and later became known as Acco Industries. The York plant today employs more than 800 people.

In 1871 David F. Stauffer took over a cake and cracker business that Jacob Weiser had begun in 1858. A good rate for the company was five barrels a day, some of which Stauffer delivered himself. The company later specialized in pretzels and helped make York the "Pretzel Capital of America."

The York Manufacturing Company was formed in 1874 and became the world's largest manufacturer of refrigerators, ice-makers, and air conditioners. That company later became the York Division of Borg-Warner Corporation, York's second biggest employer with more than 3,500 workers. In 1875 Hermann Noss' Sons, Inc., began producing paneling for buildings, such as Atlantic City's Marlborough Blenheim Hotel. Soon afterward Stephen Morgan Smith opened what would become the largest plant in the world devoted exclusively to hydraulic turbines and allied equipment. His products were also sent around the globe. The company was later sold to the Allis Chalmers Corporation and the plant currently employs about 1,900 people.

The rise of all this new business may have helped to perpetuate York's

unbroken support of Democratic candidates in Presidential elections. They favored Democrat Horace Greeley over Ulysses S. Grant in 1872, probably because Greeley supported a high tariff to protect American businessmen against foreign competition and Grant opposed it.

American inventiveness was entering an extremely active period and the new technologies and inventions found an eager public in York. In 1876 Hiram Young, owner of the local weekly newspaper, the *True Democrat* (later the *York Dispatch*), visited the Centennial Exposition in Philadelphia and brought back an incandescent lamp. He hooked it up to a battery and displayed it in the window of the newspaper office to the great interest of Yorkers.

Another man who went to the Centennial Exposition, the York dentist Dr. Charles A. Eisenhart, became intrigued with a demonstration there of transmitting a voice over the air. After returning to York, Eisenhart installed a telephone line from his office to his stable so he could call for his horse. About the same time another Yorker, W. Latimer Small, strung a telephone line from his home to Codorus Mills two miles away.

A few years later John K. Gross, who was a passenger and freight agent with the Northern Central Railway, unveiled a system of 27 telephones connected to stores and offices in York and to a central office that handled calls. Albert Galbreath started a similar exchange in Columbia and connected his lines to the community of Wrightsville. Frank A. Ziegler gave Hanover its first system the same year Gross introduced the new-fangled instrument to York. Gross sold his business in 1883 to the Southern Pennsylvania Telephone Company, which was consolidated with the Pennsylvania Telephone Company, a subsidiary of the Bell Telephone System started in 1877.

Perhaps the experience of seeing a local company swallowed up by a large system induced a group of York businessmen to establish another telephone company in 1895. Headed by Dr. Eisenhart and George B. Rudy, the group organized under the name, the York Telephone Company. Within a decade, the company had 2,600 telephones and 300 miles of pole line connecting towns and villages across York County. That company later became a part of the General Telephone Company, which established headquarters in Erie, Pennsylvania, and which still operates York's telephone system today.

As York was developing its intricate telephone system, new businesses were being added to the commercial community. In 1877 Edward C. Reineberg opened a shoe shop on South George Street. In 1880, when York housed 13,940 people and 87,841 people lived in the county, George W. Hoover and his three sons started manufacturing horse-drawn buggies in the iron-front

York's Telephone and Telegraph Company was organized in 1895 by Dr. Charles Eisenhart, a York dentist who was interested in telecommunication. These women were photographed at the telephone-company switchboard. (HSYC)

building, located on East Philadelphia Street's north side, which later became the home of the *York Dispatch*. A well-known York musician, J.O. Weaver, formed the Weaver Piano Company in 1882 and the company turned out to be the primary developer and supplier of lightweight portable pianos to army camps, hospitals, hospital ships, and USO canteens all over the world. Israel Forry Laucks established (also in 1882) the York Safe and Lock Company, which made products that were installed in the Bank of France in Paris, the Bank of China in Shanghai, Tokyo's Bank of Japan, and other financial institutions around the world.

In the late 1870s and early 1880s, two more significant businesses were begun. The first was the establishment of the City Market at 211 South Duke Street in 1878, brought about by a population increase in the town's southern parts. J.A. Dempwolf designed the 225-by-80-foot building, which, like its predecessor, the Farmer's Market, was enlarged twice. The City Market, razed after generations had used it, is said to have been one of the most architecturally pleasing buildings ever put up in York.

A few years after the City Market was established, the Arnaux Electric Light Company came to York. The company connected four arc lights to the flagstaff on the Square and they burned "with a light rivaling the daylight itself," in the words of a reporter from the *York Dispatch*. The newspaper also reports: "A large number of people gathered in the Square and neighborhood to witness the exhibition, and many were the expressions of approval and delight over the new light. . . . We ought soon to have plenty of electric light and bright streets at night, instead of the dark, dingy ones through which we have heretofore had to find our way." The time of the lamplighter igniting gas lamps in front of York taverns and stores was coming to a close.

In the late 1870s, the York community diversified in other ways as well. By 1877 increasing numbers of Jews were immigrating to York and a group of them organized under the name Beth Israel. Within two years they were holding congregational devotions in the home of Solomon Kahn of West Market Street; the officiating rabbi was Joseph Lebach. Soon afterwards the group rented a room for use as a synagogue and Hebrew school, and the congregation was established with Lebach, the Reverend Doctor Nathan Rosenau, Isador Walker, and Abram Simmons leading the services and supervising the Hebrew school. The congregation, in 1907, erected a temple on South Beaver Street in the "Little Moscow" area of York. (Hanover Jews had held services in homes as early as 1826, but the Civil War dispersed the community and a synagogue did not open there until 1953.)

Although Temple Beth Israel was the first Jewish house of worship, York's Jewish citizens had enjoyed prominence almost from the community's earliest days. Before and during the Revolution, a Jewish merchant, Elijah Etting, had operated his shop in York. Jews who left the Palatinate to escape persecution often gravitated to Pennsylvania. Finding the Pennsylvania Dutch dialect in York similar to their own language, many set down roots.

The first son of York merchant Elijah Etting and his wife, Shinah, followed his parents to Baltimore after the Revolution and became an early proponent of the "Jewish Bill," which sought to abolish discrimination against Jews desiring to hold public office. At that time holding such offices required a vow of adherence to the Christian religion and naturally excluded members of other faiths. President Thomas Jefferson appointed the Ettings' York-born son, Reuben, as United States Marshal of Maryland in 1801. The "Jewish Bill," with the young Etting's unflagging support, was adopted in 1825.

In 1879, just two years after Beth Israel was formed, another group of Jewish immigrants arrived in York, principally from Austria and Hungary. The new Jewish group, strictly Orthodox in their beliefs, established its own congregation. Anshe Hadas (People of the Faith) Congregation was chartered in 1883 and Jacob Sirovich, father of a well-known Congressman from New York, became its first rabbi.

Charles Beck, a member of Anshe Hadas Congregation, organized the Adas Israel (Congregation of Israel) for the purpose of following the Nussach Sephard of the Chasidic tradition. In 1904 the congregation erected a synagogue on South Pershing Street. Among its leaders were Jacob Feder, Samuel Williams, Benjamin Feldman, Jonas Piperberg, and Michael Leibowitz.

Two years earlier the followers of the Ashkenazic ritual of the Anshe Hadas had gathered at the home of Max Tewel, deciding to change their congregation's name to Ohev Sholom (Lovers of Peace) and to build a new synagogue. The synagogue was dedicated in 1904 with Abe Trattner as president. J.T. Ziegler and David Katz comprised the building committee.

In addition to Jews from various countries, York was benefiting from an influx of many other nationalities at this time. From the end of the 19th century to World War I, Poles, Hungarians, Czechs, Russians, and Greeks gravitated to Pennsylvania Dutch country. York became home to many of the new immigrants, especially the Italians and Greeks.

York's steady population growth made its lack of formal medical facilities increasingly burdensome, and community leaders established the building of a hospital as a high priority. York's early physicians had received their training in European medical schools; it was not until 1827 that the first American medical school was developed in Baltimore. Philadelphia had educated physicians as early as the 1760s, but few of them took up practice in York town.

In the early days of York, as in other parts of the country, medical care was usually relegated to the barber's chair. Inflammatory illnesses, such as pleurisy, bronchitis, pneumonia, and rheumatism, were common, and sometimes fatal. York town was plagued with periodic epidemics of cholera, whooping cough, and scarlet fever, and even such relatively mild afflictions as measles, dysentery, and diarrhea could have tragic results in the absence of proper medical attention.

Immigrants, who had brought old customs and beliefs from their homelands, were likely to rely on herbs or other forms of folk medicine. Such herbs as rosemary, rue, wormwood, sage, thyme, blue mint, woolly nut, fever few, and horehound were often grown in home gardens and used for medicinal purposes. From the woods, people gathered tansy, camomile, yarrow, sassafras root, penny royal, mandrake, and witch hazel, from which they concocted tonics and "cures." The practice of "powwowing," a form of witchcraft or faith healing, was also widely employed, especially by the Pennsylvania Dutch.

The coming of scientifically based medicine then was greatly welcomed in the York area and Yorkers banded together to see this needed modernization become a reality. On a blustery day in January 1880, 10 years after Lister had discovered antiseptic surgery and while Pasteur was studying bacteria and its relation to disease, Samuel Small gathered a small group of Yorkers in his office to create the York Hospital and Dispensary Association. In attendance were his son David E. Small, Jere S. Carl, Dr. Thomas Cathcart, Frank Geise, Dr. William S. Roland, and Dr. John Wiest. Small contributed a three-story building on West College Avenue and the group agreed to raise $70,000 to convert the house into a hospital. The hospital's new board of managers purchased 12 wrought-iron beds for $98 each and hired one nurse. There was no full-time physician. In 1881 Dr. A.R. Blair became the hospital's first consulting physician and Dr. James W. Kerr became the first consulting surgeon. The board of directors was made up by

Cathcart, Roland, Wiest, Blair, and E.W. Meisenhelder. A Board of Lady Managers, formed at the same time to serve in auxiliary functions, numbered Mrs. D. Pentz, Mrs. Israel Laucks, Mrs. Chauncey Black, and Mrs. A.B. Farquhar.

Physicians connected to the growing facility sought new ideas and techniques to help better serve the people of the community. Some doctors traveled to Baltimore to hear or give lectures and to sit in on seminars, and others conducted their own research in York. The most notable researcher was Dr. George E. Holtzapple, who discovered that oxygen could be used in the treatment of pneumonia. While tending to a critically ill 16-year-old boy in a Loganville farmhouse in 1885, Dr. Holtzapple, relying on his own ingenuity, rigged up an apparatus of rubber tubing, test tubes, and a spirit lamp. The lamp was used to heat a mixture of chlorate of potash and black oxide of manganese, generating oxygen which traveled through the tubing and bubbled to the surface of the water in a bucket at the patient's bedside. The oxygen saved the boy's life. Afterwards Dr. Holtzapple worked at perfecting the technique, then introduced his discovery to the medical world. Not long after that Dr. Meisenhelder began using nitrous oxide (laughing gas), but because he was worried that it might harm patients if used without extreme care, he brought a skilled anesthetist to the hospital at his own expense. Soon the hospital hired its own professional anesthetist and added a nursing school. One of the school's early graduates, Florence Gipe, left York to found the School of Nursing at the University of Maryland. York's hospital prospered from the beginning and the community supported it financially as well as with volunteer service.

In 1885 the York Hospital and Dispensary facilities were pressed into emergency service. When the York Collegiate Institute, also founded by Samuel Small and located on the same street as the hospital, caught fire, the

Below left
Temple Beth Israel, built in York in 1907, features striking stained-glass windows and "onion domes" reminiscent of Eastern European architecture. The building stands on the 100 block of South Beaver Street in York. Courtesy, Temple Beth Israel.

Below
The three-story building that housed the York Hospital and Dispensary on West College Avenue was donated by Samuel Small. A group of prominent Yorkers gathered in 1880 and agreed to raise $70,000 to convert the building into a hospital. (HSYC)

hospital volunteered shelter. Although no one was hurt in the fire, this experience inspired the Institute to lend space for the holding of classes.

Two years later the Institute was rebuilt by Small's nephew, W. Latimer Small, and George Small. (The senior Small had died just a few months before fire razed the first Institute Building.) The new building was completed using a J.A. Dempwolf design and was described by a newspaper reporter of the day as "larger, more convenient and more elaborate than the first."

If the windows in the new Collegiate Institute were any measure of its elaborateness, the building deserved the reporter's generous evaluation. Stained-glass panels were installed throughout the building by artisans and craftsmen from the J. Horace Rudy Company. The company's owner had attended the Pennsylvania Academy of Fine Arts and then worked for a Philadelphia firm as a woodcarver and engraver. His firm eventually made windows for more than 500 churches, as well as for hospitals, schools, colleges, and private homes in the Midwestern and Southeastern areas of the United States.

J. Horace Rudy's son, Charles, born in York in 1904, received his early training in his father's shop, graduated from his father's alma mater, and won major scholarly awards including a Guggenheim Fellowship. He later received awards for his sculpture and was praised by magazines such as *Life*.

York was a thriving center of activity in the 1880s. In 1884 Fluhrer's Jewelry Store opened, a Presidential election was held (Yorkers supported Democrat Grover Cleveland over Benjamin Harrison), and the 17-acre Fairmount area on the Codorus's north side was annexed to the city. But the event of the year that had the greatest local impact occurred on June 15, when heavy rains and a wind of hurricane force killed several Yorkers. The storm swept away all the structures along the Codorus, including the Pennsylvania Railroad Bridge, and caused more than $700,000 worth of property damage. In 1885 York Borough was enlarged again when the areas of Freystown, Bottstown, and Smysertown were annexed to it. The Edison Electric Light Company was formed that year, and the Eastern Market was added in the 400 block of East Market Street.

In hectic 1886 the People's Electric Light Company was formed and for the first time institutions such as the York Hospital had electric light. "Electric Light Can't Blow Out," an advertisement in the *York Dispatch* told Yorkers, and as more and more inhabitants became familiar with the non-flickering radiant new light, they had electrical lines installed in their houses and schools. The age of light had come to York and residents were quick to put its new inventions to work.

During the same year that York's second electric company came into being, Milton D. Martin, who would become a leading auto manufacturer, founded the York Spring Wagon Works on the site where the Strand Theatre would be built almost 40 years later. Money left by Martin helped in establishing another important public institution—the Martin Memorial Library.

But the biggest event of 1886 was the incorporation of the York Street Railway Company, which aided the people immensely in getting around their expanding town. The company immediately put eight closed horsecars, six open ones, 15 horses, and eight mules into service. Each driver was given a set of rules, which included a provision for ejecting stubborn tobacco smokers, "using only so much force as is necessary."

Eighteen eighty-six was also the year of the controversial market shed affair. In that year the City Council authorized George Heighes, Luther Small, and Dr. Jacob Hay to investigate the removing of the Centre Square market sheds, which many people considered eyesores. The three men advocated tearing down the sheds, which "brought forth violent opposition"

The second York Collegiate Institute building, dedicated on March 15, 1887, featured magnificent stained-glass windows made in York by the J. Horace Rudy Company. Courtesy, York College of Pennsylvania.

Right
This view of Centre Square shows the market sheds before they were destroyed in mid-1887. Christ Lutheran Church is shown at right. (HSYC)

Below right
The market sheds in the Centre Square were torn down at two o'clock in the morning on June 30, 1887, after being called a "public nuisance" in a resolution passed by city officials. The view faces the northeast corner of the Square. (HSYC)

from people who leased stands in the sheds. But on June 26 the council labeled the sheds a "public nuisance" and voted to remove them.

On June 30, at 2:00 a.m., 20 city workers brought several ropes, three horses, and seven mules to the Square to begin work. They tied one end of each rope to a shed support and the other to a horse or mule. Just as the animals were about to pull the sheds down, someone turned in a fire alarm and pandemonium broke loose. Firemen rushed to the scene, bringing with them crowds of Yorkers who thought there was a fire in Centre Square. They arrived just in time to see the shed roofs come crashing down. Great clouds of dust rose into the sky, which, seen from a distance in the moonlight, looked like smoke, alarming the latecomers even more. By 3 a.m. the sheds had all been flattened and the excitement had died down. The debris was removed the next day. Markets were held on the perimeter of the Square until the 1930s. People were then forced to go to the Farmers, City, Central, or Eastern markets.

The destruction of the market sheds prefigured the events of 1887. The

destruction was a municipal action, and so were the major events of the new year. For one thing, York was incorporated as a city almost exactly 100 years after its incorporation as a borough, but not before many years of debate on the subject. Heated discussions on the issue ensued and many people were quite vociferous in their objections.

The Central Market, another J.A. Dempwolf building, was built in 1887. Six investors invested sums ranging from $1,500 to $9,100 to build the market facing on both Beaver Street and Philadelphia Street. The building was opened in 1888 and many of the same families that leased space at the time of its opening are still operating "stands" there. By this time York was well known as a center of agricultural abundance. Tons of fresh produce, fruit, meats, and chickens were shipped out of York every year.

Outstanding local favorites developed at the markets, especially snow peas, with their tender, thin skins, and lush, red strawberries. But almost as popular among Yorkers were such seasonal favorites as the famous Pennsylvania Dutch pumpkin pie at Thanksgiving; plump, red, home-cured hams at Easter; and turkeys at Christmas. Elaborate holiday meals are still very much a part of Pennsylvania Dutch heritage. Two or three kinds of meat, and numerous vegetables, salads, breads, condiments, and desserts make up the average holiday meal, and the Pennsylvania Dutch hallmark for gracious dining is "quantity as well as quality."

York's official government had begun in 1787 when the York Borough was erected; it was really a town, but the use of the strange-sounding Pennsylvania governmental unit of borough persisted. Soon after York's erection as a borough, its burgesses asked for additional powers, including the right to issue ordinances. A supplement was passed by the General Assembly of Pennsylvania granting the new "Board of Burgesses" much greater jurisdiction than they had previously enjoyed. The board, in effect, became a town council. Until the enactment of this statute, the state legislature had been able to arbitrarily pass rules that changed the borough's laws. The sophistication which the new form of government brought with it would signal a new direction for York.

In 1859 another supplement was passed, establishing a town council and abolishing the old Board of Burgesses. The borough was then divided into five wards with two councilmen each. The councilmen served two-year terms and each ward staggered the elections, so that they voted for only one representative a year. At this time the job of second burgess was abolished

Below left
A Saturday Market Day in Centre Square in the 1890s is shown here. York's longstanding farmers' market tradition began in Colonial times and continued to play an important role in the city. Courtesy, Sunday News.

Below
Daniel K. Noel was elected the first mayor of York when it was incorporated as a city in 1887. After his two three-year terms as mayor, he devoted many more years to public service. (HSYC)

and the former chief burgess presided over the council. York was protected by a guard of watchmen headed by a night constable who passed through the streets during the night yelling the time and the weather conditions. (The job of night constable had been provided for in the original borough charter. One indication of the amount of activity in the city offices in those years was the fact that the rules for selecting the night constable changed five times while the borough form of government existed.) In 1865 the town council passed legislation that would create a police force.

By 1882 the borough had outgrown its town council form of government and in April of that year the "General Borough Law" was passed, making York subject to general Pennsylvania law. Although adopted, opponents of the law argued that York would soon outgrow even this larger form of government. The pro-city advocates campaigned for their cause enthusiastically and were able to get the issue on the November 1882 ballot. During that election the majority of York voters cast ballots for a city government. Their opponents organized a hearing before the governor, however, which resulted in his refusal to give York a city charter because it had neglected to fulfill certain technicalities in filing for the license.

Four years would pass before the issue again appeared on a public ballot. The city advocates won the election, and further objection by incorporation opponents were disallowed by the governor. Thus, almost a century after its incorporation into a borough, on January 11, 1887, York became a city in the eyes of state government.

The first mayor of the new city—Daniel Noel—was a typical York Countian. His father, Jacob Noel, had come to America from the Rhine area of Germany and had served as a private in Captain Spangler's company of York soldiers in the War of 1812, during which he was wounded at the Battle of North Point. Jacob Noel's son, Daniel, was born in York on July 7, 1820. He studied diligently and became a teacher. He taught for 12 years, then became superintendent of schools for Cumberland County. He also served Cumberland County as prothonotary for three years. He moved back to York in 1871 and was to serve two three-year terms as York's first mayor, after which Noel devoted many more years to public service before his death in 1898.

On September 24 and 25 of 1887, York held its Borough Centennial. More than 30,000 people celebrated and the borough was bedecked with flags, evergreens, and bunting for the occasion. Cannon fire and bell ringing ushered in the special 100th anniversary day, which also saw two parades. On September 24, in late morning, 3,000 schoolchildren—boys in uniform caps and girls in white—proceeded down the street. In the afternoon a parade of the military, the firemen, the secret orders, and 30 bands and drum corps marched proudly along the same route. After the parades, Governor James A. Beaver, in town for the occasion, held a reception at the Opera House. In the evening, for all of York to see, a spectacular fireworks display took place on the Public Common. The next day, the Honorable Chauncey F. Black, Pennsylvania lieutenant governor and a Yorker, concluded the celebration when he presented an oration at the Opera House.

Chauncey Forward Black was the son of Jeremiah S. Black of York. Jeremiah Black had been born in Somerset County of Scotch-Irish parents and had a distinguished career as lawyer and statesman. In 1857, while Chief Justice of the Supreme Court of Pennsylvania, he was appointed by President James Buchanan as Attorney General of the United States. Black succeeded Lewis Cass as Secretary of State in 1860.

Black's lasting claim to fame as a jurist was his brilliant defense of Lambdin P. Milligan in 1866. Milligan, with two other defendants, had been sentenced to death by a military commission in Indianapolis, where the civil

Above
Although York artist Horace Bonham passed the York County Bar, he never practiced law. Instead he went on to study art in Munich and Paris, eventually receiving recognition for both his paintings and poetry. (HSYC)

Top left
The cast of *Nittaunis, the Fairy of the Codorus* presented the play for Yorkers in a benefit at the York Opera House. (HSYC)

Top right
The York Opera House provided a variety of entertainment for Yorkers at the turn of the century. It was located on South Beaver Street near the present-day General Telephone Company. Courtesy, Sunday News.

courts were open. The case hinged not on their guilt or innocence, but on their right to be tried by a civil court rather than a military tribunal. Black, assisted by the future U.S. President James A. Garfield, won the decision of the Supreme Court, which literally marked the end of military rule by restoring the Constitution. This decision has been recognized as "a bulwark of liberty, a landmark of jurisprudence." Study of the "Ex-Parte Milligan" case is, to this day, a basic requirement for students of Constitutional law.

After Jeremiah Black's retirement from the Cabinet, he moved to York. He lived in town while "Brockie," a large mansion he commissioned, was being built two miles southwest of York. In 1873 he moved into Brockie and lived there until his death on August 19, 1883.

Chauncey Forward Black was born before his family moved to York. He attended private academies, than enrolled at Hiram College, where one of his instructors was future President James A. Garfield. The younger Black then enrolled at Jefferson College in western Pennsylvania. At age 17, when his father was appointed to Buchanan's cabinet, Chauncey followed his family to Washington. Afterwards, he returned with his family to York and opened a law office with his father. Chauncey also worked at journalism before being elected lieutenant governor. After his term was completed, he returned to his estate, Willow Bridges, southwest of York in Spring Garden Township. Black and his wife, Mary Dawson Black, lived at Willow Bridges until the death of his mother in 1897, when they moved into Brockie. Both generations of the Blacks entertained distinguished leaders of the country at Brockie, including President Garfield who was a frequent visitor.

Another prominent York family of the day was the Bonhams, who lived on East Market Street. Horace Bonham, the best known member of the family, received his early education at the York County Academy and then entered Lafayette College at Easton, Pennsylvania. Three years after his graduation in 1856, Bonham was admitted to the York County Bar. He never practiced law, but when the internal-revenue assessor's office was opened in York, he was appointed to that post by President Lincoln.

"Being a man of excellent literary training and possessed of an aesthetic nature," Bonham became interested in art and was encouraged by his first painting attempts. He went to Europe, where he studied art in Munich and in Paris. He had widely praised exhibitions in Boston and Philadelphia, and also received recognition for his poetry. Bonham's painting, *Nearing the Issue at the Cockpit*, is one of the prized pieces in the collection of the Corcoran Gallery of Art. Bonham died in York in 1892.

Elizabeth Bonham, Horace's daughter, lived in the East Market Street residence among paintings and porcelains acquired on the family's many travels, until she died in the 1960s. She left the house and its furnishings to The Historical Society of York County.

Affluence and recognition came to many other York families during this period. Henry Wasbers, Sr., a former state senator, opened a laundry and the Buckingham family started a wastepaper and rag business at 129 West Philadelphia Street. In 1888 John Mayer built a cigar factory on 63 acres on the east side of North George Street, one of the first of the many cigar factories that would soon constitute a major local industry. (A settlement called "Mayersville" soon sprang up around the factory, and in 1899 the settlement was incorporated as North York Borough.) In 1890 John T. McFall was operating one of the oddest businesses in York history, a combination hat and bicycle shop.

The year 1890 saw the city's population reach 20,793, a rise of almost one-third over the 1880 number. The county's population had grown to almost 100,000 (99,489 to be exact). The decade just beginning brought more technological advances and increased industrialization. New businesses and transportation systems sprang up as always, but not the stagecoaches or retail clothiers of earlier years. These new enterprises were machine-oriented manufacturers, who expanded the range of York's businesses and, in doing so, helped cushion the impact of the nationwide Panic of 1893. York's businesses, as in earlier panics, suffered a slowdown but the local economy remained sound.

Among the most important of the new developments of this era were the formation of the York Wagon Gear Company (founded in 1892), and the introduction of the electric trolley to city streets by the York Street Railway Company. The York Street Railway Company, in order to encourage people to use the trolleys, also gave the town parks.

Robert Cathcart Latimer, a distinguished Yorker, reminisced about the York Street Railway shortly before his death in 1974. "During the heyday of street railway prosperity," he recalls, "the local company established and maintained a recreation area southwest of town called Highland Park. It was a wooded hillside and hilltop on the north bank of the Codorus.... The

This was one of the York Railways Company's electric streetcars. (HSYC)

Park was reached by a car line that made a complete loop around it."

Latimer's memoirs tell us that the park's chief attraction was a summer theater with a stock company that performed the works of Gilbert and Sullivan and other light operas: "At least to the young people, inexperienced theatergoers that we were, the performances were a delight. The car fare each way was five cents. Admission to the theater, I think, was not more than ten cents."

Latimer also offers some rare and gentle glimpses of summertime pleasures in another railway park: "Springwood too was a wooded hillside, but the stream at the foot of the hill was a shallow brook of clear water, fine wading for the youngsters. For some of an older group it was an annual custom to walk to a small store that I think must have been at the edge of Dallastown. The fact that the walk was on the railroad track almost all the way gave it a special zest; pop and sarsaparilla bought and drunk at the store were its sufficient purpose." Brookside and Cold Springs were other parks the railway company established.

Terrible autumns and winters followed these bucolic summers. On October 6, 1893, fire destroyed several buildings on the York Fair Grounds and killed two horses. On November 19, 1895, fire destroyed the York Wall Paper Company. On September 29, 1896, a powerful cyclone destroyed the main building, the grandstand, the carriage house, and the stove buildings at the Fair Grounds.

These scattered disasters, though damaging and inconvenient, did not severely impede the actions of most people, especially those with leisure time to fill. Upper-class Yorkers began to organize some of York's first social and historical organizations. The Out Door Country Club opened in 1892, and The Historical Society of York County was established in 1895. One of the most prestigious of the new groups, however, was the local chapter of the Daughters of the American Revolution, organized on October 10, 1894, at the East Market Street home of Mrs. Henry D. Schmidt. Its members, including women of the venerable Small, Croll, Miller, Lanius, Latimer, Doudel, Spangler, Cassatt, Barnitz, Smyser, and Schmidt families, elected Mrs. Schmidt vice-president and Louise Black regent (the equivalent of president). Louise Black was the wife of Chauncey Forward Black.

The York Town Chapter of the DAR began an amibitious educational program designed to point out York's rich contributions to the Revolution and to the founding of America in general. DAR members presented papers on

Below
Highland Park was a popular stop on the trolley line. This 1899 photograph shows a group of boys posed on a long flight of steps called "Fat Man's Misery." (HSYC)

Below right
This summertime group photograph shows the York Collegiate Institute class of 1895-1896. Courtesy, York College of Pennsylvania.

Below
The York Town Chapter of the Daughters of the American Revolution, shown here, dined on April 14, 1904, in honor of the group's State Regent, Miss Frazer. (HSYC)

Below right
The Bonham House, a Victorian town house, was built in 1840 and remodeled in 1870 by Horace Bonham. Stained-glass windows and parquet floors were installed after the entire first floor was redecorated in the winter of 1867-1868. The property is owned by The Historical Society of York County and is open to the public as a museum. (HSYC)

Bottom
The second annual banquet of the YWCA's Indoor Outdoor League was held on November 10, 1909. The York chapter of the organization was founded in 1891. (HSYC)

historical topics and sponsored the placement of historic plaques in honor of various York Revolutionary heroes. The DAR is still among the important social organizations today, and its members count among their ancestors those people who settled York, participated in its development, and fought in the war that won America its independence.

One of the early families represented in the founding of York and later the local chapter of the DAR were the Smysers. The Smyser family was noted for its contributions to local and state matters throughout York's developing years. Michael, Henry, and Philip all served in the state senate during the crucial years of 1790 to 1833. Adam was on the first board of directors of the Central Market in 1887; and Edward sold John Mayer the 63 acres that would become Mayersville or North York.

Mathias Smyser was one of York County's first settlers. In 1745 he made his home in West Manchester Township. His great-grandson, Samuel, owned a section of land west of Penn Street and south of Princess Street. The area became known as Smysertown and was eventually annexed.

Although conventional businesses, such as Schmidt and Ault Paper Company (founded in 1897), and Max Grumbacher's dry-goods store (opened the next year), continued to spring up, the last years of the century generally featured establishments of a kind that had never been seen before in York.

Above
This view looking west shows Market Street Bridge during the flood of June 1889. (HSYC)

Above right
The Bon Ton Department Store opened in York in 1898 at 22 West Market Street. The store's slogan was "Walk In and Look Around." The owner, Max Grumbacher, is shown wearing a hat, circa 1899. Oil cloth at the Bon Ton was eight cents a yard and gingham was four cents a yard. (HSYC)

Below right
This 1893 view of East Market Street was taken from the Square. The P.A. and S. Small Company building is at the left. (HSYC)

A group of merchants gathered in 1897 to draw up the constitution and bylaws for the Merchant's Association of York. The organization's first slate of officers included W.H. McClellan, Isaac Bennett, C.A. Geesy, and D.H. Lafean. The association grew and a program of community involvement was adopted, creating a natural tie between York's commercial and industrial segments. As a result the group's name was changed to the York Chamber of Commerce. York was the eighth locality to acquire a charter from the national Chamber of Commerce. Alexander McLean was elected first president of the York Chamber in 1909. He was followed in office by H. Wasbers, A.B. Farquhar, J. Calvin Strayer, D. Scott Bruce, Max Grumbacher, and Walter McBlain.

The year 1891 saw the formation of an exclusive club for some of York's businessmen. Named to honor the Marquis de Lafayette, the Lafayette Club eventually took over the Philip Albright Small house on the corner of Duke and Market streets. The club still serves as an important sounding board, where community fathers can review the events of the day and stimulate action on community or business projects. Exclusivity came to York County in another form that year when John Luther Long, a Hanover resident, saw the publication of his short story, "*Madame Butterfly,*" in *Century Magazine.* The story was staged by David Belasco a couple of years later, then turned into an opera by Puccini. The now-famous opera had its American premiere at the Metropolitan Opera House in New York City in 1906.

The next year, 1899, brought to York another prestigious social organization. The York Country Club was formed by Grier Hersh, Francis Farquhar (son of A.B.), Smyser Williams, W.H. Lanius, Horace Keesey, S. Fahs Smith, and several other leading York businessmen. Hersh had laid out his

own golf course in 1894 on his estate called "Springdale." That property covered the present 800 and 900 blocks of the east side of South George Street and the estate's carriage house can be seen today at 950 South Duke Street. The Hersh home had separate wine and mushroom cellars, a large octagonal ballroom, a natural outdoor amphitheater, croquet grounds, and a conservatory crowded with exotic plants. Hersh was so enthusiastic about a country club that he erected a clubhouse (designed by J.A. Dempwolf) on land on the north side of the present-day Country Club Road, which he had bought with Francis Farquhar. He leased it, along with the grounds, to the new country club board. Those grounds, many years later, became the York College of Pennsylvania campus.

The club's nine-hole golf course was opened on July 1, 1900, and in 1915 Francis Farquhar bought Hersh's interest in the estate, which was still being leased to the club. Farquhar lived on the hill at the south side of Country Club Road and he had promised his wife that as long as they lived at their residence, called "Edgecomb," their property would front on a golf course.

In 1925 the club, outgrowing its first home, acquired land to the southwest in the Crow's Nest area, built a new 18-hole golf course, and a new clubhouse that is still used today.

The year after the local Chamber of Commerce was organized, B.M. Root founded the B.M. Root Company to manufacture woodworking machinery, becoming the first company of its kind in York. In 1899 the Dentists' Supply Company was founded.

This period ended with the grandest celebration in York's history—the Sesqui-Centennial of the erection of York County, held September 3–6, 1899. On the morning of September 4, M.B. Gibson, chairman of the committee that organized the celebration, gave an address of welcome at the Opera House. Then the Honorable John W. Bittinger gave a speech on the Germans, Robert C. Bair discussed the Scotch-Irish, and historian-teacher George R. Prowell talked about the Quakers. These three speeches highlighted "the three classes of people who composed the original settlers of York County." Though the makeup of York's population had changed considerably, there was still strong evidence of those three original groups in York's bloodline.

There were many other activities connected with the Sesqui-Centennial celebration, but the most remarkable was the September 5 industrial parade. One hundred thousand people crowded the streets to watch the parade of 168 floats. Many of the parade decorations had been created by Watt Brothers and Company. (York's industrial parades were popular community events in those days and combined the community's love of parades with its pride in the ever-growing number of highly praised industrial products.) For this parade, according to George Prowell, "Centre Square was decorated with four triumphal arches . . . forty feet wide, and twelve feet deep, so that they could be seen at a great distance. Between the arches in each angle of the square were two heroic columns, supporting Corinthian capitals and globes, stuck full of flags. These arches and columns were . . . provided with electric light. The scene at night, when the several thousand lights were lit, was very impressive and delighted the people."

It is likely that some of the music used in the Sesqui-Centennial Parade had been composed in York. Roland F. Seitz, born in Shrewsbury Township, wrote dozens of marches and other compositions, and his works were performed and recorded by some of the country's leading music groups. Seitz had been educated at Dana's Musical Institute (now a part of Youngstown State University in Ohio) and his music was often compared to John

Above
The elegance of the Colonial Hotel on York's Centre Square reflected the city's era of growth and maturity at the turn of the century. The H.S. Schmidt and Company building is shown at right. Courtesy, Sunday News.

Above right
The use of electricity added to the festive air of many of York's celebrations, including the "Moneybak" display at P. Wiest's Sons store. The arch in front of the store proclaims "Welcome Knights." (HSYC)

Right
At night, thousands of electric lights decorated the 1899 Sesqui-Centennial arches. (HSYC)

Philip Sousa's.

A little more than a year after the celebration of the Sesqui-Centennial, the community engaged itself in another joyful festivity. On New Year's Eve, 1900, hundreds of people gathered in Centre Square to await midnight. When the hands of the town clock in the steeple of Christ Lutheran Church indicated the arrival of the new century, a cannon at the soldiers' monument of Penn Common fired a salute and bells rang from churches, factories, and fire-engine houses. The city band struck up a patriotic march and Company A of the Pennsylvania National Guard fired a series of salutes. Then came fireworks, and York had welcomed itself into the 20th century.

In 1901 the Maryland & Pennsylvania Railroad, which Yorkers affectionately called the "Mom and Pop," was formed by consolidating several smaller lines. In 1902 the Carlisle Market was established at Carlisle Avenue near the York Fair Grounds.

The manufacture of cigars in York County involved 80 separate factories by 1907. The town also had become an important carriage manufacturer. As H. Dietz Keller, a great-grandson of one of the founders of York Wagon Gear and a great-nephew of another, has written: "York, in the heart of an area with natural resources of fine timber, with fine craftsmen, and with a great deal of agriculture, was a natural spot for the manufacturing of a large number of vehicles. From among its number of small carriage builders emerged several companies which later became nationally known."

The area also became known for its production of many other varied commodities, including chemicals, candies, roofing paper, silk clothing, furniture, wallpaper, machine parts, and wire products. All of this diversity and growth prompted local businessmen to form the Manufacturers' Association in 1906. A year later, Prowell describes the one-year old Manufacturer's Association as "an active and energetic body, composed of the leading manufacturers of York, who have aided in developing the material interests of the city." John C. Schmidt was elected the group's first president. Serving under him as vice-presidents were Thomas Shipley, S. Forry Laucks, and Francis Farquhar, successively.

The new century saw Yorkers voting Republican for the first time in decades, favoring Theodore Roosevelt over Democrat Alton B. Parker in 1904. At about that time the Woman's Club, which still flourishes today, started out at the home of Mrs. Grier Hersh on South George Street and Rathton Road. (The 47 founding members, incidentally, included women from the Eichelberger, Farquhar, Jessop, Smyser, and Small families.) In 1906 the York Art Club, a predecessor of the York Art Association active today, held its first meetings. Two years later the Visiting Nurse Association acquired its charter.

On April 6, 1904, York had one of its worst fires in history. A blaze swept through the York Carriage Company, claiming the lives of three city firemen. The Vigilant Company's John Henry Saltzgiver, Lewis M. Strubinger, and Horace Frank Strine all died in the blaze, which leveled the plant on North George Street. In 1928 York's Rescue Fire Company voted to take its name off a large statue that it had erected on Penn Common in 1900, rededicating it to the three men who lost their lives in the 1904 disaster and to seven other firefighters who had died in the line of duty subsequently.

After the Carriage Company fire, York's carriage industry experienced a decline. Some manufacturers saw this trend developing in the nation and, as in other times, they retooled and adapted their businesses for new products—in this case a new form of transportation, the automobile. In the next two decades, York would become one of the nation's leading auto centers.

The first stirrings of automotive interest in York arose in 1900, when, as Keller relates, "the first horseless carriage in York came down Main Street and then past the largest livery stable—chugging along, scaring the stable operator and a nearby coachman with his passengers and horses. The several large carriage and wagon builders in York realized what was happening."

Lowell W. Williams, Dietz's coauthor, takes up the story to tell about the most important car company to arise in York, the Pullman Company. "Nineteen ten and 1911 brought national fame to York's Pullman automobiles," he writes. "A [Pullman] Model 'K' was the winner in an 1,100-mile endurance race between Atlanta and New York, June 6–11, 1910. . . . On October 8, a Pullman Model 'O' won the Fairmount Park Road Race in Philadelphia." Pullman, Williams reports, began shipping automobiles to places as near as Philadelphia and as far away as Australia.

In 1914, when the town held 45,000 people and the county had more than 130,000, a healthy 10,851 worked in 247 plants to turn out almost $23 million worth of products. While York industrialists were forging state and national reputations in the automobile and other businesses, reports of the conflicts in Europe reached York. York leaders, in their board rooms and over lunch at the Lafayette Club, discussed the day's disheartening headlines. Some of them increased inventories in anticipation of future supply shortages and others reinforced manufacturing policies preparing for the worst.

The *York Dispatch*, anticipating war, took a survey of the community's resources and found that there were many factories in York that could be

A fire broke out at the York Art Store at 239 North George Street on April 21, 1912. The sign on the building across the alley advertises Coca-Cola for five cents. (HSYC)

pressed quickly into action for war production. "The plant of the W.H. Ottemiller Company has automatic machinery which could in a moment be turned to the manufacture of hand grenades," the *Dispatch* relates. "The A.B. Farquhar plant could turn out huge armored tractors and artillery carriages, and wagon bodies could be manufactured by the Pullman Company, the Bell Motor Car Company and the Martin Carriage Company. . . ." Even canteens could be made in York, it was reported.

But while war was presenting a sobering influence on community life, the city and county were still on the upswing. The Ancient Order Knights of the Mystic Chain, the Knights of Malta, the Fraternal Order of Eagles, the Brotherly Protective Order of Elks, the Order of Red Men, the Order of Odd Fellows, and the Tall Cedars of Lebanon all had York representatives in the new century. Their members made the community a center of fraternal activity. Yorkers' personal wealth had never looked better. The tax rate for that year was four mills on the dollar.

But the general prosperity could not save the once-mighty Pullman Company. As Lowell Williams tells it, "sales were down, working capital was at a low ebb, and the sterling reputation of Pullman [a reputation born of the Yorkers' devotion to fine craftsmanship] had been tarnished by some 'lemons' that had been allowed to reach the marketplace. . . . [In addition], a few crucial bad management decisions were made by 'big city experts' brought to York. However, this damage could probably have been overcome had not World War I occurred at this time. Export business 'dried up,' financing became tight and competition from well capitalized mass-production manufacturers usurped the market from the limited production, modestly funded York auto producers."

The Pullman company's death was the major industrial calamity that York suffered during the World War I period. For the most part, the five decades after the war had been amazingly good ones. York had developed most of the characteristics that remain with it today, from the architectural flavor of its streets, to the diversity of its industries and the number of its people. York, after 300 years, had achieved the mark of a mature city: stability. Despite the failure of the Pullman company, York was enjoying prosperity in generous proportions and the population was generally content.

World War I would soon change that, however.

This 1908 Pullman automobile was built in York. It is parked in front of St. John's Episcopal Church on North Beaver Street. (HSYC)

Lorie Satz, a member of the York Collegiate Institute class of 1920-1921, dressed in the style typical of fashionable young ladies in York when "the Roaring Twenties" began. Courtesy, York College of Pennsylvania.

CHAPTER VII

WORLD WAR I AND THE "ROARING TWENTIES"

The evening edition of the *York Dispatch* on April 6, 1917, used a two-column, front-page headline to declare the news: "President Proclaims War Between U.S. and Germany." Despite his election promise to keep America free from the burgeoning conflict in Europe, President Wilson decided to enter the United States in "the war to end all wars." He had requested authorization from Congress four days earlier, and on April 6, Congress voted 373 to 50 to declare war. York's Congressman, A.R. Broadbeck, was among those in favor of the act.

Another headline in the same edition of the *Dispatch* commanded Yorkers to "Enlist at Once or Be Drafted." Predictably, the command was not necessary for York. The community already had prepared for the probability of war and for sending its men again to the battlefield. Even though 4 million of the eventual 4½ million Americans who fought in World War I were draftees, most of the 6,000 men and women who served from York County were enlisted participants.

Commodore C.M. Fahs, who was in charge of the Harrisburg district of mobilization, noted that the district, of which York County was a part, had 62 applicants per day even though its daily quota was only five. "There is no lack of patriotism here," he said. Pennsylvania, in fact, led the New York State district by 700 percent in number of men signed up for the armed services. York County's draftees totaled 2,592—less than half the number of county citizens who served.

While so many of York-area men and women were engaged directly in the war efforts, county residents were aiding the cause on the home front. President Wilson called for higher food production on the nation's farms and Yorkers were prompt to act on his suggestion. Farm production was accelerated with the help of city people who volunteered to work the land, but, nevertheless, shortages soon occurred. Sugar had to be rationed at four pounds per person each month, and since many farmers sold their herds of milk cows, butter and related products were also in short supply. Most citizens, even in the city, kept their own gardens so that the shortages were little more than inconveniences.

Sadly for most Yorkers, the city's two breweries, the Keystone Brewing Company and the York Brewing Company, were forced to close their doors as a grain-conservation measure in November 1918. A *Dispatch* article, however, pointed out that there were enough alcoholic beverages to last the county until May, making Yorkers better off, in this respect, than most other communities. Theodore R. Helb, owner of the Keystone Brewing Company, announced that he would not lay off the firm's employees, but would put them to work in painting and repair jobs. In the northern part of the county, the York Haven Paper Company announced that its 300 employees would receive a five percent salary bonus to offset the increased cost of living, and other companies followed suit.

The York community supported the war effort in other ways. York bakers created a "Victory Loaf," which substituted other cereals for wheat in order to save that valuable grain for the men at the front. Campaigns were held to collect worn clothing for Belgian and French refugees and to gather linen for French hospitals. In order to ensure that the military had enough carbon, which was used in gas masks to absorb the poisonous mustard gas, Yorkers gathered peach stones, apricot pits, plum pits, olive pits, date seeds, walnut shells, hickory nut shells, butternut shells, and cherry pits for use in the manufacture of this important commodity. Yorkers adopted "heatless Mondays" and other conservation methods, and collection drives were headed up by community residents, such as Clinton W. Schultz, Charles E. Moul, C.F. Bauserman, J.V. Kleffel, M.W. Naill, Charles E. Sprenkle, and H.W. Miller.

The Woman's Club of York initiated a War Relief Committee to do sewing for French hospitals that were caring for American soldiers. Members of the Woman's Club also made garments for refugees and collected gold to sell in fund-raising drives for the hospitals. The club "adopted" four French orphans and after war's end organized the establishment of a veteran's memorial—a living row of trees lining the highway from Wrightsville to Abbottstown.

Yorkers subscribed $30.5 million to five "Liberty Loans," and leaders of the bond promotions proudly pointed out that the sum represented an average of $200 per person for the entire county. A total of $2.18 million in "War Stamps" was sold in the York Square, from a replica of the Colonial Court House (quickly renamed the "Victory House"). A War Chest was subscribed at $425,000 during the same period.

Several Yorkers achieved national prominence for their efforts on behalf of the war. Grier Hersh, president of the York National Bank and the York Gas Company, was appointed chairman of the National Defense Committee and the Liberty Loan Committee. Hersh also served as the Federal Food Administrator for York County in charge of distributing food to the hundreds of Yorkers who were without basic sustenance. Working with Hersh was John C. Schmidt, chain manufacturer and the president of the Schmidt and Ault Paper Company. Schmidt called a meeting of influential York citizens to form the local chapter of the American Red Cross. He devoted his energies full-time to the organization of the York County chapter until the spring of 1918, when he was called to Washington to head up the Chain Section of the War Industries Board.

But before the war was over, 196 Yorkers would die either on the battlefield or in hospitals. As a tribute to them, the community erected a large white replica of the "winged Victory of Samothrace" in front of the Court House. Four bronze plaques bearing the names of those who had died were installed on the Court House's pillars, and memorial services were held in churches across York County.

Several of the York volunteers had been women. Jeannette Zinn, a resident of West College Avenue and an honor graduate of York High School, had been valedictorian and class poet, and before volunteering for the service was captain of the winning team in the War Thrift Stamp contest. She died, like so many other Americans during the war, a victim of pneumonia in the United States Hospital in Liverpool, England. Her former employers at the C.H. Bear & Company furnished a room in her memory in the Girl's Club of York.

Facing page
Left
A sign displaying the slogan "Lest We Forget" on the York County Court House reminded Yorkers of their sons and daughters who fought in World War I. The *Winged Victory* statue was erected in front of the Court House in memory of York Countians who fought in the war. (HSYC)

Right
C.H. Bear, dry-goods and notions store, became Bear's Department Store, one of the most popular retail businesses in York. (HSYC)

Facing page
Left
Yorkers celebrated the end of World War I with a parade on November 16, 1918, five days after the Armistice. Courtesy, Sunday News.

Right
An emergency open-air hospital was set up on the York Fair Grounds when a flu epidemic hit the city in 1918. From the first of October 1918 to mid-January 1919, more than 6,500 cases of influenza were reported in York. (HSYC)

One of the first Yorkers who had entered the war—and one of the youngest to die—was Corporal Raymond F. Knighton. Knighton, who had lived on Walnut Street, had enlisted on July 6, 1916, at the age of 15. He was killed in France, in the Meuse-Argonne offensive, on October 4, 1918, a little more than a month before the Armistice ended the fighting on November 11.

The Yorker who most distinguished himself for heroics, however, was Captain Rodney W. Polack. A resident of the McClellan Heights section of York, Polack led his company in capturing 205 prisoners, including several German officers, before he was killed at Cunel, France, on October 14, 1918.

Toward the end of World War I, news of American victories reached York and the community began planning its Armistice celebrations. Ironically, inaccurate information triggered a false Armistice celebration in York several days before the Tuesday, November 11 signing. When reliable news came that day, however, the city and county joined the nation in exclamations of victory, including bell ringing, singing in the streets, and the banging of pot lids.

There was only one appropriate way for the community to celebrate an event as important as the Armistice: a grand parade was planned for the

WORLD WAR I AND THE "ROARING TWENTIES" • 119

following Saturday. Lining the streets to view the proceedings were 100,000 jubilant Yorkers, who applauded the 20,000 participants, including 50 bands and 13 drum and bugle corps, in the 7½-mile parade.

Undercutting the mood of celebration that the end of World War I inspired was a terrible flu epidemic that swept York between October and December of 1918. From the first of October to mid-January, when the epidemic was finally controlled, more than 6,500 cases of influenza were reported. On a single day, 2,012 children were reported home sick from York County schools. Three members of one family died within days of each other and makeshift hospitals were set up in a Beaver Street hall and also at the York Fair Grounds. Many of the community's women were active in treating the sick, including Helen V. Delaplane, who wrote a column about her experiences for the Lutheran Social Services' newsletter. "In many families," Miss Delaplane recalls, "all members were ill, so that no one was left to care for them. People were warned not to gather in crowds. All places where crowds were accustomed to assembling—movies, schools, churches, etc.—were closed. Everyone was urged to stay at home. Doctors and nurses were working at top speed. . . . Neighbors and relatives were helping each other. Under all of it was fear. Flu was a killer—what could be done? An open-air hospital seemed to be the answer. The York Fairgrounds was chosen as the site. . . . Volunteers became nurses' aides . . . the greatest number being teachers. . . . The nurse who had been appointed as [our] supervisor came down with the flu the third day." (The nurse later recovered.)

Even while York County was experiencing a terrifying flu epidemic, it was gaining in population. The 1920 census showed that 47,499 people lived in the city and 144,521 people lived in the county. And some of those people were making an impact that reached far beyond York's borders, especially in politics.

In 1919 York's state representative, Henry Lanius, who was himself blind, introduced Pennsylvania's first legislation to provide the handicapped with special education. In 1921 Samuel S. Lewis, a past president of the Vigilant Fire Company, became Pennsylvania's state auditor, initiating a 33-year political career that would see him elected or appointed state treasurer, secretary of highways, secretary of forest and waters, and lieutenant governor. A county park was named in his honor. Yorkers, in this era, were undergoing a political change that had been, perhaps, presaged in 1904, when residents broke their long Democratic trend by voting for Theodore Roosevelt rather than the Democratic candidate Alton B. Parker. Yorkers' preferences for practicality over dogma, and moderation over excess, pointed them to a different party in this election and those characteristics rule county politics to this day. Roosevelt, too, was a friendly grandfather type with sparkling eyes—in contrast to the dull Parker.

In the 1920s Yorkers supported all three Republican candidates for President, helping to elect Warren G. Harding in 1920, Calvin Coolidge in 1924, and Herbert Hoover in 1928. They were all given warm welcomes when they visited York during the decade. Harding and Hoover made campaign stops on September 27, 1920, and July 14, 1928, respectively; Coolidge visited York as President on November 19, 1926. Future President Franklin D. Roosevelt also campaigned in York in 1920. Then assistant secretary of the navy, Roosevelt had been selected as the running mate of Democratic nominee Governor James M. Cox of Ohio.

The Yorker shift to Republican loyalties had been effected, in part, by the feeling that President Wilson had gone too far in his expansion of federal power and that his zeal for reform had derailed traditional Democratic, laissez-faire business policies. But the abandonment of the Democratic

Party extended into state and local politics as well. Yorkers supported Republican gubernatorial candidates Gifford Pinchot, elected in 1922, and John S. Fisher, who was sent to the Governor's Mansion in 1926. Republican Congressmen also received York's backing, except in 1922, when Democrat Samuel Glatfelter was favored over shoe-merchant Mahlon Haines, the Republican nominee.

Haines, though a well-known York philanthropist, was probably too much of a local character for Yorkers to entrust with high office. He owned a chain of shoe stores in Pennsylvania and Maryland and called himself the "Shoe Wizard." He promised young people money if they would give up smoking immediately and forever, and he kept a small herd of buffalo on his farm for the amusement of Yorkers. Haines often sponsored essay contests, offering a $190 first prize to the student who wrote the best essay on the "Shoe Wizard's" accomplishments. Haines also waged an unsuccessful campaign to rename York's Royalist street names, including George, Princess, King, and others. But Mahlon Haines was as magnanimous as he was eccentric; he devoted himself to many community-service organizations, especially the Boy Scouts, and when he dissolved his business, he divided its assets among his 50 employees. Haines left an ersatz monument to his personality and accomplishments: a shoe-shaped house that now houses an ice cream shop and is still a tourist curiosity.

The postwar period was one of continuing prosperity for York, even though the number of industrial corporations had actually dropped to 218. But this was due to mergers and consolidations, not to a decline in growth. Those 218 factories produced finished products valued at $62,610,816, compared with a yield of $22,943,328 by the community's 247 plants in 1914.

During the late 1920s, York gained a reputation as the "Gateway to the East," because of its attractive location between Eastern and Western trade regions and because of its good transportation facilities and varied industry. The town also boasted 10 of the largest industrial plants in the United States. Those plants, according to a *Dispatch* article of 1928, led "all others in volume of production in icemaking and refrigeration machinery, bank safes and vaults, water turbines, artificial teeth, wallpaper, roofing paper, pretzels, baker's machinery, auto tire chains and commercial auto bodies."

York's prosperous automobile industry earned the community another nickname—the "Detroit of the East." During the peak of York's remarkable auto-manufacturing era, which spanned the years 1903 to 1930, there were some 30 factories in the county producing thousands of cars and trucks every year. During 1904 the Martin Parry Corporation alone turned out 20,000 vehicles. In the 1920s Martin Parry produced 65 body styles, including the Model T, which came off the factory lines at 500 a day.

This was the era, too, when York acquired a brand new hotel. Businessmen in the community had long felt the need for a high-quality modern hotel; in 1924 the Chamber of Commerce appointed a committee to study the acquisition of such a structure. A temporary board of directors was created that spearheaded a campaign to sell $1,175,000 worth of stock to cover the building costs of the new hotel. On that board were John L. Gerber, Charles H. Bear, W.S. Bond, Dr. C.P. Rice, Max Grumbacher, C. Elmer Smith, and Thomas Shipley. Land was purchased on the southwest corner of Market and Duke streets and the 198-room Yorktowne Hotel was opened on October 5, 1925. The community now could boast of an elegant downtown hotel that served both Yorkers and visitors from many miles away.

York's economic and political stability was challenged, however, by sweeping social changes—mostly affecting the town's youth—that had

begun to trouble the more conservative members of the older generation. The first issue to divide the York community was Prohibition, which had been enacted as a temporary city ordinance on July 1, 1919. Prohibition became law on January 16, 1920, when the federal Volstead Act went into effect.

But Yorkers had a family tradition of drinking that went back to Colonial days (and even further back through the families of European immigrants, especially Germans and Scotch-Irish), so Prohibition was often ignored or circumvented. Yorkers frequented speakeasies, bought bootleg liquor, or experimented with various "home brews" (which they drank themselves or sold to others). They found that "properly fermented, dandelions made a fairly decent wine with an equally decent kick." They also tried, with varying degrees of success, to make alcoholic beverages from raisins, cornmeal, vinegar, cider, and berries. Some resorted to drinking items with high alcoholic content, such as vanilla extract, cough syrups, bay rum hair tonic, and even wood alcohol. The more creative Yorkers discovered that pouring two quarts of boiling water into an old whiskey barrel, and letting it stand for awhile, produced a drink "with sufficient kick to paralyze a healthy elephant." As a result, the demand for old whiskey barrels reached unprecedented proportions.

According to a 1928 *York Dispatch*, bootlegging became so profitable that farmers spent much of their time engaged in this activity, leaving their wives sometimes to harvest the fields. Mayor E.S. Hugentugler said that bootlegging was so prevalent and accepted that he could do little to stop it, admitting that even members of the York Police Department were involved. Prohibition, at least in York, proved to be a disastrous experiment in which a majority of its citizenry simply ignored the law. An even more significant development in the "Roaring Twenties," however, was the growing schism between the generations. More and more young Yorkers became "flappers" and "sheiks," and their parents, for the most part, were not pleased.

Above, top left
Mahlon N. Haines, the "Shoe Wizard," was known for his philanthropy and was a noted figure in York for many years. The house he built in the shape of a shoe east of York is located today along busy Route 30 and remains a curiosity for passing travelers. (HSYC)

Above left
The first Pullman automobile, shown here, was built in York in 1903. York's automobile industry expanded to such an extent that the city earned the nickname "Detroit of the East." (HSYC)

Above
Members of the 1918-1919 York Collegiate Institute basketball team pose on the front steps of the school. Dr. Bruce Grove, later a well known York physician, is shown holding the ball. Courtesy, York College of Pennsylvania.

According to authors Carl E. Hatch, Joseph B. Hicks, and Richard E. Kohler, in their Martin Library booklet, "York, Pa., in the Roaring 20s" (1973): "Older women were appalled to see younger women in short skirts, low-cut blouses, rolled-down stockings and peek-a-boo waists."

Citizens registered complaints with Mayor Hugentugler, asking him to revive an old borough ordinance that made it unlawful for women "to expose their calves or shoulders or to appear on the street or in public in any dress such as attracts undue attention to the body or is in any way immodest." But the mayor refused, saying that he believed in personal liberty and thought that "people, both minors and adults, should have freedom to dress according to their individual tastes."

Another community leader who received complaints regularly was the Superintendent of York City Schools, Atreus Wanner. Wanner told the complaining citizens that he, too, was a believer in personal liberty and would, under no circumstances, institute a dress code for city schools.

The youths of York, of course, were merely responding to the "Jazz Age" ethos that F. Scott Fizgerald had chronicled in *This Side of Paradise* (1920), and which his own example helped to popularize. Movies, popular songs, novels, endless magazine articles, and especially advertising all served to reinforce the carefree, sophisticated, distinctly urban image of "Flaming Youth" that was having an effect on even America's smaller communities. Radios and automobiles also helped York out of isolation felt by many county teenagers. Although York did not yet have its own radio station, thousands owned the new entertainment box and listened to stations in Harrisburg, Washington, D.C., and other places. More people were moving into the city, too, and finding life there much more exciting than the routine of the farm.

But the changes in dress and manner, especially among women, were not well received by many York citizens. In addition to the short skirts and immodest blouses, citizens lodged complaints about the use of cosmetics. The Reverend Silas C. Swallow, a Methodist minister, sadly rebuked the "face-painting" women of the community. "In my boyhood days, about 80 years ago," the Reverend preached, "paint, powder, and rouge on a lady's lips and cheeks was so dim as to justify her denial of its presence.... Now ... it is no uncommon thing to see a lass 'a la Paree,' walking the streets with her lover, peering into a mirror held in one hand, while with the other she smears her angel face with a bag of powder, paint and rouge—meanwhile, with the escort blowing his fetid breath surcharged with tobacco smoke into the same angel's face."

In 1922 one of the town's oldest druggists told a *York Dispatch* reporter that cosmetics sales had increased 200 percent over the last few years. He went on to add that not all his customers were young women and "the way some of the old girls doll up, you can't tell them from their daughters."

In 1924, when bobbed hair became the rage, Superintendent Wanner was again besieged with demands to institute appearance codes, this time covering hair as well as dress. Didn't the Bible itself, some of the complainants urged, say that it is an abomination for a woman to cut her hair? Wanner's response once more dismayed York's conservative older generation. "The school controllers of York," he declared, "have one regulation in regard to hair ... and that is that the hair of the heads of pupils be free of pediculosis. That means, in plain words, 'cooties' are not allowed in pupils' hair."

The intensity of reaction that these changes in fashion and mores evoked was not entirely unwarranted. More than any previous generation, the young people of York—indeed of the whole country—considered themselves a distinct group. They had just been through the disrupting, emotionally devas-

Farquhar Park was the site of a large Easter egg hunt in the 1920s. Courtesy, Harry J. McLaughlin.

tating experience of World War I, and in the subsequent peacetime prosperity, they went on something of a rampage. Jazz music, speakeasies, fancy cars, and flamboyant dress were not insignificant; they were symbols of a virtual revolution in the social structure, and represented, at least to the young people, a break from the past. As authors Hatch, Hicks, and Kohler put it: "Whereas Yorkers were offended at bobbed hair, cosmetics and short skirts, they were shocked at the younger generation's smoking, vulgar dancing and petting. . . . They were horrified at rumors that the young were frequenting speakeasies and brothels. Bobbed hair, cosmetics and short skirts entailed a revolution in manners. But smoking, vulgar dancing, petting, and the spread of venereal disease involved something far more serious. This was a revolution in morals."

As in every revolution, there were counter-revolutionaries. York's first policewoman, Mabel Rozelle, was foremost among them. On a Saturday night, April 1, 1922, Officer Rozelle raided a favorite York dance hall, pulling apart dance partners and announcing that henceforth "there are certain dances that will not be tolerated by the York police department, two of which are 'The Toddle' and 'The Cheek to Cheek.'" She also set up special classes for York men, where she warned them of "flappers who looked for pickups in dance halls and who give you venereal disease."

York's movie houses and theaters were often mentioned in complaints to authorities during this era, and they, too, no doubt contributed to the "revolution in morals." To take a typical year, in 1925 the newly opened Strand Theater was offering Colleen Moore in *The Desert Flower*, with musical accompaniment provided by "Herbert Seiler at the Wurlitzer." The Orpheum featured a live show—"McIntyre and Heath, in Trumping the Ace"—and reminded patrons that Monday was "Burlesque Day" at the theater. Reginald Denny starred in the film, *California Straight Ahead*, at the Jackson Theater; and the Coliseum was hosting a Charleston Queen contest and a Fox trot-waltz competition. Yorkers could see *A Girl of the Limberlost* at the Hippodrome; Evelyn Brent was appearing on the screen at the Wizard in *Midnight Molly*; and the Scenic featured *The Hidden Menace* with Charles Hutchison.

While the majority of Yorkers, young and old, enjoyed these new diversions, and soon made visits to dance halls, and movie and vaudeville houses a part of their weekly routine, one segment of the community demonstrated strong opposition—the Ku Klux Klan. York, because of its many theaters, was being called a "banner burlesque town," and its entertainments were attracting large numbers of out-of-town visitors. Spurred on by the "old stand-pat conservatives," the Klan began waging war against the

Facing page
The Hippodrome theater at 121 West Market Street screened the film *The Serpent's Fang* in 1913. (HSYC)

Below left
A York Collegiate Institute party was held in 1920 in Mary Gotwald's barn at the rear of 153 East Market Street. Mary Gotwald is the first on the left in the back row. Courtesy, York College of Pennsylvania.

Below
The annual Halloween parade is a tradition in York. One department of the York Manufacturing Company marched in a Halloween parade in the mid-1920s dressed as clocks, with Father Time leading the group holding a sign, "Don't be Alarmed—Time Is Passing." The group assembled in front of the plant on North Hartley Street. The parade is still one of York's most popular yearly events. (HSYC)

new turpitude and the changing morals that preceded it.

A June 10, 1924, article in the *York Dispatch* tells the story of one of the KKK's many raids: "Forty hooded and gowned members of the KKK, said to be from Shrewsbury and Jacobus, attended a picnic in a woods near the Susquehanna Trail, 12 miles south of York, Saturday night, and put a stop to numerous petting parties that were in progress. . . . It is said the Klansmen rounded up a number of women who were deserted by their male escorts when the Klansmen approached. One of the ardent male wooers, however, was identified. He is a married man with several children and resides in a town in the southern part of York County. The women were taken into custody and promised the Klansmen to reform and never again return to the picnic woods."

While the Klan, in other parts of the country, were known for their violent vigilantism against blacks, Catholics, Jews, and other minorities, in York they appear to have tried to assume the role of "moral caretaker." With the exception of an occasional cross burning on a Catholic family's lawn, the group's activities in York did not have a racial tone or a strong impact. As late as the 1970s and the 1980s, though, the Klan in York County made itself visible by planning rallies and parades, many of which never came off. Perhaps the no-nonsense, law-abiding attitude of Yorkers has all along dampened the spirit of the KKK in its York mission.

But the Klan received early and vehement opposition from Mayor Hugentugler, who proclaimed: "I do not intend to tolerate in this city such an un-American organization as the KKK." The mayor may not have been as upset at the challenge to his authority that the Klan represented as he was at

This view looking west shows Market Street in 1924. The Bon Ton Department Store is in the left-hand corner. (HSYC)

their principles, since he soon began a moral crusade of his own. On October 20, 1928, he launched a campaign to break up the "canned heat" parties, which a tailor on South Hartley Street had been hosting. The daily newspapers reported arrests of several people, who were drunk on a dozen or more different alcoholic concoctions.

Other events toward the end of the decade, especially the York Sesqui-Centennial in 1927, the "Hex Murder" trial in 1928, and the stock market crash of 1929, took Yorkers' minds off the changing moral climate. But the "Roaring Twenties" had altered the social structure of the town forever, and the order and piety of its early years were significantly changed.

York's Sesqui-Centennial, marking the 150th anniversary of the time when it had been the nation's capital, gave the community an opportunity for self-congratulation. It responded by producing a lavish gala, including parades, music, decorations, and grand pageantry. But the Sesqui-Centennial was a strictly local concern. The next year a bizarre murder would bring reporters from newspapers and magazines across the country flocking to York.

On November 28, 1928, three men robbed and brutally murdered Nelson Rehmeyer, at his rural York County farmhouse. A robbery-murder, while hardly an everyday occurrence in York, was not by itself enough to send shock waves around the world. What attracted the attention of reporters was the motive for the crime: the murderers wanted to obtain a lock of Rehmeyer's hair, thereby enabling them to break a spell they believed him to have cast.

Nelson Rehmeyer was a large, powerfully built man. He stood over six feet tall and weighed close to 200 pounds. His wife had left him, taking their two daughters with her, but they made frequent visits and there was no bitterness. When the young girls were sick, they were taken to their father to be "tried for." Rehmeyer, like many of the rural folk in York County, was a practitioner of faith healing and "powwowing."

Powwowing was based on John George Hohman's book of recipes, incantations, and talismans, *The Long Lost Friend: A Collection of Mysterious and Invaluable Remedies Good for Man and Beast*. The book had been published in German in 1820, in Reading, Pennsylvania, and was widely read throughout Pennsylvania Dutch country for generations afterwards. The

Below left
This view, looking north from Centre Square, shows George Street in 1927. Paintings depicting heroes of the American Revolution were part of the city's Sesqui-Centennial celebration marking the time Congress was in York. Courtesy, Sunday News.

Below
The house of Nelson Rehmeyer in Rehmeyer's Hollow in southern York County was the site of the famous York County "Hex Murder" on November 27, 1928. Courtesy, Harry J. McLaughlin.

strongholds of powwowism (also referred to as witchcraft and "brauching") were communities, or areas of communities, where the people were largely uneducated and subject to superstitions passed down from the old country.

The three men charged with Rehmeyer's death were believers in, and sometime practitioners of, powwowism. John Blymire, 32, was a fourth-generation, self-proclaimed witch, who worked in a York cigar factory on East Princess Street. He had recently moved into town to take a room in a boarding house on Prospect Street after a series of failures. His wife had divorced him; his crops had failed; his chickens laid no eggs. He was forced to support himself at the cigar factory, and with the small amount of money he received from powwowing. But his "patients" often complained that his "trying" for them did not help, and eventually Blymire could not even perform the lowliest of witch duties: "the stopping of blood." Trying for a patient, in powwow lore, involved the recitation of chants by a witch and the offering of strange prescriptions to overcome hexes cast by another powwower, or to cure ailments or achieve ends.

Blymire had befriended John Curry, who looked several years older than his age of 14, at the cigar factory where Curry was also employed. The third man in the Rehmeyer case was Wilbert Hess, 18, whose father had a farm outside the city where he and his sons tended their plentiful crops. Mrs. Hess had a stand at the Central Market three days a week, which brought her "pin money" for the niceties of Pennsylvania Dutch life. But the Hess family, like Blymire, had been visited recently by disaster. Mr. Hess's crops had failed, his hogs had become ill, and he had suffered nervousness and loss of appetite. He visited many powwowers, convinced that someone had put a hex on him. When he consulted Blymire, he was told that a hex had, indeed, been put on his farm and Blymire assured him that for $40 he would find out who had cast the spell. Hess only had $10 and Blymire accepted the money with no complaint.

Blymire attempted to determine who had bewitched the Hess farm, but eventually visited another witch in desperation. Mrs. Nellie Noll, a resident of Lancaster County's riverside community, Marietta, was 90 years old and the most famous practitioner of powwowism in the area. For the same $10 Hess had given Blymire, she divined that the witch who had cast the spell was Nelson D. Rehmeyer of Rehmeyer's Hollow in York County's North Hopewell Township. For good measure, she added John Curry's name to the list of people Rehmeyer had hexed. She then gave Blymire instructions on how to break the spell. "Get the old witch's Bible and a lock of his hair," the River Witch said, "and bury the hair under eight feet of ground."

Blymire, accompanied by Curry, made a trip to Rehmeyer's Hollow. They sat around Rehmeyer's home chatting as old friends, and at Rehmeyer's invitation spent the night. Blymire "tried" for hours to beat down the supposed power of the man asleep above him, but to no avail. The following morning they returned to York, determined to return with help.

The next night, under a full Thanksgiving moon, the two men returned with Wilbert Hess, and what had begun as the breaking of a spell ended up in brutal murder. The three men struggled with Rehmeyer in an attempt to obtain a lock of his hair. Blymire, Curry, and Hess all struck Rehmeyer with various heavy objects; he was tied down and his shirt was set on fire. After the men left, the braying of Rehmeyer's unfed mule led a neighbor to discover the murdered man's blood-soaked and charred body.

Wilbert Hess, apparently plagued with guilt, made a full confession the next day to District Attorney Amos W. Herrman. On November 30, the *York Dispatch* carried the headline: "Murder Farmer to Get Lock of Hair to Break Spell, Three Confess."

The resulting trial, involving weeks of testimony by 34 witnesses, caused a national sensation. The city of York sat in resentful shock as the murder story, and the press reaction to it, unfolded. The *Philadelphia Record* called the Rehmeyer case "the weirdest and most curiously fascinating trial in the history of modern jurisprudence." The *New York World*, believing apparently that everyone in York was a powwower, called Yorkers "stupid clods" and "twentieth century anachronisms bound by fifteenth century superstitions." It was hinted in the national press that there were more than a thousand witches, "powwowers," hexers, or "brauchers" in York County practicing their art, using the witch's handbook, and distributing protective cloths called "himmelsbriefs."

There is no doubt that the reporters' hunger for a dramatic story blew the "Hex Murder," as it was called, out of all proportion. Most Yorkers were embarrassed that their town was suddenly being viewed as a hotbed of superstition and black magic. They knew that powwowing existed; many had been "tried for" without incident; and believers in witchcraft had largely been viewed as an eccentric, but harmless element in the community. The trial, and the unwanted attention it garnered, would change that, however. The three men who had caused the uproar were convicted of first-degree murder. Blymire and Hess were sentenced to life imprisonment, and the minor, John Curry, was given 10 to 20 years.

A wide educational campaign against the practice of witchcraft was launched, led by prominent physicians, business leaders, local reporters, and others. The York County Medical Society conducted a study of powwowing and the state departments of health and education offered help in eradicating the various superstitions and practices from Pennsylvania Dutch lore. York County Coroner L.U. Zech, in later investigations, reported seven known powwowers who practiced witchcraft as a business, and four deaths that were believed to have been caused because individuals had relied on witchcraft instead of seeking proper medical attention. Those who participated in the educational campaign asserted that "York County is not any worse or so bad as some other places in the incidence of powwowing practice," and "no witches ever were hanged in Pennsylvania for their beliefs."

With the coming of radio, television, and increased travel and educational opportunities, powwowing has all but disappeared in subsequent generations. The murderers eventually were released. Blymire, after serving 23 years, had his life sentence commuted by Governor John S. Fine, and he moved to Philadelphia where he worked as a janitor. Hess and Curry were each paroled after serving 10 years.

Forty years after the "Hex Murder" made front-page news across the nation, interest in the case was revived by a book about it by Arthur H. Lewis. Tourists and reporters trudged down the roads of southern York County looking for "Rehmeyer's Hollow." In 1969 advance men for a movie producer began gathering material and scouting locations, but the proposed film was never made, and the incident once again faded into welcomed obscurity.

While the attention of some Yorkers in the late 1920s was on powwowing, others in the community were preoccupied with more positive developments. The York Hospital board of directors announced it would begin construction, in January 1929, of a new facility on top of a hill in the Springdale section of Spring Garden Township. Coinciding with the start of construction was the annexation of the Springdale area into the city; a section of West Manchester Township became the city's 14th ward when it was also annexed.

During the same period Lee Reineberg, president of the York Chamber of Commerce, joined Mayor Jacob E. Weaver to lead efforts to acquire new

Above
Elm Beach along the Conewago between Manchester and York Haven was a popular spot for Fourth of July celebrations in the 1920s. Courtesy, Sunday News.

Facing page
Ephram S. Hugentugler was elected mayor of York in 1915, 1919, and 1923. As mayor, he refused to restrict the kinds of clothes women wore because he believed in personal liberty. (HSYC)

Christmas decorations for the city, and the York Gas Company, which had been purchased five years before by the Pennsylvania Gas and Electric Company, announced plans for a $140,000 improvement project. Conditions seemed just as favorable for the York Water Company, where president C.M. Kerr announced that water company capital stock would double from $3 million to $6 million. This was also the era of great expansion for the York Water Company, with the construction of Lake Williams. The company's reforestation program benefited the community and brought widespread notice from faraway places. In the area of transportation, the Pennsylvania Railroad was adding extra trains to its routes and handling the highest number of shipments since the war.

As a further indication of the era's prosperity, Lancaster and York counties were planning a new one and one-quarter mile long bridge over the Susquehanna at a cost of $2 million. The possibility of an airport for the York area also was being discussed. The city had $1,691,193 worth of building projects near completion and the evening newspaper reported that new shopping records had been set in the Christmas season of 1928 for downtown stores. The milling crowds that year had to dodge construction on the Square, too: the city was in the midst of building its underground comfort facilities. Above the ground, volunteers were collecting for the welfare drive to benefit York's poor people.

At the same time, 800 volunteers from 50 York churches were taking a census of the community's religious population as part of the celebration attending "the 19th Centenary of the Ministry of Jesus Christ." Heading that effort was the Reverend Doctor W.H. Feldmann of the Union Lutheran

Church who was, no doubt, pleased with the final census, which showed that more than half of York's churchgoing population was Lutheran. Helping the Lutheran minister and his large band of volunteers were numerous York companies—including the A.B. Farquhar Company, the Home Furniture Company, and the York Body Corporation—which blew their factory whistles when York churches marked the Centenary with other Christians around the world.

The jubilation, however, was in sharp contrast to events of the coming months, as America faced the impending failure of its economic system. But York, because of its healthy economy, its many locally owned and operated industries and businesses, and its fiscally conservative outlook and continued expansion, was cushioned from many of the disastrous effects that other American communities suffered from after the stock market crash of 1929. The York community maintained its hopeful spirit, drawing on the pioneer strength that had been handed down to most of the community's leaders. York was a stable center of diverse power and, while the world seemed to be falling apart around them, Yorkers worked on, convinced that this adversity, too, would pass.

Facing page
Streetcars traverse York's Centre Square in the 1920s. The speed limit is posted at 10 mph and parking is allowed for 15 minutes. Bear's Department Store is at the right. (HSYC)

Below
Smiling York residents find pleasure in the water at Elm Beach in the late 1920s, unaware of the hard times to come. Courtesy, Sunday News.

The last streetcars on Market Street, looking east from the Square, were seen in 1939. The kiosk in the background was restored and returned to the Square in the spring of 1981. Courtesy, Sunday News.

CHAPTER VIII
THE DEPRESSION YEARS

While the stock market hovered on the precipice of disaster in October 1929, York was enjoying almost unbelievable prosperity. The previous month had been a banner period for the county's cigar industry, which employed some 10,000. York Mayor Jacob E. Weaver announced that no tax increase would be necessary for the next fiscal year, and York stores and shops were still experiencing their best pre-Christmas sales ever. Banks in York were issuing record numbers of savings checks—13,072 in all—and total clearings for the year would also set new records.

Construction in the county was in high gear. A new $30-million dam project was approved for the Susquehanna River, with construction slated for spring. A new junior high school—named for York inventor Phineas Davis—was being erected in the city. Still another construction project was in the works: the new bridge, spanning the Susquehanna between Wrightsville and Columbia, less than 10 miles east of York. The concrete multiple-arch structure, which at one and a quarter miles long was said to be the longest bridge of its type in the world, joined U.S. Route 30 running from York to Lancaster. During opening day ceremonies, on October 1, 1930, crowds stood cheering on the banks of the river.

Two Yorkers were among the first to cross the newly opened bridge. A.B. Meisky, who lived on Court Avenue, drove his motorcycle across; and Guy Leber, who resided at 1206 West King Street, battled sand left over from construction to rollerskate back and forth across the length of the bridge.

Another event related to York's expanding transportation network would later close out the decade: the dedication of the York Airport, 10 miles west of York, on October 25, 1939. Thirty thousand people were on hand for the official opening of the new airfield. The field accommodated small planes traveling to and from York and was eventually heavily used by many executives of York industry and business who invested in their own planes. One York man who watched airplane traffic of the day with special interest was W.H. "Jack" Hespenheide, who had much earlier become fascinated by the science of aeronautics.

Hespenheide had first become interested in flying as a young man in the 1920s, when barnstormers had flown into York to perform their antics. He left town in 1929 to train as a pilot in Texas. When he returned, he joined four other York men—Lester Sipe, Roman Smyser, Raymond Ruth, and Addison Millard—to form the York Flying Service in 1931. Their first airfield, located east of the city on a farm owned by York historian Joseph Kindig II, became known as Fayfield. Hespenheide and his group later moved to the York Airport at Thomasville, where they operated until World War II. At that time some of the partners were wooed into service as pilot trainers.

The year 1930, however, saw about 2,500 Yorkers out of work due to the beleaguered national economy. On the brighter side, 500 people were employed on the new Safe Harbor Dam; 250 were at work on the Phineas Davis School; and still other workers were employed by the local utilities and the city, which had enacted special work programs for the jobless.

York's 62 churches, with 28,285 members, also initiated help programs, and even the Ku Klux Klan was distributing food to the unemployed.

By 1931 there were nearly 5,100 people out of work in York County. Hundreds of garments were distributed to the community's poor at a distribution center set up to aid the jobless and penniless. Even that year had its good news, though. Construction of a new sewer on the city's west end would put many people to work; 20 acres of city land was set aside for the poor to farm; hosiery mills in the county were operating on 24-hour schedules; and a United States industry study revealed that York trade had topped the $36 million mark for the previous year. The York Telephone Company, the York Oil Burner Company, the York Water Company, and the A.B. Farquhar Company all had expansion programs under way and a government loan was granted York that created 500 new jobs.

Railroad transportation was further expanded in 1932, when the Pennsylvania Railroad Company added two passenger lines to its schedule of more than 50 trains passing through York every day. Communications were also expanded, well beyond York's surrounding lands, with the city's first radio station, WORK, which went on the air in 1932. Located at 13 South Beaver Street, WORK's middle-of-the-road programming soon made it an informational and entertainment mainstay of the York community. Its news coverage won numerous state awards. (In recent years, the station has changed hands several times and, in 1981, its call letters were changed from WZIX to WOYK.)

The year 1932 saw a decline in York's jobless number as 3,000 were counted among those with relief cards. At the same time several York industries were receiving government contracts and a new paper factory was being built in York Haven.

Nineteen thirty-two was also the year of another visit by a well-known personage — even though when he came he was not yet well-known, and had he been, York would not have been pleased to receive him. Bruno Richard Hauptmann, later connected to the kidnapping and murder of the baby of American flyer Charles Lindbergh, came to York County in the late summer, several months after the Lindbergh kidnapping. He was looking for a farm property. Spring Grove realtor Clayton E. Moul showed the German emigrant several farms, but the potential buyer said that none was quite what he was looking for. Local residents later speculated that Hauptmann had probably been searching for a hideout, and that he came to York County because he knew that many of its inhabitants spoke Pennsylvania Dutch, a dialect close to his own language. The Spring Grove realtor noticed the man's picture in a national newspaper some time after his York County visit, and only then realized that he might have been an unwilling accomplice in a bizarre and sad murder.

It was the uncertainty of the times—even though the community fared better than most—that caused York once again to shift political loyalties. In 1932, Yorkers voted for a Democratic President, Franklin D. Roosevelt, for the first time in more than three decades. In 1972, a booklet by Dr. G.A. Mellander and Dr. Carl E. Hatch, both of York College, stated that, after the late 1920s, Yorkers "perceived that Republican 'laissez-faireism' if carried too far . . . could be as undesirable as dogmatic, Democratic-Wilsonian 'interventionism.'"

One of the "practical and moderate" local candidates that Yorkers favored, regardless of political affiliation, was Herbert B. Cohen, counsel for John Blymire in the hex murder trial. Like Samuel S. Lewis before him, Cohen went from membership in the Vigilant fire brigade to political success. In 1933 Yorkers elected Cohen to the State House of Representatives.

He later became State Attorney General, and a member of the Pennsylvania Supreme Court until his retirement in 1970. Cohen was active in many community activities and, among other public-service projects, he helped a group of deaf Yorkers form the York Association of the Deaf in 1934. York eventually became a center for deaf activities, led by such people as Samuel Shultz and Henry Senft, who also held offices in state and national organizations serving the deaf. The Pennsylvania Society for the Advancement of the Deaf has had state conventions in York, and York deaf people are known across the country for their enthusiastic work in improving the standard of life for the hearing-impaired.

Probably because of York's relatively sound economic state, citizens were able to devote a good deal of time in the Depression years to entertaining themselves. They did so in grand style. The York Association of the Deaf initiated a wide social program that included captioned movies and shuffleboard tournaments. The York Little Theater was begun in the winter of 1932–1933. After informal meetings at various homes of theater-minded Yorkers, the theater had its first production (of Oscar Wilde's *Lady Windemere's Fan*) on December 14, 1933, directed by two of the founding members, Ida Frances Moody and her future husband, S. Barnitz Williams. On January 24, 1934, the York Little Theater hired J.F. Foster as its first full-time director. The Little Theater was sponsored by the York Recreation Commission, and used two rooms on the second floor of the York County Academy Building for rehearsals and other dramatic activities. Early York Little Theater presidents included George Hay Kain, Jr., Gilbert A. Dietz, Lucy Smith, Cassandra S. Brown, Samuel A. Gotwalt, William C. Wanbaugh, and Alverta Herbst Keller. (In May 1956, the community group moved into the former Elmwood Theater, which after several remodeling programs still serves YLT today.)

After a night at the theater, Yorkers could go to the corner bar and have a beer, since Prohibition had been repealed on April 6, 1933. Owners of 200 restaurants, hotels, cigar stores, and drugstores flooded the Internal Revenue Service after that date for federal permits "to relieve the extreme thirst of those who obeyed the restrictions imposed by the Prohibition laws."

For those who preferred music, the York Symphony Orchestra gave its first concert on April 18, 1933, under conductor George K. Raudenbush. Seven months later, the York Symphony Orchestra announced the next year's full season, under resident conductor, Sylvan Levin. Levin was succeeded by Louis Vyner and the symphony baton was later passed on to George Hurst, Robert Mandell, Francois Jaroschy, and James C. Pfohl.

As York was finding new sources of entertainment in 1933, it also battled with economic conditions at home. Theaters cut admission prices to lure moviegoers who could no longer afford normal prices, and the York Fair also cut its entrance fees in an attempt to assist fairgoers in hard times. Twenty-four thousand Yorkers that year were given aid of some kind, ranging from foodstuffs to clothes and shoes.

York's Louis J. Appell was appointed to lead the community's National Recovery Act efforts and NRA funds brought 1,436 jobs to the York area. Twenty-six WPA projects were employing 6,112 people and, in contrast to the discouraging conditions, York was being hailed as a leader in United States production of pretzels and artificial teeth.

In early March of 1933 a banking holiday was declared by the federal government; York quietly accepted the order, although business would not be interrupted. By March 11, York banks had asked for permission to reopen and a few days later the city would share the honors with Lewistown

Above right
In 1950 the York Symphony Orchestra was photographed with Louis Vyner as conductor. Courtesy, Gazette and Daily Collection File. (HSYC)

Below
York's Strand and Capitol theaters were popular with county residents for presenting the finest in feature films. Through community support, the complex was renovated and opened as the Strand-Capitol Performing Arts Center in April 1980. Courtesy, Sunday News.

as the only two cities in Pennsylvania with all banks open and operating under near-normal conditions. York, in fact, was called a "bright spot" in Pennsylvania as far as banking was concerned, and a *Dispatch* article announcing the reopening of York banks on March 14 was even more generous with its analysis of the York economy.

"Happy days are here again," the *Dispatch*'s lead article told Yorkers, "for York banks and their thousands of depositors. With a clean bill of health from the federal government, every bank in the city opened at 9 o'clock this morning with power to resume normal banking functions . . . hoarding has become decidedly unfashionable. . . ." On the same day J.W. Gitt, chairman of the local emergency relief committee, was speaking in Harrisburg on York's successful dealings with bad times. The program, for relief board members of surrounding counties, also featured Governor Gifford Pinchot.

The 1930s were also a great time for moviegoers. Emory Myers, who was a Strand Theater projectionist from 1929 to 1970, recalls the local premiere of *Gone with the Wind* in the 1930s: "No movie ever hit York like *Gone with the Wind.* People used to line up from the front of the Strand to Bear's Department Store on the Square. Scarlett and Rhett took the city by storm."

Live performances were sometimes offered at the Strand, the Orpheum, and the York Opera House. "I remember when Abbott and Costello, the famous comedians, were there," Myers says. "They were so poor at the time that we had to give them something to eat. And then there was Sally Rand, the famous fan dancer. She was a big hit in York." The Strand discontinued its live shows in the World War II years, because Yorkers could no longer afford the increasingly high ticket prices.

M. Valerie Groff, who worked for 15 years at the Strand and Capitol theaters, recalls that York had many other entertainment opportunities, including popular concerts at Valley View Park, which "used to get such names as Gene Autry . . . and other shows were performed by the renowned Kinley Players [now at Warren, Ohio] at the York Theater. The York County Academy combined with the York Collegiate Institute in the 1930s to produce dramatic offerings at both school sites. The York Music League sponsored concerts by the Cleveland Symphony Orchestra, among others, which were held at William Penn Senior High School. Big-name groups and "home-grown" entertainment were featured at such places as the Penn Hotel, the York Country Club, the Dutch Club, the Yorktowne Hotel, and private functions sponsored by various York industries.

These entertainments were temporarily halted in 1933, however, when York was the victim of another natural disaster. On August 20 of that year, a tropical hurricane entered the Delaware coast heading west. According to Helen V. Delaplane, the hurricane "brought torrents of rain—nonstop day and night rain," which continued for four days. The Codorus Creek overflowed, bridges were under water, and all exits to York flooded. "King's Dam had broken," Miss Delaplane recalls, "causing the water to rise suddenly.... Upstream from College Avenue the Codorus makes a sharp bend to the west. In that angle the flood waters advanced from two directions. This area was the worst flooded part of York, also the most densely populated."

Two people were drowned, thousands left homeless, and there was hundreds of thousands of dollars in immediate property damage. The main plant of the Edison Electric Company was flooded, stalling the generators, and all electrical activity in the city ceased. Streetcars stopped in their tracks, lights went out, and the power outage caused further damage. The rain finally stopped at 3:15 Thursday morning, August 24, and York heaved a collective sigh of relief. According to Miss Delaplane, the flooding had "reached a peak of 13 feet 9 inches near Doll's Pontiac Garage," and stretching from there was "a great lake covering central York and far beyond on the south side." Flood damage was ultimately estimated at $4,261,000.

The *York Dispatch* termed it "the most disastrous flood in the history of the city." J.W. Gitt, the editor of the rival paper, the *York Gazette*, was determined to help the town get back on its feet after the flood. Gitt, a Hanover-educated lawyer, had bought the paper in 1915 out of receivership, and had originally intended only to revive it and profit from a resale. But in 1918 he bought another paper, the *York Daily*, merged the two morning editions, and became so involved in journalism that he never returned to law. Through his reasoned, reform-minded editorials and his civic activism, Gitt soon became an important community spokesman.

Governor Gifford Pinchot (who was a close friend of Gitt) appointed him to head up relief operations in York County. Gitt saw the flood as an opportunity to put many of the more than 10,000 people who were on relief at the time to work in a useful community project. Gitt, in a book about him, *Sweet Land of Liberty* (1975), recalls the period: "I was having a real fight with the politicians over the W.P.A. in York. Most of the politicians in the country . . . used it for political purposes. I conceived the idea that we would use it for something . . . worthwhile . . . so we put our money into digging out and widening the Codorus Creek. The people on relief were so . . . anxious to get jobs that they went down to work in the icy creek in the winter, bookkeepers and all kinds of people, with shovels and things. I'm telling you, it was terrible for awhile."

Bottom left
This calisthenics class was held at the York Collegiate Institute gymnasium in the 1930s. Courtesy, York College of Pennsylvania.

Bottom right
The August 1933 flood forced the Codorus Creek over its banks and brought havoc and destruction to the city. This photograph was taken at Beaver and North streets on August 23, 1933. The locomotive is a Pennsylvania Railroad passenger train headed for Harrisburg. Courtesy, Sunday News.

Below
J.W. Gitt was the outspoken and controversial editor of York's *Gazette and Daily* newspaper. He became a well-known and reform-minded social activist in the community. (HSYC)

Gitt also set up a commissary to feed thousands of York citizens during the Depression. Afterward he continued to serve as the community's conscience, writing forcefully against self-aggrandizing politicians and inspiring the wrath of grocers, milk dealers, coal-company owners, and anyone else who did not meet his high standards of "faith, hope, and charity."

As York began to return to normal after the flood, it resumed its nightlife. The Valencia Ballroom entertained Saturday-night crowds of up to 2,000, who came to dance to the big-band music of Duke Ellington, Benny Goodman, Glenn Miller, Cab Calloway, Tommy Dorsey, and many others. The Clooney sisters and Ozzie Nelson and Harriet Hilliard (later the well-known television team, Ozzie and Harriet) also played the Valencia, which featured a ballroom with an overhead revolving light and a bar downstairs called the Rainbow Grill. Located in the 200 block of North George Street, the Valencia entertained patrons for more than 30 years, and people came from as far as 200 miles away to take in the Valencia during its heyday.

The Valencia was owned and operated by eight members of the Tassia family, who earlier had established a fresh produce and fruit business in York. The family members formed a partnership and, in 1928, bought a huge building in the 200 block of North George Street. The building, erected in 1911, was called the Coliseum. The Tassias transformed the building into a splendid entertainment palace. The ballroom was furnished with over 700 bentwood chairs. Fourteen floor-to-ceiling murals were commissioned to decorate the ballroom and they exquisitely mirrored the Valencia's Spanish theme. On October 8, 1934, they were ready for their grand opening. Sadie Tassia was manager and her brother, Steve, was her assistant. About 40 waiters and waitresses were on hand and a half-dozen girls were on duty in the cloak room. Warming up on the newly installed stage that evening in 1934 was Mal Hallett and his orchestra, and Miss Teddie Grace, affectionately nicknamed the "sweetheart of the Dixie circuit."

Joel Michael, writing in the *York Daily Record* on the occasion of the Valencia's closing in 1973, reminded Yorkers of some of its finer moments: "The dance band could have been . . . Sammy Kaye and his Swing 'n' Sway Orchestra or Kay Kyser and his College of Musical Knowledge, or two dozen other big-name possibilities. Vaughan Monroe did York's first coast-to-coast radio commercial for Lucky Strike 23 years ago from the tiered stage of the Valencia Ballroom." In addition to the great names in American music of the time, the Valencia had its own band, the Blue Moon Orchestra. The Blue Moon was popular with York's young people, who attended the Valencia's Friday night hops. The Blue Moon Orchestra played 788 "sets" in the Ballroom.

Another York band, "The Black Diamonds," also played to "swinging

Below left
Bandleader Benny Goodman was photographed with the Valencia Ballroom's most popular hostess, co-owner Sadie Tassia. The Tassia family furnished the Valencia with ornate, Spanish-style decor. Courtesy, Harry J. McLaughlin.

Below
Red Norvo and his orchestra are seen here performing for patrons of the Valencia Ballroom. Courtesy, Harry J. McLaughlin.

and swaying" members of the community during those days when "Dance and Music" ruled the York spirit. Because it was common for young people to come to the Valencia as "stags," many romances budded at the Valencia and some of them moved into marriage. One of the young men likely to be in attendance during the Valencia's most popular evenings was a friend of the Tassias who was a reporter for the *York High Weekly*. The young journalist turned his early interest in reporting to a full-time profession and was still reporting the news and interviewing celebrities in the 1980s.

The reporter, Harry McLaughlin, generally had the company of a fellow photographer on the *York High Weekly*, William Thomas. Together they interviewed the celebrities at the Valencia, or at the Yorktowne Hotel, where many of them stayed. The more "uncooperative" stars who stayed at the Yorktowne were interviewed by the two young reporters as they made their way, often rapidly, west on East Market Street then north on North George Street to the Valencia.

The 1930s, mixed with crowd-pleasing entertainment and jolting economic news, was a study in contrasts for York. Though it had not escaped completely the impact of the Depression, York was responding well to treatment afforded by many community plans and a few national ones. By the end of 1934, things were looking bright again. The commissary, where the poor had obtained food, was closed and York County was listed 49th in the state in the number of unemployed workers. Nineteen thirty-four saw a new wire plant for York, another hosiery trade boom, and 81,818 of York County's citizens enrolled in a Sunday School program. That year also saw the visit of another President to York. President Franklin D. Roosevelt passed through the city by train after speaking at a Memorial Day program in Gettysburg. His special train slowed down as it entered the borough of West York in the late afternoon, and a crowd of cheering Yorkers greeted him as he waved from the rear platform of the train. Children placed pennies on the railroad tracks and valued them as unmatched souvenirs.

Yorkers also achieved prominence in sports during the 1930s. Dick Bachtell, and brothers Bill Good and Walter Good, were York barbell standouts and on August 3, 1936, "Little Tony" Terlazzo won the gold medal at the Olympics for weightlifting. As a featherweight, he lifted a total of 687.5 pounds, including one lift of more than twice his weight. Two other York weightlifters, John Terpak and Robert Mitchell, also competed in the Olympics, and Terpak took fifth place in his division with a total lift of 709½ pounds. Another Yorker John Grimek was named Mr. America in 1941.

In 1940 York weightlifters made a clean sweep of the National A.A.U. titles in the annual tournament in New York City. Joining Olympic competitors Terpak and Terlazzo were Steve Stanko, Joe Fiorito, and John Davis. So impressive was the Yorker weightlifting sweep that the Associated Press declared: "The city of York, Pennsylvania, can rightfully claim to be the weightlifting center of the nation today . . . ."

York's domination of weightlifting competitions came principally through efforts of Yorker Bob Hoffman. Hoffman was named a world-class athlete in 1925. He also was a world canoeing champion and later served as the U.S. Olympic weightlifting coach for 20 years. He ran the York Oil Burner Company with Yorker Ed Kraber, but his interest in weightlifting led him to begin reproducing cast-iron weights in 1932. This resulted in the formation of the York Bar Bell Company, which is still one of the largest such firms in the country.

Another Yorker who distinguished himself in sports during the 1930s was Tom Keesey, who set a national junior-college basketball scoring record of 501 points in a single season. Keesey had graduated from York High School

Below
York's young reporter, Harry J. McLaughlin, used the Valencia Ballroom as his turf to search for interviews with the famous and infamous entertainers who came to York to perform, including Ozzie Nelson and Harriet Hilliard (later Ozzie and Harriet), Kay Kyser and Ginny Simms, and Glenn Miller. Miller is shown here with reporter McLaughlin. McLaughlin would later become well-known in York for his reportage for the *Sunday Patriot News*. Courtesy, Harry J. McLaughlin.

Bottom
Tony Terlazzo from York was the first American to win an Olympic weightlifting championship when he captured the featherweight title in 1936. (HSYC)

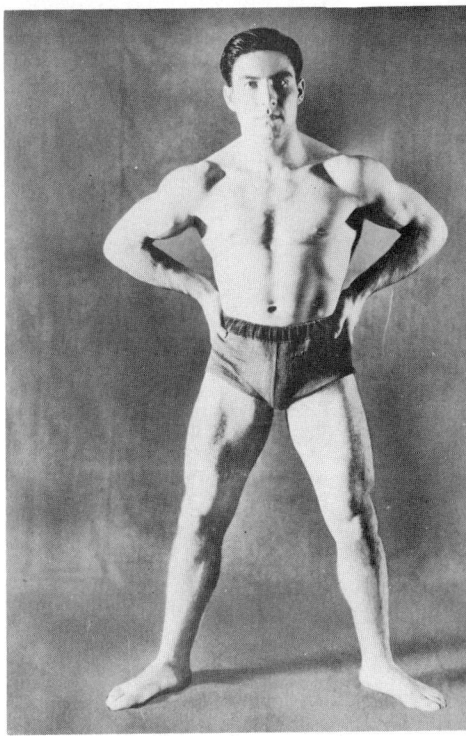

Bob Hoffman, founder of the York Bar Bell Company, helped make York the "Weightlifting Capital of the World." The Weightlifting Hall of Fame opened in York in 1981. Courtesy, Harry J. McLaughlin.

in 1937. His teammates that year included Joe "Nardie" Stock, "Hunk" Stover, Bill Hunter, and Charlie Falkler, and they were considered one of the best high-school teams in history.

While York athletes were achieving fame in sports, a York woman who had moved to Baltimore was gaining attention more akin to notoriety. The death of Pearl Snow, who had run a "high-toned" brothel in the Maryland seaport city for 35 years, was mourned by no less a personage than H.L. Mencken, American author, journalist, and linguist. He wrote about her passing in a letter to his friend Edgar Lee Masters, the writer of the *Spoon River Anthology*. "She was buried from St. John's Evangelical Church," writes Mencken, "and a large congregation was in attendance, including many public men." Snow's establishment had catered to "members of Congress, many of whom dropped over from Washington to discuss public matters with her. Her staff of interns was mainly recruited from York County, Pennsylvania, where she was born herself." Mencken immortalized another Yorker in his saucy "A Girl from Red Lion, Pennsylvania," published in 1914. That story was about a Dunkard girl who fled to Baltimore when she found herself "with child." Mencken befriended the girl and told of how she was persuaded to return home and marry her boyfriend.

As rumors of war were being sounded again in Europe, another York woman, Katherine Haviland Taylor, was bringing fame of a more respectable sort to York. She wrote more than 20 books of light fiction, including two set in her home town, *Yellow Soap* and *Nine Hundred Block*. One of her many short stories, "One Man's Journey," was made into a movie starring Lionel Barrymore and May Robson, and retitled *A Man to Remember*. York named a road after her in the Shiloh area of the county. After her death in 1941, her ashes were returned to York (from St. Cloud, Florida, where she had been living), and interred in St. John's Episcopal Churchyard. Her father, the Reverend Dr. Arthur Russell Taylor, had served St. John's as rector.

By the end of the decade, York had undergone many changes, not the least of which was a further rise in the population. The number of inhabitants in the city stood at 56,712 in 1940, a 2.6 percent increase over 1930. The county's population rose to 178,022. Local transportation in this era had been greatly improved by the building of the Pennsylvania Turnpike, which came within 20 miles of York. Buses had replaced the town's electric trolleys by 1939, and the York Street Railway became the York Bus Company. The company's employees were retrained to drive Twin Coach motor buses and the original "barns" at 520 North Hartley Street were adapted to house the buses.

Several new buildings had been added or improved during the decade. The Post Office on South George Street, built in 1912 as a memorial to the Continental Congress, underwent an enlargement program in 1940. So did the York Court House. The Crispus Attucks Association Center was dedicated, at 125 East Maple Street, to serve as a community center primarily for York's black citizens. Dr. Edward Meisenhelder, Jr., sold the West Side Sanatarium, which he had established in 1913, and it became the West Side Osteopathic Hospital in 1945 with facilities on West Market Street near the York Fair Grounds. (The hospital was renamed the Memorial Osteopathic Hospital and moved to South Belmont Street in 1961.)

All these improvements and accomplishments—in transportation, community services, public buildings, private businesses, sports, literature, and other fields—were gradually raising York to an even higher plane of prosperity. War, however, was soon to thrust York into yet another worldwide conflict. Yorkers would demonstrate the patriotism and adaptability that, by this time, were hallmarks of the community.

The residence built by the Emerton family in 1918 and 1919 for $1.6 million became the Hahn Home for Women in the 1930s. The mansion, at the corner of East Springettsbury Avenue and South George Street, remains one of York County's most elegant and magnificent buildings. (HSYC)

York celebrated the 1976 Bicentennial in its favorite fashion—with a parade down Market Street. Courtesy, Harry J. McLaughlin.

CHAPTER IX

THE RISE OF THE GREATER YORK AREA

The Japanese attacked Pearl Harbor on Sunday, December 7, 1941. The next day the *York Dispatch*, in a three-column headline, told Yorkers: "United States Suffers Heavy Losses As Japan Risks Empire In Audacious Attack on Far-flung Pacific Bases." Inside the *Dispatch* Yorkers read these editorial lines: "Now that the United States has become—without choice and as the result of treacherous and unprovoked attack—the major power in a world war the magnitude of which at the moment strains the imagination of any man to comprehend, there is a goal toward which all Americans have set their eyes undeviatingly—Victory."

Immediately, York officials conferred and named Colonel William H. Beckner Director of Energy Defense. Beckner told the community in the next day's *Dispatch*: "York is a target to the new type of warfare. For the present we do not expect long, sustained, repeated attacks. This is a war not so much of armies and navies as of production. We can get out of this mess only if we can produce." He concluded with this challenge: "York is a vital defense area, so proclaimed by the government of the United States, and industry must continue to produce defense material regardless of hardship or inconvenience to all of us."

The war effort soon reshaped daily life in York County. Individuals, groups, and industries contributed to the cause of freedom, and a plan developed in York to maximize war production was adopted nationally. The "York Plan," as it came to be known, was a new set of guidelines containing 15 points that would organize workers and machinery to greatest possible efficiency. The plan was developed by four local industrialists—William S. Shipley, W.J. Fisher, Robert P. Turner, and Warren C. Bulette—and was endorsed by the local Manufacturers Association.

S. Forry Laucks, another York industrialist, had laid the groundwork for the York Plan years earlier. In 1938 he went to Washington, D.C., and obtained the first ordnance contract for the coming war. Remembering his experiences in World War I, he did not attempt to reequip his factory for the new job, but surveyed the community to determine the extent of idle machinery. As a result, more than 45 percent of the machining operations on the gun mounts ordered from him by the government were subcontracted.

The York Plan gained considerable national publicity and York Ice Company president William W. Shipley toured the country, giving details of the plan to leaders in other communities. Many adopted the system for greater defense production.

While Americans were reading about the York Plan in the *Saturday Evening Post, Business Week*, and other publications, they also were reading about a native son who was earning recognition for himself and his community. Jacob Loucks Devers, born in York of Irish and Pennsylvania German ancestry, served in the army as commanding general of the armored forces from

August 1941 until May 1943. He was made a four-star general and was decorated with numerous military honors, during and after the war, for his extraordinary record of service. General Devers coordinated armor, infantry, air power, and supply services for the enormously important Normandy Invasions. In four and a half months after the invasion, the Sixth Army, under General Devers, liberated more than half of France, captured more than 170,000 prisoners, penetrated the Maginot Line, and boldly entered Germany.

After the war, General Devers returned to York, where he led a productive, community-oriented life. In 1949 York honored him by naming an elementary school and a road after him. He died on October 16, 1979, at the age of 92, after giving his personal papers to The Historical Society of York County.

Although war-related activity dominated the local scene, York was not just a manufacturing and fighting machine during the World War II years. People lived as normal lives as possible and the town continued to grow. Citizens formed a Young Woman's Club in 1941, and on May 30, 1942, a new City Hall was dedicated at the corner of King and Beaver streets on the site of the old St. Paul's Lutheran Church, which had been destroyed by fire. York's new city hall was built to commemorate the 200th anniversary of York's founding. It was of Colonial brick design, using white Georgian marble trim and a slate roof. The building's architects, Yorkers Robert Stair and Frederick Dempwolf, designed the lobby as a replica of the one in Philadelphia's Independence Hall, and its total cost was $225,000.

Many new community-service organizations were founded during this period. Foremost among them was the York County War and Welfare Fund, formed by the York Welfare Federation in 1943, which was responsible for raising both local welfare and national war-relief funds. During that year the federation collected $239,577; offices were provided at no charge by the

Below
Actress Hedy Lamarr came to York during World War II selling war bonds to the citizens. She is shown here outside the Yorktowne Hotel. Courtesy Harry J. McLaughlin.

Below right
Jacob Loucks Devers, a native of York, was Commander General of the European Theater of Operation and Deputy Supreme Allied Commander in the Mediterranean Theater during World War II. General Devers was largely responsible for the planning of the Normandy-area landings and was one of the country's few four-star generals. Courtesy, York College of Pennsylvania.

York Area Chamber of Commerce. The organization later became the United Way of York County.

Out where the shooting was going on, another Yorker performed an even greater—and considerably more heroic and famous—act of charity. Alexander D. Goode, rabbi of York's Temple Beth Israel from 1937 to 1942 and contributor to the York County Chapter of the American Red Cross, the Rotary Club of York, and the York YMCA, enlisted in the Navy and served as one of four chaplains on the S.S. *Dorchester*. On February 3, 1943, when the *Dorchester* was lying off the coast of Greenland, most of the crew was below deck, some because of illness, others simply because of the danger from submarine fire. Chaplain Goode was with them, busily caring for the sick crewmen, when a torpedo hit.

Orders were given to abandon ship. The men panicked and stampeded to the lifeboats. Meanwhile Chaplain Goode calmly gave his gloves to a Coast Guard officer, Lieutenant John J. Mahoney. As the *Dorchester* was sinking, Goode and the other three chaplains gave their life belts to crew members. The four chaplains, with arms joined and voices lifted in prayer, died as the *Dorchester* went down.

Later Mahoney told the story of the four chaplains, saying that the gloves Chaplain Goode had given him prevented his hands from freezing and allowed him to cling to a lifeboat for eight hours before being rescued. The story of Rabbi Goode and the other three chaplains soon circled the globe and their actions became famous as one of the war's noblest gestures.

In 1951 a 200-seat interfaith chapel was dedicated to the memory of the four *Dorchester* chaplains in Philadelphia. In 1958 the U.S. Senate posthumously awarded special Medals of Honor to the men, and in 1959 Yorkers were chosen to unveil a new tableau featuring them at the National Wax Museum in Washington. Other recognition included the naming of an elementary school for Chaplain Goode in York in 1955 and the establishment

Below left
First Lieutenant Alexander Goode, rabbi of York's Temple Beth Israel from 1937 to 1942, was one of four chaplains who drowned when the S.S. *Dorchester* sank on February 3, 1943. Goode and the other three chaplains were awarded posthumous Medals of Honor in 1958 for having given their life jackets to crew members. (HSYC)

Below
The York County town of Red Lion honored its ex-military men and women with a homecoming parade in October 1946. Courtesy, Gazette and Daily File Collection. (HSYC)

Below
"Going to the fair" has been a standard York County tradition in autumn for generations. Photographs of the York County Interstate Fair in the 1950s show the agricultural exhibitions, livestock shows, rides, and amusements on the midway. Most of these time-honored attractions have survived at the York Fair and continue in the 1980s. (HSYC)

of a national humanitarian award, the Chapel of the Four Chaplains Gold Medallion.

Before World War II ended, 10 percent of the county's population had served in the armed forces. By May 8, 1945—the day that the Allied nations proclaimed an end to the war in Europe—1,238 countians had been killed or wounded, 155 were reported missing, and 95 were being held as prisoners of war.

Because of the heavy losses, York's mayor appealed for a "simple and dignified celebration of Victory," and asked that merchants close for the afternoon to allow employees to join citywide church services. In autumn of the same year, war in the Far East ended.

After the war York, along with so many American cities, experienced a surge of industrial expansion and development. As a result the downtown area, where much of this growth was centered, began suffering from traffic congestion. A new York planning commission placed a high priority on the problem and in 1950 instituted one-way traffic on the city's main through streets: Market, King, and Philadelphia (east and west); and George, Duke, and Beaver (north and south).

While all this growth was being discussed, however, the town itself received some discouraging news. The 1950 census showed only a slight population increase of 2.6 percent over the 1940 figure, giving York 59,704 people. This proved the apex of York's population, and in succeeding decades, Yorkers would bemoan the lack of further growth. Manufacturing firms continued to move into the area, but large outside companies were purchasing many of York's already-established industries. In order to accommodate what Yorkers still hoped would be the increasingly large numbers of people and companies, the community built a new $5 million sewage-disposal plant and York school authorities began a $4.5 million expansion program.

York was not allowed to settle comfortably into its new plan of community improvements. The Korean War soon pressed York Countians into battle and called upon the talents and expertise of York leaders. The York Plan was reinstituted on a national level. A five-man group of York industrialists was named to pilot the new York Plan. William J. Fisher, president of the A.B. Farquhar Company, was named chairman and Robert P. Turner, vice-president of the New York Wire Cloth Company, was named to assist him. Both men had served on the World War II committee. Also named to the 1950 group were Stewart E. Lauer, president of the York Corporation; John H. Padden, executive secretary of the Manufacturers Association; and Beauchamp E. Smith, president of the S. Morgan Smith Company.

Thousands of Yorkers entered the service during this war. Among them was Marc Green, who introduced the games of softball and baseball to a group of youngsters in a Catholic orphanage on the island of Paengnyŏng, off the coast of western South Korea. Green had played for Little League, American Legion, and high-school teams in York before pitching on semi-professional teams and winning tryouts with the New York Yankees and the St. Louis Cardinals when he was only 16 years old.

While Green and his fellow Yorkers were gone, the town continued developing along the same lines as before. Yorkers back home were as conservative as ever: in 1952, when the issues were "Corruption, Communism and Korea," York County voted, with the nation, for Eisenhower over Stevenson.

There were, as before, new schools and further additions to old ones. In 1952 Yorker A.I. Watts acquired a license for the York Academy of Arts which, after several moves, found a home in the former Ridge Avenue School at 625 East Philadelphia Street. Pennsylvania State University opened a York branch, in 1953, in the Shiloh Elementary School Building. The York campus offered the first two years of college training to York students as well as a variety of noncredit and master's-level courses. York College of Pennsylvania received approval to award its first master's degree in 1977.

Radio station WSBA, which had gone on the air in 1942, added a television station, WSBA-TV, in 1952. That station was the first UHF station to go on the air in the East. WSBA's FM-radio counterpart was a pioneer in FM operation in the United States. WSBA merged with the Pfaltzgraff Pottery Company in 1954 and purchased the first of a number of affiliate stations, WARM of Scranton, in 1958. In 1981 WSBA Radio, under the leadership of Louis J. Appell, Jr., served as the "flagship" for 11 other stations.

By the end of the Korean War at least 29 York Countians had been killed. Total casualties, including those missing, prisoners of war, and men killed or injured in front line accidents, reached 125. About 7,000 countians were eligible after the war for Korean War bonus payments.

Those who returned to York saw a town that was beginning to take on the characteristics of a sprawling metropolis. The city, locked in on all sides by growing townships and boroughs, was experiencing a time of great strength as the county's population turned to its urbanized center city for shopping, banking, government, and entertainment facilities. A trend was developing, however, that gradually would take away a lot of the city's middle-class citizens and sap the center city of many of its most popular department stores and shops.

The move toward the suburbs by middle-class families and shopping-complex developers began in 1953 when the York County Shopping Center was planned east of the city near Haines Acres, where many city residents relocated and newcomers chose to settle. Soon after the York County Shopping Center was opened, a group of consultants studied the York area and told

Below
Softball has traditionally been one of York County's favorite sports and the city has played host to numerous national softball competitions. Ed Glacken of the York City Softball League is shown here in 1946. Courtesy, Harry J. McLaughlin.

Bottom
York in the 1950s was known for its beautiful Christmas decorations, including a huge Christmas tree in front of the York County Court House and a brilliant star hung in the middle of Continental Square. Courtesy, Gazette and Daily File Collection. (HSYC)

THE RISE OF THE GREATER YORK AREA • 149

Left
Six visitors from Arles, France, were the first members from York's sister city to come to America as guests of the York Twinning Association. Shown here in a visit to Arlington National Cemetery in September 1955 are (from the left): Rabbi Moses Friedmann, former chairman of the York Twinning Association; Jean Buon, city-council member of Arles in charge of education; Dr. Victoria Lyles, former supervisor of elementary education of York City Schools; Charles Privat, former mayor of Arles, who married a Yorker; Roger Heller from Arles; Mr. Rousset, principal of College Technique; Mademoiselle Denise Poulain, official of Bilingual World, Paris; and Madame Annette Laffe from Arles. Courtesy, York Twinning Association.

the York Area Chamber of Commerce that officials should "modernize the downtown shopping center rather than develop neighborhood centers."

In 1954 a shopping center south of York was approved, and in the same year one for the southeast was planned; a shopping center for the Fireside Terrace area was begun in September; and a fifth was approved for the 900 block of South George Street in December of that year. The town saw the planning of 11 more centers within as many years.

York became the first American city to be linked with a foreign sister city in 1954. The pioneer program with Arles, France, was established after Dr. Victoria Lyles, superintendent of the French program in elementary schools, accepted an invitation from LeMonde Bilingue in Paris to set up a people-to-people program with the 2,000-year-old city in the south of France. The program grew, and in 1957 a York exchange teacher, Margaret Boltz, married the Mayor of Arles, Charles Privat. By 1981 the birth of eight Franco-American babies and the marriages of eight Franco-American couples would be credited—at least in part—to the program.

Yorkers were also forging ties between their town and the city in England for which it was named. Because of the natural interest in the British city, America's Yorkers had adopted its nickname, the White Rose City. In the 1930s the Women's Bureau of the York Area Chamber of Commerce called for an official recognition of the designation. In ensuing years government officials and residents of America's York hosted English visitors on a regular basis.

York voted for President Eisenhower's reelection in 1956. That Eisenhower's farm was just minutes from York County's western border, and that he periodically visited York to play golf at the Country Club, only strengthened his political support locally.

Yorkers forged still another tie with the nation as a whole in the 1950s, although some Yorkers who participated in the venture—such as York Little Theater's Bert Smith—would, as Smith says, "just as soon forget it." In 1958 several Yorkers were called to do small roles in a movie that later became a classic horror picture. Smith was one of the Yorkers to appear in the science-fiction film, *The Blob*, in which Steve McQueen (in the role that launched his film career) struggles to rid humanity of an "insatiable formless creature from outer space."

But York's most famous former resident who went on to a career in the movies is Cameron Mitchell. Mitchell, the son of the Reverend and Mrs. Charles M. Mitzell of the Reformed Church in Shrewsbury, told a *York Dispatch* reporter in 1956 that a role in the York American Legion's production of *Maryland, My Maryland* and a subsequent *Dispatch* review of the show made him decide that show business would be his life's work.

Mitchell received two Oscar nominations, for his supporting roles in *Tall*

Men and *Love Me Or Leave Me*, and was nominated for Emmy Awards in television's "Oxbow Incident" and "Man on the Ledge." He has made dozens of other films and television shows, including the long-running series, "High Chaparral." Mitchell visited his home town in 1958 to see his father perform in the York Little Theatre production of *Inherit the Wind*. When his father became ill during rehearsals, Mitchell took over the role, playing to packed houses and delighted audiences.

York's connections with the outside world increased dramatically with the construction of Interstate Highway 83. The highway, carrying traffic around York between Harrisburg and Baltimore, was opened in sections from 1958 to 1961; its Route 30 bypass followed in 1970 through 1973.

In 1960 the U.S. Census Bureau reported that York, perhaps because of the traffic that I-83 was bringing to the area, now lay for the first time along the western boundary of the "supermetropolitan area" stretching from New Hampshire to Washington, D.C. The report said that the "ever-growing area" had 31.5 million inhabitants. The report also had shocking news for York city officials: for the first time ever in a census, the city itself had lost residents. Although population in the county as a whole continued to rise, the population in the city proper fell from 59,704 in 1950 to 54,504 in 1960.

The year of the 1960 census was also the year of the 1960 Presidential campaign, during which Senator John F. Kennedy stopped in York to greet throngs of townspeople at the York Interstate Fair. With Governor David L. Lawrence, County Democratic chairman Luther Yohe, and former governor (and native Yorker) George M. Leader at his side, Kennedy toured the Fair Grounds, stopping to pat the head of a donkey and to shake hands with members of the excited crowds.

Despite his campaigning Kennedy lost York County, polling 38,710 votes to Richard Nixon's 55,109. Nixon's connection with York probably served as a factor in his countywide support: his parents had resided in York County between 1946 and 1953. They bought a farm at Menges Mills so that they could be near their son, who had been elected to the House of Representatives. Nixon's younger brother Edward had graduated from West York High School.

As the 1960s began, Yorkers made plans to restore two of their prime historic properties: the Golden Plough Tavern and the General Horatio Gates house at the corner of West Market Street and North Pershing Avenue. As the preservation work on the run-down buildings started, many people in the community discovered York's historic importance. Historic York County, Inc., which later merged with The Historical Society of York County, worked with the latter organization, the Junior League, and many other organizations to bring about an awareness of history in the

Below left
John F. Kennedy visited the York Interstate Fair on a campaign tour in 1960. Courtesy, Harry J. McLaughlin.

Below
The Golden Plough Tavern and the General Horatio Gates House appear here as they looked before restoration by The Historical Society of York County. Restoration of the properties began in July 1960, and the buildings were opened to the public in June 1963. (HSYC)

community.

The area was not only preserving its past. it was also building for the present and future. Shopping centers rose on all sides of the city's borders and more people exchanged residences in the city for suburban homes. The Queensgate Shopping Center was opened and J.W. Fields Department Store opened in the North Mall.

The town had other attractions in the early 1960s, especially for young people. The drive-in restaurant at Avalong was a popular meeting place for teenagers, and the White Swan Drive-In west of York (later Clair's Restaurant) offered yet another social outlet. Their older brothers and sisters spent their time studying at York Junior College, which had an enrollment of 326, a new campus along Country Club Road south of York, and a new president, Dr. Ray A. Miller. Dr. Miller, who ran the school from 1958 to 1976, initiated a Town and Gown Concert and Lecture Series. The Town and Gown concerts attracted capacity crowds to hear, among others, flamenco guitarist Carlos Montoya, flutist Jean-Pierre Rampal, violinist Eugene Fodor, the Norman Luboff Choir, the U.S. Marine Band, pianists Ferrante and Teicher, and a group that became a widely hailed York favorite, the Preservation Hall Jazz Band. At about the same time, Dr. Frank Mussano took over the college's student-activities office and launched a program of extremely popular contemporary music concerts.

The 1960s was also the decade when women emerged to take an even more active role in York's community life. At the forefront of this move was Mary (Mrs. Charles) F. Stephenson who, as editor of the *Sunday News* women's section, reported on the burgeoning of hundreds of women's organizations in York County. She became an honorary member of many of these groups, including farm women's clubs, musical societies, hospital organizations, processional committees, church coteries, historical societies, and educational associations.

Mary Stephenson had moved to York in the 1940s to attend Thompson Business College, which had been founded in 1921. Besides her energetic work on behalf of women's groups, she became an almost legendary figure in York community life. Her collection of costumes, drawn from her everyday use as well as for special occasions, earned her such titles as "Queen of the Beaux Arts Ball" and "first woman to wear a pantsuit." She won other, somewhat dubious, titles as well. Her home-pond frog was twice the winner in York's Codorus Frog-jumping Contest. Mary Stephenson, during the 1960s, not only received recognition for her community work and professional achievements, but was a part of every major social event in York, including one of the grandest celebrations in recent history.

During the summer of 1966, the entire community threw a party for itself. The 225th Anniversary Observance of the town's founding included the participation of hundreds of Yorkers and climaxed with a grand pageant, "The York Story," presented at the York Fair Grounds. The celebration culminated on July 4, a day jammed full of celebration activities, including a spectacular fireworks show.

The summer of 1966 brought York one of its worst droughts on record. By July 15 a rainless summer had caused the York Water Company's impounding basin surface to fall 48 inches below normal. Strict water restrictions were issued to the community, and outdoor hoses, water-cooled air conditioners, and the washing of cars were banned. Despite conservation measures, however, the water company's impounding basin, by August 24, was decreasing by eight million gallons over a 24-hour period.

On September 3, 1966, President Lyndon Johnson visited the nearby York County community of Dallastown. Otis B. Morse IV, one of the press coor-

Below
President Lyndon B. Johnson made a visit to York County's Dallastown on September 3, 1966, to celebrate the community's 100th anniversary. Courtesy, Harry J. McLaughlin.

Bottom
Construction of the Peach Bottom atomic plant in southern York County is shown in 1962, five years before its opening. Courtesy, Gazette and Daily File Collection. (HSYC)

dinators for the event, estimated that more than 30,000 people, most of whom had probably come from York, turned out to greet the President.

York County saw the opening of its first large-scale nuclear power plant in 1967, under way for six years. The Peach Bottom I plant was installed on York County's southern border in the Lower Susquehanna Valley and two additional plants were planned for operation in 1972 and 1973.

In the same year that Peach Bottom I opened, cable television came to York. It was a part of the Susquehanna Broadcasting Company, which owned WSBA and its affiliate stations, along with the Pfaltzgraff Pottery Company. The cable added a half-dozen stations to Yorkers' television reception.

Yorkers' increased exposure to television programming, along with improved highways and other means of transportation, brought them ever closer, at least psychologically, to the other large metropolitan areas in their part of the country. Yorkers, who had visited surrounding cities in small numbers since the 1700s, now made frequent trips to neighboring communities. The theaters, sports facilities, restaurants, and the other attractions of Philadelphia, Baltimore, and Washington now lay within an evening's drive of York, and major recreation areas—Atlantic City, Ocean City, and Wildwood in New Jersey, and Ocean City, in Maryland—were just as conveniently situated. Soon Yorkers were agreeing with executives of large firms that had relocated in York that one of the town's biggest advantages was its location.

Three years after man's footprint was placed on the moon for the first time, the Codorus again showed men and women in York how powerless they really were. Seven to eight inches of rain drenched the city formerly known as Yorktown. As in Colonial days, the river spilled its banks, killing several York County residents and causing hundreds of thousands of dollars worth of damage. Mayor Eli Eichelberger declared a city emergency.

Rains, occurring over the night and morning hours of June 21 and 22, covered whole blocks of York housing and forced hundreds of citizens to flee their homes. A Red Cross emergency care center was set up at the Edgar Fahs Smith Junior High School.

Metropolitan-Edison workmen, responding to innumerable trouble calls, found the body of an elderly woman in the Elmwood section of York and authorities guessed that it was the body of a woman whose Camp Betty Washington Road house had been smashed and washed away by flood waters. City police, meanwhile, were scuba diving for the body of a man believed to have drowned in the city's Poorhouse Run flood-control project, and Pennsylvania Department of Transportation crewmen had run out of road barriers with which they had been closing off flooded streets.

Flood waters from the Codorus licked the brick sidewalks in front of the restored Golden Plough Tavern and General Gates House, threatening the invaluable properties with their rooms full of costly antiques. A few blocks away, in the Newberry Street neighborhood, flood waters invaded the home of an elderly York minister and destroyed a lifetime collection of papers, sermons, and books.

Rains from Hurricane Agnes created a devastating flood in downtown York on June 21 and 22, 1972. The Codorus Creek was forced over its banks and into the city streets. Courtesy, William J. Schintz.

Flood damage was set at more than $34 million, including $1.5 million worth of damage to utilities alone. As waters slowly receded clean-up operations began over the weekend of June 23.

Congressman N. Neiman Craley, who had snatched the seat of former Congressman George A. Goodling, made a petition to the Army Corps of Engineers for federal help in alleviating the problem and in expanding York's water sources for the future. Goodling regained his seat in 1966.

Fortunately the month of September brought rich rainfalls, and by October 4, bans were lifted. Water Company president George S. Schmidt thanked industries and housewives for helping to conserve water during the drought and promised that water supplies for the future were being carefully studied. The Army Corps of Engineers assisted the York community in expanding fresh-water resources.

The war in Vietnam was on everyone's mind in the late 1960s and a massive anti war rally in Washington involved the arrest of two Yorkers. On the York College campus students held a peaceful demonstration that drew a small crowd. In the Presidential election of that year, in which Vietnam was, of course, a major issue, Yorkers again favored Richard Nixon, despite a mild familiarity with Hubert Humphrey. Humphrey had visited York in 1952 and 1959, and again after the election in 1969 and 1972.

As the 1960s drew to a close, some Yorkers took a breather from politics and glowed with pride as York Countian Trudy Pedersen was named Miss Pennsylvania at the Miss Pennsylvania pageant in nearby Hershey. Her former schoolmate Margaret Louise Walker won the same title the very next year.

The breather was short-lived. Racial violence erupted in York in the summer of 1969, leaving behind thousands of dollars in property damage, 37 injured Yorkers, and two deaths. The two people killed were 27-year-old Mrs. Lillie B. Allen of Aiken, South Carolina, and York policeman Henry C. Schaad. The death of Officer Schaad was the first known killing of a city police officer in the line of duty in the history of the city. Mayor John L. Snyder imposed a curfew from 9 p.m. to 7 a.m. during the period of unrest, and members of the National Guard patrolled the streets. The national news media carried the developments of York's racial disturbances across the land.

Out of the disturbances of that summer, Yorkers established a community charrette, which led to the founding of York's community-improvement agency, the Community Progress Council, whose goal it was to halt what was seen as York's "decline." The cause for the worry was that, although the 1970 census revealed that the county had gained 32,119 people since 1960 (setting a record high of 272,455), the city's population was set at 50,355, representing a decline of more than 4,000 people. Yet another loss surprised and saddened people almost as much: the sale, in October 1970, of J.W. Gitt's nationally reputed *York Gazette and Daily*.

Journalists across the country mourned its departure from the newsstands and mailboxes of America, demonstrating that while the paper's views were not always compatible with those of Yorkers, they found a good reception in many other places. The *New York Times* said: "The *Gazette* was one of a kind . . . fifty-five years of colorful, outspoken, personal journalism have ended." The *Times* described J.W. Gitt as "an editor who crusaded unequivocally against the war, racism, and infringement of human liberties." But the *Gazette* did not disappear without a trace. After its purchase the name was changed to the *York Daily Record*, and in some respects the new paper's antecedent is quite visible in its pages.

In 1974, a few years after the sale of the *Gazette and Daily*, George

Above left
Racial unrest came to York in the summer of 1969, with two persons killed during the violent days. The National Guard patrolled the streets of the city and a curfew was enforced. Developments in York's racial problems were carried across the nation. Courtesy, William J. Schintz.

Above
The Cookes House was built in 1761 by Johannes Guckes. Some Yorkers believe that Thomas Paine lived in this house when Congress was in York. One of the oldest examples of Germanic architecture in York County, the building was recently restored and dedicated in a ceremony in May 1981.
Courtesy, Harry J. McLaughlin.

Goodling handed down his well-warmed Congressional seat to his son, William F. Goodling. The younger Goodling has served in Washington since that time, carrying on duties that include dining with world leaders as chairman of the Foreign Affairs Committee.

Congressman Goodling is best remembered in his home town of Loganville, however, not for surviving the Washington chicken-dinner circuit, but for his own chicken dinner of sorts. While still a youngster, Goodling earned a reputation as one of the area's best makers of a favorite Pennsylvania Dutch "dish," chicken corn soup. Congressman Goodling recalls preparing his chicken corn soup for various community fundraisers, and was always amazed to learn that the quantity of soup he made for sale would often be expanded by enthusiastic volunteers, who added water before delivering orders from door to door.

The migration of people and businesses out of the city continued in the late 1960s. Many people preferred the suburbs because of their attractive living conditions, such as parks and recreation areas for children. As a result of the exodus, stores in downtown York began closing or moving. In 1970 Grant's left the downtown area, followed in 1972 by Wiest's and the Golden Glow Cafeteria. In 1974 People's Drug Store, in the Colonial Hotel building, closed, as did Lehmayer's located next door to the Strand Theater, and the Thom McAn Shoe Store, located on West Market Street. In 1975 Bear's Store was sold to the Zollinger's Company. In 1976 the Strand closed, along with Les's Cafeteria, and they were followed, in 1978, by Zollinger's and the Penn Hotel.

To many Yorkers it seemed that the city itself was dying. They called on community leaders to take steps to prevent the city's further decline. The plan to save York that emerged could be summed up in one word: revitalization.

The first step that the city fathers took in revitalizing York was to give the city a new look, or rather revive its old one. In 1976 York's Office of City Planning presented its "Historic Buildings and Preservation Plan," and outlined York's architectural development. Under the direction of Planning Director Charles H. Maneval, planner Thomas M. Foust prepared an extensive report which gave new direction to city leaders. Foust stated that "most of the promotion done by [local agencies] emphasizes York's Colonial Period and its role during the American Revolution. However, in terms of the architectural character of York, little remains from the Colonial period.... In fact, probably only five or six ... buildings [still standing] were here during the Revolution, namely the Gates House and Plough Tavern at 157 and 161 West Market Street, the Cookes (Thomas Paine) House on South Penn Street at the Codorus Creek, probably the (John) Fisher house at 19 North George Street, possibly the small houses at 322 West Market Street and 22 South Beaver Street."

The report went on to say that York, in terms of surviving structures was actually an industrial town, the architecture of which was predominantly Victorian in style. In order to authentically restore York, the plan recommended: "All of the ugly siding and windows added to many downtown stores in the 1940s and 1950s would be replaced by authentic looking brick facades. Public improvements, such as trees, brick sidewalks, and appropriate street furniture, would be installed to add to the restored atmosphere."

One of the first buildings to be revived was not from the Victorian era, however. It was the Yorktowne Hotel, built in the 1920s by a group of local businessmen, who had wanted York to have a gracious building in which the town could show proper hospitality to visitors. In the mid-1970s the hotel, standing just east of the Court House, underwent extensive renovations in order to bring about what the local media and publicity people called a "return to elegance."

The nation's Bicentennial added momentum to the renaissance effort. A replica of the York County Court House, in which Congress had convened during nine months of 1777-1778, was built on the corner of Pershing Avenue and West Market Street at the Codorus Creek. C. William Dize, the York architect who designed the new York Federal Savings and Loan building, drew up the plans for the replica. York's participation in America's 200th birthday was led by the York County Bicentennial Commission. Attorney John F. Rauhauser, Jr., served as the commission's president and was the leading spirit behind York's observances.

The Bicentennial left York with much more than a replica of its first county Court House. A new pride in York's historical heritage had grown in and around the city, and Yorkers felt a new surge of honor at having played a role in national developments throughout the city's 232 years of existence. The issuance of two U.S. Postal Service stamps from York— one commemorating the 200th anniversary of the adoption of the Articles of Confederation, issued on September 30, 1977, and the other commemorating the signing of the French Alliance in York and issued on May 4, 1978—added to York's developing sense of its importance to the nation as a whole.

Yet another facet of York life was on the upswing. When Dr. Robert V. Iosue took over the presidency of York College of Pennsylvania in the fall of 1976, he emphasized the college's academic growth. Moreover, enrollment was climbing and for the first time the college faced the question of limiting it. In 1981 Dr. Iosue oversaw the construction of three new "mini-dormitories" (as the facilities were called) to alleviate the unprecedented crowding.

Even industry has expanded in recent years. In 1970 the York Labor Market area (all of Adams and York counties) had 146,700 workers; in 1978, 18,500 had been added, for a total of 165,200. Moreover, the York Area Chamber of Commerce reported in that year that retail sales for the county in 1977 had topped one billion dollars, and that almost one-third of the nation's population lived within 250 miles of York. The figures implied that the York area, or at least the county, had become a true business and population center.

In only one area did the town remain unchanged: York Countians were politically as conservative as ever. In 1976 they voted for Gerald Ford over Jimmy Carter, and in 1980 they voiced resounding support for Ronald Reagan.

One thing interrupted York's smoothly running revitalization, and most Yorkers weren't even aware of it at first. Yorkers who picked up the morning newspaper on March 28, 1979, probably had no idea that the "worst commercial nuclear power station accident in history" was taking place. Many

Facing page
Top left
A group of Yorkers celebrated the 200th anniversary of the adoption of the Articles of Confederation in 1977 by donning Colonial costumes and reenacting the patriots' crossing of the Susquehanna River. Courtesy, Sunday News.

Top right
Jimmy Carter visited the York County community of Lewisberry in 1974. Courtesy, William J. Schintz.

Bottom left
Gerald R. Ford, shown here with York College of Pennsylvania president and his wife, Dr. and Mrs. Robert V. Iosue, came to the York College campus on September 26, 1979, to speak at the Henry D. Schmidt Memorial Lecture. Courtesy, York College of Pennsylvania.

Bottom right
The York County community of Goldsboro, shown here with the Three Mile Island atomic-plant cooling towers in the background, was a focal point in "the worst nuclear power station accident in history" in March 1979. Courtesy, Sunday News.

of them, even after reading the front-page story of the emergency, went about their business with little real concern of happenings at Three Mile Island, located only 10 miles north of the center of the city.

The next day, however, the *Dispatch* said in a two-column headline, "3-Mile Island Still Leaking Radiation," and Yorkers began to worry. On the same day reports of the emergency received national attention. Telephone lines into the area were jammed, and some Yorkers vacationing outside of the city phoned for hours before reaching family members at home. Even people as far away as Arles were calling in, worried about what was going on.

On Friday, March 30, officials told preschool children and pregnant women from the four counties surrounding TMI to leave. Some Yorkers had already left the area.

A few days after the accident at Three Mile Island, experts told the American public that the effects of the TMI disaster might not be known for 40 years. Yorkers already had a hint of the accident's long-range effects. Musicians booked at area colleges refused to come into the "Three Mile Island" zone, tourism dropped sharply, and a *Dispatch* article on April 2, 1979, called the accident a "realization of a Twentieth Century Horror."

It was Wednesday, April 4, when Yorkers were told that the threat of an "immediate catastrophe" was over, but for many residents the near disaster would never be "over." Two years later, the mental-health impact of the accident was still being studied and Yorkers were hearing further reports of radioactivity from local power plants.

In the aftermath of the Three Mile Island accident, an eery shadow was cast over York County when the Philadelphia Electric Company announced it was installing dozens of sirens within a 10-mile radius of the TMI site. Other sirens were being planned for the area around the Peach Bottom Nuclear Station.

As "the country's worst nuclear-energy plant accident" faded from mem-

Above
York's "back-to-the city" project turned abandoned houses into renovated homes and signaled the urban rebirth of York. Courtesy, William J. Schintz.

Above right
At opening night of the Strand-Capitol Performing Arts Center on April 12, 1980, a capacity audience heard the York Symphony Orchestra play the National Anthem, and delighted in a memorable performance by Ella Fitzgerald. The opening of the renovated Strand symbolized a new era of revitalization for many Yorkers. Courtesy, Strand-Capitol Performing Arts Center.

ory, Yorkers turned to the business of the day. They had other problems to deal with and, regardless of the shock of the nightmare in their backyard, Yorkers showed the resiliency that is part of their heritage.

The business of nurturing the renaissance of the downtown area received top-priority attention after the Three Mile Island accident. Despite the Yorkers' revitalization efforts in the 1970s, the 1980 census showed 44,464 people in York proper compared to 50,335 in 1970—an 11 percent drop.

But York's leaders were not discouraged. The approval of downtown's new multimillion-dollar Market Way project—a plan in 1979 to turn Bear's Department Store into an $11 million shopping and entertainment complex, and the opening (on April 12, 1980) of the Strand Capitol Performing Arts Center all gave the city evidence of the hoped-for renaissance.

Like so many other structures in the downtown area, the Strand and Capitol theaters had been closed and vacated. Mayor John D. Krout stepped in when the theater buildings were threatened by the wrecking ball, and a group of community leaders assembled to transform the theaters and the Lehmayer's building south of them into a performing-arts complex. In ensuing months Yorkers gave a million dollars and hundreds of hours of volunteer work to make the restoration possible.

In 1981 the York area was a model of slow but steady growth. York's three market houses—Central, Farmers, and the New Eastern—were flourishing. The York Area Chamber of Commerce reported in 1981 that there were two York-area industries (Caterpillar Tractor Company and York Division of Borg-Warner Corporation) that employed more than 3,000 people, and that eight others employed well over 1,000. In terms of land area the county had, in 1981, 914 square miles, according to the York Area Chamber of Commerce, and the city had 5.81 square miles. The "Greater York" area had 17 square miles. The designation "Greater York" came about when the city, small in size, became completely surrounded by heavily populated townships and boroughs. In 1981 the term "York" generally meant "the Greater York Area" and the nonspecific use caused the city some awkward moments when crimes or other unpleasant incidents were tagged to "York," when actually they had occurred outside the city boundaries.

Some Yorkers complained that the city's population figures were misleading to people unfamiliar with the Greater York Area who used the city population count to appraise the area's importance and possible offerings. The situation is frequently made more complicated when "York" is used to denote "York County." Evidence of Yorkers' sensitivity to the problem can be found in the great number of businesses and other groups using the term "York Area" in their names in 1981.

One of the newest York-area groups is the Hispanic community. Father Bernard Pistone, pastor of Cristo Salvador Hispanic Catholic Church at 235 East South Street, has said that there were between 4,000 and 5,000 Hispanics in York when the church was founded in October of 1980, making up some 10 percent of the city's population. He said that most of York's

Hispanic citizens came from Puerto Rico, specifically from the towns of Adjunta, Vega, Baja, Vega Alta, Ponce, and Ajuja.

"I see the Hispanic population here growing even more in coming years," Father Pistone said. "York's industrialization has provided many opportunities for jobs and many times one member of the family will come, get a job, and then send for the rest of the family." The transition from Puerto Rico to York, Father Pistone said, is "very painful because of the language barrier and because the weather is so severe." (The county's average winter temperature is only 40.8 degrees Fahrenheit.)

Father Pistone points out that the transition is even more difficult for Puerto Ricans than for other immigrants. "The Greeks, the Vietnamese, the [other] Asians—they have come to make America their new home. They are quickly assimilated. The Puerto Ricans who come here already are Americans and they tend to hold on to ties to their native island. They can travel back and forth." Still, he says, the transition will eventually become easier, and in 10 or 15 years there will be no need for a Hispanic Catholic Church in York because the Hispanics will be assimilated into the York culture.

York is, indeed, from all indications, revitalizing itself. In February 1981, Jack Kay, Director of Community Development for York, said in a speech before the Cosmopolitan Club of York that York had "turned the corner and is coming back."

Mayor Elizabeth N. Marshall, in an address downtown on March 28, 1981, confirmed Kay's remarks: "Downtown will never be the retail center it was in the 1940s and 1950s. The Downtown area is and will be, however, a center of banking, law, cultural arts, and unique shops. York City will always be the heart of the county and the county seat and York will always hold the rich architectural beauty that makes it truly outstanding."

In commenting on the city's "rich architectural beauty," Mayor Marshall reconfirmed the city's new dedication to the promotion of York's physical uniqueness. A visiting art historian from New York City had told Yorkers that the downtown area was "like a marvelous living museum." He said the juxtaposition of Colonial, Victorian and modern buildings held a charm that was "probably more diverse and interesting than anywhere else in America." The art expert, owner of a 200-year old gallery in London with a branch in New York, visited York's Currier and Ives Gallery, housed in a "spectacular"

Below left, top and bottom
The Greater York Area is home to more than 450 houses of worship representing 45 denominations, including St. Patrick's Catholic Church on 231 South Beaver Street and Ohev Sholom Synagogue on 2251 Eastern Boulevard. Courtesy, Sunday News and HSYC.

Below
Kerry Magni, a professional dancer from York, formed the Yorktowne Dance Theatre in October 1980. The Yorktowne Dance Theatre is the first professional dance company incorporated in York to develop local talent. Courtesy, Michael Magni.

Victorian building across from City Hall, and made a stop at the Victorian home left to The Historical Society of York County by the heirs of York attorney and artist Horace Bonham. He said he was "astounded" that York "held such beauty."

With York's heightened awareness of its architectural heritage, community leaders took positive steps to earn maximum benefits from the increased interest in the city's appearance. The York Area Chamber of Commerce launched an annual two-day Victorian Heritage Festival and the city reaped considerable publicity, especially from out-of-town news media.

Yorkers are not only adjusting to taking pride in their town again, they are also working together to rebuild their center city, to strengthen the area's economy, and to promote York throughout the country. Henry R. Merges, editor of the *York Dispatch*, summed up feelings about the York community in an editorial printed on January 14, 1981. It read:

> *York County is a good place to live. One of the reasons why, perhaps the most important reason, is the jobs available to support families, churches, schools and other social institutions serving the community. York County is blessed, too, because of the diversification of its industry, supplemented by commerce and agriculture. All of these facts came to mind with the announcement that York County's unemployment rate of 6 percent is below national and state levels. It is vital that we continue to work to create conditions which will not only encourage the business we already have, but attract others as well. We must give a just day's work for a just day's pay. We must have good schools, good recreational facilities, cultural opportunities, safe streets and pride in our achievements.*

Pride in past achievements has been a guiding beacon to Yorkers in forging the community's future. Yorkers have survived everything from living among occasionally hostile Indians and the encroachment of Marylanders in the 1730s to the coming of the Klansmen in the 1920s. They have survived financial difficulties by establishing diverse businesses and industries that have shielded them from the effects of every economic problem from the panics of the 19th century to the recessions and Great Depression of the 20th century. They have survived massive takeovers from Congress's occupation in 1778 to the Confederate invasion of 1863. Yorkers have survived, as well, everything from overflowing rivers and destructive fires to a nuclear plant disaster, and it is probable that they will survive calamities as yet not seen. In recent years, the York community has survived by attracting people, whether by building new freeways, by restoring or rebuilding old landmarks, or by producing quality goods demanded around the globe.

York's experience today confirms the unwitting suggestion of the Indian deed of 1736, which stated that York County's influence would extend infinitely, ". . . to the setting of the sun." With the export of products and ideas, and the moving about of its people, that influence, indeed, seems to have no limits. This, perhaps, is the greatest achievement of all, and one which will set the stage for making York's future as magical as its past.

Below
Mitch Gibbs, a young artist from York, is shown with one of his watercolors depicting the bandstand at Farquhar Park, seen in the background. York artists, such as Virgil Sova, William A. Falkler, and Othmar Carli, have reached national and international prominence. Courtesy, Sunday News.

Below right
The Codorus Creek bike path provides a relaxing and pleasant diversion for health-conscious York citizens. Courtesy, William J. Schintz.

COLOR PLATES

The Conestoga wagon, besides serving as the freight carrier of early America, also brought early settlers to York and "... to the setting of the sun." The photo here is of a painting executed by artist William A. Falkler. Falkler is one of many York artists who give the community a lively arts atmosphere today. Courtesy, William A. Falkler.

Facing page

Top
The Titus Geesey Toy Collection of the Historical Society of York County includes this cast-iron "Overland Circus" wagon. (HSYC)

Bottom left
This painted-wood brides' box, dating from about 1750, may be found in the collection of The Historical Society of York County. (HSYC)

Bottom right
York artist Horace Bonham painted this portrait of Mary Lewis Bonham (1871-1892). Bonham's works have been cited as excellent examples of 19th-century American genre art. (HSYC)

This page

Top
With its wood-block printed borders, which have been hand-colored and stippled, this 1806 birth and baptismal record of Johannes Willem is truly a work of art. (HSYC)

Bottom
The handwritten, illuminated, watercolor birth record of Jacob N., Elizabeth B., and Joel N. Myers (1846, 1845, and 1871) is pictured here. (HSYC)

COLOR PLATES • 163

Left
An authentic reconstruction of the York County Court House, where the Continental Congress convened during its stay in York, is located at the corner of West Market Street and Pershing Avenue. It was completed in 1976 in honor of the nation's bicentennial celebration. Photo by Georg R. Sheets.

Below
A commemorative sign in front of The Historical Society of York County reminds Yorkers and informs visitors of the city's Colonial heritage. Photo by Jerry E. Sweitzer.

Facing page
The York County Court House in use today, situated downtown, was designed by well-known York architect J.A. Dempwolf. Photo by Jerry E. Sweitzer.

Left
Homes and shops in the East Market Street area of Downtown York provide a sense of Victorian charm. Many York residents consider this section one of the city's most beautiful. Photo by Jerry E. Sweitzer.

The Bonham House, now a museum owned by The Historical Society of York County, contains rooms decorated in various styles of furnishings. Pictured are the Victorian parlor (below); the fireplace and portrait of Madame de Stael by Jean Baptiste Greuze in the library (facing page, top); and the Federal dining room (facing page, bottom). (HSYC)

COLOR PLATES • 167

Facing page
The Fluhrer Building at 17 West Market Street, with its white-tile front, is one of the many fine examples of Dempwolf architecture remaining in York. Photo by Jerry E. Sweitzer.

The elegance of life in York during the Victorian era is symbolized by the Billmeyer (York) House at 225 East Market Street (right). The Italianate row house was built in 1863. Its elaborate iron fence (below) faces Market Street. Photo by Jerry E. Sweitzer.

This page
The beauty of the seasons is best reflected in the rural sections and farms of York County. Top photo by Georg R. Sheets. Bottom photo by Jerry E. Sweitzer.

Facing page
Each Tuesday, Thursday, and Saturday, the Central Market in downtown York sells fresh fruit, vegetables, meats, baked goods, colorful flowers, and York County arts and crafts. The Farmers' Market and the New Eastern Market also still operate today. Top photo by Jerry E. Sweitzer. Bottom photo by Georg R. Sheets.

COLOR PLATES • 171

Above
The Golden Plough Tavern (left) and the General Gates House (right), located at the corner of West Market Street and Pershing Avenue, are both restored properties of The Historical Society of York County. The Colonial buildings are open to visitors. Photo by Georg R. Sheets.

Left
The barroom of the restored Golden Plough Tavern is pictured here. The original building, distinguished by its half-timber construction, is believed to have been built in 1741. (HSYC)

Left
A beautiful paneled corner cupboard with the original blue paint blends nicely with the Chippendale-style chairs and dropleaf table in the dining room of the Gates House. (HSYC)

Below
Christ Lutheran Church (left) at 29 South George Street and Trinity United Church (right) at 32 West Market Street are two of the many magnificent churches found in York. Left photo by Jerry E. Sweitzer. Right photo by Georg R. Sheets.

174

Facing page
Cherry Lane, York's vest-pocket park, is the site of numerous public activities throughout the year, including a political rally in the fall (top) and Christmas caroling in December (bottom). Top photo by Georg R. Sheets. Bottom photo by Jerry E. Sweitzer.

The city of York, seen on a clear autumn afternoon from Reservoir Hill Park, south of York. The park, owned by the York Water Company, is open to the public. Photo by Jerry E. Sweitzer.

York's economy was built on a diversity of business and industry. Businesses such as Tyler & Croll once lined unpaved George Street as seen in this photograph taken about 1850. (HSYC)

PARTNERS IN PROGRESS

by Jerry E. Sweitzer

"The town of York, the seat of the American Union in our most gloomy times. May its citizens enjoy in the same proportion their share of American prosperity."

The Marquis de Lafayette, on his return visit to York in February 1825, proposed this inspiring toast wishing Yorkers a promising future.

Prosperity for York Countians had been abundant since the days of the earliest European settlement. The land was virgin and clearing the forest laborious, but the York County soil proved fertile, yielding bountiful crops and a good life for the pioneers. The settlers of German, English, Quaker, and Scotch-Irish heritage shared a common goal: to work hard and make their little town on the frontier of America a thriving community.

York grew, and soon merchants, craftsmen, and artisans flourished, all striving to create and sell superior products. The town became a borough, and with the advent of the Industrial Revolution, an innovative group of men and women set new goals for York. They were people willing to accept the changing times, and used their unique skills and ideas to establish their own businesses and industries.

Plants and firms started by one man soon employed five people, then 25, then over 100. As York became a city, more new businesses were born and some old firms died. Other industries that were becoming obsolete regrouped their interests and formed new industries based on their equipment, material, and skills.

The spirit of the early craftsmen survived into the age of machines. Business leaders and York workers still believed in manufacturing quality products, and took pride in their work. From the clocks of the early colonial days to the complex technology of today, this standard of excellence has remained solid in York businesses.

The efficiency of York industry in the 20th century became a model for the nation and the world. The "York Plan," devised by area business leaders to pool skills and machine tools to increase productivity, would be adopted quickly across the United States. Huge multinational corporations in later years would be impressed by the competence and success of York businesses and acquire them in their corporate families.

No longer was York a community on the edge of the wilderness. Products manufactured in the area were shipped and used around the world. Air conditioners, equipment for weight lifters, costumes for dancers, bricks, printing presses, boxes and containers, swimming pools, paper, labels, stoneware and dinnerware for the tables of the world—the list of products and services headquartered in York is extensive.

The variety of business and industry in York has proved a key to the steady economic growth of the area. No single industry has ever dominated York, but rather the city has become a diversified manufacturing, distributing, and agricultural center in the heart of the heavily populated East Coast region.

Floods, depressions, and the vagaries of time have pressed often upon York businesses, but through imagination, hard work, and determination, many have survived to provide jobs for Yorkers, helping them experience the prosperity Lafayette wished for them in 1825.

ALLIS-CHALMERS CORPORATION

The Allis-Chalmers manufacturing group in York consists of three separate and distinct divisions—hydro-turbines, valves, and nuclear components.

The history of Allis-Chalmers in York extends back to the 1870s, when Stephen Morgan Smith, a North Carolina native serving as pastor of York's Moravian Church, was forced to give up preaching because of a throat ailment and turned to his mechanical abilities for his livelihood. The S. Morgan Smith Company was formed with the idea of generating power from a natural source. S. Morgan Smith invented his first hydraulic turbine in 1877 and named it "Success," convinced that it was superior to older water wheels. The S. Morgan Smith Company was acquired by Allis-Chalmers on January 28, 1959.

THE HYDRO-TURBINE DIVISION

The Hydro-Turbine Division of Allis-Chalmers today is in the business of developing, manufacturing, installing, and servicing equipment and systems for the generation of hydroelectric power and for the control of flowing water. The growth and development of hydraulic turbines in both physical size and capacity has been dramatic. Units have grown in size from the 18-horsepower turbines of S. Morgan Smith's day to the world's most powerful turbines, supplied by Allis-Chalmers and rated at one million horsepower, currently installed at the U.S. Army Corps of Engineers' Grand Coulee Dam. The company's recently established Standard "Tube" Units can be used for the economical development of many smaller hydroelectrical sites.

To support this growth in the industry, Allis-Chalmers has maintained its role of technical leadership in the field of hydraulic turbines through continued research and development. The S. Morgan Smith Memorial Laboratory, opened in York in 1974, is one of the most modern hydraulic laboratories in the world and provides a base for continued hydraulic turbine development.

The division in York provides a combination of skilled employees and industrial facilities to complete the successful manufacture of hydraulic turbines and to provide the performance and reliability needed to serve customers in 36 countries worldwide.

THE VALVE DIVISION

The S. Morgan Smith Company diversified its product line in the early 1930s and began producing large metal valves based on the concept of the old cider barrel spigot. From these beginnings, the Valve Division of Allis-Chalmers has grown into the number one supplier of butterfly valves for use in fossil- and nuclear-fueled electrical generating plants. The Valve Division is also a major supplier of valves for the water and wastewater industries, helping to assure clean streams, rivers, and pure drinking water. Special valves manufactured by the division are used to control the launching of jet planes from aircraft carriers; to control high-velocity air flow in wind tunnels for proof-testing of jet engines, rockets, and aerospace components; and to control stormwater runoff in deep tunnels beneath the city of Chicago.

All of the standard and specialty products are manufactured under a stringent quality assurance program in a large facility that includes fabrication, machining, assembly, and testing areas.

THE NUCLEAR COMPONENTS DIVISION

The Nuclear Components Division, established in York in 1970, is an outgrowth of nuclear activity conducted as part of the Hydraulic Turbine Division. A rapid increase in the volume of orders in the late 1960s, especially from the U.S. Navy, created the need for a separate division to serve the expanding business.

S. Morgan Smith founded the company that was the forerunner of the Allis-Chalmers manufacturing divisions in York today.

The strictest requirements of government and industry have been met in the manufacture of reactor vessels, closure heads, thermal shields, core baskets, internals, pressurizers, purification filters, deionizers, fuel handling equipment, and accumulator tanks. The Nuclear Components Division is a significant supplier to the U.S. Navy's defense effort and is involved in the support of energy technology development in fusion power generation. The division operates at Plant Number One, located in York in an area bounded by Lincoln, Linden, and West streets.

ALLOY RODS

Alloy Rods was founded in 1940 by Edward J. Brady and had its beginning in a building located on East Prospect Street in York. Stainless steel electrodes trading under the name of Arcaloy, along with other early developments, were accepted by American industry with an eagerness which in less than five years permitted Alloy Rods to attain the distinction of being the world's largest producer of stainless steel electrodes.

By the close of World War II, the firm had outgrown its original building. In 1946 Alloy Rods moved to a newly constructed facility located west of York in West Manchester Township (Pottery Hill). The ever-increasing demand for production necessitated numerous additions and modernizations until 1969, when new plant and office accommodations were occupied in Hanover, Pennsylvania. World headquarters, completely equipped research and development laboratories, and primary manufacturing facilities remain at the Hanover location today.

Chemetron Corporation acquired Alloy Rods in 1961. After the acquisition a new line of welding electrode with flux-core interior, known as "Dual Shield," projected Alloy Rods' image even brighter within the welding industry. Other products and processes among the more than 1,000 manufactured also pioneered by Alloy Rods include shielded metal arc welding, and Atom Arc, the first iron powder, low-hydrogen electrode in the United States.

In 1967 All-State Welding Alloys was acquired by the company and is currently operating in Taneytown, Maryland. In 1969 the Welding Products Division of P&H Harnischfeger Corporation was acquired. Today, the remaining plant of that operation continues to produce welding products in Monticello, Indiana.

Allegheny Ludlum Industries acquired Chemetron Corporation and Alloy Rods in 1977. A division of the high-technology Fabricated Metals Group of this multinational corporation, Alloy Rods serves a worldwide welding electrode market.

From the very beginning, Alloy Rods has faced the future with confidence. As specialists in welding metallurgy, providing the "glue"

that holds together such diverse structures as Alaskan pipelines, bridges, buildings, power plants, and automobiles, the company has continued to increase its prominence in the American and foreign welding industry.

Whether the application is in transportation, aerospace, industrial equipment, energy, food and chemical processing, or construction, Alloy Rods looks back with pride on its record of manufacturing excellence, consistent quality, and an outstanding distributor network.

Top
Alloy Rods, founded by Edward J. Brady in 1940, was originally located on East Prospect Street, York.

Above
Today main offices of Alloy Rods are located on Wilson Avenue in Hanover.

THE J.E. BAKER COMPANY

For over 92 years The J.E. Baker Company has contributed to York County's industrial, economic, and community growth. Founded in 1889 by John Baker, the company has remained in the Baker family as a privately held corporation. The Baker Company has a long established history of serving the steel and cement industries with vital refractory products and providing raw material to agricultural markets.

Dolomite, the basic material in Baker products, was formed during the Cambrian Geologic Age from compressed deposits of calcium carbonate. The dolomite deposits are quarried and processed locally at the York Plant and at the Millersville, Ohio, division.

Originally, John Baker and a partner started a business in Wrightsville to burn lime, which was sold to the steel industry, and to local customers for plaster, whitewash, and a soil conditioner. Dolomite became an important part of steel production when Austrian magnesite was no longer available during World War I. Steel plants found they were able to extend the work life of their furnaces by burning granular dolomite. J.E. Baker responded to this need and was the first American company to offer "Standard Roasted Dolomite" used as the refractory repair and maintenance material for the banks and bottoms of open-hearth steelmaking furnaces. Baker was also the first to burn large quantities of dolomite in rotary kilns. Thus began The Baker Company's legacy of satisfying steel customers' needs with quality products and service.

The production process carries the raw product from the quarry to the York Plant where it is crushed and sold as agricultural limestone to farmers and distributors, as a fluxing agent to steel customers, and as an industrial filler for a variety of consumer products. The highest quality dolomite is fired through rotary kilns, and sold either as granular refractories, further processed into other products, or sold to the company's York-based Dolomite Brick Corporation of America (DBCA) subsidiary where it is pressed into refractory brick and sold to steel and cement companies.

The Baker Company has made a strong commitment to future growth by establishing itself in a primary position within the growing dolomite refractories market. As technology advances, the corporation anticipates changes with a program of controlled growth through innovation and new product development. In selling to the growing export market in Canada, Mexico, Central and South America, the Caribbean, and Japan, the company also contributes toward a favorable balance of trade.

Another way in which The Baker Company has shown commitment to growth is its desire for diversification. As a subsidiary of The J.E. Baker Company, Keystone Coal Company brokers coal to its parent company and other industrial concerns and utilities in Pennsylvania, Delaware, Maryland, New Jersey,

Above
The Baker One East office building is a renovated structure in York's Center Square.

Left
Turn-of-the-century quarry workers drilled rock prior to planting explosives in the Billmeyer operation.

and New York. Properties in Somerset County, Pennsylvania, owned by Keystone Coal, are used primarily for coal surface mining and tree farming. Intuition Inc., an audiovisual production company, specializes in slides, multi-image, film, and videotape presentations for industrial and commercial clients.

With a sales volume approaching $50 million, The Baker Company provides jobs for over 500 employees in the York and Ohio areas. The firm ranks employee safety as a major priority equal to product quality and production. In 1927 William H. Baker initiated an innovative program designed to cut lost time accidents by emphasizing the safe and correct way to do each job. The Baker Company is a leader in the industry in its concern for the safety and well-being of each employee.

The corporation also takes pride in its "good neighbor" policy. The company made substantial commitments to environmental control long before it came under government mandate. Its longtime support of local projects through an ongoing contributions program is made as an investment in the community.

DOLOMITE BRICK CORPORATION OF AMERICA

Dolomite Brick Corporation of America, a wholly owned subsidiary of The Baker Company, is the only producer of fired dolomite refractory brick in North America.

In the early 1960s, the use of magdolite, a fired dolomite product, began to decline in the steel industry and demand for this mainstay product of The Baker Company slowed. William Baker and his son, John Baker II, began searching for an alternate use of The Baker Company's technology and material and gained the knowledge to produce fired brick from dolomite. Raw material for the brick is the highest quality dolomite from The Baker Company's York Plant.

The initial DBCA Plant was constructed in 1964 to manufacture dolomite kiln liners, the refractory brick used to line the hot or burning zones of rotary kilns producing cement and lime. Today DBCA sells more burning zone brick to rotary cement kilns than any other American manufacturer. As the company grew in technology and capability, new brick products were introduced for the steel industry. A pitch-bonded brick that did not need to be fired was produced for the basic oxygen steel furnace and was later improved to be used in steel ladles to transport molten steel from the furnaces to other steel production operations.

An additional fired, ceramically bonded brick was developed to serve the newly emerging argon oxygen decarburizing steelmaking vessel which produces high-quality stainless steels.

DBCA today utilizes five presses and two tunnel kilns, a periodic kiln, and one tempering oven to produce its three main brick products. The bricks are stored in climate-controlled warehouses and a significant inventory guarantees immediate shipment to the company's cement and steel customers. This is backed by a technical staff which services DBCA customers and develops new products and applications for existing products.

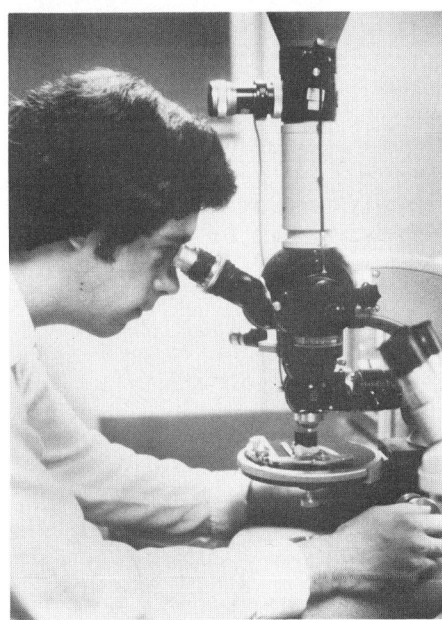

Above
Developing new products has been an essential objective of The Baker Company.

Left
This type of rigging was used during the 1920s to haul stone out of the quarries.

JNO. Z. BARTON, INC.

In the early years of his youth, John Z. Barton, a native of York, worked for the John E. Graybill Company and completed his electrical apprenticeship there. After serving in World War I, he returned to York and continued working for that firm.

Barton and an associate, Luther Doll, started a small electrical business in 1920. They opened their storefront company at 537 West Market Street and concentrated on house wiring. John Barton founded his own business in 1922, doing repair work on consumer products such as refrigerators and oil burners. Two employees who joined the firm in those early years, Chester Stump and William Strickler, would stay with the company until their eventual retirement.

Barton's electrical business weathered the Great Depression years, but not without his constant perseverance. He would often follow trucks delivering refrigerators, offering to install the machines for the new owners. He moved his business in the early '30s to 261 South George Street, to College and Stone avenues in the mid-1930s, and finally to 317 West Market Street, where it remained until the 1970s.

Barton's company served local industry in its formative years. During World War II, the electrician and his workers had industrial clients in York that included A.B. Farquhar, B.M. Root and Company, and York Hoover Body. The business was incorporated under its current name, Jno. Z. Barton, Inc., in 1953. Barton's sons, Frank L. and George H. Barton, became officers in the organization and new markets were found for the firm's electrical engineering services.

Since the early 1950s the corporation has expanded its electrical construction to include almost every conceivable type of project—industrial, commercial, institutional, underground, pole lines, high-voltage substations, sewage plants, shopping centers, housing developments, distribution centers, warehouses, paper mills, and other businesses. Jno. Z. Barton, Inc., is also engaged in the design, fabrication, assembly, and wiring of instrumentation and control panels and related work. The firm's resources include the application of microprocessors, programmable controllers, and other methods to industrial processes, energy management systems, and security systems. The company's modern, air-conditioned facilities are equipped to provide sophisticated wiring for custom panels and assemblies. The Barton company was one of the first to use computers for estimating and payroll.

The firm maintains a full-service philosophy and assumes complete responsibility for its electrical work.

Below
John Z. Barton, founder of Jno. Z. Barton, Inc., is seen in a moment of repose in this photograph taken during the 1960s.

Bottom
Charlotte Barton and young Frank Barton pose in front of the company's original location at 537 West Market Street, York (circa 1920).

The electrical design is performed by qualified and experienced personnel in accordance with the latest design codes and standards. Construction management service for electrical systems is also offered by Jno. Z. Barton, Inc.

The company moved to its present headquarters at 415 Norway Street in York in the early 1970s. More than 60 people are employed by Barton and the firm's market stretches from Vermont to South Carolina. The officers of the company are Frank Barton, president; Gary Miller, vice-president; and George Barton, secretary-treasurer. The firm is entering its third generation of operation; Thomas and Douglas Barton, grandsons of the founder, are active today in the family business.

BORGER STEEL CO.

In 1950 Ben Borger of Pottstown, Pennsylvania, and his two sons, Herbert and Samuel, purchased the York Pipe and Steel Company, a small firm that dealt in steel, pipe, and scrap metal.

eight acres of land. The company's 10 employees moved the office facilities on one day in November 1958, from the old site at 337 West College Avenue to the new 18,000-square-foot location.

The optimism of Herbert and Samuel Borger has been justified. The company's growth prompted

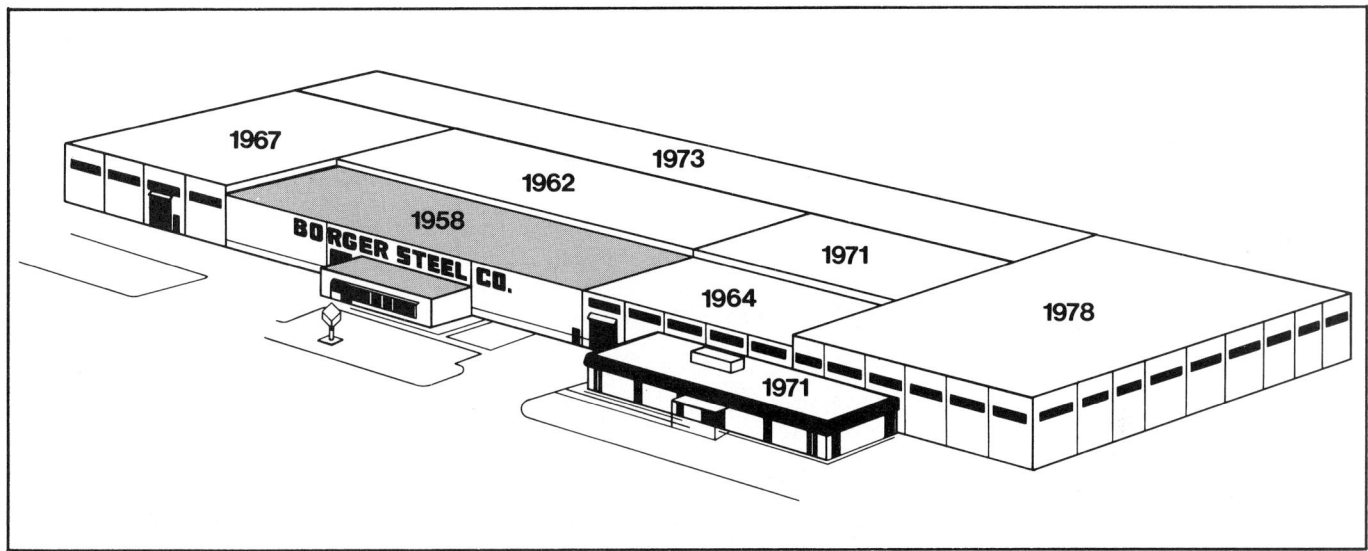

The Borgers realized that central Pennsylvania, especially York, would be an ideal location for a complete steel-service center, something not available in the region at that time. Samuel Borger was the first to move from the family's welding repair business in Pottstown to its new venture in the White Rose City. His father and brother soon followed, and together the Borgers began reorganizing their new company into a full-service distribution center, selling and processing new steel exclusively.

The business grew rapidly during the next 30 years. Shortly after the death of their father Ben in 1956, the Borger brothers changed the name of the enterprise to Borger Steel Co. The business was incorporated in 1959. Its facilities soon became inadequate to handle the large volume of steel being processed, and so, for the first of many times, expansion became necessary. In 1958 construction of a new distribution and custom-service plant was begun in East York on

additional plant expansions in 1962, 1964, 1967, 1971, 1973, and 1978. Today, Borger's Steel Service Center totals nearly 125,000 square feet and serves central and eastern Pennsylvania, as well as neighboring states, with the area's largest inventory of hot-rolled carbon steel.

Borger Steel has expanded in other ways, too. Ninety people are employed by the firm and Borger Steel operates a fleet of 14 company-owned tractor-trailers. Among the many services offered to customers are shearing, sawing, and electric eye flame-cutting.

The company has added substantially to the growth and development of industry in York County. The services offered by the firm are comparable to those found in much larger cities, and contribute significantly to the area's economy. Borger Steel Co. continues to be owned and operated by Herbert and Samuel Borger. A third generation of Borgers has joined the business and, like preceding generations, continues to look to a bright future.

Top
Current facilities of Borger Steel show the company's rapid expansion over the past 30 years.

Above
In 1950, Ben, Herbert, and Sam Borger purchased the York Pipe and Steel Company, shown here.

THE YORK AIR CONDITIONING GROUP OF BORG-WARNER CORPORATION

Ulysses S. Grant was president of the United States, Thomas Edison had not yet invented the incandescent light bulb, and it would be another two years before General George Custer would ride to meet his destiny at Little Big Horn. It was autumn of 1874 and in York, Pennsylvania, six men met to sign the articles of agreement that marked the beginning of the York Air Conditioning Group of Borg-Warner Corporation.

In its early years, the York Manufacturing Company produced a variety of machine shop and foundry products in a 3,000-square-foot plant operated by 14 employees. The hours were long and the company's potential was ill-defined but the York group was inventive, meeting customer demands for such diverse products as boilers, water wheels, steam engines, agricultural equipment, and paper-making machinery.

In 1885 they produced their first "ice machine," an innovative device for which little demand existed; ice was harvested annually from lakes and streams and held in ice houses for food preservation during the summer. The market for commercially produced ice changed dramatically with the ice famine in 1890.

Food supplies dwindled, thousands fell ill, and ice houses scrambled frantically to install refrigeration equipment to freeze their own ice. From the ice famine of the 1890s to the energy shortages of the 1980s, the York company has positioned itself to meet society's changing requirements for heating and air conditioning.

By 1904 York's fledgling marketing department listed hundreds of ice house installations, along with ice-making machinery for breweries, hotels, and cold-storage plants.

In 1897 P.H. Glatfelter, one of the founders of the company, hired Thomas Shipley, a young engineer, to serve as general manager. Under Shipley's direction, the firm concentrated on the production of ice machines, and grew from a staff of 50 employees in 1897 to a roster of 1,500 full-time workers by 1910.

The company began its international operations in the early 1900s with exports of ice plant machinery to several countries, including Cuba, Argentina, and China.

Even while concentrating its efforts on the burgeoning market for refrigeration equipment, the young company had been willing to improvise in related fields. In 1903 York Manufacturing built and installed a machine to control humidity in a blast furnace area for Carnegie Steel Company at Aetna, Pennsylvania. In 1914 York engineers developed an innovative comfort system for the Empire Theater in Montgomery, Alabama. It was the first combination of "air washing" and ventilation with the new element of refrigeration: air conditioning.

In 1927 York Manufacturing Company negotiated a merger with its 14 independently owned construction and supply companies to create the York Ice Machinery Corporation, a major manufacturer with wholly owned branches around the country.

By the early 1930s, however, refrigeration was moving into the home, and the ice houses began to close their doors. The market for commercial ice-making equipment was melting away, but the air conditioning business was beginning. York, with a history of change and innovation, met the shifting market.

In 1935, the firm moved dramatically into the home-comfort field with one of the nation's first successful room air conditioners. Within a few years self-contained units for stores, restaurants, and similar establishments gave more impetus to the growth of the air conditioning industry than any other development.

In 1942, with the company's primary focus moving away from commercial ice equipment, the firm was reincorporated as York Corporation. World War II created an urgent military demand for large refrigeration and food storage systems and temporarily delayed York's emergence as a major force in the air conditioning industry.

In the postwar period, York Corporation assumed its leadership role in the industry with a wide range of air conditioning products for homes, commerce, and industry. It continued to pioneer many industry firsts, including the first automatic ice cube maker in 1948.

In 1956 York Corporation was merged into Borg-Warner Corporation, operating briefly as a subsidiary before becoming an independent operating division of the corporation.

The company's Pennsylvania-based York Air Conditioning Group now includes many buildings and about 3,000 employees at three locations in York. The company also opened a plant in Madisonville, Kentucky, in 1974 to produce residential air conditioning products. A separate York Automotive Division in Decatur, Illinois, produces compressors for automobile air conditioners.

In 1981 the York Air Conditioning Group acquired Westinghouse Corporation's residential air conditioning business including three plants in Norman, Oklahoma; Elyria and Medina, Ohio; as well as its Luxaire, Moncrief, and Fraser & Johnston lines of heating and cooling equipment.

The York-International operation, with headquarters in York, includes manufacturing plants in England and France and joint ventures or partially owned plants in Australia, Japan, Mexico, and West Germany. York-Canada is a wholly owned subsidiary of Borg-Warner (Canada) Limited. In addition, marketing agreements with many other companies around the world provide important export opportunities for York and international recognition of the York name as one of the world's major air conditioning companies.

Today, York equipment heats and cools all types of buildings, from homes and apartments to landmarks such as the World Trade Center and the Empire State Building in New York, many of the federal government buildings in Washington, D.C., La Scala Opera House in Milan, Orly Airport in Paris, the Stock Exchange in Melbourne, Barclays Bank in London, the Hong Kong Hilton, and the National Gymnasium in Tokyo.

York products also provide fresh air and refrigeration for ships' stores in submarines. They aid petrochemical firms in the processing of fuels and chemicals, freeze ice in skating rinks, provide a precisely controlled atmosphere for many industrial processes and the operation of computers, preserve medical drugs, supply many of the cars on the highways with cooling, and preserve food in processing plants, railroad cars, trucks, and ships.

From the beginning the firm has competed in the air conditioning industry on the basis of operating costs, or efficiency, as well as first cost of equipment. Anticipating the energy shortages of the latter part of this century, however, Borg-Warner's York Group began to intensify its efforts in the late 1960s and early 1970s to develop products with greater conservation capabilities.

York was the first air conditioning and heating company to completely control heat pump operation with solid-state technology in a product line it introduced in 1976. It further enhanced its solid-state YorkGuard logic module in 1979 to provide further efficiencies in the heat pump line that is used in both residences and smaller commercial buildings.

One of the most significant developments in the history of the air conditioning industry is Borg-Warner's advanced-technology, alternating current inverter and control, called a modulator. York began work on this conservation equipment project in the late 1960s.

The company announced the results of its extensive research and field tests in 1979 and the next year began installing its most important energy-saving products: a Turbo-Modulator system that can save an annual average of 30 percent of the electricity required by a centrifugal chiller, the single largest energy-consuming component of a large building air conditioning system, and an ENMOD (ENergy MODulating) heat pump for residential application that can save up to 17 percent more energy than ordinarily is used by one of the most efficient heat pumps already available.

For more than a century, the York company has contributed innovative products to help us manage energy while, at the same time, increasing comfort in our homes, commercial, and industrial establishments. The leadership role of Borg-Warner Corporation's York Air Conditioning Group is expected to result in continued technological advances within the air conditioning industry for decades to come.

Above
Energy conservation was given a boost when York introduced the first heat pump with operation completely controlled by solid-state technology. Later improvements in its York Guard module provided increased savings in home heating and air conditioning.

Left
The original plant and office building of York Manufacturing Company in 1885. The site is now a parking lot.

THE CARPETMAN

Harold R. Helf came to York in 1941 to take a position as a carpet buyer at Gehly's Carpet House at 9 West Market Street. He had been working in the home furnishings industry since 1918 and had most recently worked in the retail business at Pomeroy's Department Store in Harrisburg. Mr. Helf stayed at Gehly's for 22 years and became the inspiration for the family carpet business known today as The Carpetman.

In 1959 Mr. Helf founded Helf Rug and Carpet Service, the first independent installation and cleaning service in the York area. It was operated until 1963, when Harold Helf and his son Larry co-founded the House of Carpet at 1756 South Queen Street in York. Larry Helf left the business for eight years—five years to work as a manufacturer's representative and three years to conduct the only carpet installation trade school in the United States.

The Carpetman was founded by the Helfs on June 14, 1971, in the railroad station building off North George Street in York. The business grew quickly and expansion necessitated a move to larger quarters at 110 South Queen Street in June 1972. One year later, a carpet remnant department was relocated at the railroad station site. Larry Helf purchased the present location for The Carpetman on November 14, 1979. The store opened for business in its new home in May 1980. The site at 700 West Market Street is familiar to many Yorkers as the H.M. Rehmeyer Building.

The Carpetman today is a family business in the truest sense of the word. The Helf family—Larry and his wife, Julia; their four sons,

Michael, Patrick, Thomas, and Stephen; and their two daughters, Lariann and Juliann—staff the retail operation. Harold Helf, the man who inspired his family's carpet business in York, died on November 30, 1976.

Larry Helf's dedication to the carpet installation field remains intact today. He is an installation consultant for Chicago Adhesive Products and travels extensively, conducting seminars for carpet installers throughout the United States.

The present facilities for The Carpetman are the largest carpet showrooms in the York area, complete with a large roll inventory and contemporary and period area rugs. A large remnant room, "The Backyards," is located near the rear of the store and is devoted to merchandising smaller pieces that have passed through the store as rolls. Helf prides himself on showing unique merchandise such as hand-made Dhurries, Iberia, and Berber qualities and machine-woven Oriental reproductions.

Left
Harold Helf was the inspiration behind the founding of The Carpetman business.

Above
The entire Helf clan is involved in The Carpetman operations.

DANSKIN, INC.

Joel and Benson Goodman established a company in New York City in 1882 to sell hosiery, leatherware, and varied children's and women's apparel.

In 1923 Herbert Goodman, the son of Joel Goodman, founded Triumph Hosiery Mills in Philadelphia. Henry Erdos was appointed general manager of the new operation in Pennsylvania, and the actual knitting of goods was begun by the firm. From 1923 to 1925, the company produced seamless hosiery only, but when a second plant was built in 1925, full-fashioned knitting was included.

Triumph Hosiery opened a new plant in York, Pennsylvania, in 1927. The operation, still located as the center part of the Danskin State Street complex, employed about 200 people. Throughout the 1930s and the 1940s, Triumph Hosiery Mills continued to produce seamless and full-fashioned hosiery of superior quality, specializing in hard-to-fit sizes. The manufacture of theatrical stockings by the company grew as well.

With the development of stretch nylon in 1949, Triumph Hosiery began research into the possibility of using this new yarn to produce dancewear. One year later, the company manufactured its first pair of stretch tights, and the "Danskin" brand name was born. The new, full-fashioned nylon stretch tights were an immediate success because they fit like a second skin and allowed full freedom of action for the wearer. Dancers soon suggested that the stretch nylon yarn would make excellent leotards and trunks, better than the cotton products then available. With some mechanical adjustments to the existing machinery, the company started to manufacture full-fashioned leotards and trunks. Specially designed machinery to produce the new garments was soon purchased.

The next major project for the firm was the development of fine-gauge knitted sweaters. Following several years of experimentation, the first line of Danskin women's and children's sweaters was manufactured, followed by a line of full-fashioned children's pants and shorts. Meanwhile, Danskin continued to produce superior seamless tights, considered to be the best in the industry.

In recent years, under the leadership of its president, Peter Goodman, and its vice-president of operations, Robert Erdos, Danskin expanded its activities into various fields of attire for the active woman and child, and created a new concept in fashion with the development of freestyle lycra swimsuits and disco clothing. Worthy of note, Danskin was presented with a special Coty Award for its "outstanding contribution to bodywear for exercise and sports." Further expansion of marketing efforts is under way as a result of the acquisition of Danskin by International Playtex, Inc., in April 1980.

Employees of the Triumph Hosiery Mills pose for this group portrait in front of the plant in 1930.

DIE-A-MATIC

Die-A-Matic, Inc., was established in 1956 as an engineering consulting firm specializing in fluid power design. Mr. and Mrs. D.E. Flinchbaugh and Mr. and Mrs. M. Stauffer founded the company and one year later were joined by Mr. and Mrs. William Gross. In 1959 the Gross family became sole owners of the company when they bought the Flinchbaughs' and Stauffers' shares of Die-A-Matic.

William Gross was the only employee of the company that first year, drawing a salary of $500 every two weeks. Offices were located in the William Christensen Steel Company building at 366 South Sherman Street, York. Die-A-Matic's first contracts were with Redco Tool and B.M. Root Company. As the engineering consulting business fluctuated, the company began selling hydraulic and pneumatic components as a jobber for established Philadelphia and New Jersey distributors.

By the early '60s, the company had found it was profitable to be a jobber/distributor. Die-A-Matic already had an inventory of products and there was no direct competition in York. The path was set for growth and expansion.

In 1964 the company obtained the direct distribution agreement for Parker Hannifin Hose and Hose Couplings in central Pennsylvania. In that same year, Die-A-Matic designed the first hydraulic dual control for use in driver education vehicles and marketed the device through the American Automobile Association in Washington, D.C. Both of these relationships remain an important part of the company's operation today.

By 1966 Die-A-Matic had become a full-line specialty house with agreements to distribute most of the products manufactured by Parker Hannifin Corporation, Helicoid Gauge, Bimba Manufacturing Company, Samuel Moore & Company, and Gast Manufacturing Corporation. In 1968 Die-A-Matic opened its first branch location, distributing identical products in the Scranton/Wilkes-Barre market. Another branch, Die-A-Matic/Maryland, followed in 1977 to serve the industrial market to the south.

Diversification from distribution began in 1971 when Die-A-Matic purchased Allgaier Shops in Arlington, Virginia, the exclusive manufacturer of all training devices for the American Automobile Association in Washington, D.C. Diversification continued when the firm formed a subsidiary company in 1978, Y/P Products, Inc., to fabricate refrigeration components sold throughout the world.

Increased specialization of products and service began in 1975, when the corporation opened its Special Products Division in a 6,000-square-foot leased facility at 321 North Duke Street, York. The new division produced power units and special fabrications using hydraulic and pneumatic components. The Special Products Division today is housed in a portion of a new 21,000-square-foot building located in the I-83 Industrial Plaza along with its sister company, Y/P Products, Inc.

The headquarters of Die-A-Matic is located at 650 North State Street, York.

Specialization continued in 1977 when another subsidiary, Mid-Atlantic Instrumentation, was formed to distribute high-quality instrumentation products primarily manufactured by Parker Hannifin Corporation. This subsidiary services the same geographical area as Die-A-Matic, but concentrates on the instrumentation market rather than the industrial market.

The firm is still controlled by the Gross family. William D. Gross, chairman of the board, is very active in the company's operation as well as community and commercial affiliations. His son, Randall Gross, now president of Die-A-Matic, joined the company in 1975. He is a director of the York Area Chamber of Commerce and, like his father, is involved in many other community activities.

Die-A-Matic is a family-owned business in its second generation. It has grown from a one-man operation serving the greater York area to a company serving an important role in the economy of central Pennsylvania, Maryland, and Washington, D.C.

DENTSPLY INTERNATIONAL

Many Yorkers know Dentsply International as "the tooth factory on College Avenue." In actuality, the York complex serves as the corporate headquarters for a worldwide enterprise engaged in a business that includes the manufacture and distribution of dental supplies and equipment, optical and medical equipment, and the retail dispensing of eyewear.

The company was originally founded on June 17, 1899, as The Dentists' Supply Company of New York. The founders, Dr. Jacob F. Frantz, John R. Sheppard, and Dean C. Osborne, started the company with an authorized capital of $10,000 and $1,000 in cash. The business was organized for the sale and distribution of dental supplies and they were later joined by an old friend, George H. Whiteley.

As the need for better artificial teeth was recognized by the profession, the businessmen soon began their own manufacture of the product. The company found itself in York early this century when the founders purchased a faltering tooth manufacturing facility, the National Tooth Company, located at 9 South Beaver Street. Executive offices moved to York in 1952 from New York City and are at 570 West College Avenue.

Artificial teeth continued to be Dentsply's primary product line until 1963, and since that time the firm has diversified as the result of a sound acquisition plan and an aggressive research and development effort. Today nearly 6,000 people work at production facilities of Dentsply International in 12 countries around the world. Over 1,100 employees work at corporate headquarters in York, making the enterprise one of the largest employers in the city.

Dentsply International manufactures a complete line of dental supplies and some equipment, producing and distributing many of the items found in dental offices and laboratories. Dental supplies produced include a full line of materials for prosthetic, restorative, and preventive dentistry, and range from artificial teeth to acrylic, porcelain, and alloy materials and from hand instruments to dental burs. The equipment products include dental prophylaxis units, stools, vacuum systems, and water recyclers.

The company's optical dispensaries in the United States sell contact lenses and eyeglasses to individuals, and many provide eye examinations. Two full-service optical laboratories fabricate eyewear prescriptions for these dispensaries and a manufacturing facility in this country produces optical equipment such as examination chairs and instrument stands.

Medical and industrial products made by Dentsply International in the United States and the United Kingdom include medical examination and treatment chairs, stretchers, stools, hospital anesthetic equipment, cardiac-monitoring equipment, medical instruments, bone cement, investment casting, industrial air grinders, acrylic materials, and related medical and industrial products.

Dentsply launched the "air age" in dentistry in 1957 with the introduction of the first high-speed air turbine handpiece. Recent introductions include a new plastic tooth material, a visible light restorative system that cures through tooth structure, and several advanced endodontic products. With a history of innovation through research, the firm is prepared for a dynamic and diversified future.

Below
Dentsply International is the foremost manufacturer of artificial teeth in the world. This photograph shows all of the employees at the College Avenue Plant in 1911.

Bottom
This early view shows the molding room for the making of artificial teeth at the Dentsply factory.

THE DROVERS AND MECHANICS BANK

York's signer of the Declaration of Independence, James Smith, maintained his residence and office for his law practice at what is now 30 South George Street when the Continental Congress met in York. His home was a meeting place of the Board of War in 1777 when John Adams of Massachusetts was its leader.

That site on South George Street today is the modern headquarters for one of York County's own financial institutions, The Drovers and Mechanics Bank. The bank gets its unusual name from the area's early days, when agriculture was the primary vocation. "Drovers" were the people who drove the cattle through the city on their way to market and "mechanics" the old-time blacksmiths who shod the horses, rerimmed the wagons, and performed other necessary tasks.

The roots of The Drovers and Mechanics Bank go back to a meeting of citizens interested in forming a bank, held at 2 p.m. on Saturday, April 28, 1883, at the Motter House in the Borough of York. A temporary organization was formed as a result of the meeting, with Israel Gross appointed chairman and William H. Bond secretary.

The bank opened for business on June 12 of that year in the 200 block of West Market Street. Later, the site was moved to 25 South George Street, where the bank occupied the first floor of a modest structure in the heart of downtown York. During the next four decades, through good times and bad, the bank continued to grow steadily. In the early 1920s the officers and directors, recognizing that the bank's growth would necessitate larger quarters, decided to search for another, more permanent location.

In 1924 the board of directors resolved to purchase the property at 30 South George Street, the historic site that remains the home of the bank. In 1958 the old Ritz Theatre at 28 South George Street was purchased, and plans were made for a new, modern banking facility.

The decade of the 1960s brought with it a sparkling new building for The Drovers. A mural by York artist Herb Leopold was commissioned for the facility and represents the many different professions served by the institution. A parking lot for bank customers was created in 1961 and the only all-weather drive-up banking facility in the area was installed.

Expansion became a key for the bank, with new branches being added—Windsor and the York County Shopping Center in 1955, Roosevelt Avenue Shoppette in 1956, Mount Rose Avenue and Hill Street in 1962, Emigsville in 1966, and Richland Avenue in 1968. The Brooks Hotel and parking lot were acquired in 1967, enabling The Drovers to provide its main office customers with adequate parking facilities and the fast, convenient service of three drive-up lanes. Branches continued to be opened, including Queensgate Shopping Center (the headquarters of administrative and operational functions for the consumer credit office) in 1975, York Haven in 1978, and Memory Lane in East York in 1981.

The official name was changed from The Drovers and Mechanics National Bank of York to The Drovers and Mechanics Bank in 1979, when the bank withdrew its membership from the Federal Reserve System and became a state-chartered institution. The bank today employs about 135 people and has assets of approximately $133 million, plus a trust department of $28 million. Thirteen members serve on its board of directors. The bank's first president was Nathan Burhan. Succeeding him were Israel F. Gross, Samuel Lichtenberger, Jacob Beitzel, James Glessner, George Jordan, A.W. Girton, and the current president, Richard M. Linder.

Below
The Drovers Bank as it appeared in the late 1920s. In 1958 the Old Ritz Theatre building at 28 South George Street was purchased, and plans were made to convert it into a modern banking facility.

Bottom
The Drovers and Mechanics Bank gained a sparkling new building during the 1960s. Located on the historic site at 30 South George Street, the bank displays a mural by York artist Herb Leopold.

EMONS INDUSTRIES, INC.

From the beginning of this century through the end of World War II, trains of the Maryland and Pennsylvania Railroad line chugged down the tracks from York, past the southern York County towns of Red Lion and Delta to a destination in Baltimore. Nicknamed the "Ma and Pa," the line carried passengers and freight on a regular route through York County for many years.

The passenger service was curtailed in the late 1940s and stopped completely in 1954. The proud short-line railroad that started in the 1870s as the Peach Bottom Railroad stared at a bleak future, facing the possibilities of an eventual death as it approached its 100th anniversary.

In 1971, six New York City businessmen were looking for the right place to invest their money. Their first venture, in 1970, was the formation of Gromar Planning and Development Corporation, a company organized to purchase control of basic types of businesses, then apply the talents of the men to the newly acquired enterprises to make them larger and more profitable. Gromar's first acquisition, the Emons Hardware Corporation, imported and distributed industrial fasteners such as screws, nuts, and bolts. Gromar later gained control of Amfre-Grant, Inc., a pharmaceutical company, and the name of the entire group of businesses was changed to Emons Industries.

The six businessmen and financiers (Robert Grossman, Joseph W. Marino, Harold Grossman, Herman Lazarus, Harvey Polly, and Vito J. Marino) discovered and purchased the "Ma and Pa" Railroad. They sold the fastener company in 1973 and devoted their energies to acquiring a fleet of freight cars using the "Ma and Pa" as a base to start. The men had visions of Emons-owned boxcars being rented to railroads and shippers around the country, much like a car rental company does today.

The management of Emons Industries sold all their other enterprises and concentrated on the rail and freight car leasing business. Corporate headquarters were moved from New York City to York in April 1976, and the Maryland and Pennsylvania Railroad gained more trackage from the Penn Central Transportation Company in the York-Hanover area that same year. Emons's leasing business grew annually, while the company began the manufacture of new freight cars in 1977 to become part of the fleet leased to railroads. The Emons concept was to rent its freight cars on a per-day basis, rather than on the standard long-term, fixed-contract method.

The growth of Emons since 1971 can be seen in its figures. From fewer than 20 employees and assets of less than $1 million, the company has grown to its current status of more than 100 employees and assets of over $95 million. The firm, like its predecessor, the "Ma and Pa," remains an integral part of the York community, serving such major industries in the area as St. Regis Paper Company, Certain-teed Corporation, Borg-Warner, and National Gypsum.

Emons Industries is a vibrant and forward-looking company in the $1-billion rail car rental industry, but it remembers its heritage and its roots in the little railroad that ran from York to Baltimore through the wilderness of rural York County.

Below
Passengers wait to board the "Ma and Pa" Railroad in this 1936 photograph. The railroad took passengers from York to Baltimore daily.

Bottom
Today Emons Industries, Inc., is a manufacturer of rail freight cars.

Emons's corporate headquarters isn't a sparkling modern building, but rather a quaint train depot built a century ago along East Market Street.

The "Ma and Pa" still runs through downtown York and south through the county, but instead of delivering passengers, slate, and mail, it is the proud flagship of the prosperous York-based Emons Industries.

EPSTEIN AND SONS, INC.

A young Polish emigrant from New York City came to York in 1917 selling picture frames. As he was passing through, he tripped over a young lady's foot on an open-air trolley. The young man made his apologies to the girl, introduced himself as Abe Epstein, and struck up a conversation. She was Helen Forner, a native Yorker.

Epstein later married the York girl, settled in the city, and became a traveling salesman. One day in 1925, he came home to York and found "For Sale" signs on his house and the five adjoining buildings. He decided to purchase all six houses himself and resell five, coincidentally beginning a career in real estate. Upon his realization that he could earn his livelihood buying and selling homes in York, Epstein opened an office in the old Gross Building at 35 East Market Street. By 1939, his business had grown so much that he needed larger quarters and moved to 56 South George Street.

His four sons joined Epstein in business in 1946 and formed the corporation, Epstein and Sons, Inc. This new enterprise, as real estate builder and developer, would provide homes for thousands of Yorkers over the ensuing 25 years. Abe Epstein was company president; Bernard Epstein, vice-president; Helen Epstein, secretary; Irwin Epstein, treasurer; and Ethel Crider, secretary-treasurer. The two younger sons, Harold and Donald, were sales representatives. All four sons were introduced to the real estate business through their father's agency, and three of them joined the company after being discharged from service in the armed forces.

Epstein and Sons is probably best known in York as the developer of Haines Acres, an area in suburban York that is home to more than 5,000 people. The Haines Acres development was started in 1954, when the Epsteins purchased a 205-acre farm in Springettsbury Township from Mahlon Haines, a well-known philanthropist. Haines agreed to donate $2,500 to the Boy Scouts of America if the development was named "Haines Acres." The first lots in Haines Acres sold for $2,500 each; the 1981 price of a lot in that same area is $20,000. The development currently consists of 1,100 homes built on approximately 800 acres.

Haines Acres is by no means the only development created by Epstein and Sons in the York area. Others include Penn Oaks South, adjoining Haines Acres; Randolph Park, Tri-Hill, Southwood Hills, and Marborough West, all in south York; and Clear Springs, Shiloh East, Andover, and Brandywine in northwest York.

Today the Epstein real estate business is still achieving one of its original goals—to keep the family together. Bernard, Harold, and Donald Epstein remain active in the agency started by their father, Abe, who died in 1963. Their brother, Irwin, died in 1973. Ethel Crider, a native of York who faithfully served the Epsteins as secretary for 50 years, is now retired. And thousands of Yorkers have the Epsteins to thank for providing them with the opportunity to enjoy comfortable homes they can call their own.

Top
Abe Epstein, founder of Epstein and Sons, first came to York in 1917.

Above
Haines Acres, a development of Epstein and Sons, today is home for thousands of Yorkers.

FUTER BROS.

In the midst of the Great Depression, two brothers—graduates of Bowman Technical School—set their sights on opening a small watch, clock, and jewelry repair shop and jewelry store in York. The landlord who rented the one-room shop to the brothers, Parke H. and Leroy C. Futer, told them outright that he thought they were crazy. After all, who had the money in York at that time to spend on "luxuries" like watches and jewelry? Undaunted by their landlord's predictions, the two men opened their store on March 1, 1932, at 166 West Market Street and began a retail enterprise that continues to flourish in the city today.

The Futer brothers chose York because they surmised it had more diversified industry at that time than any other city its size in the United States. If one business wasn't prospering, they reasoned, another would be. Armed with this determination, Parke Futer canvassed nearly all of the streets in the city on those first cold days in March 1932, asking Yorkers if they had any watches, clocks, or jewelry that needed repairing.

Business was steady from the start, despite the initial skepticism of early customers. To reassure their patrons, the Futer brothers promised that all the work they took in that first week would be ready the following Saturday.

That first Saturday arrived, and the small shop was crowded with customers. They left, fully satisfied with the service and the quality of workmanship; and the company's tradition of excellence was firmly established. In addition, the brothers obtained the cash they needed to continue their new venture—much-needed cash, it turned out, because they had started with only thirty-five dollars, all but five of which had been used to rent the shop.

In 1936, the brothers moved to a small shop on York's Continental Square. Several years later, they rented the entire corner of the square and eventually Parke Futer purchased the whole building. That structure, the Hartman Building, was reputed to be "the tallest skyscraper west of the Susquehanna River" and proved to be a fine investment.

Today, Futer Bros. Jewelry Store still occupies the southeast corner of York's Continental Square. The company that started with two employees now has a full- and part-time staff of 16. Futer Bros. continues to offer Yorkers quality repair services, custom work, and the finest lines available in jewelry, watches, glassware, china, and sterling silver.

With almost 50 years of service to the community, the family-owned business begun by the Futer brothers has seen York grow and prosper. The company, like a portion of the city, survived a disastrous flood in 1933.

Parke H. Futer owns the store today; his brother Leroy died in 1958. The family tradition is ably carried on by certified gemologist Justus H. Eigenrauch III, Parke Futer's son-in-law, who is a partner and serves as the general manager of the store. Futer Bros., registered jewelers, is a member of the American Gem Society.

Top
Futer Bros. has been located on York's Continental Square since 1936. The interior of their shop is shown here in a photograph taken soon after they moved in.

Above
The front window of the first Futer Bros. jewelry store is seen in this 1932 photograph.

FOX POOL CORPORATION

Yorkers driving on Whiteford Road in the early 1960s passed a small A-frame building that housed the executive offices of the Fox Pool Corporation. Today, drivers on busy Interstate Route 83 north of the city pass the headquarters of that same company, now located in large facilities in a modern industrial park.

Fox Pool Corporation was founded in 1957 by George Fox, who established his office at 1895 Whiteford Road. In 1968, Fox relinquished his presidency and title as chief executive officer to Donald Weir, who continues in those positions today. In 1969, Fox Pool Corporation moved its home to the I-83 Industrial Park northeast of York and initiated a series of rapid expansions. The company today is a worldwide manufacturer of in-ground vinyl-liner swimming pools and produces a quality line of Amish Country Hot Tubs. The firm also markets spas and related swimming pool, hot tub, and spa accessories.

Fox Pools attributes its phenomenal growth to its dedication to quality and engineering excellence. The company's patented Perm-X Brace construction method, backed by the only independently produced engineering report in the industry, has earned the York-based firm the reputation as "the strongest name in pools." The Perm-X Brace construction method permits pools to be built without danger of wall distortion or bowing and allows them to be easily drained at any time. This innovative method also allows pool builders to complete all surrounding decking while the pools are being constructed.

A special honor bestowed upon Fox Pools is the coveted Presidential "E" Award for outstanding success in exporting. To qualify for the award, manufacturers must show a substantial increase in exports over a 3-year period and demonstrate significant breakthroughs in particularly competitive markets, open new markets, or introduce new products into U.S. export trade. Fox Pools' receipt of the "E" Award in 1977 was the first and only by any member of the swimming pool industry.

Fox Pools has won several international awards for excellence in design from the National Swimming Pool Institute, including gold, silver, and bronze trophies and awards of merit in its highly competitive yearly contest. The company has also won awards at the Chelsea Flower Show in England and in Canadian competition as well, a record virtually unmatched by any other swimming pool manufacturer.

The firm's York facility serves as the national office and as distribution center for the Northeast. Fox Pools also has regional facilities and warehouses in Lockport, Illinois; Marietta, Georgia; and Dallas, Texas. In nearby Irving, Texas, is also the location of York Chemical Corporation, a subsidiary of the company specializing in swimming pool and water-related chemicals. Canada is served by Fox Pool Canada Limited, located in Oakville, Ontario, and the Common Market countries are served by Fox Pool International headquarters in Twyford, Berkshire, England. Quaker Plastic Corporation, a manufacturer of plastic extruded and thermo-formed products, is a subsidiary of Fox Pools located in Mountville, Pennsylvania. Fox Data Services, another York subsidiary, provides a full range of computer and programming services for local industry as well as for Fox.

The growth of this dynamic York company continues today. On April 9, 1980, groundbreaking ceremonies were held on a 92,000-square-foot facility expansion that will provide the firm with additional warehousing and manufacturing capabilities.

From its original small site on Whiteford Road in the early 1960s, Fox Pools has grown to become a worldwide company with over 250,000 square feet of sales, manufacturing, and warehousing space and has positioned itself as a leader in the billion-dollar swimming pool industry.

Top
Fox Pool Corporation was founded in 1957 by George Fox, who established this office at 1895 Whiteford Road.

Above
In 1969 Fox Pool Corporation, under the leadership of Donald Weir, moved to the I-83 Industrial Park northeast of York and started a series of rapid expansions.

THE ROY L. GEESEY AGENCY

When Roy L. Geesey founded his insurance agency back in January 1928, it seemed the only natural thing to do. After all, insurance was a family tradition for the Geeseys. Geesey's father and grandfather, both native Yorkers, were associated with Southern Mutual Fire Insurance Company, one of the few insurance companies in the area in its day.

Roy L. Geesey began his own business on the first day of 1928. The offices were in a small room on the first floor of 45 East King Street in York. Fred J. Mumma was the first, and at that time, the only assistant.

Insurance in the late '20s and the early '30s was not the complex business it is today. Agents like Geesey wrote their own policies—Geesey separated and filed his policies in a thread spool box. And the York insurance man became known for riding his bicycle around town to visit clients—a bicycle with "The Roy L. Geesey Insurance Agency" printed on its side bars.

Geesey's agency proved itself innovative by offering a number of other services, including notary, tag, and automobile financing. The agency was one of the first to develop an installment plan for car loans.

In 1929 the second-floor tenant of Geesey's building decided to move and sell the facility, giving the young insurance agent the opportunity to buy it. By 1932 the first-floor offices were expanded and John R. ("Bob") Gailey had joined the Geesey team. Spurgeon C. Lecrone joined the agency in 1936 to improve service in handling claims and other office details. Lecrone would later serve as the agency's claims manager.

Further expansion became necessary again in 1939. The second floor of the building was taken over for additional offices. A new colonial facade was constructed and this front was retained during renovations and enlargements, making the attractive building a landmark for many Yorkers.

The family insurance tradition carried over into the next two generations. J. Ray Zarfoss, son-in-law, joined the firm in 1945 and directed its growth until 1980. James R. Zarfoss, Jr., maternal

grandson, joined the family business in 1971 and today serves as its managing partner.

Over the past 53 years The Roy L. Geesey Agency has grown from a one-person office to a staff of 27, still headquartered at 45 East King Street. The agency is proud of its past performance and reputation for providing security through insurance in a friendly and professional manner.

Top
Roy Geesey (left) and his assistant, Fred J. Mumma, are shown in this 1930 photograph taken outside their office at 45 East King Street.

Above
The headquarters of The Roy L. Geesey Agency is noted for its colonial facade.

GENT-L-KLEEN PRODUCTS, INC.

"Skilled hands deserve the very best." That was, and still is, the motivation behind Claude (Bud) Strickler, Jr., the founder of Gent-L-Kleen Products, Inc., of York. His company manufactures America's finest waterless hand cleaner, a product used across the country and around the world by garage mechanics, service station attendants, factory workers, construction crews, painters, and others who need a reliable, heavy-duty cleanser.

Bud Strickler first started manufacturing his hand cleanser in the basement of his home in the Shiloh area of York County. It was 1949 and he was working full-time as a floor hand at the New York Wire Company. He called his product "Strick" and sold it to garages and service stations in the York area. Strickler went no further than seventh grade in school but his business sense told him the time was right for a new, innovative cleanser. With the help of a grade-school friend, he started his part-time manufacturing operation. Sales the first year were $800.

Strickler made major improvements in his product in 1952 to enhance its cosmetic qualities, and changed the name to "Gent-L-Kleen." He went into business for himself full-time on August 11, 1953, determined to devote all of his energies to the manufacture and sale of the waterless cleaner. His family moved to a new home in 1955, and Strickler continued the operation, still in the basement. In 1959 his company engineered and began producing a highly efficient and economical push-button dispenser.

Though relatively small compared to the giants in the soap industry, Gent-L-Kleen continued to grow, year after year. Strickler began to use manufacturers' representatives to market the product across the country. A sales manager, William (Clark) Makibbin, joined the company as president in 1957 and the business was incorporated in December 1959. Makibbin, during his 13 years at Gent-L-Kleen, was responsible for the increase in sales from $25,000 in 1957 to over $350,000 in 1970, when he retired. Today the company's annual sales exceed $2 million.

The firm made another move to a modern, 40,000-square-foot plant in the I-83 Industrial Park in July 1977. The enterprise that started with one man making hand cleanser in his basement had grown to a multimillion-dollar business with 15 employees and product sales in all 50 states and several foreign countries. Strickler's oldest son, James E. Strickler, joined Gent-L-Kleen after completing his college education in 1970 and has been increasingly active in the business as executive vice-president.

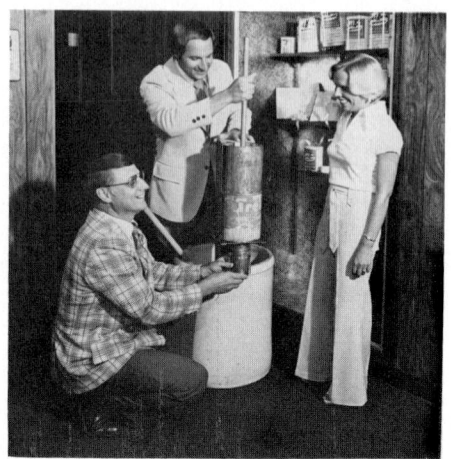

Both men's wives also work in the company, as do some of Claude Strickler's other children.

Growth has been the key to the Gent-L-Kleen story. The production capacity in 1949 was 210 pounds per hour. Today's capacity is 6,000 pounds an hour or 144,000 pounds daily. And, most importantly, the quality of the product made by Gent-L-Kleen and used by millions of people remains as consistent and as fine as it was when made by just one man.

Top
Claude Strickler, Jr. (left), founder of Gent-L-Kleen; his son, James E. Strickler; and his daughter-in-law, Karen Strickler, demonstrate the use of Gent-L-Kleen's original piece of equipment. The device consists of a 15-gallon crock and several cans, and was used to mix the waterless hand cleaner.

Above
Today, production capacity at Gent-L-Kleen is 6,000 pounds of cleanser per hour.

ARTHUR J. GLATFELTER AGENCY, INC.

From his modest start in the insurance business in 1947 as a solicitor in a local general insurance agency, Arthur J. ("Art") Glatfelter has become the founder and president of his own agency with a staff of 50 employees and premiums in excess of $15 million.

Art Glatfelter is a native of York County, born in Loganville, Pennsylvania. He was educated at Loganville Elementary School and William Penn Senior High School. In July 1942, at the age of 17, he enlisted in the United States Marine Corps, serving 25 months in the South Pacific. He was discharged in July 1946, and entered the insurance business in November 1947.

Glatfelter resolved to go into business for himself and on December 1, 1952, opened a one-man office at 62 West Main Street, Dallastown, selling all forms of insurance. He moved his operation for the first time in 1956 to R.D. No. 1, Dallastown, and 10 years later to 2449 South Queen Street, Spry. His business was still relatively small, with only four employees, when the Arthur J. Glatfelter Insurance Agency started an innovative and expansive venture in the insurance field.

That year, Glatfelter wrote his first policy especially designed for the needs of volunteer fire companies. He developed and marketed a comprehensive program, which remains to this day unique in the insurance area. The across-the-board insurance coverages provide protection for fire companies, ambulance/rescue squads, and their members in more than 40 states.

The growth of the new program required expansion for the Glatfelter Agency and necessitated two more moves—in 1973 to 1947 Security Drive and in 1976 to its present headquarters at 191 Leader Heights Road. The past five years have seen a steady increase in the number of Glatfelter employees. Once a year, the staff is treated to an all-expense-paid vacation to such exotic resorts as the Virgin Islands.

Art Glatfelter is a highly respected member of his community, active in numerous business and community organizations. He is a charter member of the Y's Men's Club of York, a YMCA service club, and served as its president for the 1954-55 term. He headed the YMCA's membership drive for two consecutive years, and has been a member of the YMCA board of directors since 1958 and is currently serving as its president.

He was chairman of the Highway Committee of the York Area Chamber of Commerce for the 1972-73 term, was elected to the Chamber's board of directors in 1972, and, after serving as its director for two years, was elected to the offices of vice-president and president. He is a member of the Sales and Marketing Executives Association and served on its board of directors. In 1976, Glatfelter was appointed to the 60-member Council of Small Businesses of the United States Chamber of Commerce, and in that year was also elected to serve on the board of directors of the International Association of Fire Chiefs Foundation.

Glatfelter credits the success of his agency to the special effort expended by his employees while serving the important needs of their clients.

The current home of the Arthur J. Glatfelter Agency is a modern office headquarters at 191 Leader Heights Road, York.

P.H. GLATFELTER COMPANY

A few weeks after President Abraham Lincoln passed through the York area on his way to battle-torn Gettysburg to deliver his now-famous speech, the P.H. Glatfelter Company was founded. On December 23, 1863, P.H. Glatfelter purchased a paper mill located in Spring Forge, Pennsylvania, at an orphan's court sale. Glatfelter, then 26 years old, was a papermaker's apprentice in a Maryland mill.

The Spring Forge mill had produced 1,500 pounds per day of newsprint from rye straw pulp back in July 1863, before the Glatfelter purchase. The town's name, Spring Forge, would later be changed to Spring Grove in 1882.

By the turn of the century the mill's capacity was up to 110,000 pounds of paper per day. In addition to overseeing the physical growth of his new company, P.H. Glatfelter pioneered the development of chemically refined wood pulps, moving the operation away from the use of rags and straw as basic papermaking raw materials.

Glatfelter played an important role in the economic growth of the York region. He was active in founding the York Manufacturing Company (now Borg-Warner Corporation), the Hanover Match Company, and the Hanover Wire Cloth Company. He was a strong advocate of community welfare and education, and became the driving force behind the construction of two churches and a public school in Spring Grove, as well as presenting a lecture hall and endowments to Gettysburg College.

His son, W.L. Glatfelter, became company president in 1907 after 20 years of managerial apprenticeship. He founded the Glatfelter Pulpwood Company, a subsidiary responsible for securing pulpwood for the mill, and expanded the firm in the vital area of raw materials supply. He built the first plant to make pulp from both hardwood and softwood, a technological milepost for the company and for the industry. As a result of this new pulp-making process, the company became widely known as a producer of high-quality book papers, a reputation still held today.

Under the direction of W.L. Glatfelter, the mill's capacity doubled to more than 200,000 pounds per day. He used his managerial skills to guide the York Manufacturing Company to an impressive fivefold increase in its capitalization. W.L. Glatfelter, like his father, was a significant influence on the religious and educational growth of the community. He was a founder of the Layman's Movement of the Lutheran Church and a president of Tressler's Orphans Home.

P.H. Glatfelter II assumed the presidency in 1930 after he literally "went through the mill," mastering every branch of the science of papermaking. He began espousing the doctrine of reforestation and managed woodlands to produce a sustained yield. The P.H. Glatfelter Company began a 1,000-acre model forest in nearby Adams County and brought farmers to view new forest management techniques. The model was Pennsylvania's first certified tree farm.

A bold 10-year expansion program, launched during the depths of the Depression, placed the company in the forefront of the paper industry. A new, large paper machine, innovations in bleaching, stream improvements, and pulp blending made the company one of the most efficient in the industry.

In the family tradition of community leadership, Glatfelter served as a director of the York Hospital, the Western Maryland Railway Company, the Pennsylvania Forestry Association, and the York Corporation, in addition to serving as the president of the Hanover Wire Cloth Company. His special interest in young people was instrumental in founding the York County Junior Achievement program.

P.H. Glatfelter III became president in 1954 after more than 15 years with the company. The next

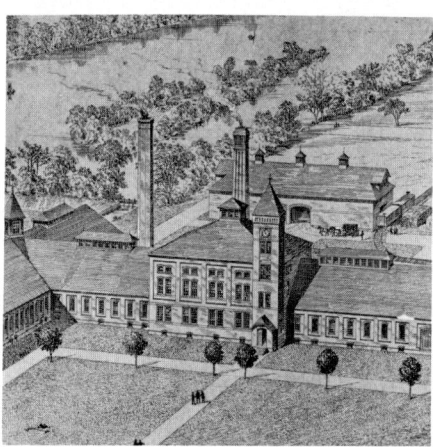

Top
The first P.H. Glatfelter paper mill office is seen in this photograph taken in the 1870s. It was the home of Louisa Auchey, standing at the gate.

Above
An 1881 illustration shows the P.H. Glatfelter paper mills in the community now known as Spring Grove. The architect was J.A. Dempwolf of York.

decade was one of expansion and modernization. Steady growth and development from forest to finished production, which was the Glatfelter tradition, continued under his leadership. His community activities included the Manufacturers Association of York, the York Area Chamber of Commerce, Western Maryland Railroad, and the York County United Fund. As with his family before him, P.H. Glatfelter III has been active in paper industry educational activities as trustee or director of the Institute of Paper Chemistry, Syracuse University Pulp and Paper Foundation, and the University of Maine Pulp and Paper Foundation.

As the P.H. Glatfelter Company concluded its first century of operation, it again expanded dramatically. A 3-year program added a new paper machine, an off-machine coater, and a 1,150-acre lake, and expanded and improved wastewater treatment and odor abatement facilities. With this expansion completed, the mill's capacity reached 200,000 tons of paper per year.

The company continued expansion in 1979, this time through the acquisition of the Bergstrom Paper Company, with mills in Neenah, Wisconsin, and West Carrollton, Ohio. Current papermaking capacities at the company exceed 500,000 tons a year, serving the growing needs of its customers in book publishing, commercial printing, catalog and directory publication, envelope and business forms manufacturing, and various other converting and technical specialty applications.

P.H. Glatfelter III remains as chairman, but in 1980, Thomas C. Norris became the first non-family member to serve as president of the company. Like those before him, Norris served a long apprenticeship with the firm and brings years of industry knowledge, company experience, and community service to the office.

The Spring Grove-based firm's commitment to environmental improvement began long before the current popular movement. Glatfelter was one of the first paper companies in the world to have a primary and secondary wastewater treatment system. In an unprecedented partnership between private industry and state government, the Glatfelter Company and the Commonwealth of Pennsylvania jointly created a 3,300-acre park with a 1,200-acre lake which provides various recreational activities for the people in the area and fresh water for papermaking. The achievements of the P.H. Glatfelter Company have not gone unrecognized. Within the past several years the company has been commended for its superior environmental efforts by the Water Pollution Control Association of Pennsylvania, the Audubon

Society, and the Izaak Walton League of America.

Throughout the Glatfelter Company's long and prosperous history, two major principles have remained steadfast—to produce the finest quality printing and writing papers utilizing technological progress, innovation, and initiative, and to participate in a wide range of interests to benefit individuals and the community. The pride P.H. Glatfelter took in his mill and in his life continues today in the company that bears his name.

A 1980 aerial view of the Spring Grove mill shows the expansion and growth of over a century of operation.

PARTNERS IN PROGRESS • 201

GREEN'S DAIRY

Kansas Utah Horner, a seller of different types of businesses, had an idea for young Clarence Green. It was 1913, and Green was anxious to find a job working outdoors. Horner had just the thing—a milk route.

For $500, Green purchased a business consisting of a horse, a wagon, a spigot-type milk can, and a list of customers. From the first day, he was concerned about the quality of the milk he delivered to his customers. When the weather turned warmer, it spoiled easily.

With $100, Green ordered a pasteurizer and scraped up enough additional cash to start a complete pasteurizing process. Some of Green's customers, however, didn't agree with the pasteurization of milk; they said it destroyed the flavor or the nutritive value. Green handled their opposition the best he could—he simply didn't tell them he used the method—and they soon discovered that his milk stayed fresher longer. Green made the opponents into believers, and started building a successful business.

The number of routes grew, and soon he added more horse-drawn vehicles and more deliverymen. By 1914 Green had purchased a Ford Touring Car-Model T with a special body to accommodate milk deliveries. Realizing the need to have his milk refrigerated before delivery, he contracted with the York Ice Machinery Corporation to install a refrigerating plant in his new building on the corner of Philadelphia and Adams streets.

A new location for his expanding business was chosen in 1924 at North Highland Avenue, the site of the main plant and headquarters today. When the building was completed, it gave Green's Dairy one of the finest facilities of its kind in the nation. Soon after the plant opened, it was evident to Clarence Green that a new method of pasteurization was needed. After some experimentation, the York Ice Machinery Corporation imported a high-temperature, short-time pasteurizer from England. Green bought one of the new devices and his dairy became the first in the United States to switch to the new method, which remains universally accepted today.

Green's Dairy was incorporated in 1947, when James O. Green, son of the founder, entered the business. Clarence Green remained active at the dairy until his death in 1973.

Today Green's Dairy, Inc., is a medium-size, independent dairy engaged in the manufacture and distribution of fluid milk products, ice cream, frozen novelties, and ice cream mix. Within recent decades, the volume of business has changed from the delivery of milk and milk products to the production of ice cream. Fifteen years ago, 95 percent of Green's business was home delivery. Today almost 80 percent of the business is devoted to wholesale ice cream.

Although ice cream and ice cream products were sold throughout the dairy's history, it wasn't until the 1960s that they became a major part of the product line. Adding to the company's growth was the acquisition of 13 milk and ice cream companies within the Green's Dairy marketing region.

The dairy presently has 10,000 home delivery customers and the bulk of the wholesale milk business is done within a 55-mile radius of York, including the tri-city area of central Pennsylvania and northern Maryland. Ice cream and frozen novelty products are distributed on a much wider geographic basis, concentrated heavily in the Philadelphia, Baltimore, and Washington, D.C., areas.

The business remains a family-run operation, with a third generation of Greens involved in the daily activities of the dairy. James B. Green and Abbie Green, son and daughter of James O. Green, serve today as the general manager and purchasing agent for Green's Dairy.

The Green's fleet of delivery vehicles in 1913 included a number of horse-drawn wagons.

HAROLD H. HOGG, INC.

Harold H. Hogg, Inc., is the outgrowth of the general contracting business established in the early 1950s by its founder, Harold H. Hogg. The present firm was organized and incorporated in 1960. In the early years, the primary emphasis was the building of homes in the York area. It has evolved into a full-service general contracting firm specializing in commercial, industrial, and multi-unit residential construction.

Harold H. Hogg, Inc., has experienced rapid but controlled growth. The current annual volume of business is many times what it was just a few years ago. The firm has aggressively pursued opportunities in a widening area from York which now includes all of south central Pennsylvania, northern Maryland, and Delaware.

Offices for the firm were moved in 1971 to the present location on Springwood Road, south of York. Operations in the attractively renovated barn began with a staff of two, but consistent growth and expansion today requires a busy organization of construction managers, engineers, and architects in the office and a large field force including field supervisors and craftsmen.

Many of the projects completed by Harold H. Hogg, Inc., are familiar ones in the York area and include manufacturing and warehouse facilities for Pfaltzgraff Pottery; the three Barley Convalescent Homes; numerous Hardee's Restaurants in central Pennsylvania and northern Maryland; the general construction for the York Federal Savings and Loan Association headquarters in downtown York; Sawmill East Raquetball Club; the 172-room Sheraton Inn East in Harrisburg; Westgate Townhouse apartments; the manufacturing addition for Sandvik-Alto Corporation; the design and construction of both new corporate headquarters and manufacturing facilities for FES (formerly Freezing Equipment Sales); Berg Electronics, Emigsville; the renovation of the Marie Ketterman Building, York Hospital; the Southern Pennsylvania Bank solar branch on Eastern Boulevard; the design and construction of new facilities for McCormick Properties, Inc., and York Graphic Services; and the Life Science Building addition, York College. Most recently, construction has begun on the York County Cerebral Palsy Home and the renovation of the former Zollinger's Department Store and Colonial Hotel into Market Way North and Market Way South, which will be key anchors in a revitalized downtown York.

A positive "can do" attitude has helped Harold H. Hogg, Inc., grow into a vital and innovative force in the York area construction marketplace. An optimistic zest for the future, flexibility, and a keen appreciation of service to the customer has kept the firm learning and expanding as an energetic leader in the future growth and prosperity of the region.

Above
The headquarters of York Federal Savings and Loan, for which Harold H. Hogg, Inc., performed the general construction, is an attractive contribution to the revitalization of downtown York.

Above left
Typical of projects by Harold H. Hogg, Inc., is the Pfaltzgraff Pottery Plant in Thomasville.

KOPPERS COMPANY, INC. MINERAL PROCESSING SYSTEMS DIVISION

Koppers is a diverse corporation, based in Pittsburgh, producing capital equipment and other products for domestic and foreign industry. The Mineral Processing Systems Division is an autonomous business unit dedicated to the design and manufacture of pulverizing equipment used to grind minerals. This York-based division was created in 1966 when Koppers acquired the Hardinge Company.

The Hardinge Company was founded in 1911 in New York by Hal W. Hardinge, a renowned consulting engineer to the mining industry. The company was formed five years after Mr. Hardinge invented the conical ball mill which was then a revolutionary grinding mill design, and remains today a mainstay in Koppers' line of mineral-processing equipment.

After the acquisition of the Steacy Schmidt Manufacturing Company in 1920, which among other products manufactured Pullman automobiles around the turn of the century, the Hardinge Company was moved to York in 1923. The company survived the Great Depression as a result of the strong leadership provided by Harlowe Hardinge, who succeeded his father as president of the firm.

The Hardinge Company remained an innovator and leader in the mineral-processing equipment industry, and in 1960, installed a 22-foot-diameter cascade mill in Sweden after taking years to develop autogenous grinding technology. This technology, which was simultaneously developed by other, much larger, companies, enabled the mining industry to process minerals such as copper and iron which are extracted from relatively low-grade ores at a much faster rate to meet worldwide demand for those minerals. However, the financial resources required to stand behind machines with selling prices approaching a million dollars each was beyond the means of the company. As a result, the Hardinge family decided to sell their business to Koppers a few years later.

Koppers has continued the Hardinge tradition of leadership in the mining equipment business. Today, Koppers produces a wide variety of large and small equipment, including three of the largest autogenous mills in existence. These mills are 36 feet in diameter and process up to 36,000 tons of iron ore per day. Several new products presently in the development stage ensure a continuation of this leadership role into the future.

Top
A 3-foot by 8-inch Hardinge conical ball mill assembled before shipment in 1914. This mill was driven by a belt riding on the pulley around the cylindrical shell of the mill at left.

Above
In 1980 this 28-foot-diameter cascade mill was installed to process uranium at Denison Mines in Ontario, Canada.

McCRORY STORES DIVISION OF McCRORY CORPORATION

One hundred years ago, the idea of buying a variety of goods at volume discounts for resale in several stores in different cities was considered innovative but risky. John Graham McCrorey was one of the country's earliest variety retailers, and together with men like Woolworth, Kress, Kresge, and Murphy, he helped to create a new class of retail store based on large-scale purchases and low-margin sales of many small but needed items.

The successful variety chains that have survived are few. McCrory Stores, headquartered in York, is privileged to celebrate its 100th anniversary in 1982. The company today incorporates four variety chains founded by determined individuals who set out to profit by supplying the right merchandise to their customers at the right price. McCrorey, along with William Walker McLellan, Harold L. Green, and John Josiah Newberry, were the founders of the stores incorporated in the present-day company.

McCrorey was born in Indiana County, Pennsylvania, in 1860 and worked on farms and in a country store in his early years. At age 22 he opened his first "five and dime" in Scottdale, Pennsylvania, with $350 he had saved and another $200 he borrowed. By the turn of the century he operated 20 stores with annual sales near $.5 million. McCrorey is said to have dropped the silent "e" from his name to reduce the cost of the gilt-lettered signs over his storefronts.

John J. Newberry of Sunbury, Pennsylvania, opened the first J.J. Newberry store in 1911. William W. McLellan, a native of Glasgow, Scotland, worked for McCrory Stores and the Kress Company before starting the McLellan chain in 1916. Harold L. Green of Connecticut bought the interests of a small line of variety retailers in 1932.

During the period of prosperity after World War I, the McCrory Corporation opened the world's largest variety store in 1922 in Brooklyn, New York. Through a series of acquisitions, the McLellan and Green stores joined the McCrory stores over the years from 1933 to 1958.

To move goods at a lower cost, a 750,000-square-foot distribution center was built in York, Pennsylvania, and opened in 1963. In 1966 the McCrory-McLellan-Green headquarters was relocated from New York City to York, resulting in a much more efficient operation.

In 1972 the J.J. Newberry Company was acquired by the McCrory Corporation, adding about 750 Newberry stores to the 650 M-M-G stores then in operation. The name of the chain was changed to "McCrory Stores" in February 1975. McCrory Stores operates about 120 retail units in Pennsylvania today and nearly 800 retail units in the United States from border to border, coast to coast.

It has been said that York and McCrory grew up together. In addition to being the headquarters for the McCrory Stores home office and distribution center, York County is also the home of five of its retail stores. York's first McCrory store opened on Market Street in 1896, and is still there today, a proud part of the York community.

Top
In 1896 McCrory's 14th store was established in York at a location on Market Street. The store still operates at that site.

Above
McCrory Stores has its national headquarters and distribution center at 2955 East Market Street, York.

MEMORIAL OSTEOPATHIC HOSPITAL

Health care after World War II was changing rapidly. A few physicians in the York area recognized the need for an osteopathic hospital to provide the newest diagnostic and therapeutic services available at the time.

M. Carl Frey, D.O. was aware that Edmond M. Meisenhelder, M.D., the owner of the West Side Sanitarium in the 1200 block of West Market Street, was looking for patient-oriented and highly skilled physicians to purchase and manage the institution according to the standards he had set 25 years before.

Dr. Frey, a surgeon and community leader, appealed to a small group of physicians to join him in raising the money to buy the facility. Thirteen osteopathic doctors, in a concentrated effort, raised $90,000 and purchased the 45-bed hospital. The charter staff members of the Westside Osteopathic Hospital, organized in 1945, were Grover F. Artman, Paul J. Brown, M. Carl Frey, James M. Hotham, Raymond Israel, Roy O. Kammer, Ernest L. Markey, James Mullen, Phillip Smith, Kenneth T. Steigelman, Rachel A. Witmyer, Paul Woolridge, and Barclay Ziegler. Within three years, the physicians gave the hospital to the community, placing control and management in the hands of the public and freeing the institution for future growth.

Public support was solicited beginning in 1958 to build a new hospital on a tract of land in Spring Garden Township, east of York. Construction for the new facility, to be named the Memorial Osteopathic Hospital, began in June 1960 and was completed in 1962. Expansion would be a hallmark of the new hospital. Four years later, a third floor was added. In 1972 the first rural medical center owned by an osteopathic hospital, the Southern Medical Center, was built in New Freedom, southern York County. A short time later the Memorial Medical Center east of the main building was erected. The North Wing, another expansion project, housed facilities for radiology, nuclear medicine, physical medicine, emergency room, and outpatient departments. Two more buildings in the Memorial Medical Center opened in mid-1981.

Today Memorial Osteopathic Hospital is a community, full-service, acute care hospital with 170 beds. The nonprofit institution employs 650 people. The hospital will observe its 20th anniversary at 325 South Belmont Street on February 25, 1982.

Memorial Osteopathic Hospital is approved and accredited by the American Osteopathic Association for the training of interns and residents. It is the first community hospital in the nation to be accredited to offer professional postgraduate courses. The hospital also participates in clinical training for R.N. candidates at York College of Pennsylvania and L.P.N. candidates from the York Area Vocational-Technical School.

The hospital was the first to have the 24-hour advanced life support unit and crew in the York community. "Lifeline"/Medic 102 was a $70,000 gift to the hospital and the citizens of York County from the volunteers of the Bird Cage Gift Shop at the hospital. The ALS program was initiated on January 21, 1980.

Other departments at MOH include surgery, nursing, pediatrics, obstetrics and gynecology, family/general practice, urology, physical therapy, respiratory therapy, emergency medicine, anesthesia, internal medicine, personnel, volunteer, public relations, dietary, housekeeping, maintenance, laboratory, radiology, and nuclear medicine.

Below
The Westside Osteopathic Hospital opened in 1945 in the 1200 block of West Market Street, York.

Bottom
Memorial Osteopathic's current, modern facility is located at 325 South Belmont Street, York.

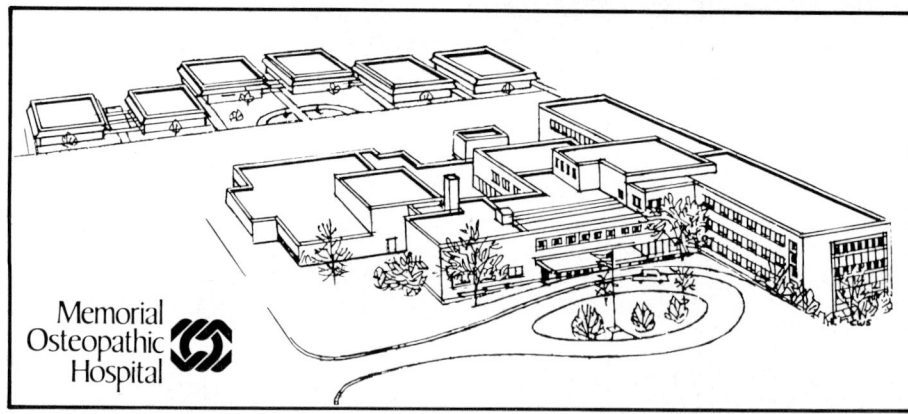

MOTTER PRINTING PRESS CO.

The Motter Printing Press Co. was founded early in 1953 by John C. Motter, a man who has spent most of his life in the manufacture of publication printing equipment. Today the company designs and manufactures high-speed web-fed printing presses and related machinery to printers of such nationally known magazines as *Reader's Digest, National Geographic, Ladies Home Journal, Parade, Redbook,* and others.

The roots of the company stretch back to 1838, when George F. Motter opened a small machine shop at the corner of Pershing Avenue and Princess Street in York. The George F. Motter's Sons business was passed down through the family for generations. John C. Motter became a journeyman machinist after serving his apprenticeship in the company in the early 1900s.

After serving in World War I, Motter returned to the George F. Motter's Sons business and developed an interest in rotogravure printing machinery. The company began manufacturing presses, the first of which was sold in 1935 and used to run a 2-color shoe ad in a Sears Roebuck catalog.

Four years before this firm went out of business, John C. Motter, with the support of his two sons, John Jr. and Frank, and a small nucleus of employees, established the John C. Motter Printing Press Co. (The name was changed in 1973.) Motter and his sons set up their engineering and sales offices on the second floor of a building on Roosevelt Avenue in York and bought the O.K. Clutch and Machinery Company building in Columbia, Pennsylvania, for manufacturing purposes. From a modest start with 61 people and 33,000 square feet of floor space, the company has experienced continual growth. Today, the parent company and its subsidiaries employ over 500 persons and occupy nearly 250,000 square feet of manufacturing and office area.

Ground was broken at 3900 East Market Street in York for the company's present facility in 1958, and in November 1966 all original operations of the firm were consolidated at this location. By this time, web-fed letterpress and offset presses had been added to the Motter line. Further expansion occurred in 1973 when the company entered the packaging market with the purchase of the Kidder Press line and the Stacy Machine Co. in Agawam, Massachusetts, and began producing flexographic, offset, and rotogravure package printing machinery. The division is now known as the Kidder-Stacy Co.

In 1976 the firm expanded its role in the packaging industry with the acquisition of the Rotographic Machinery Company of Owings Mills, Maryland. The subsidiary has added rotary die cutters and web offset presses to the Kidder-Stacy line.

Motter equipment, among the largest of its type in the world, is used to print some of the nation's most popular magazines, paperback books, mail order catalogs, and color supplements for Sunday newspapers, in addition to packaging materials for food and beverage containers. As it has for over a quarter of a century, the Motter Company will continue to operate in a manner that will provide the necessary research and development, engineering, and high-quality manufacturing for producing the type of equipment required by the graphic arts industry.

The Motter Printing Press Co. has its headquarters in a modern facility in East York.

THE NESS COMPANY, INC.

Wooden wagon wheels to axles, wheels, and rims for today's truck-trailer industry—this is the story of one of York's surviving family businesses, The Ness Company.

In a small Fairfield, Pennsylvania, factory in 1892, J. Lewis Ness and two workmen began the manufacture of wagon rims and wheels for the local trade. Ness soon discovered that his factory was too small and, for the business to grow and prosper, it would be necessary to move to a larger trading area. He made the move to York in the fall of 1893 so that his company could expand and he could solicit business in Philadelphia and New York.

Ness's new trade began to grow from his Broad Street factory. With the advent of the automobile, a line of wooden automobile wheels was included in the products manufactured by the fledgling enterprise. During the early 1920s, the local business was expanded to include a jobbing line of axles, steel rims, and garage supplies. With the increasing popularity of the automobile, the decline of the wagon wheel business was inevitable. The center of the automotive industry was moving to the Midwest, and Ness decided to discontinue the manufacturing portion of the business but to continue to supply automotive parts as a manufacturers' agency.

This new venture was only a modest success until 1934, when a manufacturers' agency partnership was formed between J. Lewis Ness and his son, Henry C. Ness, and registered in the name of the Ness Company. The partnership between father and son continued until the elder Ness's death. His widow, Josephine R. Ness, was a partner until 1946, when the partnership was dissolved. From then until 1961, the Ness Company operated under the proprietorship of Henry C. Ness. That year, a corporation was formed under the laws of the state of Pennsylvania, taking the name of The Ness Company, Inc., the name of the firm today. The corporation served as a manufacturers' agency, supplying components such as axles, wheels, rims, and suspensions to the truck-trailer industry.

In 1954, realizing the need in York for a truck-trailer service shop, the Truck Trailer Equipment Service Division was established. Located at 375 West Cottage Place, this division concentrated on repairs to all makes of truck-trailers and the mechanics were specialists in brakes and the installation of air suspensions and tag axles.

The Kelly Body Division was formed in 1964 with the purchase of the A.P. Kelly Body Works. This division, located at 501 Grantley Road, built custom truck bodies; installed lift gates, fifth wheels, and snowplows; replaced flooring in trucks and trailers; and performed many other services vital to the trucking industry, including painting and lettering.

In July 1970, Henry C. Ness, owner and president of the corporation, died and William R. McElhiney, his brother-in-law, became the new owner and president. McElhiney had joined the company in 1943. Realizing the advantages of operating from one location, the corporation built and moved into a modern facility in 1978 in the West York Industrial Park. The Truck Trailer Equipment Service and Kelly Body divisions were discontinued and only The Ness Company name was used.

Since 1960 the company has served as the exclusive sales representative for the Redco Corporation in Red Lion, Pennsylvania, manufacturer of truck rims for the transportation industry. The Ness Company continues to sell suspensions, axles, and fifth wheels, and to make repairs to truck-trailer and truck bodies.

After almost 90 years of operation, it appears that The Ness Company will remain a family-owned corporation. W. Scott McElhiney, son of the current president, and Thomas C. Wozniak, the president's son-in-law, are active in the business today and will carry on the tradition of capable leadership established by J. Lewis Ness in 1892.

Below
Henry C. Ness, right, and William R. McElhiney, his brother-in-law, are shown discussing business in this 1949 photograph.

Center and Bottom
The evolution of The Ness Company product line is shown here, from wooden wagon wheels to axles and rims for trucks.

R.S. NOONAN, INC.

Raymond S. Noonan was the general superintendent in the early 1930s for the Atlantic City Convention Hall construction project, the largest building project in the world at that time. He left that position in 1935 to come to York and establish his own construction firm, based on a principle of fair and honest treatment for clients and subcontractors. "When you buy Noonan-built, you buy the best," R.S. Noonan has said, and the phrase became the guidepost for a company that has since added over $800 million worth of construction to the American economy.

The construction firm's first home was a single room on the sixth floor of the old P.A.&S. Small Building, just off Continental Square. The company's expansion soon made it necessary to move to larger headquarters at 11 East Market Street, then again in 1948 to 26 North Duke Street, behind the Lafayette Club.

In 1968 the growing business moved to new and larger headquarters, the Noonan Building at 50 North Duke Street, formerly a seldom-used furniture warehouse that the company completely remodeled into a modern, 4-story office facility.

The R.S. Noonan company was incorporated in 1940 and by 1946 had grown into a firm with an annual business volume of $275,000. In 1952 Noonan Engineering Corporation, a group of about 40 architects, engineers, designers, and technical specialists capable of planning and developing all types of building facilities, was established as a wholly owned subsidiary. The firm today provides design and engineering requirements for the projects of R.S. Noonan, Inc.

The company by the mid-1950s was no longer just a local contractor, but was involved in operations in other parts of the country. The scope of the Noonan operation today ranges from the East Coast to the Midwest, from Canada to the Gulf of Mexico. The development of a specialization in 1955, the exclusive license to install patented underfloor warming systems to relieve frost build-up beneath floors in freezers and cold-storage warehouses, allowed the Noonan company to expand its operation coast to coast. Since 1955 R.S. Noonan, Inc., has installed these systems in more than three million square feet of floor space in the United States, Canada, and Puerto Rico.

Further diversification led the company to the development, construction, and ownership of shopping centers, including the Olmsted Plaza, Middletown, Pennsylvania, in 1959; the Queensgate Shopping Center, York, in 1962; and the Queensgate Shopping Center, Charlotte, North Carolina, in 1968.

To keep pace with developments in the industrialized system of building in the 1970s, R.S. Noonan secured a license from John Laing and Sons, London, the second largest building firm in England. Using this system, the York-based company erected condominiums and luxury apartments on the Atlantic Coast of Delaware and Maryland.

The expansion and growth of the R.S. Noonan organization led to the establishment of branch offices in Towson, Maryland, in 1965 (later relocated to Hunt Valley, Maryland, in 1974); in Greenville, South Carolina, in 1966; in Washington, D.C., in 1969; and Naples, Florida, in 1969.

Today R.S. Noonan, Inc., performs about $45 million worth of projects annually and is consistently ranked among the largest 400 general contractors in the United States. And, despite its growth and prestige, the company maintains a reputation for quality service that is highly recognized throughout the construction industry.

Buildings in York constructed by R.S. Noonan, Inc., include Memorial Osteopathic Hospital, York Hospital—Project '80, Noonan Building, York College Library, York College Gymnasium, Broad Park Manor, and Delphia House.

QUAKER CITY PAPER AND CHEMICAL CO.

Today's Quaker City Paper and Chemical Company started in 1946, when Morris Boyer and Bill Yeagley formed the Yeagley Paper Company in York. After several years of operation, Boyer and Yeagley sold their business to the Quaker City Paper Company of Philadelphia.

The bulk of the early business was the sale of coarse paper products for use in industrial and food-service applications. The first warehouse facilities were in an old 4-story building at Duke and Hay streets in York. The building had no heat. "The best that could be said for the elevator was that it was early American," one employee remembers. "The pigeons on the fourth floor left their trademark on much of our stock, but we survived."

Paul Newcomer, the current president of the company, joined the business as a salesman in 1953. In 1956 the firm moved to 1200 West Market Street in the old Black Hosiery Building, under the Franklin Discount Store. Howard Lee, the majority stockholder in Philadelphia, died in 1957, and in 1960 his widow sold the York Branch to Paul Newcomer.

A new, modern warehouse was completed at 300 North Sherman Street in February 1967. The business made another major change in 1968, when experienced personnel were hired and the company expanded into the janitor-supply business. The move proved a natural combination, since janitorial supplies and coarse paper products were often purchased by the same individuals.

The new venture increased the average size of the orders and the salesmen's time was utilized more effectively. The firm's name became outdated with the expansion, and was changed to Quaker City Paper and Chemical Company. With the acquisition of the Janitor Supply Division of Roberts and Meck in Harrisburg in 1969, the York operation was consolidated and placed firmly in the janitor-supply business.

In 1972 Quaker City acquired the coarse paper division of Andrews Paper House in York. The addition of Andrews, for many years the only paper house in the city, doubled the warehouse and office space and brought new avenues of expansion for Quaker City.

Quaker City Paper and Chemical Company today is comprised of six areas of business concentration—janitorial supplies, including equipment and chemicals; industrial packaging products, including stretch film and other packaging goods; food-service paper supplies; specialty advertising services and goods; gift packaging, including boxes and ribbons, for retail operations; and business forms.

The business has a market area of approximately 100 miles in a radius around York. About 70 people are employed in the five different areas of the company. Quaker City's headquarters is located at 300 North Sherman Street, York. In an effort to expand its operations and keep up with the progress of the area, Quaker City Paper and Chemical Company keeps an eye to the future for new and innovative specialty areas.

Headquarters for the Quaker City Paper and Chemical Company is located at 300 North Sherman Street.

I. REINDOLLAR AND SON, INC.

Sixteen cents per hour was the wage for carpenters in 1890, when Isaiah Reindollar started his contracting business in Gettysburg, Pennsylvania. And that salary wasn't necessarily measured in currency, as the carpenters were often paid in meat, clothing, hay, or other essentials.

Reindollar moved his company, I. Reindollar and Son, to York in 1907. After the founder's death in 1925, the enterprise was continued by his son, Thad, as an individual proprietorship until January 1, 1946. From this date until April 1, 1948, the firm continued under the same name but operated as a partnership between Thad Reindollar and Stewart A. Little. The business was incorporated on April 1, 1948, and today operates under the name, I. Reindollar and Son, Inc.

The transition from rough timber and wood peg construction to the modern reinforced concrete method used today was a gradual one. The efficient construction of present-day homes, public buildings, manufacturing plants, and commercial establishments conserves time and manpower and is facilitated by sophisticated equipment and prefabricated products.

I. Reindollar and Son has earned a fine reputation during its many years of service to York and York County. The company continues to be known for its excellent craftsmanship in steel and reinforced concrete construction work. Prominent structures erected by the company include York City Hall, the Yorktowne Hotel, the Martin Memorial Library, and the Historical Society of York County. Numerous educational facilities have been built by Reindollar, including William Penn Senior High School Annex, Hannah Penn Junior High School, the Dover Area Intermediate School, the Southwestern Intermediate School, and dormitories for York College of Pennsylvania. The education wing and the administration building for Christ Lutheran Church were also constructed by the York firm.

The erection of commercial structures is becoming increasingly important to I. Reindollar. The "Built by Reindollar" stamp is proudly borne by facilities that include the J.E. Baker Company office building; the office and service building for the Metropolitan Edison Company; the York toll building for General Telephone Company of Pennsylvania; the laboratory and processing building for Dentsply International, Inc.; and the Memorial Hall for the York County Agricultural Society on the York Fairgrounds.

Modern factories and warehouses are constructed by the Reindollar firm for new companies in the area, and modernization of existing plants is undertaken as well. Among the industries served by Reindollar are the York facility for Medusa Cement Company; the new plant and office site for Cole Steel Equipment Company, Inc.; warehouse facilities for AMF Inc.; plant additions and alterations to Yorktowne Paper Mills, Inc., and Yorktowne Board and Carton Company; and the hydraulics lab for Allis-Chalmers Corporation.

Hospital and medical facilities in the York area constructed by Reindollar include the 6-story nurses' quarters and auditorium for the York Hospital; the Colonial Medical Center; and the Lutheran Home for the Aged.

Today, I. Reindollar and Son, Inc., is a modern contracting company with a sophisticated in-house data processing department that handles payroll and job costing. But when it comes to quality construction and services, the firm maintains its traditional standards of excellence. As one employee said, "We're an old company with modern ways, but we keep some of those good old ways because they're still the best."

The construction of the York City Hall is shown (top) in this 1941 view of the I. Reindollar and Son crews working on the structure. The building, completed the following year, is located at West King and South Beaver streets (center).

Above
Isaiah Reindollar (right), founder of the company that bears his name, is shown with young Charles Stallsmith. Stallsmith later was active in the firm and served as chairman of the board.

SHIPLEY-HUMBLE, INC.

Like many firms in the early 1900s, today's Shipley-Humble began because of one man's vision and his talent for making things work. Thomas Shipley, a native of Jersey City, New Jersey, came to York to begin employment with the York Manufacturing Company (now the York Division of Borg-Warner) and worked his way up in the company—from general manager to vice-president, and finally to president.

Shipley's rise to the top had fulfilled all of his ambitions in the refrigeration field except one—to set up a system to market the company's products worldwide. When the directors chose not to proceed in this direction, Tom Shipley and his brothers, Samuel J. and William S., established 20 outlets around the world for York Manufacturing's air-conditioning equipment. The new company, formed in 1926, was called Thomas Shipley, Inc.

In 1929 the Shipleys sold all of their interest in the venture to York Manufacturing Company. That same year Tom Shipley, in an attempt to upgrade the area near Roosevelt Avenue across from the York Manufacturing Company's corporate offices, bought the entire block, demolished the buildings, and built Roosevelt Garage. The mammoth structure was constructed to provide parking and automobile maintenance for York Manufacturing employees. The garage also contained underground storage for 60,000 gallons of gasoline and fuel oil, and became the basis for the Shipley family's move into the petroleum supply business.

When Tom Shipley died in 1930, the Roosevelt Garage and Oil Service was passed on to his son, Samuel Hunt Shipley. In the 1930s, the business grew slowly but steadily, with the gasoline and fuel supply business becoming increasingly stronger. In 1939 Sam Shipley severed ties with York Manufacturing and purchased the York Oil Burner Company. The Roosevelt Garage was closed and sold, and the business renamed Roosevelt Oil Service. The oil company's offices were moved to Grantley Road, where they would remain until the early 1960s.

The firm's name was changed to York-Shipley, Inc., in July 1943 and the Roosevelt Oil Service became one of its divisions. The reconstructed company now manufactured, installed, fueled, and serviced oil furnaces and boilers, in addition to providing automotive fuel and supplies. Rationing during the war restricted the petroleum division's growth, but postwar sales boomed. Oil burner customers in 1948 numbered in the thousands, and the firm operated 30 Esso service stations, all within York's city limits.

The acquisition of eight local fuel companies expanded the organization. A merger with Humble-Mundis, Inc., in 1957 created another name change to the Shipley-Humble Division of York-Shipley. The various acquisitions doubled the firm's home heating business. An outgrowth was the increase in the division's "heavy oil" business, a segment which has since been a key Shipley-Humble market.

Lavern Brenneman became president of York-Shipley in 1960, and Sam Shipley served as chairman of the board. His son, William Shipley II, was the general manager of the Shipley-Humble division. Growth and expansion continued, and in 1968 the Shipley-Humble Division broke away from York-Shipley, Inc., and became an independent corporation. The manufacturing interests were sold to CompuDyne Corporation and William S. Shipley II became the first president of the new firm, Shipley-Humble, Inc.

The 1970s brought many changes to the business. Gas stations closed in the city and began opening in the suburbs. Shipley-Humble pioneered self-service gasoline stations, and in 1976 entered the grocery business by establishing Kwik Stop units with the self-serve stations. The market area expanded into Harrisburg and Lancaster and into the state of Maryland.

Today Shipley-Humble is one of the largest petroleum companies of its type in the United States, as well as one of the largest locally owned firms in York County. The company continues in the tradition of Tom Shipley to contribute strongly, day after day, to the economic and business climate of the York area.

Below
Thomas Shipley, founder of the present-day Shipley-Humble, Inc.

Bottom
The Roosevelt Garage fleet in 1935.

SNYDER AUTOMOBILE CO.

The history of the automotive industry in York is proud and illustrious, and the modern-day Snyder Auto Service Co. has carved a distinct niche in that colorful history.

At the turn of the century, a small business trading under the name, Snyder Cycle Company, sold a variety of goods to Yorkers, including bicycles, roller skates, Ediphones, and a horseless carriage livery service. The firm was started on February 12, 1898, by two brothers, Charles and Jacob Snyder. The company's first home was at 14-16 South Beaver Street.

The coming age of the automobile excited the Snyders and they began selling cars to Yorkers. Their business grew and its name was changed to Snyder Cycle and Auto Co., and Rebecca Snyder, the wife of Charles, joined the business.

As automobiles became more and more popular, the Snyder firm began to be known as one of the foremost automobile dealerships in the local area, as well as in the nation. In 1907 the Snyder operation moved to a new location at 229-31 West Market Street and the name was changed to the Snyder Auto Co.

In the early years, the Snyders were agents for makes including Pullman, White Steamer, Maxwell, Brush, Vim, Rickenbacker, Duryea, Reo, Hudson, and Olds. Success in the transportation industry even led Charles and Rebecca Snyder to design their own car, described as having "a Dissinger 2-cylinder gas engine, a leather belt, some pulleys, and a buggy."

Throughout its history, the company has been honored for its service to the transportation industry. Perhaps the most prestigious recognition came in May 1946, when Charles S. Snyder was honored with the world's automotive giants, including Ford, Olds, and Nash, at the "Golden Jubilee Celebration" of the Automotive Industry sponsored by the National Automobile Manufacturers Association in Detroit. Snyder, in addition to this recognition, was elected into the "Automobile Hall of Fame," as one of the two oldest franchised automobile dealers in the United States.

The two sons of Charles S. Snyder, Charles E. and Stuart H. Snyder, entered the business in the '30s. In 1954 the operation was incorporated under the name Snyder Automobile Co. and began to shift its focus to trucks, with the truck division operating under the trade name, Snyder Auto Service Co. Soon the franchise for automobiles would be dropped entirely. The business, a vital part of downtown York for many years, needed

Below
Today, Snyder Auto Service Co. is headquartered in a spacious building at 2150 South Queen Street.

Bottom
Snyder Automobile Co. was previously located at 229-31 West Market Street, York.

additional space to accommodate large, modern-day trucks; a new and modern facility at 2150 South Queen Street was completed in 1980.

Today the firm is the sales and service representative for numerous brands of trucks, including White, Autocar, Western Star, Iveco, and Magirus. The new, spacious 13,500-square-foot parts department, stocked with a computer-controlled inventory, is staffed with factory-trained personnel and is capable of supplying needed parts quickly.

The 12,800-square-foot service area is divided into 12 drive-through bays with individual mechanic stations to handle service and maintenance needs. Featured in the service area is a complete heavy-duty, air hydraulically controlled frame-straightening system for trucks and trailers, which

employs a precision laser optics alignments system.

The third generation of Snyders is active in the business today. Charles W. Snyder, son of Charles E. Snyder, is the sales manager, and Karl C. Snyder, son of president Stuart H. Snyder, is the company's business manager.

D.F. STAUFFER BISCUIT COMPANY, INC.

In 1871 David F. Stauffer, the son of a Mennonite minister, took over the cake and cracker business that had been founded back in 1858 by Jacob Weiser. When Stauffer entered his new venture, five barrels of crackers were considered a good volume of production per day. The delivery of the crackers was by wheelbarrow, often by Stauffer himself.

Today, the D.F. Stauffer Biscuit Company is a multimillion-dollar corporation, distributing its products nationwide and employing over 200 people. The primary products have changed from crackers and pretzels to cookies, but the business remains family-operated by the Stauffers and dedicated to a tradition of quality that dates back over 100 years.

The D.F. Stauffer Biscuit Company, originally located at 128 South George Street in downtown York, became an incorporated business in 1913 with more than 25 employees. At the time of incorporation, D.F. Stauffer brought his four sons into the business with him—Calvin, Harry, William, and D. Preston.

After the founder's death in 1921, his eldest son, Calvin, assumed the presidency. Calvin Stauffer led his family's business into a period of growth that would see the company become a leading supplier of cookies, crackers, and pretzels in the York area.

David E. Stauffer, Calvin's son, took over the leadership of the company in 1955. By 1960 the firm had outgrown its downtown York facility and moved to a new plant with 65,000 square feet. At the time of the move, the business was producing cookies, crackers, and pretzels on two oven lines and one marshmallow enrobing line.

In 1964 another third-generation Stauffer, Neil P., son of D. Preston, was elected to the position of president. In 1981 a fourth-generation Stauffer, David E. Stauffer, Jr., was elected to the presidency after the retirement of Neil P. Stauffer.

In 1970 the D.F. Stauffer Biscuit Company added about 25,000 square feet to the facilities, and in

1977 an additional 10,000 square feet of warehousing space was added. The bakery and office currently encompass about 100,000 square feet, using approximately 8.5 acres for building and parking lots.

Corporate headquarters of the D.F. Stauffer Biscuit Company today are located at Belmont and Sixth Avenue in York. The firm's present officers are David E. Stauffer, chairman of the board and secretary; David E. Stauffer, Jr., president and treasurer; Michael J. Treacy, vice-president of finance; Donald W. Hagenow, vice-president of sales; and Judith Doxsey, assistant secretary and assistant treasurer.

Today the company concentrates on developing its private label business in short-run, specialized types of cookies and aims its business at segmented markets. The firm has established a reputation as a quality and a specialty house. The Stauffers have the sophisticated equipment and the experience to make virtually every kind of cookie imaginable, pleasing cookie-lovers everywhere.

Top
In 1898 D.F. Stauffer's delivery wagon delivered crackers and other baked goods to Yorkers.

Above
D.F. Stauffer, seated in the center (with beard, coat, and tie), is seen with his employees in this 1879 photograph taken at the site of his first bakery operation at 128 South George Street, York.

TELEDYNE-McKAY

The McKay name has been associated with the chain industry since 1881, when James McKay, a native of Ireland, and his partner, Thomas Hammond, started a chain-forging and fire-welding works in Pittsburgh. McKay purchased Hammond's interests in 1887 and went into partnership with his sons, Robert J., J. Albert, and later, Thomas J. McKay. The firm continued as a partnership until 1905, when the company absorbed the Iron City Chain Works and incorporated under the name James McKay and Company.

By this time, new facilities were needed and a 10-acre plot of ground was purchased in McKees Rocks, a suburb of Pittsburgh. Buildings were erected to house fire-weld chain hammers and drop-forging shops, making it the most modern chain plant in the world at that time. The chains and forgings produced at McKees Rocks were used throughout growing industries in America. During World War I, mile after mile of anchor chain for the Liberty fleets was produced in the fire-welding plant, and the company's chains were also used for tank and truck towing, submarine nets, and mine sweeper chains. When the automobile age came after the war, a large new market for tire chains and chains for agriculture developed. Producing relatively small chains by manual fire-welding methods was too expensive, and the industry turned to electric-welded continuous lengths of chain.

In February 1919, two major independent fire-welding chain companies merged with the James McKay Company and formed the United States Chain and Forging Company. The newly merged firm began looking for a location to build an electric-weld chain plant for the automatic production of chain, ultimately deciding on York. Forty acres of land along Grantley Road in York were purchased by the company on May 21, 1919, from the Northern Central Railroad and the P.A.&S. Small Land Company. The York plant was constructed and began operations by the end of 1919. As the business grew, new and faster equipment was added to keep up with the demands for electric-welded chain and additional buildings were constructed for heat-treating, plating, and warehousing operations.

Tire chains were the primary products during the 1930s at the McKay Company, shown in the background.

The chains used on automobile tires provided the largest market for the McKay production, and that segment proved to depend on the whims of nature. The fortunes of the McKay Company (the name was changed once more in 1931) were dependent on the degree of severity of the winters in the '20s and '30s. In an effort to challenge this unpredictable element, the company began to develop new product lines, including the production of automobile bumpers and metal furniture.

The McKay Company entered the arc-welding electrode field in 1935, a move that required a great amount of research and development. By the onset of World War II, the company was firmly established in that field, supplying millions of pounds of mild and stainless electrodes for use in shipbuilding, tank construction, armor welding, and other defense industries. Large tonnages of chain from both plants were supplied to the war effort, and just three weeks after the attack on Pearl Harbor the company was one of the first in the area to be awarded the Army/Navy "E" Award, for its abilities to fulfill military demands for large quantities of chain.

After the war, the McKay Company returned to its program of development and expansion, adding new types of chains and new products in the electrode division. The old plant at McKees Rocks was phased out in 1958 and the operation transferred to York. The Automatic Welding Company of Waukesha, Wisconsin, was purchased in 1960; also, an extensive program of expansion at the York plant was begun. Concurrently, new technological efforts to increase production efficiency and expand product lines were implemented along with expanded research and engineering departments to accomplish these objectives.

In 1968 the McKay Company became a separate operation in the large and growing diversified company, Teledyne, Inc., headquartered in Los Angeles. Since that time, Teledyne McKay in York has continued the time-honored goal of manufacturing high-quality products with an emphasis on service to its customers.

PARTNERS IN PROGRESS • 215

SUSQUEHANNA BROADCASTING CO.

Susquehanna Broadcasting Co. is a diversified communications and manufacturing company with corporate headquarters at 140 East Market Street, York. Through its subsidiaries and divisions, the firm owns and operates 15 radio and television stations and three cable television companies. The York County operations of Susquehanna Broadcasting Co. include its corporate headquarters, WSBA Radio, WSBA-TV, Cable TV of York, and The Pfaltzgraff Co.

CORPORATE HEADQUARTERS

The Susquehanna Broadcasting Co. corporate headquarters are housed in seven buildings located in the heart of historic downtown York. The facilities used range from a modern office building to several restored properties dated at over 100 years old. The firm's commitment and dedication to downtown York has been demonstrated by the fact that six of the seven properties making up the corporate headquarters complex have been acquired and renovated within the past 10 years.

RADIO DIVISION

WSBA-AM began its operations in 1942 and today serves the York/Lancaster/Harrisburg region of central Pennsylvania. WSBA has achieved wide acclaim for its efforts in community service, and has a successful and envied record of programming and sales achievement.

WSBA-FM, a "beautiful music" station, made its broadcast debut in 1947 and serves the same area as its AM sister station.

The Radio Division also owns and operates radio stations in Atlanta, Dallas/Fort Worth, Miami, Orlando, Long Island, Cincinnati, Akron, Toledo, Indianapolis, and Scranton/Wilkes-Barre.

WSBA-TV

WSBA-TV is the oldest continuously operating UHF television station in the United States. A CBS affiliate, TV-43 offers a wide variety of network programming and local news to the York area.

Below left
WSBA-AM and FM headquarters are located along Route 30 east of York.

Below
Corporate headquarters for the Susquehanna Broadcasting Co. is located at a modern site at 140 East Market Street.

CABLE TV

Cable TV of York has over 30,000 subscribers and, in addition to basic cable service, also provides the York area access to Home Box Office (HBO). The company also owns and operates cable systems in Bath and Brunswick, Maine, and is currently building a system in East Providence, Rhode Island.

THE PFALTZGRAFF CO.

The Pfaltzgraff Co., the oldest family-owned pottery in continuous operation in the United States, traces its roots to the early 1800s when George Pfaltzgraff left his German Rhineland home and established a pottery in York County. Louis J. Appell, Jr., the president of today's Susquehanna Broadcasting Co., is the great-great-grandson of George Pfaltzgraff.

Today, with a distribution network throughout the United States and Canada, The Pfaltzgraff Co. is the largest manufacturer of stoneware table and gift wares in America. York County operations of the company include the corporate headquarters and design center in downtown York, manufacturing plants in West York, Thomasville, and Dover, and retail outlets at Pottery Hill and in the Village Green Shopping Center. The firm also has two plants in Adams County, Pennsylvania, and retail stores in several locations throughout the country.

Top
Pfaltzgraff pottery makers are shown in this turn-of-the-century photograph. George W. Pfaltzgraff, grandson of the founder, is standing in the boxcar door, wearing a bow tie.

Left
Pfaltzgraff's newest facility is a modern manufacturing plant and distribution center near Thomasville, Pennsylvania.

Above
Pfaltzgraff's popular Village pattern.

H.J. WILLIAMS CO., INC.

Incorporated in 1930, the H.J. Williams Co., Inc., headquartered in York, continues to operate as one of the leading firms in the heavy-construction industry throughout Pennsylvania.

During its history the H.J. Williams Co., Inc., has handled many federal, state, and municipal contracts for construction, as well as for private industry. They encompass all aspects of heavy construction for highways, bridges, dams, flood control projects, etc.

Within the past 10 years, the company has expanded through diversification and now operates a number of fully owned subsidiaries. Elderlee, Inc., located in Oaks Corners, New York; and L.S. Lee and Son of Pa., Inc., located in York, Pennsylvania, and in Elkridge, Maryland; have provided the company with facilities for producing guardrail for highways, concrete pipe, highway signs, steel fabrication, sand and gravel operations, and hot dip and mechanical galvanizing. L.S. Lee and Son of Pa., Inc., located at 1150 Greenwood Road in York, has the only mechanical galvanizing line for fasteners on the East Coast. Mechanical galvanizing is a new process of coating fasteners and other items that have long been a problem to the hot-dip galvanizer.

H.J. Williams Co., Inc., is located at South Sumner Street in West York. President R.E. Hirschman is responsible for developing the company into its present-day size. Construction performed by the firm stretches across the country, but is centered in Pennsylvania and along the East Coast. H.J. Williams Co., Inc., also has a local engineering staff and work force to handle the construction needs of local industry and individuals.

The company is currently involved in several large projects for the Pennsylvania Department of Transportation in Williamsport, Lycoming County; and Duncansville, Blair County. They have recently completed two concrete paving projects for the Florida Department of Transportation in Sarasota and Bradenton, Florida. The firm has also completed several flood control projects for the city of Lebanon, Pennsylvania.

Yorkers are familiar with the Richland Avenue Flood Control project completed by H.J. Williams Co., Inc., in 1977. The company is currently starting work on another project to benefit the revitalization of the city of York, the Boat Basin for the Codorus Creek.

The Richland Avenue Project, completed by H.J. Williams Co., Inc., is a familiar route for many Yorkers.

THE WILTON COMPANY

Metalware products manufactured by The Wilton Company of Columbia, Pennsylvania, involve natural elements, the keen skills of talented craftsmen, and the ancient method of sand molding.

Ralph Wilton, Sr., adopted the principle of sand molding and founded the Susquehanna Casting Company in Wrightsville in 1892. For over 40 years, Wilton's sand-molding foundry poured a wide range of gray-iron industrial castings.

In 1951 Ralph "Bud" Wilton, Jr., established The Wilton Brass Company and acquired another foundry in Columbia, Pennsylvania, directly across the river from the plant his father had built. The younger Wilton's foundry poured brass for industrial use.

Wilton initiated a new metalware line, the "Federal" service plate, in 1962 for use in a New York City restaurant with the atmosphere of an 18th-century English pub. The service plate was made of a new alloy called Armetale® (Latin derivation meaning "Art Metal"). The alloy, comprised of 10 different metals, produced a metal that looked and felt like pewter but had practical advantages pewter lacked.

The Armetale service plate proved popular, and a one-piece line of the dinnerware was sold in gift shops in a tri-state area surrounding the Wilton home base. Soon a new gift item, a mug, was introduced in the Armetale line. By late 1962 The Wilton Brass Company formed a retail sales division with representation in Pennsylvania, Maryland, New Jersey, Delaware, and Virginia.

Product lines continued to be introduced, and before long a number of area restaurants were using Armetale plates and mugs on their tables. In April 1963 the company formed a College Division, selling Armetale brand products to colleges and universities. By June 1963 a Premium Sales and Promotion Division was established, and the first promotional program was launched in conjunction with a noted Newark, New Jersey, brewery.

"Custom cresting," a method of personalizing the Wilton product line, was introduced in 1963. The process offered customers the opportunity to have their name, logo, or a rendering of almost any scene cast in the product itself. Armetale not only looked great, but now it could carry a message.

By 1972 the product line had grown from one item to a selection of over 300. The company that had four employees in 1962 now employed several hundred. Many of the Wilton products were designs of reproductions of original pewter pieces, created by Nathaniel Austin and other noted craftsmen of the 18th century.

A new division of metalware, created by noted designer Bruce Fox, was added in 1975. "From the fields, the waters, the forest, and the islands," was a group of primarily large, highly polished serving pieces modeled after plants and creatures in nature.

Wilton products became popular during the American bicentennial celebration in 1976, and sales growth continued during the following years. In 1977 R.P. Wilton announced the appointment of his eldest son, Fred, as chief executive officer of the family business. The name of the firm was changed to The Wilton Company, a new logo was designed to incorporate the company and its divisions, and the corporate office in Columbia and the showroom at 225 Fifth Avenue, New York, began to take on a new, more contemporary image.

As the company entered the 1980s, growth and expansion followed as new, creative product lines continued to be added. The Wilton name on a piece of metalware has come to signify quality craftsmanship and a tradition of beauty and excellence.

Top
Ralph "Bud" Wilton established The Wilton Brass Company in 1951.

Above
A place setting in the Wilton Armetale® product line.

WOLF MANAGEMENT SERVICE COMPANY

The goods in Adam Wolf's store during the 1840s were numerous and varied household goods, lumber, coal, animal feed, and according to an early ledger, "country gin."

Wolf's store opened in 1843 in the York County village of New Holland, now known as Saginaw. The proximity of the community to the Susquehanna River enabled Wolf to secure lumber to sell to his customers. Lumber was rafted down the river to Saginaw, then sold by Wolf. And, when the season came, the storekeeper joined his neighbors to catch shad in the

river, then sold them as part of his store's inventory.

In 1852 Adam's son, George Wolf, moved from the New Holland location to a site north of York along the new Northern Central Railroad. Since Mr. Wolf served as postmaster, schoolmaster, storekeeper, and railroad stationmaster, the stop on the railroad was soon known as "Mount Wolf."

The Wolf family business grew, and so did its clientele. Confederate troops stopped at Wolf's store for supplies on a raid through the county and took away almost all of the storekeeper's merchandise, paying him in Confederate dollars. Those bills today hang on the wall of Wolf Management Service Company's president, John D. Zimmerman.

As the years passed the Wolf

family concentrated its efforts on the lumber and home-building supply market. Successive companies were located in Wrightsville and York, in addition to Mount Wolf, and in the mid-1940s the business was incorporated as Wolf Supply Company.

An outgrowth of Wolf Supply Company, the Wolf Management Service Company was formed in the mid-1970s to provide a variety of administrative and managerial services for Wolf operating companies. Today Wolf Management Service Company operates from headquarters in historic downtown York at 20 West Market Street. The firm offers financial administration, personnel training and development, sales promotion, legal services, group insurance administration, safety programs, and a number of other managerial services to its associated operating companies.

Operating companies served by the Wolf Management Service group span an area from Allentown, Pennsylvania, in the north to Richmond, Virginia, in the south. More than 30 operating units are served by WMS in Pennsylvania, Maryland, Virginia, West Virginia, and Delaware.

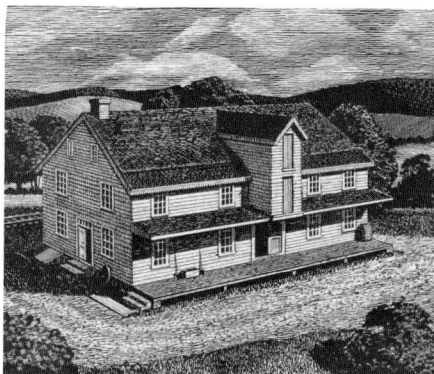

Left
Adam Wolf was the founder of a retail store in 1843 in the York County village of New Holland (now Saginaw).

Top
The George A. Wolf & Sons lumber facility, shown here in an illustration from the 1920s, was a predecessor of today's Wolf Supply Company.

Above
George Wolf, Adam's son, opened this store in the community that would later bear his name, Mount Wolf.

YORK AREA CHAMBER OF COMMERCE

With the start of the 20th century, all signs pointed to a prosperous future for the thriving and growing community of York, Pennsylvania.

Two years before, in early January 1898, a meeting was called for the merchants of York, "to perfect an organization for their better protection." On January 28, the same group met again and unanimously adopted a constitution and bylaws of the Merchants Association of York, electing J. Frank Gable president. The Association gradually developed a program of civic improvement which resulted in a merging of interests of commerce and industry in York to form the Chamber of Commerce in 1909.

"We take up odd jobs for the City that nobody else will touch," a Chamber of Commerce advertisement said in 1910. The ad boasted "Over 350 members of York's most progressive citizens—wide awake for York!!" The total membership of the Chamber has grown from that number in 1910 to nearly 1,500 members in 1981. In 1912 the York Chamber became the eighth charter member of the then-fledgling Chamber of Commerce of the United States.

The York Area Chamber of Commerce boasts a long and impressive list of projects and accomplishments since 1898 that have enhanced York and York County and made life better and more productive for its citizens: The Wrightsville-Columbia Bridge, the Crispus Attucks Center, the Yorktowne Hotel, Indian Rock Dam, York's Memorial Stadium, the Halloween Parade, the York Airport, the expansion of York Hospital, the development of the United Fund in York, the Credit Bureau, the York Area Vocational School, the County Solid Waste Authority, and the York Area Transportation Authority.

From its longtime headquarters on the third floor of the Schmidt Building on Continental Square, the Chamber in 1965 moved to its present headquarters at 13 Market Way East opposite the York County Courthouse.

It's been said, "In good times or bad, the work of the Chamber goes on. In tougher times the work of the Chamber is more important than ever." Today the Chamber of Commerce continues to serve as a dynamic, guiding force for York as it has for nearly a century. The organization is dedicated to the revitalization of downtown York and fully supports such important community projects as the exciting Market Way development.

In an effort to promote the study of economics and the free enterprise system, the Chamber, in conjunction with York College of Pennsylvania, holds a seminar for teachers in the county. The seminar culminates with the Henry D. Schmidt Memorial lecture and dinner, an event which has attracted such prominent persons as President Gerald R. Ford and political commentator William F. Buckley to York as speakers.

The York Area Chamber of Commerce has fostered several organizations over the years which have since become independent and self-sufficient: the Credit Bureau, York County Conservation Council, the Jaycees, and the Regional Planning Commission. Other organizations in the area use the Chamber of Commerce as a base of support.

The York Area Chamber of Commerce was named an accredited organization by the Chamber of Commerce of the United States in November 1976—one of only 319 accredited chambers out of more than 5,000 local chambers in the country at the time. "Wide Awake for York"—it was true in 1910 and is true for the York Area Chamber of Commerce today.

"Locate your factory in York, Pennsylvania," said the sign on an early Pullman car, made in York. The York Area Chamber of Commerce today continues to promote business and industry in York.

PARTNERS IN PROGRESS • 221

YORK BARBELL COMPANY

The York Barbell Company has been a part of weight-lifting history since 1932, when the firm first designed the York barbell since used in several Olympic Games and countless international competitions.

The success of the company has been achieved largely through the efforts of its founder and president, Bob Hoffman. Born in 1898 in Tifton, Georgia, Hoffman was often sickly as a child, once almost dying from a double blow of typhoid fever and diphtheria. Things changed, however, and he went on to become one of the greatest athletes in the Pittsburgh area.

Hoffman won many marathon races, but his greatest success was in rowing, competing as an oarsman in the 1915 National Champion "Eights," National Quartermile Championship, and the 1925 World Championship. His amazing feats in marathon racing and in rowing prompted Pittsburgh-based newspapers to dub him the "Iron Man."

A veteran of World War I, Hoffman began experimenting with boxing while in the service. He became an amateur boxer of above-average repute, sparring with Gene Tunney and George Carpentier. After the war, he settled in York and formed the York Oil Burner Company with limited capital. His own personal incentive program helped to build the business. In the early days Hoffman would often travel with just enough money for a sandwich, so if he did not sell a burner, he could not get home.

His interest in athletics never waned and he decided to sponsor the York Oil Burner Athletic Club weight-lifting team, the forerunner of today's York Barbell Club (the national weight-lifting champions for over 50 years). In conjunction with the creation of the York Barbell Company in 1932, Bob Hoffman began to publish "Strength and Health," a magazine devoted to the sport of Olympic weight lifting and to the principles of physical fitness for people in all walks of life. In the 1940s, Hoffman's company branched out into the health food business with the development of a line of vitamins and the introduction of a line of Hi-Proteen products.

The "York" name today is on more barbells around the globe than any other company name and the more than 50 Hi-Proteen products are used by amateur and professional athletes throughout the world. The York Barbell Company also markets Blue Rock Mountains Spring Water and publishes *Muscular Development*, a magazine designed for the modern body builder and power lifter.

Hoffman has used his status as publisher and editor-in-chief to become a leader in teaching what he calls "the ways of health." He has also authored 64 books and written thousands of articles.

Bob Hoffman and his York Barbell Company have become synonymous with philanthropy, in addition to business and athletics. Through Hoffman's sponsorship, United States weight-lifting teams have competed in worldwide championships. More recently Hoffman has been active in promoting softball and power lifting on local, national, and international levels. York Barbell Company now sponsors eight softball teams, and with Hoffman leading the way, York has developed one of the finest softball complexes in the world and has served as host for national championship tournaments for over a decade.

The company's philanthropic efforts stretch into other areas of community interest, including the construction of a physical therapy facility at York Hospital, donations of land to the York Area Youth Development Foundation, the development of the Bob Hoffman Memorial YMCA Camping Center, and generous contributions to the Salvation Army.

A resolution in 1971 by the International Weight-lifting Federation Congress proclaimed Bob Hoffman to be "The Father of World Weight-lifting," and befitting the honor, York has been approved as the site of the official Bob Hoffman Weight-lifting Hall of Fame. The new 34,000-square-foot facility contains an extensive collection of weight-lifting memorabilia honoring athletes from around the world who have contributed to the sport. Because of Bob Hoffman and his dedication, people from all over the world will soon be coming to York, indeed a city of champions.

Below
Bob Hoffman proudly poses with a partial collection of the medals he won in rowing and weight-lifting during the 1920s.

Bottom
During the '30s orders for barbells were shipped like this from the York Barbell Company building at 51 North Broad Street, York.

THE YORK DISPATCH

VOL. I-NO. I THE *EVENING DISPATCH* MONDAY, MAY 29, 1876

The news of the day in the borough of York was uneventful. Zion Lutheran Church's Sunday School was observing its 47th anniversary, the Western Market was expanding, and Companies A and C of the National Guard were making plans on the eve of Decoration Day to remember the war dead.

At 10 East Market Street, the publisher and editor of the new newspaper, Hiram Young, and his staff of eight assessed their new venture. For almost 12 years, Young had been publisher of the *True Democrat*, a Republican newspaper of great influence in the city and the state. With this success and his evaluation that York needed an evening newspaper, he launched the *Evening Dispatch*, later to be renamed the *York Dispatch*.

"By the fruits of your labor you shall be judged," Young wrote in the paper's first editorial. "If we give the people a good paper, they will find it out, and if we defraud them, it cannot be hid." The first edition was small—four pages with five columns of news per page. The paper sold for one cent each, six cents a week, or three dollars a year. The first front page contained a short story by Helena Dixon, entitled "John's Mother-In-Law," and an advertisement for "Choice Bananas" at P.C. Wiest's. The local news was found inside, grouped under the headlines "Latest Mail" and "Local Department."

Young had come to York from Schaefferstown, Lebanon County. Before he started his paper, he worked in a bookstore, then owned a printing shop. In 1901, 25 years after publication of his first edition of the evening newspaper, Young incorporated his business as the Dispatch Publishing Company with himself and his sons, Edward S., Charles P., William L., and John F., as the officers.

The Dispatch Publishing Company gained control of the *York Daily* in 1904 and purchased the current headquarters of the *Dispatch* at 15 and 17 East Philadelphia Street. The building, an old carriage works, features a cast-iron facade and is listed on the National Register of Historic Places.

In events that occurred around the turn of the century, the *True Democrat* became the *Weekly Dispatch*, but its publication was suspended after the acquisition of the *York Daily*. All efforts were devoted to publishing the *Daily* in the morning and the *Dispatch* in the evening. The morning paper was sold in 1918 to the Gazette Publishing Company.

The Dispatch Publishing Company today remains a business owned and controlled by the Young family. Hiram Young died in 1905 and his sons carried on the work of the company. The last of these sons, John F., died in 1947 and was succeeded as president by his son, D. Philip. D. Philip Young died in 1975 and today the firm is operated by his son and daughter, Robert L. Young as president and Pauline Young Gallatin as vice-president. Robert's sons also serve in the business—Don H. as treasurer, Michael as secretary, and Carl E. in the editorial department.

Over 50,000 people subscribe to the *York Dispatch* today, and the newspaper is published each evening except Sunday. The company also publishes the *Free Press*, a weekly paper serving 37,000 homes in southern York County and northern Maryland.

An addition has been built next to the historic *Dispatch* building to make way for larger and more efficient presses. The expansion, over 100 years after the newspaper's founding, echoes Hiram Young's vision in his first *Dispatch* editorial: "As we progress and feel able, we hope to make every necessary improvement to place the *Evening Dispatch* in the ranks of the leading daily newspapers in the country."

Top
The *Dispatch* building, dating back to the 1880s, is listed on the National Register of Historic Places.

Above
Additions to the *Dispatch* building in 1980 reflect over a century of growth and expansion by the newspaper.

YORK CONTAINER COMPANY

Robert H. Warren, Charles S. Wolf, and Reuben O. Willman, all employees of an independent manufacturer of corrugated shipping containers located in the York area, had a desire to own and manage their own enterprise.

In April 1954, the three men struck out on their own to form a local manufacturing company of corrugated packaging. Offices were set up at 303 North Sherman Street, York, and the business was operated as a 3-way partnership.

Machinery was ordered, a sales force developed, and in May 1954, the operation acquired a 15-acre site in East York on a spur of the Pennsylvania Railroad. The company was officially incorporated as the York Container Company on June 17, 1954. The payroll consisted of nine people with the starting wage for new employees at 93 cents per hour, or $37.50 per week.

Construction of the 78,000-square-foot plant was begun immediately and completed January 1955. On October 25, 1955, the company held its first sales meeting. The staff had grown to a total of 17 people with a total of over 200 years of experience in the industry.

By December 1954 the plant building, although not complete, was ready to be occupied. The company printed and joined its first container on December 15, 1954. The corrugated board was supplied by an outside converter, but production was under way. Total annual sales by the end of 1954 were $95,081.35.

The corrugator machine installations were completed in January 1955, and on January 18 of that year the first carton was completed, made from linerboard and corrugated material supplied in rolls and completely manufactured in the company's plant. The finished facility was now capable of manufacturing B or C flute products or double-wall corrugated by combining the two flutes. In May 1955 a second shift was added and production has been uninterrupted ever since.

In February 1956, an A flute machine was installed to expand the company's productive flexibility. By combining A fluted board with existing C and B flute manufacturing, York Container became one

of the first companies in the industry to offer triple-wall corrugated products to its customers.

York Container Company took its part in a historic medical event on April 25, 1958. The Salk anti-polio vaccine had just been developed and the manufacturing laboratories located in Marietta, Pennsylvania, needed cartons to ship the serum. Time was critical, but in less than a day's manufacturing time the firm delivered containers to ship $100,000 worth of the vaccine throughout the country.

By the mid-1960s, demand for the company's product had ex-

Top
The 1981 board of directors of York Container (left to right): Dennis Willman, Charles S. Wolf, Reuben Willman, Constance Wolf, Charles S. Wolf, Jr., and Samuel Willman.

The York Container Company plant on Mount Zion Road is shown in this 1954 photograph (above) and in this current photograph (right).

panded to the point that a physical plant addition was necessary. A 40,000-square-foot addition was begun in 1964 and completed in May 1965. Additional manufacturing equipment was purchased and a third shift added.

Robert H. Warren, president and one of the original founders of the business, retired in 1970. Reuben O. Willman became the chairman of the board and Charles S. Wolf became the new president and chief executive officer.

The office facilities of the York Container Company were doubled in 1980 and the existing portion renovated and improved. Design and testing facilities were expanded and new employee dining and personal areas added. Additional equipment was installed to increase production by 30 percent.

tainer Company is located near the junction of Routes 83 and 30—still on the spur of the Penn Central Railroad. By 1981 the company was manufacturing over 400 million square feet of corrugated fiberboard per year. In lineal feet, that total is enough to cross the United States four times in a continuous ribbon six feet wide.

More than 215 people are employed in various operations around the clock. These employees average more than 10 years' experience with the firm and 28 people who began in the first year of operation are still with the company.

A modern company-owned truck fleet of six tractors and 30 trailers deliver packaging throughout the day. The fleet and common carrier shipments help deliver over 12

Today York Container is a modern and widely diversified manufacturer of corrugated packaging materials. The company is capable of manufacturing packaging ranging from a carton to pack a compact car body to a wrapper small enough to pack small bottles of capsules. Order quantities vary from "one of a kind" special cartons to 40,000 or 50,000 cartons at a time. Each year over 12,000 orders are processed for more than 600 active customers.

The plant facility in York has been expanded to over 124,000 square feet on 22 acres. York Con-

trailer loads of merchandise a day throughout the continental United States and occasionally overseas.

A management team of 16 people with a total of more than 400 years of experience in the industry take part in the daily business operation. Five of these are members of the Wolf and Willman families, who still own the company and are now into the second generation of management activity. The board of directors is currently comprised of Reuben O. Willman, Charles S. Wolf, Dennis E. Willman, Samuel A. Willman, Charles S. Wolf, Jr., and Constance L. Wolf.

Top
A 1954 clipping from the York Dispatch shows R.O. Willman, Robert H. Warren, and Charles S. Wolf visiting the site of their new plant.

YORK HOSPITAL

On a cold day in January 1880, a group of York businessmen met to deal with a serious problem. The city's population was growing rapidly and the need for a hospital was becoming urgent.

To respond to the need, Samuel Small and other Yorkers created the York Hospital and Dispensary Association. Small contributed a 3-story dwelling on West College Avenue "for the medical and surgical treatment of the sick and the injured." Then he and others raised $70,000 to convert the structure into a hospital to serve York.

The first facility was modestly furnished, containing 12 wrought-iron bed frames with headboards and mattresses purchased for $98. An early visitor to the hospital in the spring of 1880 was impressed by the institution and wrote, "It is eminently suited for hospital purposes, with a yard finely shaded by fruit trees."

The maximum basic room rate was set at six dollars per week, but if the rates were too high for someone needing medical attention, they were waived entirely. It was clear that the rates would not sustain the new hospital, so a tradition of dependence on the people of York for assistance was established. Voluntary efforts of the hospital's board of directors and the hospital's auxiliary allowed the institution to begin a record of medical care for the people of York and York County. Five surgical and eight medical patients stayed overnight at the hospital's dispensary that first year, 167 "outdoor" patients were treated, and over 700 people had prescriptions filled.

In 1885, Dr. George E. Holtzapple treated a patient with pneumonia at the York Hospital, and as part of his treatment, fanned the fumes rising from the liquid in an oak bucket toward the patient. Those fumes were oxygen, and Dr. Holtzapple used it that day for the first time in recorded medical history.

The services offered by the hospital continued to grow. Affiliations with the York Collegiate Institute provided educational opportunities, the York Hospital Training School for Nurses was opened, an ambulance service was begun in 1896, and the first hospital clinic was opened in 1903.

Epidemics spread quickly throughout the city of York in those early years—smallpox in 1911, diphtheria in 1917, scarlet fever and influenza in 1918. In November of 1918, the influenza epidemic had become so contagious that emergency facilities were housed at the York Fairgrounds.

The institution's name officially became York Hospital in 1925 and a 20-acre tract of land was purchased on the southern edge of the city. Through a countywide effort to raise money, a new facility was completed and opened in September 1930. The early 1950s saw the addition of the South Wing, and expansion has continued since that time.

Medical care in the 1980s has progressed far beyond the visions of the dedicated handful of doctors and nurses who cared for Yorkers over a century ago. New techniques such as microsurgery, open-heart surgery, and the use of the CAT scanner have placed York Hospital at the vanguard of modern health care. Certain traditions from early days still remain at the hospital, however, such as the continuous process of medical education and the unstinting dedication of hundreds of volunteers contributing time and money to ensure that the people of York receive the finest medical care possible.

Top
In this photograph taken at the turn of the century, York Hospital nurses prepare food for patients from the kitchen facilities.

Above
The York Hospital ambulance in 1896 was a horse-drawn carriage.

YORKRAFT, INC.

Yorkraft, Inc., an innovative company built on creative conceptions and graphic designs, had its beginnings with a homemade Christmas card. Howard Coleman Imhoff, an artist, moved with his family to York in 1943 and went to work for a local advertising agency. Imhoff designed his family's Christmas card depicting an Amish man, his wife, and their children. Friends loved it, exclaimed to him about it, and saved it.

G. William Schaumann and his wife, Margot (the daughter of Imhoff), came to York for a visit after Schaumann was discharged from the Army Air Corps in 1945. The couple liked the area and decided to settle in York. With the encouragement of his son-in-law, Imhoff designed eight more Pennsylvania Dutch cards and had a small quantity printed in one color. In the evenings, the whole family gathered around the old kitchen table, applying watercolors by hand to the black-line art.

Schaumann traveled throughout the York and Lancaster area, selling the cards at local gift shops. The Pennsylvania Dutch tourist industry was growing, and the line of cards became an immediate success. In 1946, under the name of York Studios, Schaumann and Imhoff opened a small office over Mike's Nut Shop on South George Street. This business, too, flourished and the two men moved to the 600 block of East Market Street. York Studios was now producing 40 different items, designed by Imhoff and printed in four colors by local printers, ranging from greeting cards to notepaper, bridge tallies, placemats, and napkins.

In 1950 the business was incorporated as Yorkraft, Inc., with Howard C. Imhoff as president and G. William Schaumann as vice-president. In search of more space, the firm moved again, this time to a small 2-story building on South Albemarle Street. William C. Imhoff, son of Howard Imhoff, joined the business in 1952, and provided the knowledge of economics that would become the key to Yorkraft's success. In future years the younger Imhoff would be named vice-president and secretary-treasurer of the company.

Sales of the Pennsylvania Dutch items dwindled in the late 1950s, and the firm sought a new product line. Schaumann, attracted to the signs that once adorned small shops, inns, and taverns in early America, introduced a line of 12 Early American tavern signs at the New York Gift Show in 1959. Imhoff's colorfully designed signs were silk-screened by hand on wood and authentically antiqued. They took the gift market by surprise; Yorkraft had made the successful transition from a design studio to a manufacturer.

To broaden its horizons, Yorkraft opened a gift shop called "The Drum" in 1961. Managed by Margot Schaumann at 3550 East Market Street, the shop would later move to a larger site in the Village Green Shopping Center and win the first-place design award in the Gift Shop Design Competition in 1968, sponsored by Gifts and Decorative Accessories.

Yorkraft expanded its operation in 1964 to a 4-story, 96,000-square-foot building at 550 South Pine Street, where it currently resides. The company now produces over 450 items, including restaurant equipment, Seriglass® (a greeting card silk-screened on glass), a complete line of wooden folk art decorating accessories, and more, all executed in the distinctive style of design that has come to be Yorkraft's trademark.

Below
The family Christmas card, designed by Howard Imhoff, led to the establishment of Yorkraft.

Bottom
Howard Coleman Imhoff (1894-1972) was the founder of Yorkraft.

YORK TAPE AND LABEL CORPORATION

Two enterprising young ex-servicemen from York, Reynold B. Smith and Robert W. Trimmer, established a partnership in April 1947, under the name "York Tape Printers." They soon found themselves in the position of being industry pioneers, because their business was based on the new concept that quality printing could be added to pressure-sensitive tape, providing a remarkably convenient method of product identification, instruction, and promotion.

The two men set up their first office and plant at 600 Chestnut Street in York. Much of their knowledge was to be gained only through experimentation, trial, and error. Flexography, a method of printing long rolls of material by using flexible plates mounted around continuously turning cylinders, was still in the developmental stages. Materials and supplies were limited and often unsuitable. The standard printing inks of the time did not dry quickly enough, and the early wooden cylinders warped and cracked with use.

Smith and Trimmer developed their own methods, experimented with new materials, and built and modified printing presses to meet the needs of the company. Through Trimmer's expertise in building and running the presses and Smith's ability in administration and sales, the partners slowly made their business dream a reality.

Within the first three years, York Tape Printers moved twice to accommodate additional equipment and a growing staff. The first move was to Salem Avenue, followed by a move to Springdale Avenue. In 1952 the company relocated to its present site at 1953 Stanton Street, occupying 5,000 square feet and gradually renting more and more available space as the business continued to expand.

The search for new market opportunities led to new products and increasing sales. With the demand for consecutively numbered pressure-sensitive tapes evident, the partners discovered a way to manufacture and sell them competitively, creating a line that was a mainstay of the firm in its early years.

In the early 1950s the company's sales amounted to one million dollars, with over 80 percent of the business coming from three types of tape products. The staff then numbered about 30. By the mid-1950s, Smith began to develop a new product line, innovative in the printing and converting industry. The venture was die-cut, "pick-off" pressure-sensitive labels carried on a release liner. The labels would prove to be ideal for packaging, promotion, and product design. The partners met delivery for their first multimillion-label order by running the presses continuously for weeks—days, nights, and weekends. Later, more efficient methods of speedy high-volume printing would be devised.

A short time later York Label Corporation was formed. In the 1960s, the Stanton Street building, now corporate headquarters, and a second plant in Columbia, South Carolina, were purchased. The Columbia plant helped to supply the southern textile industry, a large user of identification tapes and labels. Trimmer sold his share of the company to Smith in 1965 and retired to Arizona. Today, operating as York Tape and Label Corporation, the firm is still wholly owned by the original founder, Reynold Smith.

The years have witnessed many changes and additions for the innovative, "home-grown" enterprise. A new plant in Cornwall, Pennsylvania, has increased total manufacturing space. Production capacities have been expanded to include letterpress and sophisticated screen printing. Flexographic presses have been modernized to incorporate embossing, hot stamping, and other processes. The product lines have diversified to include

Below
The first home of York Tape Printers was a small building at 600 Chestnut Street, York.

Bottom
Today the corporate headquarters of York Tape and Label Corporation is located at 1953 Stanton Street.

rigid plastic nameplates, display windows for electronic devices, and custom-fabricated presentation cases. With the increase in production, a machine systems department has been added to provide all types of automatic labeling services. A trained, specialized sales force works out of numerous offices across the country and a highly skilled production staff is hired from the nation's top technical schools, as well as from the local area. Today sales approach $15 million and employees number almost 300.

THE YORK WATER COMPANY

In 1816, residents of every small town lived in fear of the cry of one word—"FIRE!"

York in the early 1800s was a cluster of brick and frame buildings centered a few blocks around Continental Square. The city was in constant danger of being ravaged by fire, so a group of citizens decided to meet and plan to safeguard York against this ever-present threat.

In the winter of 1815-1816, some York men gathered at the Indian King Tavern on High Street (now the Dauphin Deposit Trust Company site on West Market Street). At this tavern owned by Colonel George Hay, the Yorkers decided upon a simple idea to meet the city's water needs—to pipe water by gravity from a nearby spring to a reservoir, with auxiliary mains used to serve the most populated area of the city.

Few precedents existed for the Water Company experiment, since only 25 water systems were operating in America at the time. The men invested their own private capital, and on February 23, 1816, a charter was granted to the York Water Company. This charter makes the York company the oldest investment-owned water system in Pennsylvania under continuous management.

The first meeting of the 30 stockholders was held on March 18, 1816. During the rest of that year and into the next, three miles of wooden pipes were installed to serve 118 customers. Land containing springs was purchased in the area along what is now Rathton Road east of Queen Street. Logs with diameters of 14 to 20 inches were cut in the forests up along the Susquehanna River. More than 12,000 of these logs were then floated down the river during spring floods, and hauled by wagons from Wrightsville to York.

These logs were the first water mains for the York Water Company. Holes of 3- and 4-inch diameters were bored by manpower and hand tools, then connected together by iron ferrules. The wooden pipes lasted several generations, and even today, an old wooden pipe will occasionally be discovered during construction, still in good condition.

The age of iron and steel brought new development and prosperity to York and more expansion to the York Water Company. The original wooden water mains were replaced with cast-iron pipes. York's growth soon taxed the use of the company's springs, and in 1848, to meet the needs of the community, the firm built a pumping station on the south side of the Codorus Creek near the current intersection of Penn Street and Kings Mill Road.

The York Water Company kept pace as the city increased its population to nearly 34,000 by the end of the century. A 117-acre tract of land south of Country Club Road was purchased for a new reservoir and land on the south branch of the Codorus was acquired for a new pumping station and a cleaner source of water. Two years later, in 1897, the first water was pumped from Brillhart's Station into the east basin of the new reservoir. A newspaper of the day reported that the christening was greeted with "the booming of a small cannon and a rousing cheer."

The foresight of the York Water Company continued into the new century. Recognizing the perils of contaminated water, the company instituted filtered water in 1899 and chemically purified water in 1910. The first impounding dam, Lake Williams, was completed in 1913 and assured a plentiful supply of water for many years. A second reservoir, Lake Redman, was built in 1966 during the most severe drought in the memory of many York County residents.

The tradition of conservation management, planning, and service to York and York County continues today, with more than 125,000 people benefiting from the insights of the men who met in Hay's tavern back in 1816.

Below
The construction of a clear-water basin, started as a sedimentation basin, is shown in this 1894 photograph. The York Water Company served about 50,000 people that year.

Bottom
Today the twin clear-water basins, located in Reservoir Park overlooking the city of York, are a familiar site to area residents.

ACKNOWLEDGMENTS

A volume three or four times the size of this one could only hint at the vast richness of York's heritage. One of the author's chief frustrations in putting this volume together, in fact, concerned the selection of facts and stories. The process of making those selections was both enhanced and made more difficult by the fact that The Historical Society of York County and other resource facilities are so heavily endowed with materials on York history. The Society alone houses hundreds of thousands of documents, photographs, maps, books, and other records—presenting an intimidating but exciting challenge to the researcher and author.

The making of such a book demands not only access to resources, but also the efforts and cooperation of many people. I was fortunate from the outset to have the keen talents and dedication of Jerry E. Sweitzer, the illustration editor and writer of the business biographies found in the last chapter of *To the Setting of the Sun: The Story of York*. A native of York County who counts among his ancestors some of York County's earliest settlers, Jerry sometimes spent hours and days tracking down a single needed photograph or map. His work in this volume speaks eloquently for itself.

With experience as a newspaper reporter and an innate destiny to create stories as my foremost credentials, I needed desperately the assistance of distinguished historians who would keep my facts as honest and my stories as straight as is humanly possible. Again I was blessed with assistance of the highest caliber. The York Area Chamber of Commerce's Publications Committee, made up of York's leading historians, nurtured the project under the sound and reasoned guidance of Attorney Byron H. LeCates—himself a former president of The Historical Society of York County and a historian with intuitive knowledge of York's past. Committee members Landon Charles Reisinger, Helen Miller Gotwalt, Judge Richard E. Kohler, Attorney John F. Rauhauser, and James Rudisill gave many hours to ensure the authenticity of the manuscript. Landon Reisinger, particularly, spent innumerable hours of painstaking effort with the author in combing the chaff from the grain and the nearly correct from the correct—especially in the section of the book chronicling York's Colonial period.

The personnel and officers of The Historical Society of York County—Mrs. Charles (Mimi) Brimfield, Douglas C. Dolan, Mary C. Wells, Patricia A. Tomes, Scott J. Atwood, Joela M. Donley, Steven K. Young, and Gail M. Shank—were magnanimous with their assistance to me and to the book's illustration editor. Mrs. Margo Atwood, Mrs. Dorothy Lagunowich, and Mrs. Susan Beecher made available the resources of York College archives; and Phyllis Doutrich and Elizabeth Brooks provided hospitable aid at Martin Memorial Library. I also am most grateful to the members of the John C. Schmidt family for access to their private library and to other resources they lent cheerfully.

The files of the *York Dispatch* and the expertise of *Dispatch* personnel—Henry Merges, Shirley Shaffer, Steven Hevner, Terry Holland, George Laird III, Jean Farlow, Anita Gray, Steve Swartzbaugh, and Ruth Quinlivan—were of invaluable help.

I am indebted as well to *York Daily Record* staff members Joel Michael and Eli Sliver, and to *York Sunday News* editor Gordon A. Freireich and staff members Mrs. Mary Stephenson, Scott Miller, and Glenn Dietz. Harry McLaughlin and Jerry Gleason of the York Bureau of the *Sunday Patriot News* also contributed freely of their time, and additional aid was given by Harry McLaughlin who allowed us to use photographs from his extensive collection. Tanya Wood, William Schintz, and Linda Reis of the William Penn Memorial Museum also lent photographic material; and Marguerite Eriksson and Walt Partymiller were valuable resource people in the compilation of this history.

Many York business and community leaders helped the author establish an initial perspective for this work by sharing ideas and knowledge and by lending additional materials. Among those people were: Charles S. Wolf, John C. Schmidt, Dr. Carl Hatch, Dr. Robert Terry, Dr. Sardari Khanna, Mr. and Mrs. Sidney N. Rosenfeld, V.T. Kartorie, Sally Summers, George Brown, Harold W. Anderson, Arthur E. Young, Harris Sacks, Kay Wilt, Larry L. LaPrairie, Mr. and Mrs. William Bittinger, Carl F. Neu, Allen I. Samuelson, Donald M. Shaffer, Amy Bittinger, Allan M. Dameshek, Mrs. William H. Kain, Elizabeth Brown, and Anne Marden.

I owe a special note of thanks to Ruthe F. Craley, William A. Falkler, and Barbara Marchese for their generous contributions, and to my sister, Rose Shoff, who typed the manuscript—again and again. Special expressions of my gratitude must also go to my family, friends, colleagues, and clients who persevered with me through the many months of research and writing.

This book could not have been published without the support of the York Area Chamber of Commerce and its enthusiastic president Carl F. Neu. The Chamber staff members—Carol Himes, Carol Murphy, Tammy Barnhart, Grace Loucks and Betty Little McCarty—have my deep thanks for their patient assistance, as does Dr. Robert V. Iosue whose suggestion that I write the book led to this publication.

My editors at Windsor Publications—Randy Smoot, Barbara Marinacci, and Lissa Sanders—deserve eloquent commendations for courage and patience in dealing with a decidedly non-historian author. Warm thanks should also be extended to the other people at Windsor Publications who contributed in many ways to the making of this book: Karen Story, business biography editorial director, and Phyllis Gray, editorial assistant; Teri Davis Greenberg, picture editor, and Anna R. Igra and Jana Wernor, assistant picture editors; Kathy Cooper, editorial coordinator; David Seidman, copy editor; and Tracey Benedict, typist.

Finally, this book is dedicated to some very special people: Beth Ann and Connie Shoff; Scott and David Wynegar; Kelly, Joy, and Ryan Hershey; and Timothy Knaub.

If this volume stirs a greater appreciation of York's heritage; if it stimulates the reader toward further study of the York community's history; if it is entertaining and informative—then it has served its purpose and made all our efforts worthwhile. The story of York is an exciting and magical affair, and to have shared in its telling has been a most rewarding and satisfying experience. I trust the reader experiences some of that excitement and some of that magic as the pages of this book are turned.

GEORG R. SHEETS

BIBLIOGRAPHY

Biddle, Gertrude Bosler, and Lowrie, Sarah Dickinson. "Notable Women of Pennsylvania." Philadelphia, Pennsylvania: University of Pennsylvania, 1942.

Cadzow, Donald A., "Archaeological Studies of the Susquehannock Indians of Pennsylvania." Harrisburg, Pennsylvania: Pennsylvania Historical Commission, 1936.

Carter, W.C., and Glossbrenner, A.J. "History of York County From Its Erection to the Present Time: 1729-1834." Harrisburg, Pennsylvania: Aurand Press, 1930.

Commager, Henry Steele. "Documents of American History." New York, New York: Appleton-Century-Crofts, 1934.

Country Club of York. "History of the Country Club of York: 1899-1975." York, Pennsylvania: p.p., 1975.

Downer, Alan S. "The Memoirs of John Durang, American Actor—1785-1816." Pittsburgh, Pa.; University of Pittsburgh Press for The Historical Society of York County, 1966.

Dudrear, Albert, Jr. "The Dudrear-Dodderer Family." York, Pa.: p.p., 1976.

Eichelberger, A.W. "Eichelberger Family Record: 1693-1900." Hanover, Pennsylvania: Hanover Herald Print, 1901.

Engle, William H. "History of the Commonwealth of Pennsylvania." Philadelphia, Pennsylvania: E.M. Gardner, 1883.

Farquhar, A.B. "The First Million—the Hardest: An Autobiography." New York, New York: Doubleday, Page and Company, 1922.

First Presbyterian Church of York, Pennsylvania. "Two Hundred Years: 1762-1962." York, Pennsylvania: p.p., 1962.

Fisher, George G. "Ordinances of the Borough and City of York." York, Pennsylvania: Gazette Printing Company, 1896.

Fortenbaugh, Robert. "The Nine Capitals of the United States." York, Pennsylvania: York Graphic Services, 1975.

Freed, Theodore F., and Rosenmiller, W.F.O. "Pictorial History of Pleasure and Commercial Vehicles Manufactured in York County, Pennsylvania." York, Pa.: 1977.

Friedman, Rabbi Moses N. "York Jewish Bicentennial." York, Pennsylvania: p.p., 1955.

"Gazette and Daily." York, Pennsylvania: various dates of publication.

Gibson, John. "History of York County, Pennsylvania." Chicago, Illinois: F.A. Bartley Publishing Company, 1886.

Gordon, General John B. "Reminiscences of the Civil War." New York, New York: Charles Scribners Sons, 1903.

Gotwalt, Helen Miller. "Crucible of a New Nation—First York County Court House, 1754-1841." York Pennsylvania: York County Bicentennial Commission, p.p., 1976.

Greiman, Edward A. "Memoirs." York, Pennsylvania: Graphic Services and White Rose Engravings Company, p.p., 1968.

Hall, Clifford J., and Lehr, John P. "York County and the World War." York, Pennsylvania: p.p., 1920.

Hardt, P. "The Self-Taught Conveyancer or Farmers' and Mechanics Guide." Baltimore, Maryland: Shaffer and Maund, 1819.

Hartman, Terry. "The Folkculture of Pennsylvania Dutch Farmers' Market." Washington, D.C.: National Endowment for the Humanities, n.p., 1978.

Hatch, Carl E., Hicks, Joseph B., and Kohler, Richard E. "York, Pa. in the Roaring Twenties." York, Pennsylvania: Martin Library, p.p., 1973.

Hawkins, Charles A., and Landis, Housten E. "York and York County—A Sesqui-Centennial Memento." York, Pennsylvania: York Daily Press, 1901.

Heisey, John W. "York County in the American Revolution." York, Pennsylvania: The Historical Society of York County, 1971.

Jones, Jeri L. "York County Pennsylvania Geologic Guide." York, Pennsylvania: York Rock and Mineral Club, p.p., 1980.

Kain, Emily. "The Women's Club of York, Seventy-five Years." York, Pennsylvania: p.p., 1975.

Kent, Barry C. "Discovering Pennsylvania's Archaeological Heritage." Harrisburg, Pennsylvania: Pennsylvania Historical and Museum Commission, 1980.

Kindig, Joseph III. "Architecture in York County." York, Pennsylvania: The Historical Society of York County, p.p., 1979.

Lafayette Club. "The Lafayette Club Murals." York, Pennsylvania: p.p., 1962.

Latimer, Robert Cathcart. "Reminisces of York, 1891-1901." N.p.

Lewis, Arthur H. "Hex." New York, New York: Trident Press, 1969.

Lutheran Social Services, South Region. "The Messenger." York, Pennsylvania: n., n.d.

Miller, Lewis. "Sketches and Chronicles." York, Pennsylvania: The Historical Society of York County, p.p., 1966.

Moore, Frank, ed. "Diary of the American Revolution." New York, New York: Charles Scribner, 1860.

Morning Journal. York, Pennsylvania: various dates of publication.

Nye, W.S., and Redman, John G. "Farthest East—Wrightsville, Pa." York, Pennsylvania: p.p., 1963.

Olson, McKinley C. "J.W. Gitt's Sweet Land of Liberty." New York, New York: Jerome S. Ozo, 1975.

Patriot News. Harrisburg, Pennsylvania: various dates of publication.

Peckham, Betty. "The Story of a Dynamic Community—York, Pennsylvania." York, Pennsylvania: York Area Chamber of Commerce, 1945.

Peckham, Betty. "York, Pennsylvania: A Dynamic Community Forges Ahead." York, Pennsylvania: York Area Chamber of Commerce, 1957.

Pennsylvania Gazette. York, Pennsylvania: various dates of publication.

Prowell, George R. "History of York County, Volume I." Chicago, Illinois: J.H. Beers and Company, 1907.

Rupp, I. Daniel. "History of Lancaster County." Lancaster, Gilbert Hills, 1844.

Schlegel, Philip J. "Recruits to Continentals: A History of the York County Rifle Company, June 1775-1777." York, Pennsylvania: The Historical Society of York County, p.p., 1979.

Secor, Robert. "Pennsylvania, 1776." College Park, Pennsylvania: Pennsylvania State University, 1976.

Small, Cassandra Morris. "Letters of '63." Detroit, Michigan: Stair-Jordan-Baker, Inc., 1929.

Sunday News. Lancaster, Pennsylvania: various dates of publication.

Taub, Lynn Smolens. "Greater York in Action." York, Pennsylvania: York Area Chamber of Commerce, 1968.

"Yearbook of the Historical Society of York County For the Year 1941: Notes and Documents Concerning the Manorial History of the Town of York." York, Pennsylvania: The Historical Society of York County, p.p., 1941.

York City Fire Department. "History of the York Fire Department, 1776-1976." Marceline, Missouri: Walsworth Publishing Company, p.p., 1976.

INDEX

Italicized numbers indicate illustrations

A
Abbottstown 85, 90, 118
Acco Industries 98
Adams, John *64*, 65
Adams, Samuel *47*
Adams County 16, 57, 65, 66, 156
Adas Israel Congregation 101
Addagyjunkquagh (Indian) 13
Adlum, John 26
Adlum, Joseph 27
Agriculture 22, 24, 42-43, 56
Albright, Anna Maria Ursula Duenckle 44
Albright, Philip 44
Allen, Lillie B. 154
Allis Chalmers Corporation 98
Almshouse 66, 67
American Chain Company 98
American Legion, York 150
American Red Cross, York County Chapter 147
Andrews, John 55, *56*
Anshe Hadas Congregation 101
Appell, Louis J., Jr. 137, 149
Armand, Charles (Marquis de la Rouerie) 57
Armand's Legion 57
Armor, Thomas 29, 36
Armstrong, John, Jr. 61
Arnaux Electric Light Company 100
Asbury, Francis 58
Automobile industry 114, 115, 121
Avalong 152

B
Bachtell, Dick 141
Bacon, Samuel 61
Baer, Jacob 97
Baer, John H. 97
Bailey, William 58
Bair, Robert C. 112
Baltimore & Ohio Steam Railway Company 74, 76, 77
Baltimore Company 73
Baptiste, Ezekiel 83
Barnitz, Anna Barbara Spangler 25
Barnitz, Catherine Hay 25
Barnitz, Charles 25, 67, 76
Barnitz, David Grier 25
Barnitz, George 83
Barnitz, Jacob 83
Barnitz, John 25
Barnitz, John George Charles 25
Bartgis, Matthias 59
Barton, Thomas 27, 29
Batwell, Daniel 55

Bauer, Martin 18
Baugher, Frederick 78
Bauserman, C.F. 118
Bay, Andrew 29
Bear, Charles H. 121
Bear's Department Store 118, *119*, 132, *133*, 138, 155
Beaver, James A. 106
Beck, Charles 101
Beckner, William H. 145
Bedford 21
Beidinger, Nicholaus. See Bittinger, Nicolas
Bell Motor Car Company 115
Bennett, Isaac 111
Bennett, Joseph 16
Bentz, Matilda 66
Bentz, Sophia 66
Berghous A. 90
Bermudian (town) 43
Beyer, Joseph 18
Biddle, Nicholas 76
Billmyer, George 69
Billmyer (York) House *169*
Bishop, John 22
Bittinger, Christian 36
Bittinger, John W. 112
Bittinger, Nicolas 23, 36
Bixler, Jacob 59
Black, Chauncey Forward 106, 107, 109
Black, Jeremiah S. 106
Black, Louise 109
Black, Mary Dawson 102, 107
Black Diamonds, The 140
Black Horse Inn and Tavern 21
Blair, A.R. 101, 102
Blue Moon Orchestra 140
Blunston, Samuel 15
Blymire, John 128, 129, 136
Boltz, Margaret 150
Bond, W.S. 121
Bonham, Elizabeth 108
Bonham, Horace *107*, 108, 110, 160, 163
Bonham, Mary Lewis *162*, 163
Bonham House 110, *166*, *167*
Bon Ton department store 48, 49, *111*, 126
Borg-Warner Corporation, York Division of 98, 158
Bott, Hermanus 22
Bottstown 22, 103
Boudinot, Elias 46
Braddock, Edward 28, 29
Bradley, Margaret 66
Brethren in Christ 43, 44
Broadbeck, A.R. 117
Brockie (mansion) 107
Brookside Park 109
Brown, Cassandra S. 137
Bruce, D. Scott 111
Brule, Etienne 10, 11

Buchanan, James 106
Buehler's Hotel 73
Bulette, Warren C. 145
Buon, Jean *150*
Burgoyne, John 50
Burroughs, Thomas H. 81
Butler, Richard 71

C
Calvert, Cecilius (Lord Baltimore) 12, 33
Calvert, Charles (fourth Lord Baltimore) 16
Campbell, John 58, 59, 63
Camp Scott 93
Camp Security 41
Canadochly settlement 14
Canals 75-76
Cantler, David 61
Capitol Theater *138*, 158
Carl, Jere S. 101
Carl, Michael 23
Carli, Othmar 160
Carlisle 21, 28, 45
Carlisle Market 113
Carlton, John *25*
Carroll Township 81
Carter, Jimmy 156, *157*
Carter, W.C. 17, 70
Cass, Lewis 106
Cassatt, David 61, 67, 71
Cassatt Building 95
Caterpillar Tractor Company 158
Cathcart, Robert 59, 63
Cathcart, Thomas 101, 102
Cayuga Indians 11
Cazenove, Thomas 62
Central Market 104, 105, 110, 128, 158, 170, *171*
Centre Square 22, 23, 24, 25, 26, 32, 40, 44, 46, 48, 52, 53, 58, 62, 63, 72, 77, 81, 82, 84, 85, 87, 91, 92, *94*, 103, *104*, *105*, 111, 112, 113, 127, 131, *133*
Chalfont, Edward J. 84
Chalfont, James 75
Chamber of Commerce, York Area 111, 112, 121, 129, 147, 150, 156, 158, 160
Chambersburg 90
Chanceford Township 81
Chandler, David 23, 31
Charles I (king of Great Britain) 12
Charles II (king of Great Britain) 12
Cherry Lane *174*, 175
Chester County 16, 18, 90
Children's Home 97
Christ Lutheran Church 18, 23, *24*, 31, 46, 55, 66, *85*, 104, 113, *173*
Churches and synagogues: Adas Israel Congregation, 101; Anshe Hadas Congregation, 101; Christ Lutheran Church, 18, 23, *24*, 31, 46, 55, 66, *85*, 104, 113, *173*; Church of

the Brethren 43; Cristo Salvador Hispanic Catholic Church, 158; First English Lutheran Church, 42, *58*, 59; First Moravian Church, 27, 36, *37*, 55, 66; First Presbyterian Church, 39, *58*, 59; First Reformed Church, 42; German Evangelical Lutheran Church, 23, *24*, *58*, 59, 66; German Reformed Church, 24, 31, 53, 62, *63*, 67; Methodist Episcopal Church, 57, 58, 62, *63*; Ohev Sholom Synagogue, 101, *159*; St. John's Episcopal Church, 27, 51, 55, 56, *58*, 59, *115*, 142; St. John's German Lutheran Church, 95; St. Matthew's Lutheran Church, 24; St. Patrick's Church, 43, *70*, *159*; St. Paul's Lutheran Church, 95, 146; Second English Lutheran Church, *58*, 59; Temple Beth Israel, 100, *102*, 147; Trinity Reformed Church, 24; Trinity United Church, *173*; Union Lutheran Church, 131-132; Warrington Friends Meeting House, *28*; York Friends Meeting House, *30*, 98; Zion Reformed Church, 36, 46
Church of the Brethren 43
City Hall 10, 146, 160
City Market 95, 100, 104
Civil War 89-93
Clark, Henry 26
Clark, John 44, 59, 63
Cleveland, Grover 103
Clockmaking industry 24
Clubs and organizations: American Legion, York, 150; American Red Cross, York County Chapter, 147; Chamber of Commerce, York Area, 111, 112, 121, 131, 147, 150, 156, 158, 160; Cosmopolitan Club, 159; Daughters of the American Revolution, York Town Chapter, 109, 110; Dutch Club, 138; Eagles, Order of, 115; Elks, Order of, 115; Girl's Club of York, 118; Historical Society of York County, The, 66, 68, 69, 108, 109, 110, 146, 151, 160, 163, 164, 166, 172; Historic York County, Inc., 151; Knights of Malta, 115; Knights of the Mystic Chain, 115; Lafayette Club, 111, 114; Manufacturers Association, 114, 145, 148; Merchant's Association of York, 111; Odd Fellows, Order of 115; Out Door Country Club, 109; Red Men, Order of, 115; Rotary Club, 147; Tall Cedars of Lebanon, 115; United Way, 147; Visiting Nurse Association, 114; Woman's Club of York, 114, 118; Women's Bureau, 150; YMCA, 97, 147; York Art Association, 114; York Art Club, 114; York Association of the Deaf, 137; York Country Club, 111, 138, 150; York County Agricultural Society, 88; York County Colonization Society, 83; York County Medical Society, 129; York Music League, 138; York Twinning Association, 150; York Welfare Federation, 146; Young Woman's Club, 146; YWCA, 110
Coaler, Andrew 22
Cochran, Thomas E. 90
Codorus (steamboat) 54, 73
Codorus Creek 10, 18, 21, 22, 24, 26, 44, 51, 55, 58, 61, 62, 68, 73, 76, *78*, 97, 103, 108, 139, 153, 155, 156; bike path, *160*
Codorus Frog-jumping Contest 152
Codorus Furnace 29, *30*
Codorus Mills 99
Codorus Navigation Company 72, 73; seal of, *72*
Codorus Township 43
Cohen, Herbert B. 136, 137
Cold Springs Park 109
Colebrookdale 44
Coliseum Theater 124, 140
Collins, Samuel 66
Colonial Hotel 94, *113*, 155
Columbia 99
Columbia, Lancaster & Philadelphia Railroad 77
Commonwealth National Bank 46
Conestogoe Indians 13
Conewago Creek 24, 43, 131
Conewago Falls 73
Conewago Turnpike 66
Connolly, Frank P. 96
Conojehela Valley 14
Conrad, Hal 32
Continental Square 21, 22, 95, 149
Conway, Thomas 50, 51
Conway Cabal 49, 51, 52, 63
Cookes House 52, *155*
Cookson, Thomas 21, 22, 59
Coolidge, Calvin 120
Cope, Gilbert 30
Cosmopolitan Club 159
Court House: (1754) 25, 26, 40, 41, 45, 46, 47, 48, 49, 52, 53, 65, 69; (1839) 62, *63*, *80*, 81, 84, 87, 88, 92, 118, *119*, 143, 149, 156, 164, *165*; reconstruction of Colonial, 22, *25*, 118, 156, *164*
"Cow Insurrection" 59
Cox, James M. 120
Cox, Thomas 25
Craley, N. Neiman 154
Craley 16
Cresap, Thomas 14
Crispus Attucks Association Center 143
Cristo Salvador Hispanic Catholic Church 158
Croll, Christopher 22
Cruise, Walter 36, 38
Cumberland County 28, 29, 106
Currier and Ives Gallery 159
Curry, John 128, 129

D
Dale, James A. 82
Dallastown 109, 152
Daughters of the American Revolution, York Town Chapter 109, 110
Davis, Gardner and Webb foundry-machine shop 73
Davis, John 141
Davis, Phineas 74, 76, 135
Day, John 25
Deane, Silas 53
Deane, Simeon 52
Delaplane, Helen V. 120, 139
Delaware River 10, 11
Delroy 14
Delta 16
Dempwolf, Frederick 95, 146
Dempwolf, J.A. 95, 100, 103, 105, 112, 164, 169
Dempwolf, Reinhart 95
Dentist's Supply Company 112
Depression, Great 135-140
Devers, Jacob Loucks 145, *146*
Dickens, Charles 85, *86*
Dick's Bloomery 29
Diehl, John Adam 18
Dietz, Gilbert A. 137
Dietz, Jacob 81
Digges, John 16
Digges Choice 16
Dill, James 44
Dill, John 36
Dill, Matthew 25, 39
Dillsburg 25, 36
Dingee and Company, W.W. 88
Distilling industry 24-25, 117
Dixon, Jeremiah 33
Dize, C. William 156
Domville, Paul 13
Donaldson, Joseph 36
Dongan, Thomas 13 19
Doudel, Jacob 31
Doudel, Michael 31, 36, 37, 38, 40, 61-62, 67, 73, 87
Douglas, Stephen 89
Dover Township 24, 86, 87
Drovers and Mechanics Bank 46
Duffield, George 46
Dunkards (German Baptists) 43, 44, 82
Dunn, Robert 71
Dunn, William 84
Durang, Ferdinand 70
Durang, Frederick 42
Durang, Jacob 41
Durang, John 40, 41, 42, 70
Dutch Club 138

INDEX • 233

Dutch settlement 11

E
Eades, Benjamin 70
Eagles, Order of 115
Early, Jubal 90, 92
Eastern Market 103, 104
Easton 21, 107
East Prospect 14
Edgecomb (residence) 112
Edie, James 59
Edie, John 59
Edison Electric Light Company 103, 139
Education 55-56, 58-61, 71, 81, 97-98, 148-149. *See also* Schools and Colleges
Edwards, Evan 44
Eichelberger, Eli 153
Eichelberger, George 41
Eichelberger, Jacob 41, 73, 83
Eichelberger, Lydia Worley 41
Eichelberger, Martin 22, 23, 36, 41, 44
Eichelberger, Michael 22, 79
87th Regimental Band, Pennsylvania Volunteers 89
Eisenhart, Charles A. 99
Eisenhower, Dwight D. 148
Elgar, John 54, 73, 76, 89
Elizabeth Moore's Inn 46
Elks, Order of 115
Elm Beach 131, *132*
Elm-spring farm 67
Elmwood 153
Elmwood Theater 137
Engle, Jacob 43
English settlement 11, 12-14
Erie 99
Etters 16
Etting, Elijah 100
Etting, Reuben 100
Etting, Shinah 100
Evangelical Zeitung, Die (newspaper) 79
Evans, Fitz James 95
Ewell, R.S. 90
Eyster, George 30
Eyster, Weiser and Company 78

F
Fahs, C.M. 117
Fairmount 103
Fairmount Park Road Race 114
Fairview Township 81
Falkler, Charlie 142
Falkler, William A. 160, 161
Farmer's Market 97, 100, 104, 158, 170
Farquhar, A.B. 88, 89, 90, *91*, 93, 111
Farquhar, Elizabeth Jessop 89, 102
Farquhar, Francis 111, 112, 114
Farquhar Company, A.B. 88, 132, 136, 148; plant of, 115
Farquhar Park *130*, 131, 160
Fayfield 135
Feder, Jacob 101
Federal Fire Company 56
Feldman, Benjamin 101
Feldmann, W.H. 131
Fields Department Store, J.W. 152
Fine, John S. 129
Fiorito, Joe 141
Fireside Terrace 150
First English Lutheran Church 42, *58*, 59
First Moravian Church 27
First Pennsylvania Regiment 38
First Presbyterian Church 39, *58*, 59
First Reformed Church 42
Fisher, Charles 52, 53
Fisher, John 20, 24, 25, 52, 53, 63
Fisher, John S. 121
Fisher, William J. 145, 148
Fisher house 155
Floods: (1817) 71-72; (1933) 139; (1972) 153-154
Fluhrer Building 95, *168*, 169
Fluhrer's Jewelry Store 103
Ford, Daniel 75
Ford, Gerald 156, *157*
Fort Duquesne 65
Foster, J.F. 137
Foust, Thomas M. 155
Franklin, Benjamin 28, *29*, 49, 52, 53
Franklin, William 28
Franklin County 39
French and Indian War 28-29, 35, 36, 39
Frey, Tobias 89
Frey, William 89
Freystone 89, 103
Friedman, Moses *150*

G
Gage, Thomas 35
Galbreath, Albert 99
Gardner, John 83
Gardner, Martin 66
Gardner, Peter 17
Garfield, James A. 107
Gates, Horatio 36, *49*, 50, 51, 52
Gates House *23*, 51, *151*, 153, 155, *172, 173*
Geesy, C.A. 111
Geise, Frank 101
Gelwicks, Frederick 23
General Borough Law 106
General Telephone Company 107
Gentzler, Waldo Emerson 60
George II (king of Great Britain) 21
George III (king of Great Britain) 35, 38, 55
Gerber, John L. 121
German Evangelical Lutheran Church 23, *24*, *58*, 59, 66. *See also* St. Matthew's Lutheran Church
German Lutheran School 44, 55
German Reformed Church 24, 31, 53, 62, *63*, 67
German settlement 14-15, 18
Gettysburg 36, 61, 85, 91, 93, 141
Gettysburg College 60, 61
Gettysburg Pike 90
Gibbs, Mitch *160*
Gibson, John 25
Gibson, M.B. 112
Gipe, Florence 102
Girl's Club of York 118
Gitt, J.W. 138, *139*, 154
Glacken, Ed *149*
Glatfelter, Millard E. 60
Glatfelter, Samuel 121
Globe Inn 69, 72
Glossbrenner, A.J. 17, 70
Golden Lamb Tavern 42
Golden Plough Tavern 22, *23*, 51, *151*, 153, 155, *172*
Goldsboro 16, 78, 156
Good, Bill 141
Good, Walter 141
Goode, Alexander D. *147*
Goodling, George A. 154, 155
Goodling, William F. 155
Goodridge, William C. 84
Gordon, John B. 90, *91*, 92
Gotwald, Mary *124*
Gotwalt, Jacob 95
Gotwalt, Samuel A. 137
Governor's Mansion 121
Grafius, Abraham 66
Grant, Ulysses S. 89, 99
Graybill, Jacob (Crebill) 22
Greeley, Horace 99
Green, Marc 148
Grieger, Henry 67
Grier, David 44, 62
Griest, Amos 84
Griest, Margaret Garrettson 84
Griffith, W.H. 67
Grimek, John 141
Grist, John 14
Grist Creek 14
Groff, M. Valerie 138
Groll, Christian 18
Gross, John K. 99
Grove, Bruce 122
Grumbacher, Max *111*, 121
Grumbacher's dry-goods store 110
Guckes, Johannes (Cookes) 52, 155
Guinston 27
Gunmaking industry 30

H
Hahn, Michael 36
Hahn Home for Women *143*
Haines, Mahlon N. 121, 122; house of, 121, *122*
Haines Acres 149

Hall, Thomas 16
Hallam Furnace and Forge 29
Hallam Township 73, 81
Hamilton, Hance 25, 26, 29
Hamilton Bank annex 46
Hancock, John 45, *46*, 49
Hand, Edward 40
Hanover Borough 23, 24, 36, 39, 43, 66, 81, 99, 100, 111, 139
Hantz, Jacob 86
Harding, Warren G. 120
Harnish, Samuel 81
Harrisburg 13, 59, 65, 66, 72, 73, 75, 77, 86, 87, 90, 96, 117, 123, 138, 139, 151
Harrison, Benjamin 1.
Harrison, William Henry 79
Hartley, Catherine *45*
Hartley, Thomas 36, 44, *45*, 50, 57, 59, 62, 63, 65
Hartman, Daniel 87
Hartmann, John 85
Hartmann Building *85*
Hatch, Carl E. 123, 124, 136
Hath, Robert Gamel 27
Haughy, Thomas 27
Hauptmann, Bruno Richard 136
Hay, George 89, 90
Hay, Jacob 67, 103
Hay, John 25, 70, 93
Hay, Julia Maul 25
Hay's Addition 70
Health care 101-102
Heighes, George 103
Helb, Theodore R. 117
Heller, Roger *150*
Hendricks, Henry 22
Hendricks, James 13, 14
Hendricks, John 13, 14
Hendrickson, Cornelius 10, 11
Henneisen, John 67
Henry, John Joseph 57
Henry, Patrick 50
Herrman, Amos W. 128
Hersh, G. Edward 67
Hersh, Grier 67, 111, 112, 118
Hersh, Mrs. Grier 114
Hespenheide, W.H. Jack 135
Hess, Wilbert 128, 129
Hetrich, Christian 66
Hex murder 127-129
Heyer, Valentine 17
Hicks, Joseph B. 123, 124
Highland Park 108, 109
Hinsman, Joseph 22
Hippodrome Theater 124, *125*
Historical Society of York County, The 66, 68, 69, 108, 109, 110, 146, 151, 160, 163, 164, 166, 172
Historic York County, Inc. 151
History of York County (book) 17
Hoffman, Bob 141, *142*
Hohman, John George 127

Hoke, Samuel (Hoake) 22
Holtzapple, George E. 102
Home Furniture Company 132
Hooke, Frederick 59
Hoopes, Robert 44
Hoover, George W. 99
Hoover, Herbert 120
Hopewell Township 81
Hotels, inns, and taverns: Black Horse Inn and Tavern, 21; Buehler's Hotel, 73; Colonial Hotel, *94*, *113*, 155; Elizabeth Moore's Inn, 46; Globe Inn, 69, 72; Golden Lamb Tavern, 42; Golden Plough Tavern, 22, *23*, 51, *151*, 153, 155, *172*; Penn Hotel, 138, 155; White Hall Hotel, 79, 86; Yorktowne Hotel, 121, 138, 141, 146, 156
Hub Store 88
Hudson, Henry 10
Hugentugler, Ephram S. 122, 126, *130*, 131
Humphrey, Hubert 154
Hunt, Levi Clarence 60
Hunter, Bill 142
Hurricane Agnes 153; destruction caused by, *153*
Hurricane of 1933 139
Hurst, George 137

I
Indians 9-13, 19, 22, 28, 32-33. *See also individual tribes*
Indian Steps 32
Indian Steps Museum 32, 33
Influenza epidemic of 1918 118, 120
Inman, Henry 12
Inners, Christian 81
Iosue, Robert V. 156, *157*
Iron industry 29-30, 86
Iroquois, Five Nations of the 11, 12, 13, 19
Irvine, William 45
Irwin, Elisabeth 26
Irwin, George 57

J
Jackson Theater 124
Jacobus (town) 126
Jail: (1756) 26; (1768) 26
Jameson, David 29
Jaroschy, Francois 137
Jefferson, Thomas 100
Jessop, Edward 89
Jessop, Jonathan 24, 56, 73, 76, 84, 89
"Jewish Bill" 100
Jewish residents 100-101
Johnson, Lyndon B. *152*
Johnston, Samuel 27, 31, 33, 44
Johnston, William 58
Joice, John 71
Jones, Robert 26

K
Kahn, Solomon 100
Kain, George Hay, Jr. 137
Katz, David 101
Kay, Jack 159
Kean, John 36
Keesey, Horace 111
Keesey, Tom 141
Keith, Governor 15
Keller, Alverta Herbst 137
Keller, H. Dietz 113, 114
Kennedy, John F. *151*
Kenny, James 44
Kerr, C.M. 131
Kerr, James W. 101
Key, Francis Scott 70
Keystone Brewing Company 117
Kindig, Joseph, II 135
Kindig, Joseph E., III 18
King, Adam 72
King's Dam 139
Kirk, Elisha 24
Kirk, Jacob 81
Kirkwood, Daniel 61, *81*, 82
Kleffel, J.V. 118
Klein, Jacob 26
Kline, John 73
Klinefelter, Samuel 60
Knighton, Raymond F. 119
Knights of Malta 115
Knights of the Mystic Chain 115
Kohler, Richard E. 123, 124
Korean War 148, 149
Kottcamp, Christian Charles 96
Kottcamp, Harry 96
Kraber, Ed 141
Kraut, Christoph 18
Kreutz Creek 14, 17
Kreutz Creek settlement 14, 23
Kreutz Creek Valley 16, 17
Krout, John D. 158
Ku Klux Klan 124, 126-127, 136
Kurtz, George P. 61
Kurtz, John 46

L
Lafayette, George Washington 72
Lafayette, Marquis de 49, 51, *52*, 57, 72, 111
Lafayette Club 111, 114
Lafean, D.H. 111
Laffe, Madame Annette *150*
Lake Williams 131
Lamarr, Hedy *146*
Lamberville, John de 11
Lancaster 32, 41, 45, 52, 65, 66, 135
Lancaster County 14, 16, 21, 25, 28, 29, 31, 43, 90, 128, 131
Landys, Samuel 17
Langworthy, Edward 46
Lanius, Christian 87
Lanius, Henry 120
Lanius, W.H. 111

Latimer, Lissie 91
Latimer, Robert Cathcart 108, 109
Laub, Michael 22
Laucks, Israel Forry 97, 100
Laucks, Mrs. Israel 102
Laucks, S. Forry 114, 145
Lauer, Stewart E. 148
Lauman, Christian 62
Laurel Fire Company 49, 52, 56
Laurens, Henry 46, 48, *49*, 50
Lawmaster, Frederick 30
Lawrence, David L. 151
Leader, George M. 151
Lebach, Joseph 100
Leber, Guy 135
Lee, Arthur 38
Lee, Richard Henry 38, 48
Lee, Robert E. 90, 91, 93
Lehmayer, Nathan 87
Lehmayer's 87, 155
Leibowitz, Michael 101
Leightner, Ignatius 30, 31
Lenhart, Godfrey 24, 47, 58
Lever, John 30
Levin, Sylvan 137
Lewis, Ellis 16
Lewis, James 67
Lewis, Samuel S. 120, 136
Lewisberry 16, 156
Lewistown 137
Lincoln, Abraham 89, 93
Lindenberger, John 71
Lischy, Jacob 23, 24
Livingston, Philip *53*
Loeffler, George Lewis 62
Loganville 102, 155
Long, John Luther 111
Long Level 11, 12
Long Lost Friend, The (book) 127
Loucks, George 73
Louis XIV (king of France) 35
Lovell, James 46, 52
Lower Chanceford Township 32, 81
Lower Susquehanna Valley 153
Lutheran Theological Seminary 61
Lyles, Victoria 150

M
McAllister, Archibald 44
McAllister, Mary Dill 39
McAllister, Richard 25, 38-39, 44
McBlain, Walter 111
McClellan, W.H. 111
McClellan Heights 119
McFall, John T. 108
McFeeson, John 16
McKinley, William 93
McLaughlin, Harry J. *141*
Maclay, William 62
McLean, Alexander 111
McLean, Archibald 33, 46
Madison, James 69
Magni, Kerry *159*

Mahoney, John J. 147
Manchester Township 24, 59, 131
Mandell, Robert 137
Maneval, Charles H. 155
Manufacturers Association 114, 145, 148
Marietta 128
Market Sheds 69, *104*
Market Street Bridge *111*
Marshall, Elizabeth N. 159
Marsh Creek 36
Martin, Milton D. 103
Martin Carriage Company 115
Martin Memorial Library 103
Maryland & Pennsylvania Railroad 113
Mason, Charles 33
Mayer, John 108, 110
Mayer, Lewis 79
Mayersville 108, 110
Meem, John 26, 47
Meisenhelder, E.W. 102
Meisenhelder, Edward, Jr. 143
Meisky, A.B. 135
Mellander, G.A. 136
Memoir of John Durang (book) 41
Memorial Osteopathic Hospital 143
Menges Mills 151
Merchant's Association of York 111
Merges, Henry R. 160
Methodist Episcopal Church 57, 58, 62, 63
Meyer, Solomon 65, 73
Michael, Joel 140
Mifflin, Thomas 50, 52
Millard, Addison 135
Miller, H.W. 118
Miller, Henry 31, 36, 37, 40, 44, 61, 62, 63
Miller, Henry, Jr. 61
Miller, Lewis 41, 56, *68*, 69, 70, 72, 89, 91, 93
Miller, Ray A. 152
Milligan, Lambdin P. 106
Milling industry 24, 78
Minshall, Thomas 27
Mitchell, Cameron 150, 151
Mitchell, Robert 141
Mitzell, Charles M. 150
Mohawk Indians 11
Monaghan Township 81
Monocacy Road 18, 22, 24
Monoghan settlement 36. *See also* Dillsburg
Monroe, James 83
Moody, Ida Frances 137
Moore, Mary 46
Moravian residents 42
Morgernstern, Philip 42
Morris, Charles 57, 83
Morris, George S. 61
Morris, John Gottlieb 57
Morris, Robert Hunter 22

Morse, Otis B., IV 152
Mott, Lucretia 83
Moul, Charles E. 118
Moul, Clayton E. 136
Mundorf, Peter 62
Mussano, Frank 152
Myers, Elizabeth B. 163; birth record of, *163*
Myers, Emory 138
Myers, Jacob N. 163; birth record of, *163*
Myers, Joel N. 163; birth record of, *163*

N
Naill, M.W. 118
Nearing the Issue at the Cockpit (painting) 107
Newberrytown 16
Newberry Township 16, 81, 84
New Eastern Market 158, 170
New Freedom 16
New Holland 66, 86
New Oxford 85
Newspapers: *Evangelical Zeitung, Die,* 79; *Pennsylvania Chronicle and York Weekly Advertiser,* 59; *Pennsylvania Gazette,* 49, 58; *Pennsylvania Herald and York General Advertiser,* 59; *Pennsylvania Journal,* 37; *People's Advocate,* 79, 81; *Republicanische Herald, Der,* 79; *Sunday News,* 152; *Sunday Patriot News,* 141; *True Democrat,* 99; *York Daily Record,* 73, 81, 139, 140, 154; *York Dispatch,* 32, 99, 100, 103, 114, 117, 121, 122, 123, 126, 128, 138, 139, 145, 150, 157, 160; *York Gazette and Daily,* 65, 72, 73, 81, 82, 90, 139, 154; *York High Weekly,* 141
New York Wire Cloth Company 148
Nine Hundred Block (book) 142
Nixon, Edward 151
Nixon, Richard 151, 154
Noel, Daniel K. *105*, 106
Noel, Jacob 106
Noll, Nellie 128
Northern Central Railroad 78
North Hopewell Township 128
North Mall 152
North York Borough 108, 110
Noss' Sons, Inc., Herman 98

O
Odd Fellows, Order of 115
Odd Fellows Hall *88*
Ohev Sholom Synagogue 101, *159*
Oneida Indians 11, 19
"One Man's Journey" (short story) 142
Onondaga Fort 11
Onondaga Indians 11, 19
Onvesant, Matthias 22

Orpheum Theater 124, 138
Ottemiller Company, W.H. 115
Out Door Country Club 109

P
Padden, John H. 148
Paine, Thomas 52, *53*, 155
Palatines 42
Panic of 1837-1839 79
Panic of 1893 108
Parker, Alton B. 114, 120
Parry Corporation, Martin 121
Peach Bottom atomic plant *152*, 153, 157
Peach Bottom Township 16, 39, 62, 81
Pedersen, Trudy 154
Penn, Granville 25
Penn, John 19, 58
Penn, John, Jr. 58-59
Penn, Richard 19, 33
Penn, Thomas 19, 31, 33
Penn, William *12*, *13*, 14, 15, 18, 19, 25
Penn Common 88, 92, 113, 114
Penn Hotel 138, 155
Pennington, James W.C. 84, 85
Pennsylvania Academy of Fine Arts 103
Pennsylvania Chronicle and York Weekly Advertiser (newspaper) 59
Pennsylvania Colonization Society 83
Pennsylvania Department of Transportation 153
Pennsylvania Gas and Electric Company 131
Pennsylvania Gazette (newspaper) 49, 58
Pennsylvania (German) Dutch residents 82
Pennsylvania Herald and York General Advertiser (newspaper) 59
Pennsylvania Historical Commission 12
Pennsylvania Journal (newspaper) 37
Pennsylvania Railroad Company 136, 139; bridge of, 103
Pennsylvania State Arts Council 95
Pennsylvania State University, York 148
Pennsylvania Telephone Company 99
Pennsylvania Turnpike 143
Pentz, Mrs. D. 102
People's Advocate (newspaper) 79, 81
People's Electric Light Company 103
Peters, Richards 52
Peters, William 31
Pfohl, James C. 137
Philadelphia 21, 42, 65, 66, 75, 76, 84, 90, 95, 99, 101, 103, 107, 114, 129, 147, 153
Philadelphia Millinery 96
Phineas Davis School 135
Pickering, Timothy 47, 52
Pidgeon, Joseph 14
Pietists. *See* Dunkards
Pigeon Hills 14
Pigeon Hills settlement 16
Pinchot, Gifford 121, 138, 139
Piperberg, Jonas 101
Pistone, Bernard 158, 159
Pitt, James 27
Pittsburgh 65, 77
Polack, Rodney W. 119
Poorhouse Run flood-control project 153
Population figures: (1800) 65; (1820) 72; (1830) 75; (1850) 87-88; (1860) 89; (1880) 99; (1890) 108; (1914) 114; (1920) 120; (1940) 143; (1950) 148; (1960) 151; (1970) 154; (1980) 158
Post Office 143
Potomac River 23
Poulain, Denise *150*
Privat, Charles *150*
Prohibition 122; repeal of, 137
Prospect Hill Cemetery 53, 83
Prowell, George R. 29, 36, 47, 73, 79, 86, 98, 112, 114
Public Common 69, 88. *See also* Penn Common
Pulaski, Casimir 52, 53, 55
Pulaski's Legion 55
Pullman Company 115

Q
Queensgate Shopping Center 152

R
Railroads 74, 76-77, 85-86, 136. *See also* Baltimore & Ohio Steam Railway Company; Columbia, Lancaster & Philadelphia Railroad; Maryland & Pennsylvania Railroad; Northern Central Railroad; Pennsylvania Railroad Company; Wrightsville & Gettysburg Railroad Company; York-Wrightsville Railroad
Railroad Station House 62, *63*
Ramona Restaurant 24
Rankin, John 16
Raudenbush, George K. 137
Rauhauser, John F., Jr. 156
Reading 21, 44, 66, 127
Reagan, Ronald 156
Red Lion 147
Red Men, Order of 115
Reed, William 69
Rehmeyer, Nelson 127, 128; house of, *127*
Rehmeyer's Hollow 127, 128, 129
Reineberg, Edward C. 99
Reineberg, Lee 129
Reisinger, Ray 96
Reistertown 85
Religion 23-24, 27-28, 31, 43-44, 57-59, 71, 82, 100-101. *See also* Churches and synagogues
Reminiscences of the Civil War (book) 91
Republicanische Herald, Der (newspaper) 79
Rescue Fire Company 114
Reservoir Hill Park 175
Revolutionary War 35-41, 44-45, 50, 69-70
Rice, C.P. 121
Ridge Avenue School 148
Roberts, T. 59
Robinson, Andrew 67
Robinson, Penrose 78
Roland, William S. 101, 102
Roosevelt, Franklin D. 120, 136, 141
Roosevelt, Theodore 93, 114, 120
Root, B.M. 112
Root Company, B.M. 112
Rosenau, Nathan 100
Ross, George 44
Ross, James 39, 40
Rotary Club 147
Roth, John 36, 37, 41
Rousset, Mr. *150*
Rozelle, Mabel 124
Rudy, Charles 103
Rudy, George B. 99
Rudy, J. Horace 103
Rudy Company, J. Horace 103
Rush, Benjamin 52
Russel, William 44
Ruth, Raymond 135

S
Safe Harbor Dam 135
St. Clair, John 29
St. John's Episcopal Church 27, 51, 55, 56, *58*, 59, *115*, 142
St. John's German Lutheran Church 95
St. Matthew's Lutheran Church 24
St. Patrick's Church 43, *70*, 159
St. Paul's Lutheran Church 95, 146
Saltzgiver, John Henry 114
Satz, Lorie *116*
Scenic Theater 124
Schaad, Henry C. 154
Schall, James 75
Scherer, Jacob 18
Schlegel, Philip J. 36, 37
Schmeiser, Georg 18
Schmeiser, Mathias. *See* Smyser, Mathias
Schmidt, George S. 154
Schmidt, John C. 67, 72, 83, 98, 114, 118
Schmidt, Mrs. Henry D. 109

INDEX • 237

Schmidt and Ault Paper Company 110, 118
Schmidt and Company, H.S. 113
Schmucker, Samuel S. 61
Schools and colleges: German Lutheran School, 44, 55; Pennsylvania Academy of Fine Arts, 103; Pennsylvania State University, York, 148; Phineas Davis School, 135; Ridge Avenue School, 148; Shiloh Elementary School, 149; Smith Junior High School, Edgar Fahs, 153; Thompson Business College, 152; University of Pennsylvania, 55, 60, 61; West York High School, 151; William Penn Senior High School, 138; York Academy of Arts, 148; York College of Pennsylvania, 25, 55, 56, 63, 112, 136, 149, 156; York Collegiate Institute, 61, 98, 102, 103, 124, 138, 139; York County Academy, 55, 56, 59, *60*, 61, 66, 71, 77, 81, 82, 84, 85, 97, 107, 137, 138; York High School, 118, 141; York Junior College, 152
Schultz, Clinton W. 118
Schultz, Heinrich 18
Schultz, John 81
Schultz, Valentine 18
Schwaab, Georg. *See* Swope, George
Schwaab, Michael. *See* Swope, Michael
Scotch-Irish settlement 15-16
Second English Lutheran Church *58*, 59
Second Pennsylvania Regiment 38
Seitz, Roland F. 112
Seneca Indians 11, 19
Senft, Henry 137
Sesqui-Centennial celebration 94, 112, 113, 127
Shaffer, Addison 98
Shawnee Indians 32
Sheridan, Philip Henry 89
Shiloh Elementary School Building 149
Shipley, Thomas 114, 121
Shipley, William S. 145
Shipley, William W. 145
Shrewsbury Township 81, 112, 126, 150
Shugart, Zachariah 22
Shultz, Christina 16
Shultz, Johann 16; house of, *17*
Shultz, Martin 17; house of, 16
Shultz, Samuel 137
Simmons, Abram 100
Singer house 96
Sipe, Lester 135
Sirovich, Jacob 101
Sitler, Jacob 57
Slagle, Christopher (Schlegel, Christoffel) 23

Slavery 66, 83. *See also* Underground Railroad
Small, Alexander 87
Small, Anna Maria Ursula 44
Small, Cassandra Morris 91, 93
Small, David 90, 101; house of, *96*
Small, George 44, 73, 77, 103
Small, Isabel Cassatt 98
Small, Joseph 81
Small, Luther 103
Small, Peter 66
Small, Philip Albright 61, 77, 78, 90
Small, Samuel 61, 77, 78, 90, 95, *98*, 101, 102, 103
Small, Sarah Latimer 77
Small, W. Latimer 90, 91, 99, 103
Small and Smyser iron works 86
Small and Son, George 78
Small Company, P.A. and S. 44, 61, 78, 90, 95, 111
Small house 111
Smith, Beauchamp E. 148
Smith, Bert 150
Smith, Bruce B. 10
Smith, C. Elmer 121
Smith, Edgar Fahs 61
Smith, James 29, 30, 36, 38, *39*, 46, 59, 62
Smith, John *8*, 10
Smith, John Allen 60, 61
Smith, Lucy 137
Smith, Matthew 39, 40
Smith, S. Fahs 111
Smith, Steven Morgan 98
Smith Company, S. Morgan 98, 148
Smith Junior High School, Edgar Fahs 153
Smyser, Adam 87, 110
Smyser, Edward 110
Smyser, Henry 110
Smyser, Mathias 18, 110
Smyser, Michael 110
Smyser, Philip 110
Smyser, Roman 135
Smyser, Samuel 88, 110
Smyser-Royer Company 86
Smysertown 103, 110
Snow, Pearl 142
Snyder, John L. 154
Snyder, Simon 69, *70*
Somerset County 106
Southern Pennsylvania Telephone Company 99
Sova, Virgil 160
Spangler, Baltzar 21, 22, 24, 25, 31, 61
Spangler, Baltzar, Jr. 27, 61
Spangler, Daniel 67
Spangler, George 68
Spangler, Jacob 72, 73
Spangler, Kaspar 24
Spangler, M.H. 72
Spangler, Michael 70

Spangler, Rudolph 24, 31
Spangler, S.H. 31
Sprenkle, Charles E. 118
Sprigg, George H. 67
Springdale 112, 129
Springettsbury Manor 13, 21, 25; map of, *15*
Springfield Township 81
Spring Garden Band 87, 89
Spring Garden Township 107, 129
Spring Grove 14, 136
Springwood 109
Stair, Christopher 81
Stair, Robert 146
Standard Chain Company
Stanko, Steve 141
Stanton, Edwin M. 93
Stauffer, David F. 98
Stephenson, Mary F. 152
Steuben, von, Baron Friedrich Wilhelm Ludolf Gerhard Augustin 52
Stevens, Thaddeus 61, *71*, 81, 84, 85
Stevenson, George 25, 26, 31, 33
Stevenson, Robert 38
Stock, Joe "Nardie" 142
Stoddard, Benjamin 44, 51
Stoer, Christian 62
Stoer, Peter 67
Stony Brook 14, 16, 17
Stover, "Hunk" 142
Strand-Capitol Performing Arts Center 138, 158
Strand Theatre 87, 103, 124, *138*, 155, 158
Strayer, J. Calvin 111
Strine, Horace Frank 114
Strubinger, Lewis M. 114
Stuke, Arnold 22
Stuke, Nicholas 22
Sully, Thomas 56
Sunbury 21
Sunday News (newspaper) 152
Sunday Patriot News (newspaper) 141
Sun Fire Brigade 32, 49, 56. *See also* Laurel Company
Susquehanna and TideWater Canal 75, 76
Susquehanna Broadcasting Company 153
Susquehanna River 9, 10, 11, 12, 13, 14, 15, 16, 18, 21, 23, 24, 25, 29, 32, 33, 36, 43, 45, 53, 54, 59, 62, 63, 65, 66, 71, 72, 73, 75, 77, 87, 90, 131, 135, 156
Susquehanna Trail 126
Susquehanna Valley 9, 10, 11, 19, 75
Susquehannocks 8, 9, *10*, 11, 12, 13, 32, 33
Swallow, Silas C. 123
Swedish settlement 11
Swope, Eva 46
Swope, George 18, 22, 25

Swope, Michael 22, 38, 44, 46, 79

T
Tall Cedars of Lebanon (organization) 115
Tannenberg, David 66
Tanner, Jacob 44
Tassia, Sadie *140*
Taylor, Arthur Russell 142
Taylor, Katherine Haviland 142
Taylor, Zachary 87
Temple Beth Israel 100, *102*, 147
Terlazzo, Tony *141*
Terpak, John 141
Tewel, Max 101
Theaters: Capitol Theater, *138*, 158; Coliseum Theater, 124, 140; Elmwood Theater, 137; Hippodrome Theater, 124, *125*; Jackson Theater, 124; Orpheum Theater, 124, 138; Scenic Theater, 124; Strand Theater, 87, 103, 124, *138*, 155, 158; Wizard Theater, 124; York Theater, 138
Thomas, William 141
Thomasville 135
Thompson, William 39
Thompson Business College 152
Thompson's Battalion 39, 40
Three Mile Island atomic plant 156, 157, 158
Trattner, Abe 101
Trinity Reformed Church 24
Trinity United Church *173*
True Democrat (newspaper) 99
Trumbull, John 52
Turner, Robert P. 145, 148
Tuscurora Indians 19

U
Underground Railroad 83-85
Union Fire Brigade 56. See also Vigilant Fire Company
Union Lutheran Church 131-132
United States Army Hospital 92
United Way 147
University of Pennsylvania 55, 60, 61
Updegraff, Joseph 31

V
Valencia Ballroom 140, 141
Valley View Park 138
Van Buren, Martin 79
Vandersloot, John Edward 32, 33
Variety Iron Works 86
Victorian Heritage Festival 160
Vietnam War 154
Vigilant Fire Company 56, 114, 120, 136
Visiting Nurse Association 114
Volstead Act 122
Vyner, Louis 137, *138*

W
Wagner, Daniel 36, 46, 59, 63
Wagner, Samuel 67
Wagner, William 2, 6, 67, 69, 70, 78
Wagonmaking industry 30
Walker, Andrew 44
Walker, Isador 100
Walker, Margaret Louise 154
Wanbaugh, William C. 137
Wanner, Atreus 123
War of 1812 61, 70, 106
Warrington Friends Meeting House 28
Warrington Township 81
Wasbers, Henry, Sr. 108, 111
Washington, George 31, 36, 37, 38, 39, 40, 44, 45, 49, 50, 51, 52, 57, 63, 65, 68
Washington Borough 9, 10, 14
Washington Hall 88
Washington Township 43
Watson, Patrick 25
Watt, Andrew 96
Watt, Richard 95, 96
Watt and Brother 96
Watt Brothers and Company 112
Watts, A.I. 148
Wayne, Anthony 44, 45, 57
Weaver, Daniel 30
Weaver, J.O. 100
Weaver, Jacob E. 129, 135
Weaver Piano Company 100
Webster, James 96
Webster, Richard Watt 96
Weigel, Nathanial 95
Weightlifting Hall of Fame 142
Weiser, Charles 87
Weiser, Jacob 98
Welsch, Jacob 22, 24
Welsch, Samuel 24
Welsh, Henry 67
Welshantz, Conrad 30
Welshantz, Joseph 30
West Chester 30
West Manchester Township 88, 110, 129
West Manheim Township 81
West Side Osteopathic Hospital 143
West Side Sanatarium 143
West York Borough 141
West York High School 151
Whisler, Ulrich 21
White, Thomas 90
White, William 46
White Hall Hotel 79, 86
Widagh (Indian) 13
Wiest, John 101, 102
Wiest, Peter 86, 87
Wiest's Department Store 86, 87, *113*, 155
Wilcocks, Henry 59
Wilkinson, James 40, 50, 51
Willem, Johannes 163; birth and baptismal record of, *163*
William Penn Museum 13

William Penn Senior High School 138
Williams, Israel 71
Williams, Lowell W. 114, 115
Williams, S. Barnitz 137
Williams, Samuel 101
Williams, Smyser 111
Willis, William 26, 83; house of, *83*
Willow Bridges 107
Wilmouth, Margaret 26
Wilson, Woodrow 117, 120
Winans, Ross 76
Winter, C.F. 97
Winter, John 97
Wise, John 81
Wizard Theater 124
Wolf, A. and E. 86
Wolf, E.I. 77, 78, 81
Wolf Supply Company 87
Woman's Club of York 114, 118
Women's Bureau 150
Woodyear, Thomas 67
WORK-radio 136
World War I 114-115, 117-119
World War II 145-148
WOYK-radio 136
Wright, James 22
Wright, John, Jr. 22, 25, 84
Wright, Phebe 85
Wright, William 84, 85
Wright's Ferry 36, 62. See also Wrightsville
Wrightsville 25, 62, 66, 71, 77, 84, 90, 91, 92, 99, 118, 135
Wrightsville & Gettysburg Railroad Company 85
Wrightsville-Columbia Bridge *90*
WSBA-radio 149
WSBA-TV 149, 153
WZIK-radio 136

Y
Yellow Soap (book) 142
YMCA 97, 147
Yocumtown 16
Yohe, Luther 151
"York" (locomotive) *74*, 76
York, Carlisle and York Springs Episcopal Church 29
York, Duke of 12
York Academy of Arts 148
York Airport 135
Yorkana 14
York Art Association 114
York Art Club 114
York Art Store 114
York Association of the Deaf 137
York Bank 2, 6, 67, 79
York Bar Bell Company 141, 142
York Barrens 16
York Body Corporation 132
York Borough Centennial 106
York Brewing Company 117

INDEX • 239

York Bus Company 143
York Carriage Company 114
York City Band 87
York City Softball League 149
York College of Pennsylvania 25, 55, 56, 63, 112, 136, 149, 156
York Collegiate Institute 61, 98, 102, 103, 124, 138, 139; basketball team of 1918-1919, *122;* class of 1895-1896, *109;* class of 1920-1921, 116; second building of, *103*
York Corporation 148
York Country Club 111, 138, 150
York County Academy 55, 56, 59, *60,* 61, 66, 71, 77, 81, 82, 84, 85, 97, 107, 137, 138
York County Agricultural Society 88
York County Bank 87
York County Colonization Society 83
York County Gas Company 87
York County Interstate Fair 88, 92, 137, 148, 151
York County Jail 41
York County Medical Society 129
York County Rifle Company 36
York County Shopping Center 149
York County War and Welfare Fund 146
York Dail Record (newspaper) 73, 81, 139, 140, 154
York Depot 89
York Dispatch (newspaper) 32, 99, 100, 103, 114, 117, 121, 122, 123, 126, 128, 138, 139, 145, 150, 157, 160
York Fair Grounds 109, 113, 118, 120, 143, 152
York Fire Department 56
York Flying Service 135
York Friends Meeting House *30,* 98
York Gas Company 118, 131
York Gazette and Daily (newspaper) 65, 72, *73,* 81, 82, 90, 139, 154
York Haven 16, 66, 87, 131, 136
York Haven Paper Company 118
York Haven turnpike 79
York High School 118, 141
York High Weekly (newspaper) 141
York Hospital *102,* 103, 129; association of, 101
York Ice Company 145
York Junior College 152
York Little Theater 137, 150, 151
York Manufacturing Company 98, 124
York Music League 138
York National Bank 95, 118
York Oil Burner Company 136, 141
York Opera House 106, *107,* 112, 138
York Paint and Hardware Company 86

York Plan 145, 148
York Police Department 122
York Railways Company 108; streetcar, *108*
York Recreation Commission 137
York Riflemen 31
York Rifles 89
York Safe and Lock Company 100
York Spring Wagon Works 103
York Square 100, 118, *134,* 138
York Street Railway Company 103, 108, 143
York Symphony Orchestra 137, 138, *158*
York Telephone and Telegraph Company 99
York Telephone Company 99, 136
York Theater 138
Yorktowne Dance Theatre 159
Yorktowne Hotel 121, 138, 141, 146, 156
York Trust Company 95
York Twinning Association 150
York Wagon Gear Company 108, 113
York Wall Paper Company 109
York Water Company 71, 77, 131, 136, 152, 154, 175
York Welfare Federation 146
York-Wrightsville Railroad 85
Young, Edward 71
Young, Hiram 99
Young Woman's Club 146
YWCA 110

Z
Zech, L.U. 129
Ziegle, Gottlieb 75
Ziegle, Thomas A. 89
Ziegler, Frank A. 99
Ziegler, Georg 18
Ziegler, J.T. 101
Ziegler, Jacob 18
Ziegler, Philip 18
Zimmerman, Georg Adam 18
Zinn, Jeannette 118
Zion Reformed Church 36, 46
Zorger, Frederick 30

PARTNERS IN PROGRESS INDEX

Allis-Chalmers Corporation 178
Alloy Rods 179
Baker Company, J.E. 180-181
Barton, Inc., Jno. Z. 182
Borg-Warner, York Division of 184-185
Borger Steel Co. 183
Carpetman, The 186
Commonwealth National Bank 187
Curtain Call Costumes, Inc. 188

Danskin, Inc. 189
Dentsply International 191
Die-A-Matic 190
Drovers and Mechanics Bank, The 192
Emons Industries, Inc. 193
Epstein and Sons, Inc. 194
Fox Pool Corporation 196
Futer Bros. 195
Geesey Agency, The 197
Gent-L-Kleen Products, Inc. 198
Glatfelter Agency, Inc., Arthur J. 199
Glatfelter Company, P.H. 200-201
Green's Dairy 202
Hogg, Inc., Harold H. 203
Koppers Company, Inc. 204
McCrory Stores Division of McCrory Corporation 205
Memorial Osteopathic Hospital 206
Motter Printing Press Co. 207
Ness Company, Inc., The 208
Noonan, Inc., R.S. 209
Quaker City Paper and Chemical Co. 210
Reindollar and Son, Inc., I. 211
Shipley-Humble, Inc. 212
Snyder Auto Service Co. 213
Stauffer Biscuit Company, Inc., D.F. 214
Susquehanna Broadcasting Co. 216-217
Teledyne-McKay 215
Williams Co., Inc., H.J. 218
Wilton Company, The 219
Wolf Management Services Company 220
York Area Chamber of Commerce 221
York Barbell Company 222
York Container Company 224-225
York Dispatch, The 223
York Hospital 226
Yorkraft, Inc. 227
York Tape and Label Corporation 228
York Water Company, The 229

THIS BOOK WAS SET IN
OPTIMA AND PALADIUM TYPES,
PRINTED ON
70 LB. GLATFELTER PAPER
AND BOUND BY
MAPLE-VAIL BOOK
MANUFACTURING GROUP,
YORK, PENNSYLVANIA.
COVER AND TEXT DESIGNED BY
ALEXANDER D'ANCA
LAYOUT BY
JERI BERMAN
AND LISA SHERER